LOGIC DESIGN THEORY

NRIPENDRA N. BISWAS

Indian Institute of Science

 PRENTICE HALL, Englewood Cliffs, New Jersey 07632

Library of Congress Cataloging-in-Publication Data

Biswas, Nripendra Nath. (date)
    Logic design theory / Nripendra N. Biswas.
        p.   cm.
    Includes bibliographical references and index.
    ISBN 0-13-524398-X : $44.25
    1. Logic design.   2. Logic, Symbolic and mathematical.   I. Title.
TK7888.4.B57   1993   92-33732
621.39'5—dc20   CIP

Acquisitions editor: Peter Janzow
Editorial/production supervision and
    interior design: Maria McColligan
Copyeditor: Barbara Zeiders
Cover design: Wanda Lubelska
Prepress buyer: Linda Behrens
Manufacturing buyer: Dave Dickey
Supplement editor: Alison Munoz

Printed in the United States of America

10 9 8 7 6 5 4 3 2 1

ISBN 0-13-524398-X

Prentice-Hall International (UK) Limited, *London*
Prentice-Hall of Australia Pty. Limited, *Sydney*
Prentice-Hall Canada Inc., *Toronto*
Prentice-Hall Hispanoamericana, S.A., *Mexico*
Prentice-Hall of India Private Limited, *New Delhi*
Prentice-Hall of Japan, Inc., *Tokyo*
Simon & Schuster Asia Pte. Ltd., *Singapore*
Editora Prentice-Hall do Brasil, Ltda., *Rio de Janiero*

To my wife, Reba

CONTENTS

Contents

Contents   vii

CHAPTER 12 FUNDAMENTAL-MODE SEQUENTIAL MACHINES   277

PREFACE

Over the last several years all of us who are in the field of computer science and engineering have become aware of the tremendous impact that very-large-scale integration has made in our respective areas. The field of logic design (also known more formally as switching theory) is no exception. A decade ago, everything seemed to have reached a final and stable form in this area. However, VLSI changed all that. With its introduction, many new devices were invented, and many new technologies came into existence. All this called for new approaches in the domain of switching theory. Perhaps most important was the shift in the number of variables from the small to the very large. This singular fact started a chain reaction resulting in the development of new algorithms for logic design whose various procedures are *computer-aided* rather than manually operated. It also introduced many new structures for logic synthesis such as PLAs and others. The VLSI chip also demanded new and revolutionary techniques of fabrication, compaction, testing, and fault tolerance. Consequently, new subjects such as fault-tolerant computing, design for testability, and built-in self-test have evolved.

Another difficulty faced by modern logic designers is that most problems, such as minimization of Boolean functions, folding of PLAs, and many others have been proven to be NP-complete. Perhaps the only practical way to develop algorithms for handling such problems is to adopt the divide-and-conquer approach. A good exposure to the various steps in the development of such an algorithm becomes a great asset to students. With this in mind, I introduce the CAMP algorithm (Chapter 4) in such a manner that it serves as a good example for the development of a computer-aided procedure that illustrates this approach.

It is now evident that there is a wide gap between the prevailing textbooks on logic design (or switching theory) and the various new topics and approaches that must be discussed to introduce students to the special problems posed by VLSI. In this book I have made a modest attempt to bridge this gap. A modern book on logic design theory would be incomplete unless the new topics and approaches are included. On the other hand, because of the very large volume of literature published on these various issues, it is impossible to deal with all the aspects in a single book. I have therefore discussed a few typical procedures that will introduce the readers to these new and exciting topics of logical design. In this respect, Chapter 4, Tabular and Computer-Aided Minimization Procedures; Chapter 7, Programmable Logic Arrays; Chapter 8, Design for Testability; and Chapter 11, Incompletely Specified Sequential Machines, deserve special mention.

At present, the subject of switching theory is a core course for students of electrical and computer engineering. In my opinion, the subject should also be a requirement for students of computer science. I sincerely believe that many young computer scientists are missing a subject of fundamental importance by not studying switching theory in their undergraduate or graduate courses. Most of the algorithms developed by computer scientists are now based on graph theory. A good and ingenious blending of graph *and* switching theories is clearly needed. After all, what is switching theory? As Kohavi has rightly said in the preface of his book *Switching and Finite Automata Theory* (McGraw-Hill, 1975): "It provides techniques useful in a wide variety of applications and helps develop *a way of thinking* that leads to understanding of the structure, behavior, and limitations and capabilities of logical machines." Thus switching theory helps in the development of this *way of thinking* by giving it an algebraic and formal form that is amenable to mathematical manipulation. Hence a good knowledge of switching theory is as valuable to computer scientists as to computer engineers. There are many instances where a switching theoretic algorithm is much simpler than one developed by the application of graph theory alone. The FCM way of achieving maximum folding of PLAs (Chapter 7) and the bunch and reduce algorithm for the state minimization of incompletely specified sequential machines (Chapter 11) are typical examples of the simplicity and effectiveness of switching theoretic algorithms.

The book is intended primarily as a textbook for senior undergraduate and graduate students in the disciplines of computer engineering and science. However, while writing this book, I also have in mind a large number of computer engineers and scientists in industrial research and development laboratories who are now dealing with various aspects of logic design but had no opportunity to go through a formal course on the subject. This book is ideal for such engineers and scientists who are eager to find a reference work that covers not only the fundamental principles of logic design but also introduces some of the challenging aspects of the VLSI technology.

I have included a large number of worked-out examples. All important results and conclusions have been stated as theorems and are rigorously proved. At the same time, new concepts and techniques have been presented in a simple and straightforward manner. I do not, however, discuss VLSI devices, circuits, layout, or fabrication technologies. These are discussed in the many books devoted to VLSI design.

In its manuscript stage, this book was used extensively at the Indian Institute of Science, Bangalore, India, and at the Center for Advanced Computer Studies at the University of Southwestern Louisiana. I hope it will be a useful textbook for students and a helpful self-study volume for engineers and scientists engaged in VLSI, CAD, and related laboratories in industrial research centers.

I am thankful to many persons who have helped me in many ways in bringing my class notes to the present form of this book. Notable among them are Professor Subrata Dasgupta and Dr. Terry M. Walker of the Center for Advanced Computer Studies at the University of Southwestern Louisiana. I have also received substantial help in writing some of the chapters from two of my former students, now colleagues, Dr. James Jacob and Dr. S. Srinivas. Mr. R. Vijayendra deserves special mention for doing an excellent job in preparing the artwork for this book.

I also express my appreciation to Gordon and Breach, Science Publishers, New York, for their permission to use materials from my book *Introduction to Logic and Switching Theory* that develop the background of the classical switching theory used in this text. I am also grateful to the Institute of Electrical and Electronics Engineers, New York, Taylor & Francis Ltd., London, UK, and the Indian Academy of Sciences, Bangalore, India, for their permission to reproduce materials from some of my papers published in *IEEE Transactions and Conference Proceedings, International Journal of Systems Science,* and *Sadhana, Academy Proceedings in Engineering Sciences,* respectively. Many thanks also to the variety of people at Prentice Hall who worked hard to make the production of this book a possibility.

Bangalore, India   **Nripendra N. Biswas**

1

Boolean Algebra

1.1 INTRODUCTION

In our day-to-day life we come across many situations where we arrive at the solution of a problem simply by thinking. In such an instance we generate a thought process in our mind, the end result of which is a logical decision. Obviously, ordinary algebraic and arithmetic calculations do not help us to solve this category of problems. It will be a great help if a way can be found to codify the various thoughts in some kind of algebra that is amenable to systematic manipulation. Then our method of thinking, which seems random, can be made systematic and the solution can be arrived at much more easily. Boolean algebra, which evolved from a classic paper of George Boole (Boole, 1854), is such an algebra. With the passage of time Boolean algebra has emerged as a powerful tool and forms the foundation of many theories of computer science and engineering.

To illustrate our point more vividly, let us consider a very familiar problem. Professor P has authored four papers with four of his students—A, B, C, and D—in the following manner:

Paper 1 is authored by P and A.
Paper 2 is authored by B, C, and P.
Paper 3 is authored by D, A, and P.
Paper 4 is authored by P, C, and D.

These four papers have been accepted for an international conference. The conference requires that each paper be presented by one of its authors. Professor

P himself is too busy to attend the conference. To encourage the students, he wants to send all four of them, so that each can present one paper. He writes to the director of the institute requesting approval of travel and other grants to the four students. But unfortunately, due to a paucity of funds, the director requests that the professor send the minimum number of students. The professor and students sit down together and after some thinking come to the conclusion (the solution of the problem) that A and C should be sent so that all four papers can be presented at minimum cost.

It is interesting to note that this problem can be expressed formally and the solution arrived at by the use of switching theory (see Example 3.6.1 and Problem 4.12). Switching theory, the theoretical foundation on which all of the principles of logical design have been built, is based on Boolean algebra. Hence a detailed study of Boolean algebra is essential for a good understanding of the basic principles of logic design.

1.2 POSTULATES OF BOOLEAN ALGEBRA

A Boolean algebra can be shown to be a special case of a lattice. It can also be developed independently with the help of Huntington's postulates. In this book we follow the latter approach.

Definition 1.2.1. A set B of elements $(a, b, c, \ldots)$ with an equivalence relation (denoted by $=$), two binary operations, one of them denoted by $+$ and the other denoted by $\cdot$ (or simply by conjunction), and a unary operation, complementation (denoted by $'$), is a *Boolean algebra* if and only if the following postulates are satisfied.

P.1 *Associativity:* The $+$ and $\cdot$ operations are associative:

$$(a + b) + c = a + (b + c) = a + b + c$$

$$(ab)c = a(bc) = abc$$

P.2 *Commutativity:* The $+$ and $\cdot$ operations are commutative:

$$a + b = b + a$$

$$ab = ba$$

P.3 *Distributivity:* The two operations are distributive over each other:

$$a + bc = (a + b)(a + c)$$

$$a(b + c) = ab + ac$$

P.4 *Identity elements:* There exists an identity element (denoted by 0, called zero) for the $+$ operation and another (denoted by 1 and called one or unity) for the $\cdot$ operation within B such that

$$a + 0 = a$$

$$a1 = a$$

P.5 *Complement:* Each member of B has a complement within B such that if a' is the complement of a, then

$$a + a' = 1$$

$$aa' = 0$$

It should be noted that 0 and 1, which denote the two identity elements of the Boolean algebra, should not be misinterpreted as the numbers 0 and 1 of ordinary algebra. It should also be mentioned here that as in an ordinary algebra, so also in a Boolean algebra, the $\cdot$ operation is performed before the $+$ operation. Thus

$$a + bc = a + (bc) \neq (a + b)c$$

1.3 FUNDAMENTAL THEOREMS

Theorem 1.3.1   Closure of Identity Elements.   For all $a \in B$, $a + 1 = 1$ and $a0 = 0$

Proof

$$
\begin{aligned}
a + 1 &= (a + 1)1 && \text{by P.4} \\
&= (a + 1)(a + a') && \text{by P.5} \\
&= a + 1a' && \text{by P.3} \\
&= a + a' && \text{by P.4} \\
&= 1 && \text{by P.5}
\end{aligned}
$$

$$
\begin{aligned}
a0 &= a0 + 0 && \text{by P.4} \\
&= a0 + aa' && \text{by P.5} \\
&= a(0 + a') && \text{by P.3} \\
&= aa' && \text{by P.4} \\
&= 0 && \text{by P.5} \qquad \text{Q.E.D.}
\end{aligned}
$$

Theorem 1.3.2   Equality Theorem.   For all $a,b,c \in B$, if $a + b = a + c$ and $ab = ac$, then $b = c$.

Proof

$$
\begin{aligned}
b &= 1b && \text{by P.4} \\
&= (a + a')b && \text{since } 1 = a + a' && \text{by P.5} \\
&= ab + a'b && && \text{by P.3} \\
&= ac + a'b && \text{since } ab = ac && \\
&= ac + a'b + 0 && && \text{by P.4} \\
&= ac + a'b + a'a && && \text{by P.5} \\
&= ac + a'(b + a) && && \text{by P.3} \\
&= ac + a'(a + b) && && \text{by P.2} \\
&= ac + a'(a + c) && \text{since } a + b = a + c && \\
&= ac + a'c + aa' && && \text{by P.3 and P.2} \\
&= ac + a'c + 0 && && \text{by P.4}
\end{aligned}
$$

$$= c(a + a') \qquad \text{by P.3}$$
$$= c1 \qquad \text{by P.5}$$
$$= c \qquad \text{by P.4} \qquad \text{Q.E.D.}$$

Theorem 1.3.3   Complementarity Theorem.   For all $a,b \in B$, if $a + b = 1$ and $ab = 0$, then $a = b'$ and $b = a'$.

Proof
$$a + b = 1 = a + a' \qquad \text{by P.5}$$

Also,
$$ab = 0 = aa' \qquad \text{by P.5}$$

We have
$$a + b = a + a' \quad \text{and} \quad ab = aa'$$

By Theorem 1.3.2, $b = a'$. $\qquad$ Q.E.D.

Again,
$$a + b = 1 = b + b'$$

and
$$ab = 0 = bb'$$

We have
$$b + a = b + b' \quad \text{and} \quad ba = bb'$$

By Theroem 1.3.2, $a = b'$. $\qquad$ Q.E.D.

Theorem 1.3.4.   The identity elements 0 and 1 are complements of each other.

Proof. Since 0 and 1 are $\in B$, by P.4,
$$1 + 0 = 1 \quad \text{and} \quad 01 = 0$$

Therefore, by Theorem 1.3.3, $0 = 1'$ and $1 = 0'$. $\qquad$ Q.E.D.

1.4 UNIQUENESS PROPERTIES

Theorem 1.4.1.   The identity elements 0 and 1 are unique.

Proof. If 0 is not unique, then let there be two 0's, 0_1 and 0_2. Since $0_1 \in B$ and 0_2 is an identity element, then by P.4,
$$0_1 + 0_2 = 0_1$$

Similarly, since $0_2 \in B$ and 0_1 is an identity element,
$$0_2 + 0_1 = 0_2$$

Therefore,

$$0_1 = 0_1 + 0_2 = 0_2 + 0_1 = 0_2$$

Similarly, it can be shown that

$$1_1 = 1_1 1_2 = 1_2 1_1 = 1_2 \qquad \text{Q.E.D.}$$

Theorem 1.4.2. The complement of an element is unique.

Proof. If the complement of an element is not unique, then let the element a have two complements, a_1 and a_2. Therefore, by P.5,

$$a + a_1 = 1 \quad \text{and} \quad a + a_2 = 1$$

Also,

$$aa_1 = 0 \quad \text{and} \quad aa_2 = 0$$

Hence

$$a + a_1 = a + a_2 \quad \text{and} \quad aa_1 = aa_2$$

Therefore, by Theorem 1.3.2, $a_1 = a_2$. \qquad Q.E.D.

1.5 LAWS OF BOOLEAN ALGEBRA

Theorem 1.5.1. The law of involution holds good in Boolean algebra. That is, for all $a \in B$, $(a')' = a$.

Proof. Let $a' = b$; then $(a')' = b'$. Now, by P.5,

$$b + b' = 1 \quad \text{and} \quad bb' = 0$$

Also,

$$a + a' = 1 \quad \text{and} \quad a'a = 0$$

Hence we have

$$b + b' = b + a \quad \text{and} \quad bb' = ba$$

Therefore, by Theorem 1.3.2, $b' = a$. That is, $(a')' = a$. \qquad Q.E.D.

Theorem 1.5.2. The law of idempotence holds good in Boolean algebra. That is, for all $a \in B$, $a + a = a$ and $aa = a$.

Proof

$$\begin{aligned}
a + a &= a1 + a1 &&\text{by P.4} \\
&= a(1 + 1) &&\text{by P.3} \\
&= a1 &&\text{by Theorem 1.3.1} \\
&= a &&\text{by P.4}
\end{aligned}$$

Again,

$$aa = aa + 0 \qquad \text{by P.4}$$
$$= aa + aa' \qquad \text{by P.5}$$
$$= a(a + a') \qquad \text{by P.3}$$
$$= a1 \qquad \text{by P.5}$$
$$= a \qquad \text{by P.4} \qquad \text{Q.E.D.}$$

Theorem 1.5.3. The law of absorption holds good in Boolean algebra. That is, for all $a, b \in B$,

$$a + ab = a \quad \text{and} \quad a(a + b) = a$$

Proof

$$a + ab = a1 + ab \qquad \text{by P.4}$$
$$= a(1 + b) \qquad \text{by P.3}$$
$$= a1 \qquad \text{by Theorem 1.3.1}$$
$$= a \qquad \text{by P.4}$$

Again,

$$a(a + b) = aa + ab \qquad \text{by P.3}$$
$$= a + ab \qquad \text{by Theorem 1.5.2}$$
$$= a \qquad \text{Q.E.D.}$$

1.6 DeMORGAN'S THEOREM

Theorem 1.6.1. $(a + b)' = a'b'$ and $(ab)' = a' + b'$.

Proof

$$(a + b) + a'b' = (a + a'b') + b$$
$$= (a + a')(a + b') + b \qquad \text{by P.3}$$
$$= (a + b') + b \qquad \text{by P.5 and P.4}$$
$$= a + (b' + b)$$
$$= a + 1 \qquad \text{by P.5}$$
$$= 1 \qquad \text{by Theorem 1.3.1}$$

Again,

$$(a + b)(a'b') = a(a'b') + b(a'b') \qquad \text{by P.3}$$
$$= (aa')b' + a'(bb')$$
$$= 0b' + a'0 \qquad \text{by P.5}$$
$$= 0 \qquad \text{by P.4}$$

Therefore, we have

$$(a + b) + a'b' = 1 \quad \text{and} \quad (a + b)(a'b') = 0$$

Therefore,

$$(a + b)' = a'b' \qquad \text{by Theorem 1.3.3}$$

Similarly, it can be shown that

$$(ab) + a' + b' = 1 \quad \text{and} \quad (ab)(a' + b') = 0$$

Therefore,

$$(ab)' = a' + b' \qquad \text{by Theorem 1.3.3} \qquad \text{Q.E.D.}$$

1.7 THE INCLUSION (IMPLICATION) RELATION

Definition 1.7.1.   For all $a,b \in B$, an *inclusion* can be defined in two ways:

a is included in (or simply "in") B if and only if $a + b = b$.

Alternatively,

a is included in B if and only if $ab = a$.

When a is in b, then a is said to imply b. Hence the inclusion relation is also called the implication relation. When a is in b, that is, when a implies b, then a is said to be an *implicant* of b, and b is said to *cover* a. The relation a is in b is written as

$$a \leqslant b \quad \text{or} \quad b \geqslant a$$

Theorem 1.7.1.   The inclusion relation is reflexive. That is, for all $a \in B$, $a \leqslant a$.

Proof

$$aa = a \qquad \text{by Theorem 1.5.2}$$

Therefore,

$$a \leqslant a. \qquad \text{Q.E.D.}$$

Theorem 1.7.2.   The inclusion relation is transitive. That is, for all $a,b,c \in B$, if $a \leqslant b$, and $b \leqslant c$, then $a \leqslant c$.

Proof. If $a \leqslant b$, then $ab = a$, and if $b \leqslant c$, then $bc = b$. Now

$$
\begin{aligned}
ac &= (ab)c &&\text{since } a = ab \\
&= a(bc) \\
&= ab &&\text{since } bc = b \\
&= a &&\text{since } ab = a
\end{aligned}
$$

Therefore, $a \leqslant c$. \qquad Q.E.D.

Theorem 1.7.3. The inclusion relation is antisymmetric. That is, for all $a,b \in B$, if $a \le b$ and $b \le a$, then $a = b$.

Proof. If $a \le b$, then $ab = a$, and if $b \le a$, then $ba = b$. Therefore, $a = ab = ba = b$. Q.E.D.

It is interesting to note that *Theorem 1.7.3 is also an equality theorem,* as it defines a sufficient condition where two elements a and b are equal.

1.8 BOUNDS OF BOOLEAN ALGEBRA

Theorem 1.8.1. For all $a \in B$, $0 \le a \le 1$.

Proof. By P.4,

$$a + 0 = a \quad \text{and} \quad a1 = a$$

Therefore, $0 \le a$ and $a \le 1$. Q.E.D.

This theorem shows that the identity elements 0 and 1 constitute the lower and upper bounds, respectively, for all the elements of a Boolean algebra.

1.9 DUALITY IN BOOLEAN ALGEBRA

Notice that each of the five Huntington postulates that form the basis of Boolean algebra is presented in a pair of equations. An important property exhibited by the pairs is that one element of a pair can be obtained from the other by interchanging the $+$ and $\cdot$ operations and the identity elements 0 and 1. This property is known as the *principle of duality,* and one of the pair of equations is called the *dual* of the other.

Theorem 1.9.1. Every theorem in a Boolean algebra has its dual, which is also true.

Proof. Consider any theorem and the various steps that prove this theorem. Now interchange $+$ and $\cdot$ and 0 and 1 in the theorem and also in every step of the proof. By the principle of duality, the new theorem is the dual of the previous theorem, and since every step in the proof of the new theorem is the dual of the steps in the proof of the previous theorem, the proof is also valid. Q.E.D.

1.10 BOOLEAN CONSTANTS, VARIABLES, AND FUNCTIONS

We are quite familiar with the nature and definitions of constants, variables, and functions in an ordinary algebra. There are five arithmetic operations—addition, subtraction, multiplication, division, and exponentiation—and all the operands are integers or real numbers. These numbers are the constants in an ordinary algebra, as they do not change their values during the process of computation. The variables, usually denoted by letters such as a, b, c, or x, y, z, can take up the value of any of the constants, and may have different values during the process of computation. In a Boolean algebra also, the same definitions apply to the constants and variables. However, there is a significant difference between ordinary and Boolean algebra regarding the number of constants. Another difference is that the arithmetic operations of the ordinary algebra need not satisfy the closure property, whereas both the binary and unary operations of Boolean algebra must satisfy the closure property. Let us work out a few examples of Boolean algebra that will make our observations clear and obvious.

Example 1.10.1

Show that the set of numbers having all eight factors of 30, that is, {1,2,3,5,6,10,15,30}, together with the two operations LCM and HCF, constitute a Boolean algebra. Which ones are the identity elements? Define the complementation operation, and find the complement of all the elements.

Solution Let LCM be denoted by + and HCF by ·, so that

$$5 + 6 = \text{LCM}(5,6) = 30$$

$$5 \cdot 6 = \text{HCF}(5,6) = 1$$

Tables 1.10.1 and 1.10.2 define the + and · operations on all the elements. The tables prove the following:

1. The LCM and HCF operations are closed and therefore qualify to be binary operations.
2. The LCM and HCF operations are also associative and commutative and therefore satisfy P.1 and P.2 of Boolean algebra.
3. From the tables it can also be verified that the two operations are fully distributive and therefore satisfy P.3. For example,

$$3 \cdot (6 + 10) = 3.30 = 3$$

$$3 \cdot 6 + 3 \cdot 10 = 3 + 1 = 3$$

Again,

$$(3 + 6) \cdot (3 + 10) = 6.30 = 6$$

$$3 + 6 \cdot 10 = 3 + 2 = 6$$

4. The tables also show that the identity elements for the + and · operations are 1 and 30, respectively, since for any element a,

$$a + 1 = a \quad \text{and} \quad a \cdot 30 = a$$

5. The complement of an element a can be obtained by dividing 30 by the element. That is,

$$a' = 30/a$$

For example, if $a = 10$, then $a' = 30/10 = 3$. Table 1.10.3 gives the complements.

TABLE 1.10.1

LCM	1	2	3	5	6	10	15	30
1	1	2	3	5	6	10	15	30
2	2	2	6	10	6	10	30	30
3	3	6	3	15	6	30	15	30
5	5	10	15	5	30	10	15	30
6	6	6	6	30	6	30	30	30
10	10	10	30	10	30	10	30	30
15	15	30	15	15	30	30	15	30
30	30	30	30	30	30	30	30	30

TABLE 1.10.2

HCF	1	2	3	5	6	10	15	30
1	1	1	1	1	1	1	1	1
2	1	2	1	1	2	2	1	2
3	1	1	3	1	3	1	3	3
5	1	1	1	5	1	5	5	5
6	1	2	3	1	6	2	3	6
10	1	2	1	5	2	10	5	10
15	1	1	3	5	3	5	15	15
30	1	2	3	5	6	10	15	30

TABLE 1.10.3

a	1	2	3	5	6	10	15	30
a'	30	15	10	6	5	3	2	1

It can now easily be verified that

$$a + a' = \text{identity element for } \cdot = 30$$
$$a \cdot a' = \text{identity element for } + = 1$$

For example, if $a = 3$, then

$$3 + 3' = 3 + 10 = 30$$
$$3 \cdot 3' = 3 \cdot 10 = 1$$

This example is quite instructive, as it brings out the salient properties of a Boolean algebra in a simple manner. It is significant to note that the foregoing

TABLE 1.10.4

+	a	b	c	d
a	a	b	c	d
b	b	b	d	d
c	c	d	c	d
d	d	d	d	d

TABLE 1.10.5

·	a	b	c	d
a	a	a	a	a
b	a	b	a	b
c	a	a	c	c
d	a	b	c	d

example of a Boolean algebra has eight constants or elements. Such an algebra is often called an eight-element or eight-valued Boolean algebra.

Example 1.10.2

Show that the four sets $\{\Phi\}$, $\{1,2\}$, $\{3,4,5\}$, and $\{1,2,3,4,5\}$, together with the union, intersection, and complementation operations, constitute a four-valued Boolean algebra. What are the identity elements?

Solution Let $a = \{\Phi\}$, $b = \{1,2\}$, $c = \{3,4,5\}$, and $d = \{1,2,3,4,5\}$. Tables 1.10.4 and 1.10.5 show the result of the union and intersection operations among the four elements. Let union be denoted by $+$ and intersection by $\cdot$. These two tables show that:

1. $+$ and $\cdot$ qualify to be binary operations.
2. a is the identity element for $+$, and d is the identity element for the $\cdot$ operation.
3. The complements for a, b, c, and d are d, c, b, and a, respectively.

It can also be verified from the tables that P.1, P.2, and P.3 are also satisfied. Hence the four given sets constitute a Boolean algebra that has four elements or constants and therefore is a four-valued Boolean algebra.

1.11 TWO-VALUED BOOLEAN ALGEBRA: SWITCHING ALGEBRA

We have just seen examples of an eight-valued and a four-valued Boolean algebra. Is it possible to have a two-valued Boolean algebra? Let us examine this question carefully. If a two-valued Boolean algebra exists, the two elements must be the two identity elements. Let 0 and 1 be the two elements. They should also be the complement of each other. By Theorem 1.3.4 the identity elements are, in fact, complements of each other. Now we must find two tables defining the $+$ and $\cdot$ operations.

Since 0 and 1 are in B, and 0 and 1 are identity elements, then by P.4,

$$0 + 0 = 0$$

$$1 + 0 = 1$$

Also,

$$0.1 = 0$$

$$1.1 = 1$$

Again, by Theorem 1.3.1,

$$0 + 1 = 1$$

$$1 + 1 = 1$$

Also,

$$0.0 = 0$$

$$1.0 = 0$$

The equations above satisfy P.1, P.2, and P.3 and also give us Tables 1.11.1 and 1.11.2, which define the $+$ and $\cdot$ operations. Therefore, the two elements 0 and 1 with the $+$ and $\cdot$ operations as defined by Tables 1.11.1 and 1.11.2, respectively, indeed constitute a two-valued Boolean algebra. This is an outstanding and revolutionary result for an electrical engineer engaged in the design of digital circuits, where the various devices, signals, and pulses assume only two states, which we shall call the logical 0 and logical 1 states. In the next two sections we shall see how contact and electronic gate circuits are examples of two-valued Boolean algebra. As these gates and contacts are the basic elements of a switching circuit, two-valued Boolean algebra is called *switching algebra*.

TABLE 1.11.1

+	0	1
0	0	1
1	1	1

TABLE 1.11.2

$\cdot$	0	1
0	0	0
1	0	1

1.12 ELECTRONIC GATES AND MECHANICAL CONTACTS

Let us first consider electronic gates.

Definition 1.12.1. An electronic circuit that has one or more inputs and one output, and in which the electrical condition of the output at any time is dependent on those of the inputs at that time, is called an *electronic gate*.

In switching circuits it is so arranged that the inputs and output of an electronic gate can assume one of only two distinct values. We call one of these values the logical 0 and the other the logical 1. It is possible to design two types of electronic gates to perform the two binary operations, the $+$ operation as

Gate Symbol	Contact Network	Truth Table
OR Gate $f = x+y$	OR Connection $f = t_{12} = x + y$	OR function $\begin{array}{cc\|c} x & y & f \\ 0 & 0 & 0 \\ 0 & 1 & 1 \\ 1 & 0 & 1 \\ 1 & 1 & 1 \end{array}$
AND Gate $f = xy$	AND Connection $f = t_{12} = xy$	AND function $\begin{array}{cc\|c} x & y & f \\ 0 & 0 & 0 \\ 0 & 1 & 0 \\ 1 & 0 & 0 \\ 1 & 1 & 1 \end{array}$
NOT Gate $f = x'$	NOT Connection $f = t_{12} = x'$	NOT function $\begin{array}{c\|c} x & f \\ 0 & 1 \\ 1 & 0 \end{array}$

Figure 1.12.1 Symbols and truth tables of electronic gates and contact networks

defined by Table 1.11.1 and the $\cdot$ operation as defined by Table 1.11.2. We have already specified that the inputs and outputs of the gates will be either 0 or 1.

An electronic gate that produces an output satisfying Table 1.11.1 is called an *OR gate* and is represented as shown in Fig. 1.12.1. Its outputs for the four different combinations of its inputs are as given in Fig. 1.12.1. Such a table is called a *truth table* for the OR gate. The reason such a gate is called an OR gate will be clear from the truth table. It can be seen from this table that the output of the OR gate is 1 when either *a or b* (or both) are 1.

The electronic gate that performs the $\cdot$ operation is called an *AND gate* because the output is 1 only when both *a and b* are 1. Its symbol and truth table are given in Fig. 1.12.1. It must be remembered that in addition to the two binary operations, a Boolean algebra must have the unary operation of complementation. The gate that performs such an operation is called an *INVERTER gate,* as it will be evident from its truth table (Fig. 1.12.1) that it inverts the input. Unlike AND or OR gates, the inverter gate, which is also called a *NOT gate,* has only one input.

Thus the OR, AND, and NOT gates performing the $+$, $\cdot$, and complementation operations constitute a two-valued Boolean algebra. It is interesting to note that the $+$ and $\cdot$ operations have been called LCM and HCF operations in the eight-valued Boolean algebra of Example 1.10.1, and union and intersection operations in Example 1.10.2. It will be quite appropriate to call the $+$, $\cdot$, and complementation operations of the two-valued Boolean algebra of the electronic gates the OR, AND, and NOT operations. As these operations are logical in nature, these three operations are called *logical operations,* and the gates are called *logic gates.*

We shall now see that the familiar mechanical contacts also form a two-valued Boolean algebra when certain conventions are observed. For the purpose of this development we shall, for the time being, confine our attention to two simple types of contacts, a make contact and a break contact, which are defined as follows:

Definition 1.12.2. A *make contact* (Fig. 1.12.1) has two terminals and provides an open path betweeen them when it is in normal, that is, unoperated condition, and provides a closed path in the operated condition.

Employing the conventions followed in electrical circuits, an open path will also be called an *open circuit,* and a closed path will be called a *short circuit.*

Definition 1.12.3. A *break contact* (see contacts y' and z' of Fig. 1.12.3) has two terminals and provides a closed path between them when it is in the normal, that is, unoperated condition, whereas in the operated condition it provides an open path.

Definition 1.12.4. A *transfer* or *changeover contact* (Fig. 1.12.1) has three terminals and combines the functions of a make contact and a break contact.

The conventions to be followed are that when a contact is in normal condition it is considered to carry the logical 0 signal, and when in the operated condition it is considered to carry the logical 1 signal.

Consider next the condition of the path between 1 and 2 in Fig. 1.12.1, where two make contacts, x and $y,$ have been connected in parallel and then in series. The different conditions of the path for various conditions of the two contacts are given in the adjoining truth table. It is significant to note that the truth table of the parallel connection is identical to that of the OR gate. Therefore, the parallel connection performs the $+$ operation of Table 1.11.1, that is, the logical OR operation. Similarly, the series connection has the same truth table as the AND gate, and therefore performs the logical AND operation. The complementation operation is performed by providing a mechanical coupling between a make and a break contact so that they operate simultaneously, or by a transfer contact. It can be seen from the transfer contact of Fig. 1.12.1 that when x is closed, x' is open, and vice versa.

Thus the contact networks, like electronic gates, also constitute a two-valued Boolean algebra. The two-valued Boolean algebra is a special class of Boolean algebra, and because of its application in switching circuits, is also called

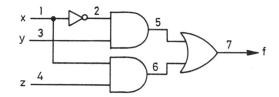

Figure 1.12.2 Gate network.

switching algebra. The principles of logic design are based on this switching algebra and therefore formally constitute what is known as *switching theory.*

We shall now work out a few examples to illustrate how the gate and contact networks represent Boolean functions (also called *switching functions*).

Example 1.12.1

Compute the switching function represented by the gate network of Fig. 1.12.2. Also compute the truth table of the network.

Solution   Mark the seven different lines of the figure as shown. Use F_i to represent the output at point i. Then

$$F_2 = x'$$
$$F_5 = F_2\, y = x'y$$
$$F_6 = xz$$
$$F_7 = F_5 + F_6 = x'y + xz$$

Therefore, $f = F_7 = x'y + xz$. Hence the gate network of Fig. 1.12.2 represents the Boolean function $f = x'y + xz$. Once f is computed, the truth table can easily be computed by calculating f for all combinations of x, y, and z. For example, for $x = 0$, $y = 0$, and $z = 0$, $f = 1.0 + 0.0 = 0 + 0 = 0$; for $x = 0$, $y = 0$, and $z = 1$, $f = 1.0 + 0.1 = 0 + 0 = 0$; and so on (see Table 1.12.1).

Example 1.12.2

Compute the Boolean function represented by the contact network of Fig. 1.12.3. Also compute the truth table representation of the network.

TABLE 1.12.1

x	y	z	f
0	0	0	0
0	0	1	0
0	1	0	1
0	1	1	1
1	0	0	0
1	0	1	1
1	1	0	0
1	1	1	1

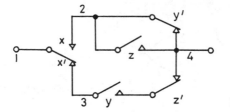

Figure 1.12.3 Contact network.

Solution Mark all the terminals as shown. Now $f_{12} = x$, $f_{24} = y' + z$, $f_{13} = x'$, $f_{34} = yz'$, and

$$\begin{aligned} f_{14} &= f_{124} + f_{134} \\ &= f_{12}f_{24} + f_{13}f_{34} \\ &= x(y'+z) + x'(yz') \\ &= xy' + xz + x'yz' \end{aligned}$$

Alternatively,

$$\begin{aligned} f_{14} &= f_{124}\,(\text{via }y') + f_{124}\,(\text{via }z) + f_{134} \\ &= xy' + xz + x'yz' \end{aligned}$$

Once f_{14} has been computed, the truth table can be computed by calculating f_{14} for all combinations of x, y, and z, as done for Example 1.12.1 (see Table 1.12.2).

TABLE 1.12.2

x	y	z	f_{14}
0	0	0	0
0	0	1	0
0	1	0	1
0	1	1	0
1	0	0	1
1	0	1	1
1	1	0	0
1	1	1	1

REFERENCES

BOOLE, G. *An Investigation of the Laws of Thought.* New York: Dover Publications, Inc., 1854.

HILL, F. J., AND G. R. PETERSON. *Switching Theory and Logical Design,* 3rd ed. New York: John Wiley & Sons, Inc., 1981.

KEISTER, W., A. E. RICHIE, AND S. H. WASHBURN. *The Design of Switching Circuits.* Princeton, N.J.: D. Van Nostrand Company, 1962.

Kohavi, Z. *Switching and Finite Automata Theory,* 2nd ed. New York: McGraw-Hill Book Company, 1978.

Miller, R. E. *Switching Theory,* Vol. I. New York: John Wiley & Sons, Inc., 1966.

Phister, M., Jr. *Logical Design of Digital Computers.* New York: John Wiley & Sons, Inc., 1959.

Shannon, C. E. A symbolic analysis of relay and switching circuits, *AIEE Trans.,* Vol. 57, 1938, pp. 713–723.

Shannon, C. E. The synthesis of two-terminal switching circuits, *Bell Syst. Tech. J.,* Vol. 28, No. 1, January 1949, pp. 59–98.

Whitesitt, J. E. *Boolean Algebra and Its Applications.* Reading, Mass.: Addison-Wesley Publishing Co., Inc., 1961.

PROBLEMS

1.1. Prove the following identities.

   (a) $a + a'b = a + b$

   (b) $ab + bc + a'c = ab + a'c$ (consensus theorem)

1.2. If $a \leq b$, show that each of the following relations holds.

   (a) $a' + b = 1$

   (b) $ab' = 0$

   (c) $b' \leq a'$

1.3. Given $a = b'c + bc'$, show that

$$a' = bc + b'c'$$

$$b = a'c + ac'$$

$$c = a'b + ab'$$

1.4. Prove that the number of elements in a Boolean algebra is always even.

1.5. The number of elements in a Boolean algebra is given by 2^n, where n is a positive integer excluding 0. Is this statement true? If yes, prove it as a theorem; otherwise, give a counterexample.

1.6. By repeated application of Theorem 1.6.1, prove the generalized DeMorgan's theorem, which is stated as follows: If in a Boolean function every element is replaced by its complement and the operations $+$ and $\cdot$ are interchanged, then the resulting function is the complement of the original function. That is, if $g = f(x_1, x_2, \ldots, x_n, +, \cdot)$, then $g' = f(x_1', x_2', \ldots, x_n', \cdot, +)$.

1.7. With the help of the theorem proved in Problem 1.6, find the complement of the following functions.

$$f_1 = (a + b)c + c'd$$

$$f_2 = a'b'c' + a'b(c + d')$$

$$f_3 = a(b + c'(d + e'))$$

1.8. The dual of a Boolean function can be defined as follows: If in a Boolean function the binary operations ($+$ and $\cdot$) and the identity elements (0 and 1) are interchanged, then the resulting function is the dual of the original function. That is, if $g = f(x_1, x_2, \ldots, x_n, 0, 1, +, \cdot)$, then $g^D = f(x_1, x_2, \ldots, x_n, 1, 0, \cdot, +)$. Find the dual of the following functions:

$$f_1 = xyz + x'y'z$$

$$f_2 = (x + y')z + x'yz'$$

$$f_3 = x'(y + z'(x + y'))$$

1.9. If a function and its dual are the same, the function is called a self-dual function. Check if any one or more of the following functions are self-dual.

$$f_1 = a(b' + c') + b'c'$$

$$f_2 = (a + b + c)(a' + b' + c)$$

$$f_3 = ab + bc + c'd$$

$$f_4 = b'(a'c' + ac) + b(a'c + ac')$$

1.10. Prove that if $g = f(x_1, x_2, \ldots, x_n)$, then $g^D = f'(x_1', x_2', \ldots, x_n')$.

1.11. Prove that the identity elements 0 and 1 of a Boolean algebra are duals of each other. (*Hint:* Express 0 and 1 as $0 = aa'$ and $1 = a + a'$.)

1.12. Four sets a, b, c, and d, with the union, intersection, and complementation operations, constitute a four-element Boolean algebra. If $a = \{3,4,9,10\}$ and $b = \{3,9\}$, find c and d.

1.13. Construct a four-element Boolean algebra where the elements are integers and LCM and HCF are two binary operations.

1.14. The eight letters in the word WILMARTH constitute an eight-element Boolean algebra. W and H are the identity elements for the $+$ and $\cdot$ operations, respectively. The complements of W, I, L, and M are H, T, R, and A, respectively. Derive two tables defining the $+$ and $\cdot$ operations.

1.15. Tables defining the $+$ and $\cdot$ operations of an eight-element Boolean algebra consisting of the eight letters TMWALKER are given below. Determine the identity elements and the complementation table. Also find pairs of elements where one of the pair implies the other.

+	T	M	W	A	L	K	E	R
T	T	M	W	A	L	K	E	R
M	M	M	L	K	L	K	R	R
W	W	L	W	E	L	R	E	R
A	A	K	E	A	R	K	E	R
L	L	L	L	R	L	R	R	R
K	K	K	R	K	R	K	R	R
E	E	R	E	E	R	R	E	R
R	R	R	R	R	R	R	R	R

·	T	M	W	A	L	K	E	R
T	T	T	T	T	T	T	T	T
M	T	M	T	T	M	M	T	M
W	T	T	W	T	W	T	W	W
A	T	T	T	A	T	A	A	A
L	T	M	W	T	L	M	W	L
K	T	M	T	A	M	K	A	K
E	T	T	W	A	W	A	E	E
R	T	M	W	A	L	K	E	R

1.16. Two algebraic systems are said to be isomorphic if and only if they are identical except for the labels and symbols representing their elements and operations. Show that the Boolean algebras of Example 1.10.2 and Problem 1.15 are isomorphic. Establish a one-to-one correspondence between their elements and operations.

1.17. Show that the four-element Boolean algebras of Example 1.10.1 and Problem 1.13 are isomorphic. Establish a one-to-one correspondence between their elements and operations.

1.18. Calculate the switching functions realized by the gate networks shown in Fig. P.1.18.

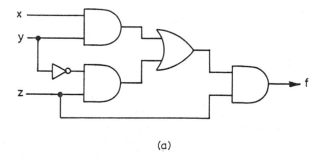

(a)

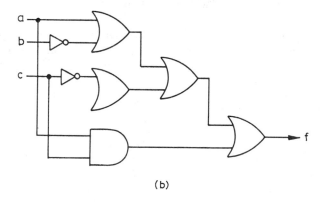

(b)

Figure P.1.18

1.19. Calculate the switching functions realized by the contact networks shown in Fig. P.1.19.

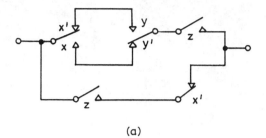

(a)

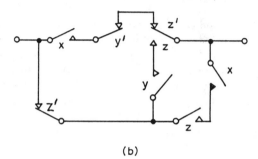

(b)

Figure P.1.19

1.20. Design gate and contact networks to realize the following switching functions:

$$f_1 = (x + y)'z + x'y$$

$$f_2 = (a' + b + c)(a + c') + b'c$$

$$f_3 = a'bc + abc + d$$

1.21. Compute the truth tables of the three functions of Problem 1.20.

1.22. The combination of a make and a break contact x and x' (Figs. 1.12.1 and P.1.19), known as a *transfer* or *changeover contact,* performs the complementation operation of the variable x; that is, when $x = 0$, x' must be 1, and when $x = 1$, x' must be 0. Is this condition satisfied by the transfer contact *always*? If not, why? Can you design a modified transfer contact where the deficiency just now found by you will not exist?

1.23. A two-valued Boolean algebra consisting of elements a and b and the three set operations of union, intersection, and complementation is isomorphic to switching algebra. If $a = \{2,7\}$, find b.

2

Boolean Functions and Logical Operations

2.1 INTRODUCTION

We have seen how electronic gates that form the basic switching elements for logic design can realize Boolean functions. Some fundamental terms, forms, and definitions relating to Boolean functions and expressions will now be studied. We shall also see how many other logical operations besides AND, OR, and INVERSION can be derived. A systematic study of the fundamental properties of these operations will show why for the practical design of logic circuits, gates performing some of these other operations are preferred to AND and OR gates.

2.2 THE NORMAL FORM

Definition 2.2.1.   A Boolean variable in the true form or in the complemented form is called a *literal*. Thus, a, a', b, b', and so on, are literals.

Definition 2.2.2.   The Boolean product of two or more literals is called a *product term*.

Definition 2.2.3.   The Boolean sum of two or more literals is called a *sum term*.

Definition 2.2.4.   When a Boolean function appears as a sum of several product terms, it is said to be expressed as a *sum of products* (SOP). The SOP form is also called the *disjunctive normal form* (DNF).

$$f(abcd) = a' + bc' + cd$$

is an example of the SOP form or DNF.

Definition 2.2.5.   When a Boolean function appears as a product of several sum terms, it is said to be expressed as a *product of sums* (POS). The POS form is also called the *conjunctive normal form* (CNF).

$$f(abcd) = (a + b)(b + c + d)$$

is an example of the POS form or CNF.

A Boolean function that is neither in the disjunctive nor in conjunctive normal form can be converted to such a form by applying P.4 of Chapter 1.

Example 2.2.1

Express the following functions in normal forms.

(a) $f_1 = a'b' + b(c + d')$
(b) $f_2 = (a' + b)(a + cd)$

Solution

(a) $f_1 = a'b' + bc + bd'$
(b) $f_2 = (a' + b)(a + c)(a + d)$

2.3 THE CANONICAL FORM

Definition 2.3.1.   When each of the terms of a Boolean function expressed either in SOP or POS form has all the variables in it, it is said to be expressed in *canonical form*.

Here also, by the idempotence law of Boolean algebra, the canonical form cannot have the same term more than once. The canonical SOP form is called the *disjunctive canonical form* (DCF), and the canonical POS form is called the *conjunctive canonical form* (CCF).

Example 2.3.1

Express each of the following functions in a canonical form:

(a) $f_1 = ab'c + bc' + ac$
(b) $f_2 = (a + b)(b + c')$
(c) $f_3 = a + a'(b + c')$

Solution

(a) $f_1 = ab'c + bc'(a' + a) + ac(b + b')$
    $= ab'c + a'bc' + abc' + abc + ab'c$

$$= ab'c + a'bc' + abc' + abc$$
(b) $f_2 = (a + b + cc')(b + c' + aa')$
$$= (a + b + c)(a + b + c')(a + b + c')(a' + b + c')$$
$$= (a + b + c)(a + b + c')(a' + b + c')$$
(c) $f_3 = a + a'(b + c')$
$$= a + a'b + a'c'$$
$$= a(b + b')(c + c') + a'b(c + c') + a'c'(b + b')$$
$$= (ab + ab')(c + c') + a'bc + a'bc' + a'bc' + a'b'c'$$
$$= abc + abc' + ab'c + ab'c' + a'bc + a'bc' + a'b'c'$$

In the examples above, f_1 and f_3 have been expressed in the disjunctive canonical form, and f_2 in the conjunctive canonical form.

2.4 FUNDAMENTAL PRODUCTS AND SUMS

Definition 2.4.1. A product term of n variables is called a *minterm* of n variables. Thus $a'b'c'$ and $ab'c'$ are minterms of three variables.

Since each variable can appear in a minterm in one of the two forms, true or complemented, the number of all possible minterms of n variables is 2^n. A minterm is also called a *fundamental product*.

If a 0 is written for a complemented variable and a 1 for the uncomplemented variable, each minterm can be expressed as a binary number. Each minterm is then designated as m_i, where the subscript i is the decimal value of the binary number. These are shown in Table 2.4.1 for the three-variable case.

Definition 2.4.2. A sum term of n variables is called a *maxterm* of n variables. Thus $a' + b + c + d'$ and $a + b + c + d$ are maxterms of four variables.

TABLE 2.4.1   MINTERMS

Minterms ($n = 3$)	Corresponding binary number representations	Corresponding symbolic representations
$a'b'c'$	000	m_0
$a'b'c$	001	m_1
$a'bc'$	010	m_2
$a'bc$	011	m_3
$ab'c'$	100	m_4
$ab'c$	101	m_5
abc'	110	m_6
abc	111	m_7

Like the minterms, the number of maxterms is also 2^n for n variables. A maxterm is also called a *fundamental sum*. It is customary to designate each maxterm by M_i, where i is the decimal equivalent of the binary number representation of a maxterm, as shown in Table 2.4.2 for the three-variable case. It should be noted that in the maxterms we have written a 0 for a variable in the true form, and a 1 for a variable in the complemented form. This is the opposite of the procedure we followed in the case of minterms. It can easily be verified that the complement of m_i is M_i, and vice versa; that is,

$$m'_i = M_i \quad and \quad M'_i = m_i$$

From the definitions of minterm and maxterm it is evident that the *disjunctive canonical form of a Boolean function is a sum of minterms, and the conjunctive canonical form is a product of maxterms*. Thus

$$f_1 = a'b'c' + a'b'c + abc$$
$$= m_0 + m_1 + m_7$$

and

$$f_2 = (a + b + c)(a' + b' + c)(a' + b' + c')$$
$$= M_0 M_6 M_7$$

This has led to another convenient way of writing the canonical form wherein the m's or M's are not written at all. Thus

$$f_1 = \Sigma(0,1,7)$$

and

$$f_2 = \Pi(0,6,7)$$

Here the decimal numbers (which are subscripts of the m's or M's) identify the

TABLE 2.4.2 MAXTERMS

Maxterms ($n = 3$)	Corresponding binary number representations	Corresponding symbolic representations
$a + b + c$	000	M_0
$a + b + c'$	001	M_1
$a + b' + c$	010	M_2
$a + b' + c'$	011	M_3
$a' + b + c$	100	M_4
$a' + b + c'$	101	M_5
$a' + b' + c$	110	M_6
$a' + b' + c'$	111	M_7

particular terms, Σ indicates that the terms are minterms and the function is a summation, and Π indicates that the terms are maxterms and the function is a product.

The minterms and maxterms have certain distinctive properties that are very useful in the manipulation of Boolean functions. These are now stated in the following theorems. The proofs of these theorems are left to the reader.

Theorem 2.4.1. The sum of all 2^n minterms of n variables is 1. That is,

$$\sum_{i=0}^{2^n-1} m_i = 1$$

Theorem 2.4.2. The product of any two n-variable minterms, which are different, is 0. That is,

$$m_i m_j = 0 \qquad \text{when} \quad i \neq j$$

Theorem 2.4.3. Let the set of all the 2^n minterms of n variables be partitioned into two subsets, and let f_i be the sum of members of one partition, so that $f_i = \Sigma m_i$, and f_j be the sum of members of the other partition, so that $f_j = \Sigma m_j$, then

$$f_i = f_j'$$

Theorem 2.4.4. $m_i^D = M_2 n - 1 - i$.

The theorems above show the important properties of minterms. Maxterms also exhibit similar properties. These are stated in the following four theorems.

Theorem 2.4.5. The product of all 2^n maxterms of n variables is 0. That is,

$$\prod_{i=0}^{2^n-1} M_i = 0$$

Theorem 2.4.6. The sum of any two n-variable maxterms, which are different, is 1. That is,

$$M_i + M_j = 1 \qquad \text{if} \quad i \neq j$$

Theorem 2.4.7. Let the set of all n-variable maxterms be partitioned into two subsets, and let f_i be the product of all members of one partition, so that $f_i = \Pi M_i$, and f_j be the product of all members of the other partition, so that $f_j = \Pi M_j$. Then

$$f_i = f_j'$$

Theorem 2.4.8. $M_i^D = m_2 n - 1 - i$.

Although all these theorems can be proved independently, this is not really necessary. It can easily be seen that the theorems regarding maxterms are the duals of the theorems regarding minterms.

2.5 DISJUNCTIVE AND CONJUNCTIVE CANONICAL FORMS

It has been mentioned earlier that the disjunctive canonical form is the same as the sum of minterms and the conjunctive canonical form is the same as the product of maxterms. It is interesting to note that if a function is expressed in the DCF, it can also be expressed in the CCF, and vice versa. This is illustrated by working out a few examples.

Example 2.5.1

Express the following functions in the other type of canonical form.

(a) $f_1 = a'bc + ab'c' + abc$
(b) $f_2 = a'b'c'd' + a'bc'd + a'bcd'$
(c) $f_3(abc) = M_3 M_4 M_5$

Solution (a) $f_1(abc) = m_3 + m_4 + m_7 = f_i$ say. By Theorem 2.4.3, the complementary function

$$f_i' = f_j(abc) = m_0 + m_1 + m_2 + m_5 + m_6$$

Therefore,

$$f_i = f_j' = m_0'm_1'm_2'm_5'm_6'$$
$$= M_0 M_1 M_2 M_5 M_6$$

(b) $f_2(abcd) = m_0 + m_5 + m_6 = f_i$, say. Hence by Theorem 2.3.3 the complementary function

$$f_i' = f_j(abcd) = \Sigma(1,2,3,4,7,8,9,10,11,12,13,14,15)$$

Therefore,

$$f_j' = m_1'm_2'm_3'm_4'm_7'm_8'm_9'm_{10}'m_{11}'m_{12}'m_{13}'m_{14}'m_{15}'$$

Therefore,

$$f_2 = f_j' = \Pi(1,2,3,4,7,8,9,10,11,12,13,15)$$

(c) $f_3(abc) = M_3 M_4 M_5 = f_i$, say. Now

$$f_i' = f_j = M_0 M_1 M_2 M_6 M_7$$

Again,

$$f_j' = M_0' + M_1' + M_2' + M_6' + M_7'$$

Therefore,

$$f_3 = f_j' = \Sigma(0,1,2,6,7)$$

The result of these examples can be stated in the form of a theorem as follows.

Theorem 2.5.1. A Boolean function expressed as a sum of minterms or as a product of maxterms can be converted into the other form as given by

$$\Sigma m_i = \Pi M_j \quad \text{and} \quad \Pi M_i = \Sigma m_j$$

where the subsets i and j are two partitions of the entire set of 2^n subscripts of either m's or M's.

The procedure to be followed in proving Theorem 2.5.1 should be obvious from the worked-out examples above.

From this theorem it can be concluded *that any Boolean function can be expressed in both the disjunctive and conjunctive canonical forms.*

2.6 BINARY, OCTAL, AND HEXADECIMAL DESIGNATIONS

Consider a Boolean function f expressed as a sum of minterms, so that

$$f = m_0 + m_1 + m_3 + m_6$$

This can be rewritten as follows:

$$f = 0 \cdot m_7 + 1 \cdot m_6 + 0 \cdot m_5 + 0 \cdot m_4 + 1 \cdot m_3 + 0 \cdot m_2 + 1 \cdot m_1 + 1 \cdot m_0$$

When the coefficients of the minterms arranged as above, that is, in descending order from left to right, are written, the resulting binary number is called the *binary designation* of the function. Thus f can also be expressed as

$$f = (0 \quad 1 \quad 0 \quad 0 \quad 1 \quad 0 \quad 1)_2$$

It is interesting to see now that once the binary number designation of a function is known, it is very easy to write its CCF, that is, its product-of-maxterms form. Theorem 2.5.1 gives the relation between the DCF and CCF of a Boolean function. It is

$$\Sigma m_i = \Pi M_j$$

Now, in the binary number designation there are 1's for the i terms. Hence the 0's are the j terms. Therefore, those maxterms that appear in the CCF can be found by knowing the values of j's. Thus the CCF can be written by noting the locations of 0's in the binary designation.

Example 2.6.1

A three-variable Boolean function has a binary number designation 10101100. Find its DCF and CCF.

Solution The eight positions will be occupied by the minterms and maxterms as follows:

m_7	m_6	m_5	m_4	m_3	m_2	m_1	m_0
M_7	M_6	M_5	M_4	M_3	M_2	M_1	M_0
1	0	1	0	1	1	0	0

Those minterms where the binary designation has 1's will appear in the DCF of the function, and those maxterms where the binary designation has 0's will appear in the CCF of the function. Hence

$$f = m_2 + m_3 + m_5 + m_7 \qquad \text{(DCF)}$$
$$= M_0\, M_1\, M_4\, M_6 \qquad \text{(CCF)}$$

This shows that the binary number designation is a very convenient way of representing a function, as it has inherent in it both the DCF and the CCF.

A compact way of remembering or writing the binary number designation is to express the binary number as an octal number. From our knowledge of interconversion between the binary and octal numbers, this is easily carried out by bunching the bits of binary number in groups of 3. In the three-variable case, since there is no ninth position, it is filled by a 0, while converting from binary to octal, and the 0 at the ninth position is omitted after converting from octal to binary.

Example 2.6.2

Express the following function in its CCF and find its octal designation.

$$f = \Sigma(2,3,6)$$

Solution It is a three-variable function. Therefore, its characteristic number will be determined by writing 1's below m_2, m_3, and m_6 and 0's below others.

m_7	m_6	m_5	m_4	m_3	m_2	m_1	m_0
0	1	0	0	1	1	0	0

Noting the 0's in the characteristic number, the CCF of the function is $M_0\, M_1\, M_4\, M_5\, M_7$. Since $(001,001,100)_2 = (114)_8$, its octal designation is 114.

Example 2.6.3

Express the function, whose octal designation is 256, in both types of canonical forms, and write the truth table of a circuit that realizes the function.

Solution $(256)_8 = (010,101,110)_2$. Therefore, it is a three-variable function, and its binary form (omitting the 0 at the extreme left) is 10101110. Therefore, its DCF is $m_1 + m_2 + m_3 + m_5 + m_7$ and CCF is $M_0\, M_4\, M_6$.

The circuit of the function produces a 1 output when a fundamental product or a minterm is 1; the truth table can be written from the DCF or the sum of the minterm form. It is shown as Table 2.6.1.

2.7 SELF-DUAL FUNCTIONS

Definition 2.7.1. If a Boolean function is equal to its dual, then the function is called a *self-dual* (SD) function.

For example, consider the two functions

$$f_1 = ab + ac + bc \quad \text{and} \quad f_2 = \Sigma(0,3,5,6)$$

TABLE 2.6.1 TRUTH TABLE OF
THE FUNCTION $(256)_8$

x	y	z	f
0	0	0	0
0	0	1	1
0	1	0	1
0	1	1	1
1	0	0	0
1	0	1	1
1	1	0	0
1	1	1	1

$$\begin{aligned} f_1^D &= (a + b)(a + c)(b + c) \\ &= (a + bc)(b + c) \\ &= ab + ac + bc = f_1 \end{aligned}$$

Therefore, f_1 is self-dual.

$$\begin{aligned} f_2^D &= m_0^D m_3^D m_5^D m_6^D \\ &= M_{7-0}\, M_{7-3}\, M_{7-5}\, M_{7-6} \\ &= M_7\, M_4\, M_2\, M_1 \\ &= m_0 + m_3 + m_5 + m_6 = f_2 \end{aligned}$$

Therefore, f_2 is also self-dual.

In the examples above we have actually calculated the dual of the function and then verified if it is equal to the function. The following theorem enables us to determine a self-dual function without actual computation but observing two properties in its sum-of-minterms form.

Theorem 2.7.1. An n-variable Boolean function f is self-dual if and only if its sum-of-minterms form:
(a) Has exactly 2^{n-1} number of minterms
(b) For each $m_i \in f$, $m_{2^n-1-i} \in f'$

In other words, if $f = \Sigma m_i$, then $f' = \Sigma m_{2^n-1-i}$.

Proof. Let $f = \Sigma m_i$. Then

$$\begin{aligned} f^D &= \Pi m_i^D = \Pi M_{2^n-1-i} \\ &= \Pi M_k \qquad \text{where} \quad k = 2^n - 1 - i, \quad N(k) = N(i) \\ &= \Sigma m_p \qquad p \neq k \end{aligned}$$

and

$$N(p) = 2^n - N(k) = 2^n - N(i)$$

where $N(p)$ = number of m_p's
  $N(k)$ = number of M_k's
  $N(i)$ = number of m_i's

Now $f = f^D$ if and only if

$$\Sigma m_i = \Sigma m_p$$

This is possible if and only if

$$N(i) = N(p) = 2^n - N(i)$$

Hence $N(i) = 2^{n-1}$.   Q.E.D. (a)
  Again, since $f = \Sigma m_i = \Sigma m_p$,

$$f' = \Sigma m_k = \Sigma m_{2^n-1-i}$$ Q.E.D. (b)

Example 2.7.1

Determine the self-duality of the functions f_1 and f_2 discussed above with the help of Theorem 2.7.1.

Solution Expressing f_1 in its DCF,

$$f_1 = \Sigma(3,5,6,7)$$

The number of minterms of the three-variable function is $4 = 2^2$. Again, if $f_1 = \Sigma m_i$, then

$$\Sigma m_{2^n-1-i} = \Sigma(4,2,1,0) = f_1'$$

Hence f_1 is self-dual.

$$f_2 = \Sigma(0,3,5,6)$$

Let $f_2 = \Sigma(0,3,5,6) = \Sigma m_i$, say. The number of minterms in $f_2 = 4 = 2^2$. Again,

$$\Sigma m_{2^n-1-i} = \Sigma(7,4,2,1) = f'$$

Hence f_2 is also self-dual.

Corollary 2.7.1A. In an n-variable function there are exactly 2^k self-dual functions, where $k = 2^{n-1}$.

The proof of the corollary is left as an exercise for the reader.

2.8 LOGICAL OPERATIONS

So far we have discussed only two logical operations, AND and OR, involving two or more variables, and one logical operation, NOT (INVERSION), involving only one variable. Except for the NOT operation, the other two operations are defined by a two-variable truth table. As there are altogether 16 functions of two variables, it is possible to define many more logical operations. Notable among these, which have found practical applications, are the NAND, NOR, and EXCLUSIVE-OR operations. Like the AND and OR, each of these also has a distinct symbol for its representation. The NAND, NOR, and EXCLUSIVE-OR

TABLE 2.8.1 TRUTH TABLES FOR NAND, NOR, AND XOR OPERATIONS

a	b	NAND $(ab)'$	NOR $(a + b)'$	XOR
0	0	1	1	0
0	1	1	0	1
1	0	1	0	1
1	1	0	0	0

operations between variables a and b are expressed as $a \uparrow b$, $a \downarrow b$, and $a \oplus b$, respectively. These are defined in the truth table of Table 2.8.1. It can be seen that the NAND is NOT of AND, NOR is NOT of OR, and in the EXCLUSIVE-OR, the function becomes 1 only when either a or b is 1 and not both: hence the name EXCLUSIVE-OR. The ordinary OR operation is really the INCLUSIVE-OR. We discuss some basic properties of these operations in the following sections.

2.9 NAND OPERATION

It will be interesting to investigate if NAND operation can be one of the two binary operations to form a Boolean algebra. For this let us see if the NAND operation is associative and commutative. In equation form NAND can be defined for two and three variables as follows:

$$a \uparrow b = (ab)' = a' + b'$$

$$a \uparrow b \uparrow c = (abc)' = a' + b' + c'$$

Now

$$a \uparrow b = a' + b' = b' + a' = b \uparrow a$$

Thus the *NAND operation is commutative:*

$$(a \uparrow b) \uparrow c = ((ab)'c)' = ab + c$$

Again,

$$a \uparrow (b \uparrow c) = (a(bc)')' = a' + bc$$

Hence

$$(a \uparrow b) \uparrow c \neq a \uparrow (b \uparrow c)$$

Thus it can be seen that the *NAND operation is not associative*, and therefore it cannot satisfy postulate P.1 of Boolean algebra, and hence cannot form a Boolean algebra.

However, a very useful property of the NAND operation is stated as the following theorem.

Theorem 2.9.1. A Boolean function expressed in the sum-of-products (AND–OR) form can also be expressed in NAND–NAND form.

Proof. Without any loss of gnerality, let the theorem be proved by taking the particular function

$$f = abc + def$$

Now

$$
\begin{aligned}
f &= ((abc + def)')'\\
&= ((abc)'(def)')'\\
&= ((a \uparrow b \uparrow c)(d \uparrow e \uparrow f))'\\
&= (a \uparrow b \uparrow c) \uparrow (d \uparrow e \uparrow f) \qquad\qquad \text{Q.E.D.}
\end{aligned}
$$

This theorem tells us that any AND–OR realization of a Boolean function can be converted into a NAND–NAND realization by replacing all the AND and OR gates by NAND gates.

Another interesting fact is that a two-input NAND gate can act as an INVERTER gate if the variable is fed to both the inputs. This follows from the equation

$$a \uparrow a = (aa)' = a'$$

Thus the AND–OR–NOT realization of the function $f = ad' + bd + a'cd$, shown in Fig. 2.9.1(a), can be realized by an all–NAND network, shown in Fig. 2.9.1(b).

2.10 NOR OPERATION

NOR operation can be expressed in equation form as follows:

$$a \downarrow b = (a + b)' = a'b'$$

$$x_1 \downarrow x_2 \downarrow \cdots \downarrow x_n = (x_1 + x_2 + \cdots + x_n)' = x_1'x_2' \cdots x_n'$$

Like NAND operation, *NOR operation is commutative but not associative.* Hence NOR operation also cannot form a Boolean algebra. Also note that

$$a \downarrow b = a'b' = (a' + b')^D = (a \uparrow b)^D$$

Therefore, *NOR and NAND operations are duals of each other.* Hence we also have the dual of Theorem 2.9.1 in Theorem 2.10.1. It plays an important role in the synthesis of NOR–NOR networks.

Theorem 2.10.1. A Boolean function expressed in the product-of-sums (OR–AND) form can also be expressed in NOR–NOR form. Thus if

$$f = (a + b + c)(d + e + f)$$

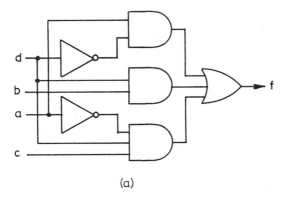

(a)

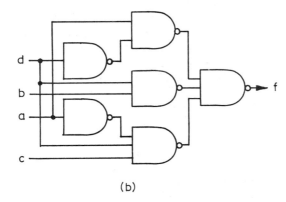

(b)

Figure 2.9.1 (a) $f = ad' + bd + a'cd$ implemented by AND–OR–NOT gates; (b) f implemented by NAND gates only.

then

$$f = (a \downarrow b \downarrow c) \downarrow (d \downarrow e \downarrow f)$$

Like the NAND gate, *a two-input NOR gate can also act as an INVERTER gate.*

2.11 EXCLUSIVE-OR OPERATION

From the truth table the EXCLUSIVE-OR (XOR) operation can be expressed in the form of the following equation:

$$a \oplus b = a'b + ab'$$

Let us now investigate if the XOR operation is commutative and associative. For this it can be seen that the XOR function is identical to the sum-modulo-2 function. Therefore, in the truth table of $a \oplus b = c$, the bits of column c are the mod-2 sum of the a and b bits. Hence if columns a and b are interchanged, c remains unaltered. This shows that

$$a \oplus b = b \oplus a$$

Hence *the XOR operation is commutative.* Again, since column c gives the mod-2 sum of columns a and b, if column c is interchanged with a, then a will give the mod-2 sum of columns b and c. Therefore, if

$$a \oplus b = c$$

then

$$c \oplus b = a$$
$$a \oplus c = b$$
$$a \oplus b \oplus c = 0$$

Again, if $a \oplus b \oplus c = d$, then

$$(a \oplus b) \oplus c = d$$
$$a \oplus (b \oplus c) = d$$

Hence *the XOR operation is also associative.* Thus XOR operation satisfies postulates P.1 and P.2 of Boolean algebra.

Now, let us check if like the INCLUSIVE-OR operation, XOR and AND operations are mutually distributive over each other: that is, if

$$a \oplus bc = (a \oplus b)(a \oplus c)$$
$$a(b \oplus c) = ab \oplus ac$$

Now

$$
\begin{aligned}
a \oplus bc &= a'(bc) + a(bc)' = a'bc + ab' + ac' \\
&= a'bc + ab'c + ab'c' + abc' + ab'c' \\
&= \Sigma(3,4,5,6)
\end{aligned}
$$

Again,

$$
\begin{aligned}
(a \oplus b)(a \oplus c) &= (a'b + ab')(a'c + ac') \\
&= a'bc + ab'c' \\
&= \Sigma(3,4)
\end{aligned}
$$

TABLE 2.11.1 USEFUL IDENTITIES OF EXCLUSIVE-OR OPERATION

1. $a \oplus b = a'b + ab' = (a' + b')(a + b)$
2. $(a \oplus b)' = a'b' + ab = (a' + b)(a + b') = a \oplus b' = a' \oplus b$
3. $a(b \oplus c) = ab \oplus ac$
4. $a + b = a \oplus b \oplus ab = a \oplus a'b$
5. $a \oplus a = 0$
6. $a \oplus a' = 1$
7. $a \oplus 0 = a$
8. $a \oplus 1 = a'$
9. $a \oplus a \oplus \cdots \oplus a = 0$ for even number of a's
10. $a \oplus a \oplus \cdots \oplus a = a$ for odd number of a's

TABLE 2.12.1 FUNCTIONALLY COMPLETE SETS

Set	Identities showing realizations of operations		
	AND	OR	NOT
AND, NOT	—	$a + b = (a'b')'$	—
OR, NOT	$ab = (a' + b')'$	—	—
XOR, AND	—	$a + b = a \oplus b \oplus ab$	$a' = a \oplus 1$
NAND	$ab = (a \uparrow b) \uparrow (a \uparrow b)$	$a + b = (a \uparrow a) \uparrow (b \uparrow b)$	$a' = a \uparrow a$
NOR	$ab = (a \downarrow a) \downarrow (b \downarrow b)$	$a + b = (a \downarrow b) \downarrow (a \downarrow b)$	$a' = a \downarrow a$

Therefore, $a \oplus bc \neq (a \oplus b)(a \oplus c)$. Proceeding in a similar manner, it can be verified that $a(b \oplus c) = ab \oplus ac$. Hence whereas the AND operation is distributive over the XOR operation, the XOR operation is *not* distributive over the AND operation. Therefore, the *XOR and AND operations cannot form a Boolean algebra*.

Like the NOR and NAND gates, a two-input XOR gate can also act as an INVERTER when the variable to be inverted is fed to one of the inputs and a 1 is fed to the other input. This is because

$$a \oplus 1 = a'1 + a1' = a'$$

If instead of 1, 0 is fed to the other input, the XOR gate behaves as a "transparent" gate and simply passes the variable a as it is to the output. This is because

$$a \oplus 0 = a'0 + a0' = a$$

Some useful properties of the EXCLUSIVE-OR operation, including those already mentioned, are listed as identities in Table 2.11.1.

2.12 FUNCTIONALLY COMPLETE SETS

Definition 2.12.1. A set of operations is called a *functionally complete set* if and only if any Boolean function can be expressed by operations belonging to the set only.

For example, the set of operations {AND, OR, NOT} is obviously functionally complete. In fact, to prove any other set of operations to be functionally complete, it should be shown that its members can express the three operations of AND, OR, and NOT. That the sets {AND, NOT}, {OR, NOT} {XOR, AND}, {NAND}, and {NOR} are functionally complete are shown by the identities performing the AND, OR, and NOT operations as listed in Table 2.12.1.

It can be seen that the NAND and NOR operations alone form a functionally complete set. It is therefore possible to implement any switching function using only one type of gate, either NAND or NOR. Hence these two operations are also known as *universal operations,* and these gates are used much more extensively than other gates in the synthesis of combinational logic circuits. A detailed study of logic synthesis using these and other types of gates and modules is presented in Chapter 5.

REFERENCES

BISWAS, N. N. *Introduction to Logic and Switching Theory*. New York: Gordon and Breach, Science Publishers, Inc., 1975.

KOHAVI, Z. *Switching and Finite Automata Theory,* 2nd ed. New York: McGraw-Hill Book Company, 1978.

MCCLUSKEY, E. J. *Logic Design Principles*. Englewood Cliffs, N.J.: Prentice-Hall, 1986.

PROBLEMS

2.1. Express the following functions in both conjunctive and disjunctive canonical forms.
  (a) $f_1 = a + bc$
  (b) $f_2 = ab + a'c + bd$
  (c) $f_3 = (x + y')(x' + z')$
  (d) $f_4 = (x + y + z)(x' + y')$

2.2. Express the following functions as products of maxterms.
  (a) $f_1 = \Sigma(1,2,4,7)$
  (b) $f_2 = \Sigma(0,2,3,4-10)$
  (c) $f_3 = \Sigma(6,8,10,12)$
  (d) $f_4 = \Sigma(0-5,6-12,16,18-21)$

2.3. Express the following functions as sums of minterms.
  (a) $f_1 = \Pi(2,3,6)$
  (b) $f_2 = \Pi(0-4,7)$
  (c) $f_3 = \Pi(1,2,3,8,10,12)$
  (d) $f_4 = \Pi(1,3-6,8,10-12,14,18)$

2.4. Express each of the functions shown in the truth table first as a sum of minterms and then as a product of maxterms.

a	b	c	d	f_1	f_2	f_3	f_4
0	0	0	0	0	1	0	1
0	0	0	1	1	0	1	0
0	0	1	0	1	0	1	0
0	0	1	1	1	1	1	0
0	1	0	0	0	1	0	1
0	1	0	1	1	0	0	1
0	1	1	0	0	1	0	0
0	1	1	1	0	1	0	1
1	0	0	0	1	0	1	0
1	0	0	1	1	0	0	1
1	0	1	0	0	1	1	1
1	0	1	1	1	0	0	0
1	1	0	0	0	1	1	0
1	1	0	1	0	1	0	1
1	1	1	0	0	0	0	1
1	1	1	1	1	1	1	0

2.5. Express the complements of the functions in Problem 2.2 as products of maxterms, and complements of the functions of Problem 2.3 as sums of minterms.

2.6. Find the binary, octal, and hexadecimal designations of the functions of Problem 2.4.

2.7. Express the following functions in both CCF and DCF.
  (a) $f_1 = (237)_8$ **(b)** $f_2 = (126)_8$ **(c)** $f_3 = (423)_8$
  (d) $f_4 = (1234)_{16}$ **(e)** $f_5 = (23A2)_{16}$ **(f)** $f_6 = (ABCD)_{16}$

2.8. Find which of the following functions are self-dual.
  (a) $f_1 = (226)_8$ **(b)** $f_2 = (161)_8$ **(c)** $f_3 = (237)_8$
  (d) $f_4 = (A456)_{16}$ **(e)** $f_5 = (EAA9)_{16}$ **(f)** $f_6 = (A2BA)_{16}$

2.9. For each of the following functions find the value of x so that the function is self-dual. Is the value of x unique?
  (a) $f_1(abc) = ab' + b'c + x$
  (b) $f_2(abcd) = a'bc' + (a' + bc')d + x$
  (c) $f_3(abcd) = (0,3,4,5,6,8,14,x)$
  (d) $f_4 = (E6x8)_{16}$

2.10. A three-variable function realized by a network of NOR gates remains unaltered when all the NOR gates of the network are replaced by NAND gates. Find the function realized by the network. Does the function have a unique value? If not, find at least one more function that could have been realized by the network.

2.11. Starting from the definition of an XOR function in equation form, that is, knowing $a \oplus b = a'b + ab'$, prove that if $a \oplus b = c$, then $a \oplus c = b$.

2.12. An INHIBIT operation denoted by the symbol $*$, say, can be defined by the equation $a * b = a'b$. Prove that the INHIBIT operation alone is functionally complete.

2.13. Write the truth table of the function f, where $f = a + b + c$.

2.14. Show that the odd-parity function p of an n-bit code $(b_n b_{n-1} \cdots b_2 b_1)$ is given by

$$p = b_n \oplus b_{n-1} \oplus \cdots \oplus b_2 \oplus b_1$$

2.15. An opposite minterm can be defined as follows:

> **Definition P.2.15.** For every minterm m_i of an n-variable function, there is a minterm m_{2^n-1-i} which will be called the *opposite* minterm of m_i. The pair of minterms m_i and m_{2^n-1-i} are mutually opposite to each other.

It is obvious that the sum of the decimal designation of a pair of opposite minterms is $2^n - 1$, and therefore

$$m_i + m_{2^n-1-i} = 11 \cdots 11$$

Now prove the following theorem and its corollary.

> **Theorem P.2.15.** A Boolean function f is self-dual if and only if the function f and its complement are such that $f = \Sigma m_i$, and $f' = \Sigma m_{2^n-1-i}$.

> **Corollary P.2.15A.** An n-variable Boolean function is self-dual if and only if it can be expressed as a sum of exactly 2^{n-1} number of minterms that do not have even a single pair of opposite minterms.

3

The Karnaugh Map

3.1 INTRODUCTION

The Karnaugh map is a very convenient and ingenious way of representing a switching function. The original idea of representing a switching function in a coordinate system was conceived by Veitch (1952). It was then modified by Karnaugh (1953) in a form that is now so well known as the Karnaugh map. Theoretically, switching functions of any number of variables can be represented on the map. But for practical purposes the map is used for functions of only up to six variables. Although the main objective of representing a switching function on the map was to express the function in its minimized form, the map is an extremely powerful tool for many other analytical investigations of the properties of switching functions. In fact, no one could have been more prophetic than Karnaugh himself when he made the following observation in his reply to Caldwell's remark about his paper (Karnaugh, 1953).

> The map method, in its present form, is likely to be useful in two ways: As a pedagogic device, for the introduction of ideas about logic circuits and their synthesis, and also a desk top aid to the working engineer. In making full use of the human facility for recognizing geometric patterns at a glance, the map method supplies a number of shortcuts to synthesis that are not as easily found by other methods.

I am tempted to mention here that when Karnaugh made the observation above in 1953, perhaps he hardly realized that one day his map would be more powerful as a pedagogic tool than as a minimization method. As we shall see later in the book, there are immunerable instances where many new concepts valid for even hundreds of variables, which otherwise appear very complex and abstract, can be visualized on a four- or a five-variable map with astounding

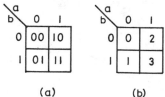

(a) (b) **Figure 3.2.1** Two-variable map.

simplicity and clarity. I therefore have no hesitation in asserting that a thorough study of the various aspects and potentials of the Karnaugh map will be very rewarding to an engineer or a scientist engaged in the development and perfection of VLSI design.

3.2 THE KARNAUGH MAP

We have seen in Chapter 2 how a switching function given in any form can ultimately be expressed in the disjunctive canonical form, that is, as a sum of minterms. We also know that for an n-variable function there are 2^n minterms. The Karnaugh map for n variables has 2^n cells. Each of these cells is assigned a distinct coordinate number, which precisely defines the position of the minterm where it should be plotted. For example, consider the two-variable (a,b) map as shown in Fig. 3.2.1. It can be seen from the two-variable map that it has two columns 0 and 1, and also two rows 0 and 1. We also know that the four minterms of a two-variable function ($a'b'$, $a'b$, ab', and ab) can be written in the binary designation as 00, 01, 10, and 11. Therefore, if the two columns represent the two binary values that the variable a can assume, and the two rows the two binary values that variable b can assume, then the four minterms when plotted on the four cells of the map will occupy the positions as shown in Fig. 3.2.1(a). This shows how the four minterms are assigned four distinct locations on the map. If we want to use the decimal designation of the minterms, the designations of cells of the two-variable Karnaugh map are as shown in Fig. 3.2.1(b). By

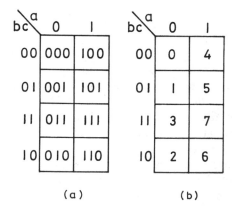

(a) (b) **Figure 3.2.2** Three-variable map.

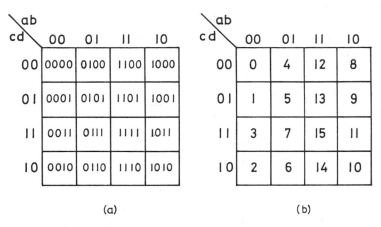

(a)

(b)

Figure 3.2.3 Four-variable map.

arguing in the same manner, it can be verified that a three-variable Karnaugh map can be shown as in Fig. 3.2.2. A four-variable map is shown in Fig. 3.2.3. For the sake of completeness it should be mentioned here that a three-variable Karnaugh map can also be drawn as shown in Fig. 3.2.4. However, throughout the book we use the form as given in Fig. 3.2.2, as this form is coincident with the left half of the four-variable map as shown in Fig. 3.2.3.

The most important and significant feature of all the two-, three-, and four-variable Karnaugh maps above is that there is a change of only one bit when we go from one row (column) to a row (column) immediately next to it. We shall now define an important parameter of these maps.

Definition 3.2.1. Two columns (rows) of a Karnaugh map are said to be logically *adjacent* (or simply adjacent) to each other if their variable coordinates differ in only one bit.

It can be seen that all columns (rows) which are physically adjacent in two-, three-, and four-variable maps are also logically adjacent according to Definition 3.2.1. In addition, it can be verified that the top and bottom rows and the leftmost

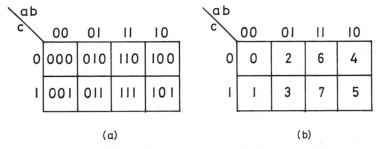

(a)

(b)

Figure 3.2.4 Alternative forms of the three-variable map.

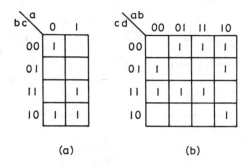

Figure 3.2.5 (a) Function $f_1 = \Sigma(0,2,6,7)$ and (b) function $f_2 = \Sigma(1,3,4,7-10,12,15)$ plotted on maps.

(a)   (b)

and rightmost columns of a four-variable map are also adjacent according to the definition, although they are not physically adjacent.

If a Boolean function is given as a sum of its minterms (that is, in its disjunctive canonical form), then the function is plotted on the map by writing 1's on those cells which represent the minterms that are present in the function. No 0's are usually written for cells representing absentee minterms but are meant by implication.

Example 3.2.1

Represent the following functions on a Karnaugh map.

(a) $f_1(abc) = \Sigma(0,2,6,7)$
(b) $f_2(abcd) = \Sigma(1,3,4,7-10,12,15)$

Solution The functions f_1 and f_2 are as shown in Fig. 3.2.5(a) and (b), respectively.

If a function is not given in its DCF, then it can first be expanded algebraically in the canonical form and then plotted on the map. However, such a function can also be plotted directly on the map without carrying out the algebraic expansion. For this, let us study how a product term that is not a minterm appears on a map. Take, for example, the product term abc and see how it looks on a four-variable map. When abc is expressed as a sum of minterms of a four-variable function, we get

$$abc = abc(d' + d)$$
$$= abcd' + abcd$$
$$= \Sigma(14,15)$$

So when abc is plotted on a four-variable map, it appears as shown in Fig. 3.2.6. It is interesting to note that the two 1's in the map of Fig. 3.2.6 are in adjacent cells and form a cluster. For the cluster as a whole, the coordinate values of variables a, b, and c are 1, whereas the coordinate values of variable d are both 0 and 1. For this reason the variable d gets eliminated and does not appear in the product term. Arguing in a similar manner, it can be shown that a product term of two variables will appear as a cluster of four 1's on a four-variable map, and a product term of only one variable will appear as a cluster of eight 1's on a four-variable map. A few typical clusters of two, four, and eight 1's are shown in Fig. 3.2.7.

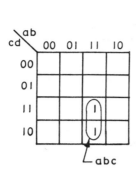

Figure 3.2.6 Product term *abc* appears as a cluster of two 1's on a four-variable map

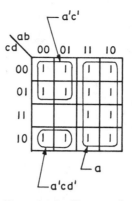

Figure 3.2.7 Clusters of two, four, and eight 1's on a four-variable map.

Example 3.2.2

Plot the following functions on the Karnaugh map.

(a) $f_1(abcd) = ab' + a'bc$
(b) $f_2(abcd) = c'd' + a'bd$
(c) $f_3(abcd) = b'c + d + abc'$

Solution The solution for the functions above are as shown in Fig. 3.2.8(a), (b), and (c), respectively.

Example 3.2.3

Express the following functions in their disjunctive canonical forms and determine if there is any relation among them.

$$f_1(wxyz) = x(w' + z) + w'yz$$

$$f_2(wxyz) = x(w'y'z' + z)$$

$$f_3(wxyz) = w'x'yz + w'xz' + xz$$

Solution Expressing f_1 and f_2 in the SOP form, we have

$$f_1 = w'x + xz + w'yz$$

$$f_2 = w'xy'z' + xz$$

Now, plotting f_1, f_2, and f_3 on the map as shown in Fig. 3.2.9(a), (b), and (c), we see that

$$f_1 = \Sigma(3,4,5,6,7,13,15)$$

$$f_2 = \Sigma(4,5,7,13,15)$$

$$f_3 = \Sigma(3,4,5,6,7,13,15)$$

From this it can be concluded that

$$f_1 = f_3, \quad f_2 < f_1, \quad \text{and} \quad f_2 < f_3$$

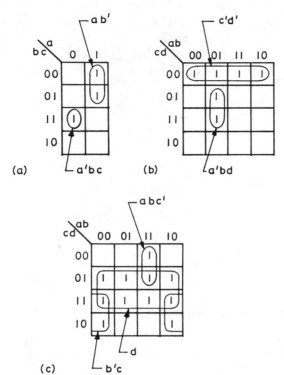

Figure 3.2.8 Solutions of Example 3.2.2.

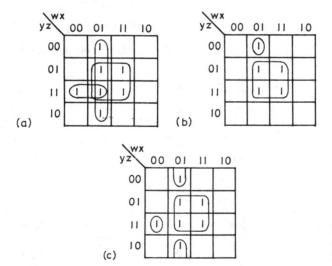

Figure 3.2.9 Map method of determining disjunctive canonical forms.

Definition 3.2.2. If two switching functions are such that one is included in or equal to the other, then the two functions are said to be *comparable*.

In the three functions of Example 3.2.3, all three functions are comparable to one another.

3.3 CUBES AND THE KARNAUGH MAP

If we study a three-dimensional cube as drawn in a three-dimensional Cartesian coordinate system (Fig. 3.3.1), we notice that (a) it has 2^3 vertices; (b) every vertex can be designated by a 3-bit binary number and therefore also by one of the 2^3, or 8, decimal digits from 0 to $2^3 - 1$; (c) every vertex has three adjacent vertices whose coordinates differ by only one bit; and (d) every vertex has an opposite vertex whose coordinates differ in all the three bit positions.

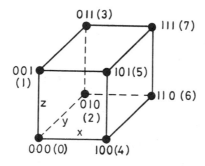

Figure 3.3.1 Binary designations of the eight vertices of a three-dimensional cube.

Generalizing, an *n*-dimensional hypercube, or simply an *n*-cube, will have the following properties.

1. An *n*-cube has 2^n *vertices.*
2. Every vertex of an *n*-cube can be designated by an *n*-bit binary number and therefore also by one of the 2^n decimal digits from 0 through $2^n - 1$.
3. Every vertex of an *n*-cube has *n adjacent* vertices, whose coordinates differ by only one bit. All other vertices are called *distant* vertices.
4. Every vertex of an *n*-cube has one distant vertex whose coordinates differ in all *n* bit positions. Such a vertex is called an *opposite* vertex.
5. An *n*-cube can be expressed as a combination of 2^1 number of $(n - 1)$-cubes, 2^2 number of $(n - 2)$-cubes, 2^3 number of $(n - 3)$-cubes, . . . , or 2^n number of 0-cubes.

It is interesting to note that while any *n*-cube $(n > 3)$ cannot be drawn geometrically in an *n*-dimensional Cartesian coordinate system, it can very conveniently be represented in an *n*-variable Karnaugh map. For example, Fig. 3.3.2 shows the Karnaugh map representation of a four-variable function that has two 2-cubes, one 1-cube, and one 0-cube.

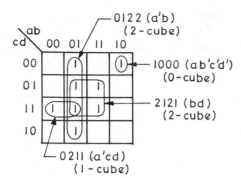

Figure 3.3.2 Four-varaible function having two 2-cubes, one 1-cube, and one 0-cube.

A close observation of the Karnaugh map representation of cubes will reveal the following:

1. In an *n*-variable map a 0-cube represents an *n*-variable minterm. A 0-cube therefore has *n* binary bits.

2. A 1-cube on a map is a cluster that is a combination of two adjacent minterms (0-cubes). Consequently, a 1-cube in an *n*-variable map has $n - 1$ variables. To represent the variable eliminated, the digit 2 is used throughout this book. Hence, to represent a cube of dimension 1 and above, a ternary notation (0, 1, and 2) is used. Note that in Fig. 3.3.2 the 0-cube $ab'c'd'$ is represented by 1000, whereas the 1-cube $a'cd$, a product term from which the variable *b* has been eliminated, is represented by 0211. Similarly, a 2-cube is a product term of $(n - 2)$ variables and will have two 2's in it, since two variables are eliminated from it by the combination of two 1-cubes, or four 0-cubes (see, for example, the 2-cube 0122 or $a'b$ in Fig. 3.3.2).

3. An α-cube in an *n*-variable map will have α 2's in its cubical notation. It is a product term of $(n - α)$ variables and is a result of the combination of 2^1 $(α - 1)$-cubes, 2^2 $(α - 2)$-cubes, . . . , or $2^α$ 0-cubes.

We can not only represent the cubes on the Karnaugh map, but can also find their mutual dispositions by observing the map. In Fig. 3.3.3(a) we can observe that all three cubes are disjoint and each cube is adjacent to two other cubes. Figure 3.3.3(b) shows four disjoint cubes. The cube $a'cd$ (0211) is adjacent to the cube $a'bc'$ (0102) and also to the cube abd (1121). Figure 3.3.3(c) shows two mutually intersecting cubes, the cube cd (2211) and the cube bc (2112). The cube of intersection, that is, the subcube that is common to the two intersecting cubes, is obtained by the product of the two cubes. In this case the cube of intersection is bcd (2111). Sometimes a cube may be entirely included in another cube. Thus, if cube *a* is within cube *b* $(a < b)$, then *a* is said to *subsume* or *imply* *b* and *b* is said to *cover* *a*. *a* is also called an *implicant* of *b*.

3.4 PRIME CUBES

Consider the switching function

$$f = a'b' + bd + ab'$$

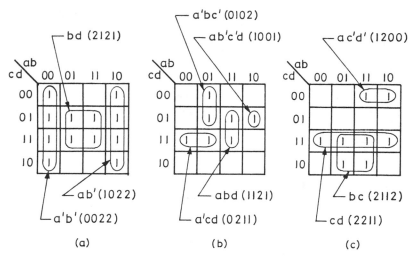

Figure 3.3.3 Mutual dispositions of cubes from the map.

This function is a sum of three cubes, as has been shown in Fig. 3.3.3(a). It can easily be seen in the map and also by carrying out the algebraic summation that the two cubes $a'b'$ and ab' can combine to form a larger cube b'. Again, the cube bd can expand into the two other cubes to form a bigger cube, d. The cubes b' and d which are formed by either combination or expansion among the three given cubes of the function are the largest cubes that can be formed in this function. Each of these cubes is called a *prime cube* or a *prime implicant* of the function. It should be mentioned here that *the process of combination can be viewed as a special case of expansion, where one cube expands into the whole of another cube of the same dimension.* We may now define a prime cube as follows.

Definition 3.4.1. A cube of a given function that cannot grow larger by expanding into other cubes of the function is called a *prime cube* (PC) or a *prime implicant* (PI) of the function.

It can easily be verified that in Fig. 3.3.3(a) none of the three cubes shown is a prime cube; in (b) the cubes $a'bc'$ and $a'cd$ are prime cubes, whereas the cubes abd and $ab'c'd$ are not prime cubes; and in (c) all three cubes are prime cubes.

We shall now define three different types of prime cubes that are encountered in a switching function.

Definition 3.4.2. If among the minterms subsuming a prime cube, there is at least one that is covered by this and only this prime cube, then the prime cube is called an *essential prime cube* (EPC) or an *essential prime implicant* (EPI). In Fig. 3.3.2 all four cubes shown are essential prime cubes.

Definition 3.4.3. The subcube of an essential prime cube that is covered by this and only this EPC is called a *distinguished cube* (DC). The minterms subsuming a distinguished cube are called *distinguished minterms*. Note that the limiting dimensions of a DC within an EPC of dimension α are 0 and α.

Definition 3.4.4. If each of the minterms subsuming a prime cube is covered by other essential prime cubes, then the prime cube is a *redundant prime cube* (RPC) or a *redundant prime implicant* (RPI). In Fig. 3.4.1(a), the prime cube $b'c$ is an RPC, whereas the two other prime cubes ab' and $a'c$ are EPCs.

Definition 3.4.5. A prime cube, which is neither essential nor redundant, is called a *selective prime cube* (SPC) or a *selective prime implicant* (SPI).

Among the minterms subsuming such a prime cube, there is at least one that is covered neither by an EPC nor by this and only this prime cube. It is therefore obvious that the minterm must be covered by another selective prime cube. Therefore, *the existence of one selective prime cube implies the existence of another*. And these two SPCs covering the same minterm appear as two interconnecting links of a chain. In Fig. 3.4.1(b) the two intersecting prime cubes $b'c$ and $a'c$ constitute an SPC chain. It can be seen that the minterm 1 can be covered either by the SPC $b'c$ or by $a'c$.

Quite often a switching function may have a number of SPCs covering some or all of its minterms. In such a case there are two subsets of the SPCs that can cover the minterms. For example, in the function of Fig. 3.4.2, the minterms 6, 7, 14, and 15 are covered by an EPC, whereas the minterms 1, 5, 9, and 11 are covered by the five SPCs shown in solid and dashed lines. The five SPCs form a closed SPC chain. Among these SPCs, there are two subsets that can cover the four minterms 1, 5, 9, and 11. One of the subsets has two SPCs shown by the solid lines and the other subset has three SPCs shown by the dashed lines. Obviously, if we choose the former subset of the SPCs, then we can express this given function as a sum of three product terms. On the other hand, if we chose

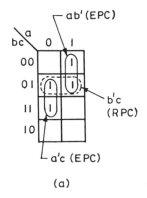

(a)

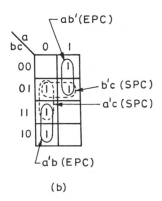

(b)

Figure 3.4.1 (a) Essential and redundant prime cubes; (b) essential prime cubes and a pair of selective prime cubes forming a chain.

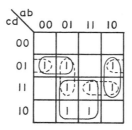

Figure 3.4.2 Two subsets of SPCs cover the minterms 1, 5, 9, and 11. All five SPCs form a closed SPC chain.

the other subset (shown by dashed lines), then the function can be expressed as a sum of four product terms. We shall see very soon that the former expression will be more economical to implement than the latter. Consequently, the selection of the proper subset of the SPCs is an important goal of any minimization algorithm.

3.5 MINIMUM SUM OF PRODUCTS

We have already seen that a switching function can always be expressed as a sum of product terms, that is, as a sum of cubes. If we now want to design a gate circuit to realize the switching function, then it is obvious that every product term or cube will need one AND gate, and the number of input lines to the AND gate will be equal to the number of literals in the product term. Thus if we want the circuit to be most economical: then first, the number of AND gates should be minimum, and second, the number of input lines to each AND gate should also be minimum. Since to make the circuit most economical is one of the important objectives of a circuit designer, it is imperative to express every switching function with a minimum number of product terms and a minimum number of literals. Such an expression for a switching function is called the *minimum sum-of-products* (MSOP) *form*. The various methods by which this objective is achieved are known as *minimization methods* or *algorithms*.

From the definitions and properties of prime cubes studied in the preceding section it can be concluded that the MSOP form of a switching function must be a sum of prime cubes only. Again among these prime cubes, we must have (a) all essential prime cubes, (b) no redundant prime cubes, and (c) the cheaper subset of selective prime cubes. In the Karnaugh map, these can be recognized very easily by careful observation. However, a good rule to follow is to choose the prime cubes in ascending order of their dimension, that is, first choose the 0-cubes, then the 1-cubes, then the 2-cubes, and so on. For example, while minimizing the function shown in Fig. 3.5.1, namely

$$f = \Sigma(1,3,4,5,8,9,13,15)$$

one must not be tempted to select the cluster of four containing the minterms 1, 5, 9, and 13, as this 2-cube $c'd$ turns out to be an RPC, since the four 1-cubes

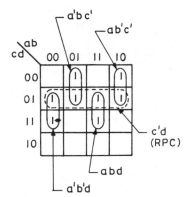

Figure 3.5.1 $f = \Sigma(1,3,4,5,8,9,13,15)$ plotted on map.

shown in the figure are all EPCs and cover all the minterms subsuming the 2-cube $c'd$. In Fig. 3.5.2(a) the function

$$f = \Sigma(1,3,5,7,8,10,12,13,14)$$

has two EPCs and one SPC chain constituted by the cubes abc' and $bc'd$. In this case both these SPCs are 1-cubes and therefore have the same number of literals. Hence any one of them can be included in the MSOP form of the function. This function therefore has two valid solutions. In Fig. 3.5.2(b) the function

$$f = \Sigma(0,1,3,4,5,6,7,11,14)$$

has three EPCs and also one SPC chain constituted by the SPC $a'd$ and the SPC $a'bc$. Here, however, one of the SPCs in the chain is a 2-cube, whereas the other is a 1-cube. Therefore, to minimize the number of literals in the MSOP form, we must choose only the SPC of larger dimension $a'd$ to be included in the solution. Hence in this case the function has only one solution. Sometimes we may

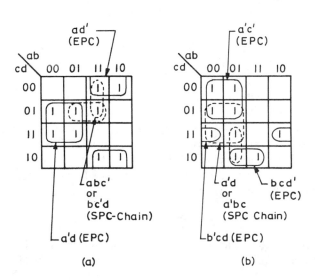

(a)

(b)

Figure 3.5.2 (a) $f = \Sigma(1,3,5,7,8,10,12,13,14)$ and (b) $f = \Sigma(0,1,3–7,11,14)$ plotted on maps.

The Karnaugh Map   Chap. 3

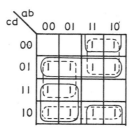

Figure 3.5.3 $f = \Sigma(1-3,5-10,12-14)$ exhibits cyclic prime cubes.

encounter functions that do not exhibit any EPC or RPC and contain only SPCs. One such function,

$$f = \Sigma(1,2,3,5,6,7,8,9,10,12,13,14)$$

is shown in Fig. 3.5.3. Such functions are said to exhibit *cyclic prime implicants* and are known as *cyclic functions*. In such functions the SPC chain is closed and have invariably two equally valid solutions. For example, in the function of Fig. 3.5.3 the subset of the SPC chain shown by the solid-line SPCs is one valid solution ($f = a'c + c'd + ad'$), while the SPCs shown by the dashed lines constitute the other valid solution ($f = ac' + a'd + cd'$).

3.6 MINIMUM PRODUCT OF SUMS

If we are interested in obtaining the minimum product-of-sum form of a given switching function, this can be done by following a very simple procedure. After plotting the function on the map, minimize not the 1's but the 0's. This will yield the minimum sum-of-product form of the complementary function. As an example, the 0's of the function as given in Fig. 3.4.2 have been plotted on the map of Fig. 3.6.1 and minimized to obtain the MSOP form. Thus

$$f' = c'd' + b'd' + a'b'c + abc'$$

Now, by applying DeMorgan's theorem,

$$f = (c + d)(b + d)(a + b + c')(a' + b' + c)$$

This expession is the minimum product-of-sum (MPOS) form of the function as given in Fig. 3.4.2.

Sometimes the reverse situation is encountered. The function is given in the

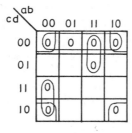

Figure 3.6.1 Minimization of the complementary function to obtain the MPOS form.

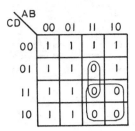

Figure 3.6.2 Solution of Example 3.6.1.

product-of-sum form, and the minimized expression is required in the sum-of-product form. Consider the following example.

Example 3.6.1

Solve the problem of paper presentation with the minimum number of students described in Section 1.1.

Solution Note that all combinations of students needed for presenting the four papers are given by the expression

$$A \text{ AND } (B \text{ OR } C) \text{ AND } (D \text{ OR } A) \text{ AND } (C \text{ OR } D)$$

This can be expressed as a Boolean function of four variables A, B, C, and D with $+$ as the OR connective and $\cdot$ (or simply conjunction) as the AND connective. Thus

$$f(ABCD) = A(B + C)(D + A)(C + D)$$

Now f must be expressed in the minimum sum-of-product form to yield the solution. For this, the complement of f is found by DeMorgan's theorem.

$$f' = A' + B'C' + A'D' + C'D'$$

Plotting this function f' on the map and minimizing the 0's (Fig. 3.6.2), we get

$$f = AC + ABD$$

Therefore, the four papers can be presented either by A and C, or by A and B and D. Obviously, the minimum number is 2, which means that A and C must go to the conference to present all four papers.

3.7 DON'T-CARE TERMS

It must be clear by now that the Karnaugh map is a representation of a switching function expressed in the form of a truth table or as the sum of minterms or as the sum of arbitrary cubes. In all the maps that we have discussed so far, in each cell we have plotted either a 1 (shown on the map) or a 0 (not shown but meant by implication). This means that for such functions the output of the circuit is clearly specified to be either 1 or 0. Such functions are called *completely specified functions*. There may be many practical cases, however, where the output of a circuit cannot be precisely specified. Very often this happens due to the simple fact that all input combinations may not occur in a practical situation. For example, if the input variables of a function $f(abc)$ represent the conditions of the red, yellow, and green lights of a traffic signal, we know that the variables a

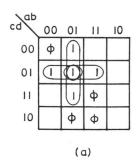

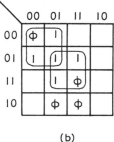

(a)   (b)   **Figure 3.7.1** Don't-care terms.

and c can never be 1 simultaneously. Therefore, the input combination where a and c are both 1 will never occur and the exact value of the function for these input combinations cannot be specified. Such functions are known as incompletely specified functions. The input combinations for which the function is not specified are shown by plotting a ϕ on the corresponding cell of the map. It is obvious that while minimizing, the value of ϕ can be assumed to be either 1 or 0. Since the circuit designer does not care for the exact value of these cells and chooses either 1 or 0 to suit the objective of obtaining the minimum solution, these terms are known as *don't-care terms*. The minterms for which the function has the value ϕ are also known as don't-care minterms.

Although these terms are known as don't-care terms, these are very much sought-after terms by the logic designers, as these are very helpful in minimizing the cost of a switching function. To illustrate this point, consider the situation shown in the map of Fig. 3.7.1. The true minterms of the function are 1, 4, 5, 7, and 13, whereas the don't-care minterms are 0, 6, 14, and 15. If the MSOP form of this function is obtained by ignoring the don't-care minterms, the solution is the sum of four 1-cubes, as shown in Fig. 3.7.1.(a). On the other hand, if the don't-care terms are taken into consideration, and the minterms 0 and 15 are assumed to be 1's and the minterms 6 and 14 to be 0's, the solution becomes the sum of two 2-cubes as shown in Fig. 3.7.1(b). It is obvious that the latter solution is much cheaper to implement. This example shows the usefulness of the don't-care terms.

3.8 FIVE- AND SIX-VARIABLE MAPS

The five-variable map is drawn as two separate four-variable maps, as shown in Fig. 3.8.1. Each of the two four-variable maps is a map for the four variables x_2, x_3, x_4, and x_5. They differ in the value of the first variable x_1; in one of the maps $x_1 = 0$, and in the other, $x_1 = 1$. Decimal designations of the cells can be computed following the same procedure as in other maps. These are as shown in Fig. 3.8.1. Similarly, the six-variable map consists of four four-variable maps, as shown in Fig. 3.8.2. Each of the four-variable maps is a map of the four variables x_3, x_4, x_5, and x_6. They differ in the coordinates of the first two variables, x_1 and x_2, as shown in Fig. 3.8.2. The figure also shows the decimal designations of the various cells, which are computed in the usual manner. The minimization on these maps is carried out by following simple procedures. First the function on

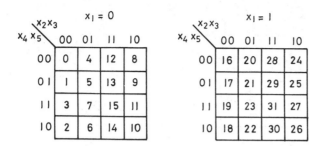

Figure 3.8.1 Five-variable map.

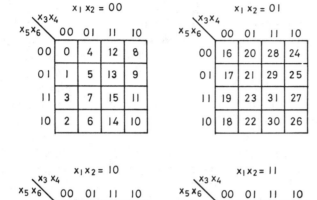

Figure 3.8.2 Six-variable map.

each individual four-variable map is minimized in the same way as is done in a four-variable map. Next, identical patterns on adjacent maps are identified. It should be seen that in a five-variable map, both maps are adjacent, as they differ in only one variable: x_1. On the six-variable map, each map is adjacent to two other maps. It can easily be verified that identical patterns, that is, identical cubes formed on two adjacent maps, can combine to eliminate one variable. Identical cubes formed on all four maps in the six-variable map can combine to eliminate two variables. These are illustrated in the following two examples.

Example 3.8.1

Minimize on the map the following five-variable function:

$$f(x_1\ x_2\ x_3\ x_4\ x_5) = \Sigma(0,1,4,5,6,13,14,15,22,24,25,28,29,30,31)$$

Solution The solution has been shown in Fig. 3.8.3. It can be seen that the cube 21121 ($x_2\ x_3\ x_5$) and the cube 22110 ($x_3\ x_4\ x_5'$) are each the result of combination of two identical cubes on the two maps.

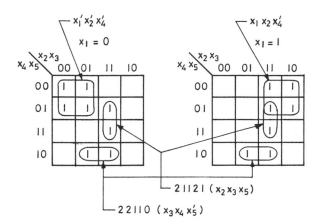

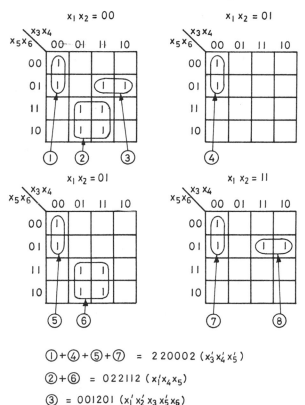

Figure 3.8.3 Minimization of $f = \Sigma(0,1,4-6,13-15,22,24,25,28-31)$ on a five-variable map.

Example 3.8.2

Minimize on the map the six-variable function

$$f(x_1\,x_2\,x_3\,x_4\,x_5\,x_6) = \Sigma(0,1,6,7,9,13,14,15,16,17,32,33,38,39,46,47,48,49,57,61)$$

Solution The plotting of the function on the six-variable map and the solution obtained have been shown in Fig. 3.8.4. It can be seen that the cubes 1, 4, 5, and 7

①+④+⑤+⑦ = 220002 ($x_3' x_4' x_5'$)

②+⑥ = 022112 ($x_1' x_4 x_5$)

③ = 001201 ($x_1' x_2' x_3 x_5' x_6$)

⑧ = 111201 ($x_1 x_2 x_3 x_5' x_6$)

Figure 3.8.4 Minimization of $f = \Sigma(0,1,6,7,9,13-17,32,33,38,39,46-49,57,61)$ on six-variable map.

are identical cubes located on the four maps. Hence they combine to produce a single cube 220002 (x_3' x_4' x_5'). Similarly, cubes 2 and 6 combine to produce the cube 022112 (x_1' x_4 x_5). Cubes 3 and 8, although identical, are not located on adjacent maps. Hence they do not combine with each other and produce two individual cubes, 001201 (x_1' x_2' x_3 x_5' x_6) and 111201 (x_1 x_2 x_3 x_5' x_6), in the solution.

3.9 MULTIPLE-OUTPUT MINIMIZATION

So far we have discussed the minimization of single switching functions. Most practical circuits, however, have more than one output for the same set of input variables. Such functions are known as *multiple-output functions*. The minimization of multiple-output functions is a very complex problem and is discussed in greater detail in Chapter 7. In this section we describe the map method of minimization of such functions when the number of variables is limited to four or five or at most six.

Consider the four-input, three-output function, shown in the truth Table 3.9.1. The three individual functions are shown in three individual four-variable maps in Fig. 3.9.1. The main objective of multiple-output minimization is to express all the output functions in a minimum number of product terms. Obviously, this can be done if the same product term can be shared by more than one output. This objective is achieved on the map by intuition and observation, which the human brain is highly capable of. This has been done in the case of the multiple-output function of Table 3.9.1 in Fig. 3.9.1(a), and we see that the three functions

TABLE 3.9.1

a	b	c	d	f_1	f_2	f_3
0	0	0	0	0	1	0
0	0	0	1	1	1	0
0	0	1	0	0	1	0
0	0	1	1	0	1	0
0	1	0	0	0	0	0
0	1	0	1	1	1	0
0	1	1	0	0	0	0
0	1	1	1	1	1	1
1	0	0	0	0	0	1
1	0	0	1	1	0	1
1	0	1	0	0	0	1
1	0	1	1	0	0	1
1	1	0	0	0	0	0
1	1	0	1	1	0	1
1	1	1	0	0	0	0
1	1	1	1	1	1	1

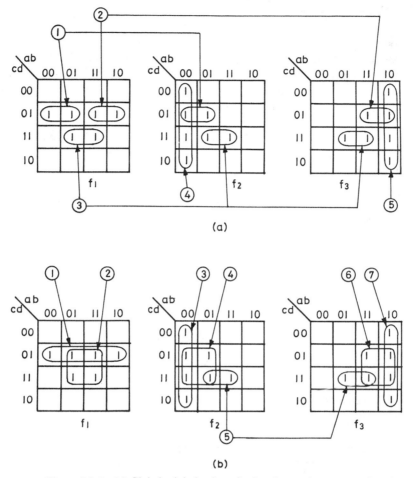

Figure 3.9.1 (a) Global minimization of a four-input, three-output function yields a five-product-term solution; (b) individual minimization of the same function yields a seven-product-term solution.

can be expressed by five product terms, of which two are shared by two functions and one by all three functions. It should be mentioned here that if the three functions would have been individually minimized, the resulting solution would have contained seven product terms, of which only one could be shared by functions f_2 and f_3 [Fig. 3.9.1(b)].

The human brain is undoubtedly the best minimizer of a multiple-output function. Unfortunately, as it depends on visual observation, its application is limited to functions of smaller number of variables, which can conveniently be plotted on the map. Whenever the number of variables becomes large, as is the case in VLSI implementations, we must develop algorithms that are programmable. This development has proved to be an extremely difficult task and is discussed in more detail in Chapter 7.

3.10 UNATE FUNCTIONS

Now that we are quite familiar with the minimum sum-of-product form of a switching function and also the three types of prime cubes, we may discuss in this section an interesting class of switching functions known as unate functions. A significant property of this class of functions is that every unate function consists of only essential prime cubes.

Definition 3.10.1. If, in the minimum sum-of-product form of a switching function, each variable appears either in its true form or its complemented form, but not both, then the function is called a *unate function*.

The true and complemented forms are also called positive and negative forms, respectively.

Example 3.10.1

Determine which of the following functions is (are) unate functions.

(a) $f_1(x_1x_2x_3) = \Sigma(3,4\text{--}7)$
(b) $f_2(x_1x_2x_3x_4) = x_1'x_2 + x_1x_2x_4 + x_1'x_2'x_3'x_4$
(c) $f_3(x_1x_2x_3x_4) = \Sigma(1,4,5,9,13,15)$

Solution Minimizing on the map (not shown), we get

(a)
$$f_1 = x_1 + x_2x_3$$

Here all the three variables are in the true form. Hence the function is a unate function.

(b)
$$f_2 = x_1'x_2 + x_2x_4 + x_1'x_3'x_4$$

Here the variable x_1 is in the complemented form, x_2 is in the true form, x_3 is in the complemented form, and x_4 is in the true form. Therefore, f_2 is a unate function.

(c)
$$f_3(x_1x_2x_3x_4) = x_3'x_4 + x_1'x_2x_3' + x_1x_2x_4$$

Here the variable x_1 is in both forms. Therefore, the function is not unate.

Definition 3.10.2. If in the minimum sum-of-product form of a switching function, a variable x_i is only in the positive (negative) form, then the function is said to be *positive* (*negative*) in x_i. If it appears in both positive and negative forms, then the function is said to be *mixed* in x_i.

Theorem 3.10.1. A switching function is unate if and only if it can be expressed as a sum of essential prime cubes, all intersecting at a common subcube.

Proof. IF (Sufficiency): Let C_1, C_2, ..., C_n be essential prime cubes intersecting at the subcube C_s. Then an EPC C_i can be obtained by eliminating one or more variables from C_s. Therefore, a variable x_j appearing in any C_i must be in the same form as it appears in C_s. Hence the variable x_j must appear only in one form whenever it appears in an EPC C_i. Hence the function is unate.

Q.E.D

ONLY IF (Necessity): Let the MSOP form of a unate function U consists of prime cubes $C_1, C_2, \ldots, C_n$. Then, by Definition 3.10.2, no variable of U appears in both true and complemented forms. Therefore, $C_1 C_2 \ldots C_n \neq 0$. Hence all the prime cubes intersect at a common subcube C_s, given by $C_s = C_1 C_2 \ldots C_n$. Again, consider two cubes C_i and C_j intersecting at the subcube C_{ij}. Then each of the two cubes C_i and C_j has at least one minterm outside C_{ij} which is distinct to that cube. This holds good for all pairs of the cubes $C_1, C_2, \ldots, C_n$. Hence each cube has at least one minterm outside C_s which is covered by only that cube. Therefore, each of the cubes $C_1, C_2, \ldots, C_n$ is an essential prime cube. Hence a unate function can be expressed as a sum of EPCs, all intersecting at a common subcube.   Q.E.D.

Note that the function f_2 of Example 3.10.1, shown in Fig. 3.10.1(a) in the given SOP form, has in its MSOP form [see Fig. 3.10.1(b)] three EPCs all of which intersect at the common minterm 5 ($x_1' x_2 x_3' x_4$), which is a 0-cube.

It should be mentioned here that to detect the unateness of a switching function, it is not always necessary to reduce it to its MSOP form. The unateness can also be determined from another property of switching functions known as 1-monotonicity, which is defined below.

Definition 3.10.3.   A switching function f is *1-monotonic* in the variable x_i if the residue functions $\mathrm{RF}_0(x_i)$ and $\mathrm{RF}_1(x_i)$ are comparable. Further,

if $\mathrm{RF}_0(x_i) > \mathrm{RF}_1(x_i)$, then f is negative in x_i;

if $\mathrm{RF}_0(x_i) < \mathrm{RF}_1(x_i)$, then f is positive in x_i; and

if $\mathrm{RF}_0(x_i) = \mathrm{RF}_1(x_i)$, then x_i does not appear in the MSOP form of the function.

Definition 3.10.4.   If a switching function is 1-monotonic in all its variables, then the function is called a 1-monotonic function.

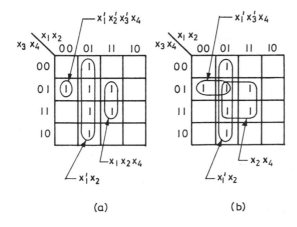

(a)   (b)

Figure 3.10.1   (a) Function f_2 in the given SOP form; (b) function f_2 in the minimized MSOP form.

It is now evident from the definition of 1-monotonic function above that such a function will always be either positive or negative in a variable x_i. Therefore, a 1-monotonic function is also unate. Hence sometimes these two terms are used interchangeably.

Consider the function f_2 of Example 3.10.1. Let us detect if it is 1-monotonic. The function has been given as $f_2 = x_1'x_2 + x_1x_2x_4 + x_1'x_2'x_3'x_4$. Now the residue functions of x_1, $RF_0(x_1)$ and $RF_1(x_1)$ are obtained by substituting 0 and 1, respectively, for x_1 in the function f_2. Thus

$$RF_0(x_1) = f_2(0x_2x_3x_4) = x_2 + x_2'x_3'x_4$$

$$RF_1(x_1) = f_2(1x_2x_3x_4) = x_2x_4$$

Now

$$RF_0(x_1)RF_1(x_1) = (x_2 + x_2'x_3'x_4)(x_2x_4)$$
$$= x_2x_4$$
$$= RF_1(x_1)$$

Therefore, $RF_0(x_1) > RF_1(x_1)$. Hence f_2 is negative in x_1. Similarly, it can be shown that $RF_0(x_2) < RF_1(x_2)$, $RF_0(x_3) > RF_1(x_3)$, and $RF_0(x_4) < RF_1(x_4)$. Therefore, f_2 is positive in x_2, negative in x_3, and positive in x_4. Hence the function is 1-monotonic, that is, unate.

REFERENCES

KARNAUGH, M. The map method for the synthesis of a logic circuit, *AIEE Trans. Part I, Commun. Electron.,* Vol. 72, No. 9, November 1953, pp. 593–598.

KOHAVI, Z. *Switching and Finite Automata Theory,* 2nd ed. New York: McGraw-Hill Book Company, 1978.

McCLUSKEY, E. J. *Logic Design Principles.* Englewood Cliffs, N.J.: Prentice-Hall, 1986.

VEITCH, E. W. A chart method for simplifying truth functions, *Proc. ACM,* Pittsburgh, May 2–3, 1952, pp. 127–133.

PROBLEMS

3.1. Plot the following functions on the Karnaugh map and thereby express them in their disjunctive canonical forms.
  (a) $f_1 = a + b'$
  (b) $f_2 = a + b'c$
  (c) $f_3 = x_1 + x_2 x_3' + x_3' x_4$
  (d) $f_4 = wx + x'y + w'z$

3.2. Show that the functions f_1, f_2, and f_3 are comparable when:
  (a) $f_1 = x_1'x_2 + x_1'x_2'x_4 + x_1x_2x_3$
  (b) $f_2 = x_1'x_3'x_4 + x_2x_3x_4 + x_1'x_2x_4'$
  (c) $f_3 = x_1'x_2 + x_1'x_4 + x_2x_3$

3.3. Express the functions of Problem 3.1 in their conjunctive canonical forms.

3.4. Plot the following functions on maps, determine all the prime cubes, and classify them into essential, redundant, and selective prime cubes.
(a) $f_1 = \Sigma(1,2,5,6,7)$
(b) $f_2 = \Sigma(2,4,5,6)$
(c) $f_3 = \Sigma(1,3,5,7,9,10,12,13)$
(d) $f_4 = \Sigma(3,4,8,9,10,12-15)$

3.5. Minimize the folowing functions on the map. In each case, state how many EPCs and SPCS are in the MSOP form of the function.
(a) $f_1 = \Sigma(0,1,2,4)$
(b) $f_2 = \Sigma(1,3,5,6,7)$
(c) $f_3 = \Sigma(0,1-4,5,8,10,12,13-15)$
(d) $f_4 = \Sigma(2,4,6-9,10,12,15)$
(e) $f_5 = \Sigma(0,3,5,8,9,11,12,15)$
(f) $f_6 = \Sigma(0-4,6-9,12-15)$

3.6. Plot the following cubes on maps, and express them as a sum of minterms.
(a) 0122   (b) 11221   (c) 2102   (d) 012122

3.7. The cube 0021 is a subsuming cube of all four of the following functions. In each function, state if the cube is a prime cube. If it is not a prime cube, then find the expanded cube of which 0021 is an implicant. In each such function, list the other cubes into which 0021 expands to form a prime cube.
(a) $f_1 = 0021 + 0102 + 1202 + 2110$
(b) $f_2 = 0021 + 0102 + 2111$
(c) $f_3 = 0021 + 2101 + 1021 + 2110$
(d) $f_4 = 0021 + 2101 + 1212$

3.8. Plot the following functions on map, and minimize them. Express them in cubical form.
(a) $f_1 = 0122 + 2122 + 0121$
(b) $f_2 = 2121 + 0110 + 2112 + 1201$
(c) $f_3 = 1012 + 2221 + 0121 + 2102$
(d) $f_4 = 0121 + 2001 + 2112 + 0212 + 1212$

3.9. Find the MSOP form for each of the following functions. In each case, state if the solution is unique; if not, give all the solutions.
(a) $f_1 = \Sigma(8,9,10,13,15) + \phi\Sigma(0,4,6,12,14)$
(b) $f_2 = \Sigma(5,9,14,15) + \phi\Sigma(0,1,7,8,11-13)$
(c) $f_3 = \Sigma(0,3,7,11,13) + \phi\Sigma(2,4,6,12)$
(d) $f_4 = \Sigma(2,8,9,10-12) + \phi\Sigma(3,6,13-15)$

3.10. Express the functions of Problem 3.9 in their MPOS forms.

3.11. Minimize the following functions.
(a) $f_1 = \Sigma(2,4,9-12,19-26,29,31)$
(b) $f_2 = \Sigma(7-11,16-20,22,29,30)$
(c) $f_3 = \Sigma(1,3,6,9,22-29,36-40,45,51)$
(d) $f_4 = \Sigma(0-6,13-16,17-20,25-29,41-48,57-60)$

3.12. Construct four-variable functions having the given properties. Wherever it is not possible to construct a function, explain why.
(a) A function consisting of EPCs only.
(b) A function consisting of RPCs only.
(c) A function consisting of SPCs only.
(d) A function consisting of EPCs and RPCs only.

(e) A function consisting of EPCs and SPCs only.

(f) A function consisting of RPCs and SPCS only.

3.13. For each of the following statements, state if it is true or false. If true, prove it as a theorem; otherwise, give a counterexample.

(a) A function consisting of only EPCs has a unique MSOP form.

(b) A function consisting of only EPCS and SPCs cannot have a unique MSOP form.

(c) A function consisting of only EPCs and a closed SPC chain cannot have a unique MSOP form.

(d) A function consisting of only SPCs cannot have a unique MSOP form.

(e) A function that has a unique MSOP form also has a unique MPOS form.

3.14. Find a method of detecting a self-dual function on a map. Apply your method to determine which of the following functions are self-dual.

(a) $f_1 = ab + bc + ac$

(b) $f_2 = \Sigma(0,3,5,6)$

(c) $f_3 = \Sigma(0,2,5,6,8,11,12,14)$

(d) $f_4 = \Sigma(1,3,7,9,10,13,14,15)$

(e) $f_5 = \Sigma(0,1,5\text{--}7,11,12,15,17,18,21\text{--}23,27\text{--}29)$

3.15. Solve Problem 2.8 with the help of a map.

3.16. Find on a map all the MSOP forms of the following function.

$$f = \Sigma(1,3,4,5,10,12,14,18,19,21,23,24,26,28,29)$$

3.17. With the help of a map, determine which of the following functions are unate.

(a) $f_1 = \Sigma(3,4\text{--}7)$

(b) $f_2 = \Sigma(1,4\text{--}7,13,15)$

(c) $f_3 = \Sigma(1,5\text{--}7,11\text{--}13,15)$

(d) $f_4 = \Sigma(1,4,5,7,9,12,13,15,29,31)$

(e) $f_5 = \Sigma(2,8\text{--}13,15\text{--}18,23\text{--}25,27\text{--}31)$

3.18. Solve Problem 3.17 without the help of a map.

3.19. Express each of the "nonunate" functions of Problem 3.17 as a sum of the minimum number of unate functions.

3.20. Express each of the functions of Problem 3.5 as a sum of the minimum number of unate functions.

3.21. A four-variable unate function has four EPCs, of which two are 0121 and 0112. Find the DCF of the function.

3.22. A four-variable unate function has one 1-cube and two 2-cubes, intersecting at minterm 15. Find the MSOP form of the function. How many functions having this specification are there? Show all of them on separate maps.

3.23. Construct four-variable functions having the following specifications. If impossible, give reasons.

(a) A function having five minterms and four EPCs, none of which is a 0-cube.

(b) A cyclic function whose complement is not a cyclic function.

(c) A cyclic function whose complement is also a cyclic function.

(d) A function that is both unate and self-dual.

4

Tabular and Computer-Aided Minimization Procedures

4.1 INTRODUCTION

As we discussed in Chapter 3, the map method of minimizing a Boolean function is very efficient and accurate for a smaller number of variables. If, however, the number of variables exceeds six, it is very difficult to recognize the solution cubes on the map. In such a situation tabular methods must be used. Another advantage of all tabular methods is that they are programmable and therefore can be developed as a CAD (computed-aided design) tool. The most extensively used tabular method is the Quine–McCluskey (QM) algorithm. But even this method becomes inadequate in a very large scale integration (VLSI) environment. Nevertheless, a thorough understanding of the QM method is absolutely essential for developing any other algorithm suitable for the design of VLSI circuits and systems.

4.2 QUINE–McCLUSKEY ALGORITHM

The tabular method known as the Quine–McCluskey algorithm was proposed by Quine (1952) and improved by McCluskey (1956). In Quine's method, the Boolean

Some materials in this chapter are reproduced by permission of the IEEE, New York, USA, from author's papers mentioned at References, Biswas (1984, 1986, and 1990), from their publications, *Proceedings, 21st Design Automation Conference*, 1984, and *IEEE Trans on Computer-aided Design of Integrated Circuits and Systems*, 1986 and 1990.

function to be minimized is first expressed as a sum of minterms or 0-cubes. All minterms are arranged one after another to form a table, which we shall call table T_0 (see Table 4.2.1). Each minterm of this table is then compared with the rest to see if one variable can be eliminated by the combination of two minterms. For example, when the minterm $a'bc'd$ is combined with the minterm $a'b'c'd$, it yields the product term $a'c'd$ since

$$a'bc'd + a'b'c'd = a'c'd$$

McCluskey pointed out that it is not necessary to compare each minterm with all the other minterms. He showed that two minterms will combine if there is one and only one variable in the true form in one of the minterms and in the complemented form in the other. This improvement, suggested by McCluskey, considerably reduced the number of comparisons and therefore significantly improved the efficiency of the method. Let us now illustrate the various steps of the QM method by minimizing the Boolean function

$$f_1 = \Sigma(0,1,3,5,7,8,9,10,13,14,15,17,21,25,29)$$

First we define the term weight of a cube.

Definition 4.2.1.   When a cube is expressed in a form where a true variable is denoted by a 1, a complemented variable by a 0, and an eliminated variable by a 2, the number of 1's in the cube is called its *weight*.

For example, the five-variable minterm 21(10101), which is a 0-cube, has a weight 3, and the five-variable 2-cube 02121 has a weight 2.

In the QM method, the minterms (0-cubes) are arranged in ascending order of their weights to form table T_0. Thus table T_0 can have several partitions, having minterms of weights 0, 1, 2, and so on.

Table T_0 of our example function f_1 is shown in Table 4.2.1. The minterm 0 is in the first partition of weight 0. The second partition of weight 1 has minterms 1 and 8. The third partition of weight 2 has minterms 3, 5, 9, 10, 17, and so on. While constructing table T_1 from table T_0, the minterm 0 of the partition of weight 0 is to be compared with only the two minterms 1 and 8 of the next partition only. These two comparisons generate the 1-cubes (0,1) and (0,8) in table T_1. Similarly, the minterms of partition of weight 1 need to be compared with the minterms of the next partition of weight 2 only. These comparisons generate six 1-cubes of weight 1 in table T_1. After all comparisons are completed, we get table T_1, containing only 1-cubes. Comparing in a similar manner table T_1 generates table T_2, which has only 2-cubes. Table T_2 generates table T_3, having only one 3-cube. No further table can be generated.

Note that the weight difference of 1 is a necessary but not a sufficient condition for the combination of two cubes in a table. For example, the five-variable minterm 3(00011) having weight 2 in table T_0 will combine with 7(00111) but not with 13, 14, 21, and 25, although all have weight 3. Similarly, the five-variable 1-cube 00021 (1,3), having weight 1, will combine with the 1-cube 00121 (5,7) of the next partition but not with others, although they have weight 3. Thus,

TABLE 4.2.1 COMBINATION TABLES FOR $f_1 = \Sigma\,(0,1,3,5,7\text{--}10,13\text{--}15,17,21,25,29)$

T_0

	x_1	x_2	x_3	x_4	x_5	
0	0	0	0	0	0	✓
1	0	0	0	0	1	✓
8	0	1	0	0	0	✓
3	0	0	0	1	1	✓
5	0	0	1	0	1	✓
9	0	1	0	0	1	✓
10	0	1	0	1	0	✓
17	1	0	0	0	1	✓
7	0	0	1	1	1	✓
13	0	1	1	0	1	✓
14	0	1	1	1	0	✓
21	1	0	1	0	1	✓
25	1	1	0	0	1	✓
15	0	1	1	1	1	✓
29	1	1	1	0	1	✓

T_1

	x_1	x_2	x_3	x_4	x_5	
(0,1)	0	0	0	0	2	✓
(0,8)	0	2	0	0	0	✓
(1,3)	0	0	0	2	1	✓
(1,5)	0	0	2	0	1	✓
(1,9)	0	2	0	0	1	✓
(1,17)	2	0	0	0	1	✓
(8,9)	0	1	0	0	2	✓
(8,10)	0	1	0	2	0	A
(3,7)	0	0	2	1	1	✓
(5,7)	0	0	1	2	1	✓
(5,13)	0	2	1	0	1	✓
(5,21)	2	0	1	0	1	✓
(9,13)	0	1	2	0	1	✓
(9,25)	2	1	0	0	1	✓
(10,14)	0	1	2	1	0	B
(17,21)	1	0	2	0	1	✓
(17,25)	1	2	0	0	1	✓
(7,15)	0	2	1	1	1	✓
(13,15)	0	1	2	1	1	✓
(13,29)	2	1	1	0	1	✓
(14,15)	0	1	1	1	2	C
(21,29)	1	2	1	0	1	✓
(25,29)	1	1	2	0	1	✓

T_2

	x_1	x_2	x_3	x_4	x_5	
(0,1,8,9)	0	2	0	0	2	D
(1,3,5,7)	0	0	2	2	1	E
(1,5,9,13)	0	2	2	0	1	✓
(1,5,17,21)	2	0	2	0	1	✓
(1,9,17,25)	2	2	0	0	1	✓
(5,7,13,15)	0	2	1	2	1	F
(5,13,21,29)	2	2	1	0	1	✓
(9,13,25,29)	2	1	2	0	1	✓
(17,21,25,29)	1	2	2	0	1	✓

T_3

	x_1	x_2	x_3	x_4	x_5	
(1,5,9,13, 17,21,25,29)	2	2	2	0	1	G

while comparing cubes belonging to one partition with those of the adjacent partition of a QM table T_α, every variable position must be checked to make sure that the two cubes differ in *one and only one* position and have identical symbols (0, 1, or 2) in all other positions.

Following these procedures table T_0 generates table T_1, and then table T_1 generates table T_2, and so on, until a table T_α is reached, where no cube of table T_α will combine with another cube to generate a table $T_{\alpha+1}$ having $(\alpha + 1)$-cubes. Here the procedure for the generation of successive combination tables terminates. In our illustrataive example, after table T_0, T_1, T_2, and T_3 have been generated, no table T_4 can be generated.

Another precaution that must be taken while generating tables T_2, T_3, and so on, is the avoidance of adding a cube more than once in the table. Take, for example, the cube 02002 (0,1,8,9) in table T_2. This tube is generated twice by the cubes of table T_1, once when (0,1) combines with (8,9) and again when (0,8) combines with (1,9). But because of the idempotence law, the 2-cube (0,1,8,9) must appear only once in table T_2. Hence every time a 2-cube is generated by the 1-cubes of table T_1, it should be checked that it has not been generated already. Only a 2-cube generated for the first time should be written in table T_2. It is interesting to note that every 2-cube of table T_2 will be generated twice by the 1-cubes of table T_1. This can easily be verified. For example, take the 2-cube 20201 (1,15,17,21). This will be generated when (1,5) combines with (17,21), and again when (1,17) combines with (5,21). Similarly, each 3-cube of table T_3 will be generated thrice. In our example function the only 3-cube 22201 (1,5,9,13,17,21,25,29) of table T_3 will be generated for the first time when (1,5,9,13) combines with (17,21,25,29) and again when (1,5,17,21) combines with (9,13,25,29), and finally, when (1,9,17,25) combines with (5,13,21,29). In general, the following theorem regarding the number of multiple generation of an α-cube can be stated.

Theorem 4.2.1. An α-cube of table T_α $(\alpha > 0)$ is generated α times by the $(\alpha - 1)$ cubes of table $T_{\alpha-1}$.

The reader may easily prove this theorem.

While generating various tables of the QM method, whenever a cube in a table combines with another cube, the two cubes are checked off ($\checkmark$). Hence after all the tables are generated, the cubes without the check mark are the largest cubes that do not combine with any other cube of the function. Hence by Definition 3.4.1 these are the prime cubes. In function f_1 there are seven such cubes, marked A to G. We must now determine which are the essential, redundant, and selective cubes among these. For this purpose, another table, called the *prime cube* (PC) *table,* is formed. Table 4.2.2 shows the PC table for function f_1.

In the first column of this table all the PCs, A to G, are written. The subsequent columns are headed by all the minterms of the function. If a prime cube PC_i covers a minterm m_j, a cross is placed at the intersection of the row of PC_i and the column of m_j. After all crosses have been placed, the PC table shown in Table 4.2.2 is obtained. Now look for single-cross columns in this table. Column

TABLE 4.2.2 PRIME CUBE TABLE

Prime cubes	⓪	①	③	⑤	⑦	⑧	⑨	10	⑬	14	15	⑰	㉑	㉕	㉙
A 8,10						X		X							
B 10,14								X		X					
C 14,15										X	X				
*D 0,1,8,9	X	X				X	X								
*E 1,3,5,7		X	X	X	X										
F 5,7,13,15				X	X				X		X				
*G 1,5,9,13,17, 21,25,29		X		X			X		X			X	X	X	X

TABLE 4.2.3 SELECTIVE PRIME CUBE TABLE

Prime cubes	⑩	⑭	15
A 8,10	×		
*B 10,14	×	×	
C 14,15		×	×
*F 5,7,13,15			×
A < B			

0 is such a column. Hence the minterm 0 is covered only by the PC *D*. Hence, by Definition 3.4.2, *D* is an essential prime cube (EPC). All the minterms covered by *D* are then circled. Minterms 0, 1, 8, and 9 get circled in this process. Following this procedure, PCs *D*, *E*, and *G* are chosen as EPCs, and all minterms except 10, 14, and 15 get covered. Each of the remaining PCs of Table 4.2.2 is obviously either an RPC or an SPC. A proper subset from among these PCs must be chosen to cover the minterms 10, 14, and 15. To do this, another table, called a *selective prime cube* (SPC) *table,* is formed with all the rest of the PCs as rows and the uncovered minterms as columns (see Table 4.2.3).

4.3 THE DOMINANCE RELATION

In most SPC tables the minimum subset of SPCs is selected with the help of the dominance relation.

Definition 4.3.1. In an SPC table, if a row *I* has crosses in all columns where another row *J* has crosses, and there is at least one more column with a cross under *I* but not under *J*, row *I* is said to dominate row *J*. In other words, between the pairs of rows *I* and *J*, *I* is the *dominating row* and *J* is the *dominated row.*

Applying this definition in the SPC table, Table 4.2.3, among rows *A*, *B*, and *C* which form a group of PCs of the same dimension, that is, all are 1-cubes, we find that row *A*(8,10) is dominated by row *B*(10,14). Hence if row *B* is selected, it will cover all minterms of row *A* and also at least one extra minterm. Moreover, since *A* and *B* are of the same dimension, they have the same number of literals, and therefore are said to have the same *cost*. Note that a PC of dimension α has higher cost than a PC of dimension greater than α. Therefore, the deletion of row *A* (which is a dominated row) does not affect (in fact, helps) in obtaining the minimum cover. These observations are stated in the following theorem.

Theorem 4.3.1. A row in an SPC table that is dominated by another row of the same or smaller cost can be deleted from the SPC table.

Note that in Table 4.2.3, row A is dominated by row B, and row F is dominated by row C. But whereas A can be deleted, being of the same cost as the dominating row B, F cannot be deleted, as it has a lower cost than the dominating row C. When row A is deleted, column 10 becomes a single-cross column, and therefore the SPC $B(10,14)$ must be chosen to cover the minterm 10. With the selection of B, minterms 10 and 14 get covered (circled in Table 4.2.3). Now minterm 15 can be covered by either C or F. Since F is the larger cube, it is chosen. This leads to the choice of B and F to cover all the minterms of the SPC table. Hence the minimum sum solution of function f_1 is

$$
\begin{aligned}
f_1 &= (\text{EPCs}) + (\text{SPCs}) \\
&= (D + E + G) + (B + F) \\
&= (0,1,8,9) + (1,3,5,7) + (1,5,9,13,17,21,25,29) + (10,14) + (5,7,13,15) \\
&= 02002 + 00221 + 22201 + 01210 + 02121 \\
&= x_1'x_3'x_4' + x_1'x_2'x_5 + x_4'x_5 + x_1'x_2x_4x_5' + x_1'x_3x_5
\end{aligned}
$$

4.4 CYCLIC FUNCTIONS

In the example function f_1 worked out in the preceding section, a proper subset of the SPCs was chosen by applying the dominance relation among rows. There are many functions where in the SPC table, at a certain stage, no row may dominate another, resulting in a deadlock. Such functions are called *cyclic functions*. Here the proper subset of the SPCs are to be chosen by a different method, called the *branching method*. Consider the function

$$f_2 = \Sigma(2,6,13,14,15,18,26,30)$$

While minimizing this function by the QM method, only tables T_0 and T_1 can be formed. Eight PCs (all in table T_1) are generated. These are $A(2,6)$, $B(2,18)$, $C(6,14)$, $D(18,26)$, $E(13,15)$, $F(14,15)$, $G(14,30)$, and $H(26,30)$. The PC table identifies $E(13,15)$ as an EPC. The SPC table then becomes as shown in Table 4.4.1.

TABLE 4.4.1 SPC TABLE

	②	⑥	14	18	26	30
*$A(2,6)$	×	×				
$B(2,18)$	×			×		
$C(6,14)$		×	×			
$D(18,26)$				×	×	
×$F(14,15)$			×			
$G(14,30)$			×			×
$H(26,30)$					×	×
		$F < C$	$F < G$			

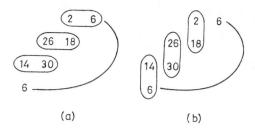

Figure 4.4.1 Cyclic function as a closed SPI chain: (a) horizontal subset as a valid solution; (b) vertical subset as another valid solution.

(a)   (b)

In this table only $F(14,15)$ gets deleted, being dominated by both G and C. But even after deleting F, no single $\times$ column can be found. Hence the dominance relation fails to yield any solution. This is the indication that the function has become cyclic and that the SPC chain is a closed one (Fig. 4.4.1). In the QM method any one of the remaining PCs of Table 4.4.1 is now selected as an SPC of the solution. Let us choose $A(2,6)$. This PC and the two minterms covered by it are then removed. Now the dominance relation can be applied to the rest of the table (Table 4.4.2). This results in having two other SPCs $D(18,26)$ and $G(14,30)$ included in the solution set. If in Table 4.4.1 we would have chosen $B(2,18)$ while branching, we would have got the other valid solution set, consisting of the three SPCs $B(2,18)$, $C(6,14)$, and $H(26,30)$. Hence the function has two valid solutions:

$$f_2 = \text{EPC} + \text{SPCs} = E + \{A + D + G\}$$
$$= (13,15) + \{(2,6) + (18,26) + (14,30)\}$$

or

$$f_2 = \text{EPC} + \text{SPCs} = E + \{B + C + H\}$$
$$= (13,15) + \{(2,18) + (6,14) + (26,30)\}$$

It is interesting to note that the two valid SPC subsets are the horizontal and vertical subsets of the closed SPC chain, as can be seen in Fig. 4.4.1(a) and (b), respectively.

TABLE 4.4.2 REDUCED SPC TABLE

	14	18	26	30
B (2,18)		X		
C (6,14)	X			
*D (18,26)		X	X	
*G (14,30)	X			X
H (26,30)			X	X
	$B < D$		$C < G$	

4.5 THE DEGREE OF ADJACENCY AND ESSENTIAL PRIME CUBES

The Quine–McCluskey method finds the minimum sum of cubes of a switching function in three steps. In the first step it generates all the prime cubes in combination tables T_0, T_1, and so on. In the second step it identifies all the essential prime cubes from the PC table. In the third and final step it selects the minimum SPC subset from the SPC table by successive applications of the dominance relation, with branching, if need be. We have already seen (Theorem 4.2.1) how in the first step all the terms starting from table T_2 onward are generated more than once. This results in much wasteful computation. The second step is computationally more expensive. Here, first a matrix of p rows and m columns is generated, where p is the number of prime cubes and m is the number of minterms. Then each column of this matrix is scanned in search of single-cross columns. The third step is also expensive, as the dominance relation has to be applied a number of times. On the whole, the QM method is a computationally expensive algorithm. In 1971, Biswas (1971) introduced the concept of a new parameter called the degree of adjacency (DA) and showed that with its help an EPC can be identified as soon as it is generated in one of the combination tables, T_0, T_1, . . . This entirely eliminates the PC table and therefore all the computation associated with it. The DA is defined as follows:

Definition 4.5.1. The number of times a minterm combines with other minterms of the switching function is called the *degree of adjacency* (DA) of the minterm.

It can be seen that the DA of a minterm can easily be determined while generating table T_1 from table T_0. For example, for function f_1 (table T_0 of Table 4.2.1) the minterm 0 has a DA of 2, as it has combined with two minterms, 1 and 8. Similarly, the minterm 1 has a DA of 5, as it has combined with five minterms, 0, 3, 5, 9, and 17. An essential prime cube (EPC) can now be identified with the help of the following theorem.

Theorem 4.5.1. If a minterm of DA α generates a term in table T_α, then the term is an essential prime cube.

Thus the minterm 0, which has a DA 2, has generated the term (0,1,8,9) in table T_2. Hence the term (0,1,8,9) is an essential prime cube. Similarly, since the minterm 3 having a DA 2 (it combines with only 1 and 7) has generated the term (1,3,5,7) in table T_2, the term (1,3,5,7) is an EPC.

Sureshchander (1975) made a further improvement and showed that even the combination tables need not be generated. He was the first to develop a fast technique (Sureshchander, 1975) for the minimization of switching function, utilizing the concept of degree of adjacency. Later, many authors developed techniques based on the DA concept. Notable among them was the directed search method of Ryne et al. (1977). A common and significant feature of all these methods was the complete elimination of the combination and two cover tables, the PC and the SPC tables. This was a significant departure from the philosophy of Quine and McCluskey and resulted in the development of techniques where the minimum sum can be determined with considerably less computation. In all these methods the EPCs can be determined accurately by a theorem that is a restatement of Theorem 4.5.1 (see Theorem 4.6.1). However, the determination of the minimum subset of the SPCs posed a serious hurdle. The CAMP algorithm developed by the author to overcome this hurdle is discussed in the next section.

4.6 THE CAMP ALGORITHM

The CAMP (computer-aided minimization procedure) algorithm was developed by the author in 1984 (Biswas, 1984). It was further improved in 1990 (Biswas, 1990). Although the improved version, called CAMPII, is adequate for minimizing a single-output switching function, some of the salient features of CAMPI, together with relevant definitions and theorems, will be described for proper understanding of CAMPII. A detailed study of the CAMP algorithm is very useful from another viewpoint. It introduces to the reader various obstacles and pitfalls that must be overcome while developing a CAD package.

CAMPI minimizes single functions. The function to be minimized is expressed as a sum of minterms, and these minterms are input to the program in their decimal designations. Let the function to be minimized be the four-variable function

$$f_3(abcd) = \Sigma(1,3,5,7,9,10,13,14,15)$$

as plotted on the map in Fig. 4.6.1. The computer program takes up the first minterm in the list, 1, and calculates its degree of adjacency. For this the minterm is converted into its binary form and each bit is complemented one at a time. In this process the minterm generates all its adjacent minterms one by one. Thus 0001(1) will generate 1001(9), 0101(5), 0011(3), and 0000(0). In the function, 9, 5, and 3 are present but 0 is absent. Hence 1 has a degree of adjacency 3 in this function, and its three *directions* of adjacency are 9, 5, and 3. When 9 and 1 combine, we get the product term from which the variable *a* is eliminated. This will be written by replacing the bit under *a* by 2. Thus we get 2001. Similarly, when 1 combines with 5 and 3, the product terms or cubes 0201 (variable *b* eliminated) and 0021 (variable *c* eliminated) are produced, respectively. It is therefore possible that the minterm 1 may combine with other minterms in the function and can produce a cube from which all three variables corresponding to the three adjcency directions are eliminated. The resulting cube *d* or 2221 in the ternary notation (where 2 indicates the absence of the corresponding variable) may turn out to be a cube in the solution. But whether this cube will really find a place in the final solution is not yet known. Hence this cube (product term) is called a candidate solution cube (CSC).

Definition 4.6.1.   A minterm *m* in the list of minterms constituting a Boolean function $f(m < f)$ having an adjacency α produces a *candidate solution cube* (CSC), with α 2's in place of the variables that get eliminated every time it combines with another minterm of the function.

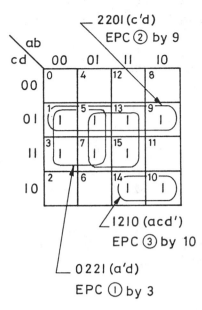

Figure 4.6.1 Function $f_3\,(abcd) = \Sigma(1,3,5,7,9,10,13,14,15)$ plotted on map.

When two n-variable minterms combine, they produce a 1-cube of $n - 1$ variables. Hence it can easily be verified that an m-cube from which m variables have been eliminated is the result of the combination of 2^m minterms (0-cubes). Thus the four-variable ($abcd$) minterms 1(0001), 5(0101), 9(1001), and 13(1101) produce the two-variable product term $c'd$, that is, the 2-cube 2201.

Definition 4.6.2.   The set of 2^m n-variable minterms whose combinations produce a product term of $n - m$ variables or an m-cube will be called the *set of subsuming minterms* (SSM) of the product term or m-cube.

It now follows that the SSM of a product term or the cube expressed in ternary (0,1,2) form can be obtained by replacing the 2's with all combinations of 0's and 1's. Thus the SSM of the cube 02102 is obtained by replacing the two 2's by four binary combinations, as shown in Table 4.6.1.

Theorem 4.6.1.   A candidate solution cube (CSC) is an essential prime cube (EPC) of the switching function if the set of subsuming minterms of the

TABLE 4.6.1

Cube	Binary combinations	SSM	Decimal designation
02102	00	00100	(4)
	01	00101	(5)
	10	01100	(12)
	11	01101	(13)

CSC is within the function (SSM $< f$), that is, if the CSC is wholly within the function.

Corollary 4.6.1A. The candidate solution cube (CSC) of a minterm having degree of adjacency (DA), either 0 or 1, is an essential prime cube (EPC).

Proof. The proof of the corollary follows from the fact that when the DA is 0, the minterm is itself the CSC and its SSM, and is therefore in f. When the DA is 1, the SSM of the CSC are the two minterms that combine to produce the CSC and hence are in f. Q.E.D.

Theorem 4.6.2. If the SSM generated by the CSC of a minterm is not wholly in f, then the minterm is covered by at least two intersecting prime cubes.

Proof. If the SSM generated by the CSC of a minterm is not wholly in f, then all adjacent minterms are not in a single cube. Therefore, the minterms must be in at least two cubes. Each of these cubes may represent either an essential, a redundant, or a selective prime cube, with the minterm (generating the CSC) as a common minterm. Hence the minterm must be covered by at least two intersecting prime cubes. Q.E.D.

In the first phase of the CAMPI algorithm all the EPCs are selected one after another. The program takes up the first minterm in the list and calculates its DA and CSC. Both the DA and CSC are stored in their respective arrays. If the DA turns out to be either 0 or 1, the CSC is selected as a *solution cube* (SC) of the solution, and the minterm(s) subsuming the SC is(are) flagged off. If the DA is 2 or more, the program computes its SSM from the corresponding CSC and checks if the SSM is in f. If the SSM is in f, the CSC is an EPC (Theorem 4.6.1). It is then stored as a solution cube of the solution and all the members of the SSM are flagged off. If the SSM is not in f, the CSC is not a product term of the solution (Theorem 4.6.2), but it is still saved for possible future use. The program then goes to the next minterm in the list that has not yet been flagged off, and repeats the procedure until the entire list of true minterms is scanned.

It should be obvious from Theorems 4.6.1 and 4.6.2 that at the end of phase I of the program, the following situation prevails.

1. All EPCs have been selected and stored or printed out as cubes of the solution.
2. All minterms covered by EPCs and RPCs, if any, have been flagged off.
3. Only those minterms that are covered by SPC chains alone remain uncovered. But the program has already computed and stored their DAs and CSCs.

Phase II of the algorithm determines the selective prime cubes. Obviously, SPCs are generated by the minterms that remain uncovered by the EPCs. The algorithm takes up these minterms one by one in ascending order of their degrees of adjacency, which have already been calculated in phase I. If a minterm with a DA value of α generates an EPC, the EPC will always be an α-cube. On the other hand, a minterm with a DA value of α that generates an SPC will produce a cube of dimension between 1 and $\alpha - 1$. An attempt must be made to generate the highest-dimension cube. Consider the switching function f_3 shown on the Karnaugh map of Fig. 4.6.1. Here, in phase I, minterm 3 with a DA of 2 finds the EPC 0221 ($a'd$), minterm 9 with a DA of 2 the EPC 2201 ($c'd$), and minterm 10 with a DA of 1 the EPC 1210 (acd'). These three EPCS cover all minterms except 15. Hence phase II of the program must find a largest-dimension SPC to cover the minterm 15. The CSC generated by the minterm has the following form:

$$2 \quad 1 \quad 2 \quad 2$$

Let us write above each of the 2's that minterm which combines with the minterm 15 to eliminate the variable at the bit position occupied by the 2:

$$7 \qquad 13 \quad 14$$

$$2 \quad 1 \quad 2 \quad 2$$

We note that the adjacency in the position of the first 2 is in the direction of 7, that of the second 2 is in the direction of 13, and that of the third 2 is in the direction of 14. Also, it can be seen from the map that the largest cube that covers 15 is obtained by expanding in the directions of 7 and 13 and discarding the direction of 14. Hence the 2's under 7 and 13 must be retained, and the 2 under 14 must be replaced by the original bit of the minterm. Hence the largest cube that is an SPC is given by

$$2 \quad 1 \quad 2 \quad 1$$

Thus we must find a way to determine those adjacencies that participate in forming the cube of the SPC. For this purpose CAMPI follows a heuristic procedure, called the *column difference* (CD) *procedure*. Following this procedure the cube 2121 (5,7,13,15) is chosen as the SPC to cover 15.

For function f_3 of Fig. 4.6.1, all three adjacency directions of 15—that is, 7, 13, and 14—were covered. There may be other cases where one or more adjacency directions may remain uncovered. Consider function f_4 as plotted and solved on the map of Fig. 4.6.2. Here the minterm 15 is in a situation similar to that of minterm 15 of Fig. 4.6.1, with the exception that after phase I of the program, two of its adjacency directions, 7 and 13, become covered, whereas direction 31 remains uncovered. Hence although the CD heuristic will recommend that direction 31 be discarded, it must be made (since it is still uncovered) the most deferred direction in the ordering of discarding the adjacency directions. CAMPI has a mechanism by which the uncovered adjacency directions are made the most deferred directions that must be discarded.

In phase II the program takes up the minterms of one particular DA value at a time, starting from the DA value of 2 to the maximum value DAMAX. Even when taking up the minterms of one particular value of DA, it takes a minterm if at least one of its adjacency directions has been covered by an already selected EPC or SPC. This procedure, called *passport checking,* is useful in avoiding the generation of superfluous solution cubes. For cyclic functions, no minterm among the SPC generating minterms will have any passport. Here the first minterm

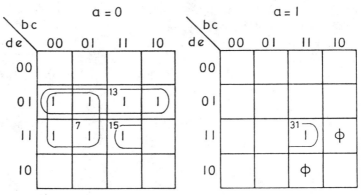

Figure 4.6.2 Function f_4 $(abcde)$ = $\Sigma(1,3,5,7,9,13,15,31)$ + $\phi\Sigma(27,30)$ plotted on map.

(among the SPC generating minterms) with minimum value of DA is taken up, and an SPC to cover this minterm is selected. This is the procedure for *branching*.

Don't-care minterms are also included in the function. But unlike the true minterms, they are flagged off as covered minterms right from the beginning. Consequently, they participate in the calculation of DA and formation of SSM but do not initiate any action in any phase of the algorithm.

The description above is a brief review of the salient features of the various procedures of the CAMPI algorithm. With these procedures CAMPI produces the minimum sum-of-product form in most cases. To illustrate a few cases where the algorithm fails, consider the following two functions:

$$f_5(abcde) = \Sigma(0,2\text{--}7,9\text{--}16,18,19,23,25,26,30)$$

$$f_6(abcd) = \Sigma(0,2,4\text{--}7,11,13,15) + \phi\Sigma(1,12)$$

Function f_5 is shown in Fig. 4.6.3. The map also shows the five EPCs that will be generated in phase I of the algorithm. After the first phase only the minterm 11 remains uncovered. The CD heuristic of CAMPI will get the 2-cube 02012 ($a'c'd$) as the cube covering the minterm. But it can easily be seen from the map that this is not the largest cover. The largest cube covering 11 is the 3-cube 02212 ($a'd$) having the SSM {2,3,6,7,10,11,14,15}. Thus the CD heuristic fails in this case. In CAMPII we therefore do not use the CD heuristic, but a deterministic approach, based on the following theorem.

Theorem 4.6.3. A minterm m_e can be excluded from the candidate solution cube (CSC) generated by a minterm m_g by discarding a 2 in the ith position of the CSC (that is, by replacing the 2 by the original bit at the ith position of m_g) if

$$b_e^i \oplus b_g^i = 1$$

where b_e^i and b_g^i are the bits at the ith positions of m_e and m_g, respectively.

Proof. If $b_e^i \oplus b_g^i = 1$, then b_e^i and b_g^i are different. Hence when the 2 at

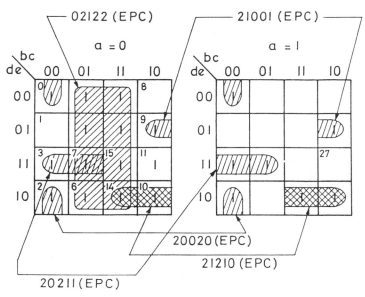

Figure 4.6.3 Function f_5 (*abcde*) $= \Sigma(0,2–7,9–16,18,19,23,25,26,30)$ plotted on map.

the ith position of CSC is replaced by b_g^i, the new CSC and m_e will have differing bits at the ith position. Therefore, the two cubes will be disjoint and therefore mutually exclusive.   Q.E.D.

To implement this theorem, we construct first the *matrix of absentee minterms* (MAM), and then an *exclusion matrix* (EM) by computing $b_e^i \oplus b_g^i$ for all minterms of the MAM under all 2's of the CSC. Thus for the function f_5 of Fig. 4.6.3, we get the EM shown in Table 4.6.2, where "ADs" means "adjacency directions."

TABLE 4.6.2

m_g 11	0	1	0	1	1
ADs	27	3	15	9	10
Present		√	√	√	√
CSC	0	2	2	2	2
MAM 1	0	0	0	0	1
8	0	1	0	0	0
EM 1	—	1	0	1	0
8	—	0	0	1	1
Discard			×		

From EM we find the minimum number of columns that will exclude all the absentee minterms. As a first step to achieving this, all the columns that are dominated by another column should be eliminated, and then the minimum number of columns from the remaining columns should be chosen. Here the first and fourth columns are dominated by the third column. Hence, if the third 2 is discarded, we exclude both the minterms 1 and 8, and get the largest cube, 02212 ($a'd$), as the solution cube.

Now consider the function f_6 plotted on the map of Fig. 4.6.4. Here the two EPCs (shown shaded in Fig. 4.6.4) will be computed in the first phase of CAMP. In the second phase the program takes up minterm 7 (since 7 has a DA of 3, and 5 a DA of 4). Its three adjacent directions are 15, 5, and 6, and its CSC can be computed to be 2122, as shown in Table 4.6.3.

From the map the SSM of the CSC is

$$SSM = \{4–7, 12–15\}$$

and the set of absentee minterms SAM = {14}. Hence CAMPI will search for a 2-cube SPC to cover 7. It will first discard the first 2 from left to right, that is,

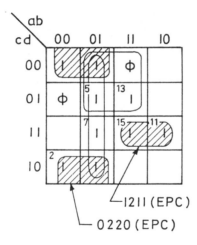

—1211 (EPC)

— 0220 (EPC)

Figure 4.6.4 Function f_6 ($abcd$) = $\Sigma(0,2,4,-7,11,13,15) + \phi\Sigma(1,12)$ plotted on map.

TABLE 4.6.3

m_g 7	0	1	1	1
ADs	15	3	5	6
Present	✓		✓	✓
CSC	2	1	2	2

direction 15, and will select the cube 0122 (4,5,6,7) as a solution cube. The program then comes to the only remaining uncovered minterm, 13, and following the same procedure, will choose the 2-cube 0202 (4,5,12,13) as another solution cube. Thus we get two cubes, shown unshaded in Fig. 4.6.4, in the second phase. As can be verified on the map, this is not the minimum subset of the SPCs. There is a single SPC, the cube 2121 (5,7,13,15), which gives the minimum solution. This failure on the part of CAMPI to yield the minimum solution is due to the fact that it has a mechanism to cover all the uncovered adjacent minterms, but not the uncovered distant minterms (as defined below), which in this example is the minterm 13.

Definition 4.6.3. In a CSC of dimension α generated by a minterm m_g, a minterm having a distance [number of positions where one minterm has a 0(1) and the other minterm a 1(0)] of 1 from the m_g is an *adjacent minterm*. All other minterms having a distance greater than 1 are called *distant minterms*.

Definition 4.6.4. In a CSC of dimension α generated by a minterm m_g, there is only one minterm that has a distance α from the m_g. This distant minterm will be called the *opposite minterm*.

In CAMPII, therefore, the algorithm is so modified that all the uncovered minterms in a CSC except the opposite one are covered, irrespective of whether they are adjacent or distant. For this reason, a *matrix of uncovered minterms* (MUM) is constructed. For function f_6 of Fig. 4.6.4, this is shown as in Table 4.6.4. In this table "ACSC" means "augmented CSC."

The following theorem is then applied to identify the 2's, which must be retained if we want to cover all the minterms of MUM.

Theorem 4.6.4. To cover a minterm m_c in the CSC generated by minterm m_g, each of the 2's of the CSC in the ith position must be retained if

$$b_c^i \oplus b_g^i = 1$$

where b_c^i and b_g^i are the bits at the ith position of m_c and m_g, respectively.

Proof. When $b_c^i \oplus b_g^i = 1$, the bits at the ith position of m_c and m_g are different. Hence if the 2 of the CSC at the ith position is replaced by b_g^i, the resulting CSC and m_c will be two disjoint cubes, and therefore mutually exclusive. Hence 2 at the ith position must be retained. This must be applied to 2's at all ith positions for which $b_c^i \oplus b_g^i = 1$, so that m_c is not rendered disjoint by any one of the ith positions satisfying this relation.   Q.E.D.

This theorem is applied by constructing an *inclusion matrix* (IM) of the uncovered minterms, MUM. Like the exclusion matrix (EM), each row of IM is also obtained by carrying out an EXCLUSIVE-OR operation with each row of

TABLE 4.6.4

	0	1	1	1
m_g 7	0	1	1	1
ADs	15	3	5	6
Present	√		√	√
CSC	2	1	2	2
MUM 5	0	1	0	1
13	1	1	0	1
IM 5	0	—	1	0
13	1	—	1	0
Retain	√		√	
ACSC	3	1	3	2
MAM 14	1	1	1	0
EM 14	—	—	—	1
Discard				×
VSPC	3	1	3	1
SC	2	1	2	1

MUM with the generating minterm m_g. It is obvious that the elements of the IM are computed only under the 2's of the CSC of the m_g. For function f_6 the IM will be as shown in Table 4.6.4.

Applying Theorem 4.6.4 it can be seen from the IM that the 2's in directions 15 and 5 must be retained to cover the minterms 15 and 5. These 2's are therefore augmented to 3, and we get what we shall call the *augmented candidate solution cube* (ACSC). Now the MAM and EM are computed. Since 3's cannot be discarded, the EM is constructed under the 2's of the ACSC. The one-row EM of function f_6 indicates that the 2 in the direction of 6 must be discarded to exclude the minterm 14. When this is done the cube 3131 is obtained as a solution cube. Such an SPC will be called a valid SPC, which may be defined as follows:

Definition 4.6.5. A selective prime cube that covers all the uncovered minterms, both adjacent and distant (except the opposite minterm), and excludes all the absentee minterms will be called a *valid selective prime cube* (VSPC).

Before printing, the program reconverts all 3's into 2's, and the SC is printed out as 2121. The CAMPII printout for function f_6 is shown in Table 4.6.5.

TABLE 4.6.5 CAMPII PRINTOUT OF f_6

MINTERM	DA	SOLUTION CUBE
2	2	0220
11	1	1211
7	3	2121

THE FUNCTION HAS 2 EPCS AND 1 SPCS

It is important to mention here that each row of the EM must have at least one 1. If in the EM even a single row fails to generate at least one 1, the dual purpose of covering all the uncovered minterms and excluding all the absentee minterms of the CSC cannot be achieved. In such a situation the program abandons the minterm and goes to the next minterm having a passport. If after scanning all the SPC-generating minterms in the list, no minterm generates any VSPC, the program comes to the branching mode and generates an SPC cover without trying to cover all the uncovered minterms. During the process of generating the VSPCs, as soon as a VSPC is generated all the minterms covered by the VSPC are flagged off and the program starts scanning once again from the beginning of the list of minterms in ascending order of DA. Quite often it may happen that a minterm which did not generate any VSPC in the previous scan will now generate one, as some of the minterms within its CSC that were uncovered during the previous scan will now become covered.

We shall now discuss an important situation that must be taken care of during the process of generating a VSPC. We may come across an IM where a row has 1's under all 2's of the CSC. According to Theorem 4.6.4, in order to include the particular minterm that generates such an all-1 row, all 2's of the CSC must be retained. However, it is known that the maximum dimension of SPC is $\alpha - 1$, where α is the degree of adjacency of the minterm and therefore the number of 2's in the CSC. Hence an SPC cannot be generated by retaining all 2's of a CSC. It is therefore not possible to cover a minterm that generates an all-1 row in the IM. In the algorithm, therefore, we delete such a row from the IM and then proceed to find the conditions for including the rest of the rows. It can easily be verified that the minterm which generates the all-1 row in the IM is the opposite minterm within the CSC of the generating minterm m_g. This result is stated as the following theorem, the proof of which is obvious.

Theorem 4.6.5. A VSPC can never cover an opposite minterm if it is present in its candidate solution cube (CSC).

Corollary 4.6.5A. If an all-1 row is generated in the IM, it must be deleted and the rest of the IM should be processed.

While processing an SPC, the matrix for the uncovered minterm (MUM) and the corresponding inclusion matrix (IM) is processed first. This indicates which of the 2's of the CSC must be retained. This information is incorporated by augmenting these 2's (which must be retained) to 3's. A CSC with some 3's and some 2's is called an *augmented candidate solution cube* (ACSC). The matrix for the absentee minterms (MAM) and its corresponding exclusion matrix (EM) are then processed. If in the EM there is even a single row having no 1, the particular absentee minterm that generates this row cannot be excluded. Hence in such a situation no VSPC exists, the minterm is abandoned, and the program goes to the next minterm having a passport. The switching function $f_7(abcde) = \Sigma(1-4,6-13,15,19,23,27,31)$ plotted in Fig. 4.6.5 illustrates this situation. After all EPCs are identified in phase I, the program comes to phase II and first takes up minterm 4, which does not have a passport. Then it comes to 2. Although 2 has a passport, it fails to obtain a VSPC. The same situation continues with 6 and 8. When 12 is taken up next, it does not have a passport. Then it takes up 13, and it gets the VSPC, 01202 (8,9,12,13). It is interesting to note that while processing the minterm 13, it encounters the minterm 10, which is an opposite minterm in the CSC of 13. Hence it is deleted according to Theorem 4.6.5. After the VSPC covering 13 has been found, the minterms 8, 9, 12, and 13 are flagged off. The program now comes to 4 again and selects the VSPC (4,6); then it comes to 2 and selects the VSPC (2,3,10,11). With this all the minterms are covered and the minimum solution shown in Fig. 4.6.5 is obtained. The CAMPII printout for function f_7 is shown in Table 4.6.6.

If no VSPC can be generated after scanning all the SPC-generating minterms, the program goes into the branch mode. Here the first uncovered minterm having the least DA is processed. Obviously, in this mode the formations of MUM and therefore of IM are suspended. Only the MAM and EM are processed. After a

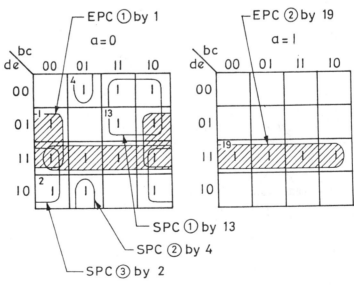

Figure 4.6.5 Function f_7 $(abcde) = \Sigma(1-4,6-13,15,19,23,27,31)$ plotted on map.

Minimization Procedures   Chap. 4

TABLE 4.6.6 CAMPII PRINTOUT OF f_7

MINTERM	DA	SOLUTION CUBES
1	2	02021
19	3	22211
- - - -	- - -	- - - - - - - - -
13	3	01202
4	2	00120
2	3	02012

THE FUNCTION HAS 2 EPCS and 3 SPCS

cover is found, the program reverts to the normal mode. There may be cases where the program goes to the branch mode more than once.

The importance of Theorem 4.6.5 will be evident from the example of function f_7. But for this theorem the algorithm would have gone to the branch mode and might have ended by selecting four instead of the minimum three SPCs.

It can be seen that CAMPII always gets the minimum solution covering all the uncovered minterms, both adjacent and distant, in the normal mode. In the branch mode where the choice of the branching minterm is arbitrary, the solution may not be minimum in some cases. Theorem 4.6.5 allows it to switch to the branch mode only when it is inevitable. The MAM and EM of CAMPII ensure the largest possible dimension for each cube of the solution.

Example 4.6.1

Find the CAMPII printout when it minimizes the example function of the Quine–McCluskey algorithm,

$$f_1(x_1x_2x_3x_4x_5) = \Sigma(0,1,3,5,7–10,13–15,17,21,25,29)$$

Calculate DA, SSM, and so on, with the help of a map.

Solution From the map (Fig. 4.6.6) it can be seen that the minterm 0 with DA 2 will generate the EPC 02002 (0,1,8,9), the minterm 3 with DA 2 the EPC 00221 (1,3,5,7), and the minterm 17 with DA 3 the EPC 22201 (1,5,9,13,17,21,25,29). This completes phase I of the program. The algorithm then takes up the minterm 10 with DA 2. It will be processed as shown in Table 4.6.7.

After selection of this VSPC the minterms 10 and 14 are flagged off. The program now takes up the minterm 15 with DA 3. It will be processed as shown in Table 4.6.8. Hence the printout will be as shown in Table 4.6.9.

Note that the solution obtained is the same as in the classical QM algorithm.

Example 4.6.2

While finding the SPCs in phase II of the problem above, what happens if the program comes first to the minterm 14, another minterm with DA 2, instead of the minterm 10?

Solution It starts processing the minterm 14 as an SPC-generating minterm, as shown in Table 4.6.10. As the ACSC does not have a single 2, m_g 14 does not have a passport. The program now abandons this minterm and goes to 10, another minterm

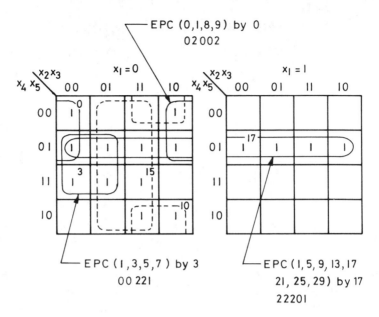

EPC (0,1,8,9) by 0
02002

EPC (1,3,5,7) by 3
00 221

EPC (1,5,9,13,17
21, 25, 29) by 17
22201

Figure 4.6.6 Function $f_1 = \Sigma(1,3,5,7–10,13–15,17,21,25,29)$ plotted on map shows three EPCs and two CSCs.

TABLE 4.6.7

m_g 10	0	1	0	1	0
ADs	26	2	14	8	11
Present			√	√	
CSC	0	1	2	2	0
MUM 14	0	1	1	1	0
IM 14	—	—	1	0	—
Retain			√		
ACSC	0	1	3	2	0
MAM 12	0	1	1	0	0
EM 12	—	—	—	1	0
Discard				×	
VSPC	0	1	3	1	0
SC	0	1	2	1	0

TABLE 4.6.8

m_g 15	0	1	1	1	1
ADs	31	7	11	13	14
Present		√		√	√
CSC	0	2	1	2	2
MUM					
MAM 4	0	0	1	0	0
6	0	0	1	1	0
12	0	1	1	0	0
EM 4	—	1	—	1	1
6	—	1	—	0	1
12	—	0	—	1	1
Discard					×
VSPC	0	2	1	2	1
SC	0	2	1	2	1

TABLE 4.6.9

MINTERM	DA	SOLUTION CUBE
0	2	02002
3	2	00221
17	3	22201
10	2	01210
15	3	02121

THE FUNCTION HAS 3 EPCS AND 2 SPCS

with DA 2. Thereafter the computing proceeds as shown in the solution of Example 4.6.1.

4.7 SPIs AND THE MINIMIZATION COMPLEXITY OF SWITCHING FUNCTIONS

From what we have discussed so far it is quite evident that irrespective of the algorithm used, a switching function having a large proportion of SPCs compared to EPCs, will be more complex and time consuming to minimize. Based on

TABLE 4.6.10

m_g 14	0	1	1	1	0
ADs	30	6	10	12	15
Present			$\checkmark$		$\checkmark$
CSC	0	1	2	1	2
MUM 10	0	1	0	1	0
15	0	1	1	1	1
Retain			$\checkmark$		$\checkmark$
ACSC	0	1	3	1	3

this experience we may even define a quantitative parameter to express the minimization complexity of a switching function.

Definition 4.7.1. The *minimization complexity* (MC) is defined as follows:

$$MC = \frac{\text{number of SPCs}}{\text{number of EPCs} + \text{number of SPCs}}$$

If a switching function has only EPCs and no SPCs, the value of MC is 0. On the other hand, if a function has only SPCs and no EPCs, the value of MC is 1. Thus the quantitative value of MC varies between the limits 0 and 1

4.8 VLSI AND THE INADEQUACY OF THE MINTERM-BASED ALGORITHM

So far we have discussed the Quine–McCluskey and CAMP algorithms for the minimization of Boolean functions. Both of these algorithms and many others reported in the literature require that the switching function to be minimized first be expressed as a sum of minterms. Such algorithms are called minterm-based algorithms. These are quite efficient and adequate as long as the switching function to be minimized is limited to, say, 12 variables, so that the program does not handle more than about 3000 minterms. When the number of variables increases beyond 12, as will be the case in a VSLI environment, the run time of the program increases enormously and becomes quite impractical. Quite often a minterm-based algorithm has a front-end processor that converts a switching function given in the form of an equation (that is, as a sum of cubes) into a form that is a sum of minterms. For a function of a very large number of variables, even this conversion time becomes quite appreciable.

To explain the inadequacy of the minterm-based algorithm, consider the following switching function, which is a 20-variable function.

$$f_8 = x_1x_2 + x_3x_4x_5x_6x_7x_8x_9x_{10}x_{11}x_{12}x_{13}x_{14}x_{15}x_{16}x_{17}x_{18}x_{19}x_{20}$$

Both the Quine–McCluskey and CAMP algorithms will require it to be expressed as a sum of minterms. It is obvious that the first term, x_1x_2, is a sum of 2^{18} minterms and the second term is the sum of 2^2 minterms. So table T_0 of the QM algorithm must have $2^{18} + 2^2$ rows, which should also be partitioned in order of increasing weights. Even the subroutine or subprogram that prepares this partitioned table will require enormous time. The reader can also imagine the formidable time that may be taken by the algorithm to produce the subsequent combination and PC tables that are required to obtain the minimized form.

In the CAMP algorithm, to print out the EPC x_1x_2, the program will, among other things, have to generate its SSM having 2^{18} rows and will have to invoke the search routine 2^{18} times before it can come to the conclusion that the entire SSM is present. This is the situation for a very simple switching function having only two EPCs. For a more complicated function having a number of EPCs and SPCs, the situation goes virtually out of control. It will now be obvious that a minterm-based algorithm is highly inadequate in a VLSI environment, where the number of variables to be handled will invariably be large.

To overcome this difficulty, an algorithm that can handle the switching function as a sum of cubes must be developed. This fact was recognized by scientists working at IBM, and the first cube-based algorithm, known as MINI, was reported in 1974 (Hong et al., 1974). Thereafter, quite a few cube-based algorithms were developed. We discuss these in more detail in Chapter 7. It should be mentioned here that just as a good knowledge of the Quine–McCluskey method is essential to developing the CAMP algorithm, so a sound understanding of the principles and theorems of the CAMPII algorithm are very necessary to develop a cube-based algorithm.

4.9 CUBE-BASED ALGORITHMS

In a cube-based algorithm, the cubes are processed directly, that is, without converting them as the sum of minterms. For example, let a function be given as

$$f_9 = x_1'x_3 + x_1'x_2'x_3' + x_1x_3x_4 + x_1'x_3'x_4'$$

When expressed as a sum of cubes, the function becomes

$$f_9 = 0212 + 0002 + 1211 + 0200$$

These cubes have been plotted in the Karmaugh map of Fig. 4.9.1(a). A cube-based algorithm should now process the four cubes directly and produce at the end the minimized form shown in the map of Fig. 4.9.1(b). Thus the minimized form is the sum of three cubes:

$$f_9 = x_1'x_2' + x_1'x_4' + x_3x_4$$
$$= 0022 + 0220 + 2211$$

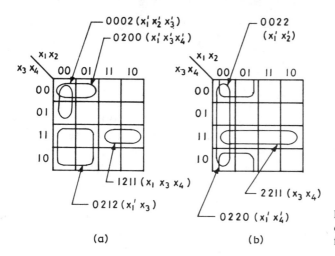

Figure 4.9.1 (a) Function f_9 as a sum of four cubes; (b) f_9 in the minimized form is a sum of three cubes.

Each cube-based algorithm has its own way of obtaining the minimum solution. However, in the next section we discuss some basic cubical operations whose concepts are essential for proper understanding of a cube-based algorithm.

4.10 CUBICAL OPERATIONS

We have already seen in Section 3.3 that two cubes may have four different dispositions and how these can be recognized by simple observation on the map. Here we see how they can be detected by performing some bit-by-bit operations when the cubes are expressed in ternary notation. As bit-by-bit operation can be performed for any number of variables, these are quite suitable when the function is of a large number of variables. The four dispositions are:

1. *Intersection:* Two cubes C_i and C_j will intersect with each other if they do not have even a single variable appearing in the complemented form in one cube and in the true form in the other. Thus in a four-variable function $f(abcd)$, the cubes $abc(1112)$ and $cd(2211)$ will be intersecting. Hence in bit-by-bit comparison of two intersecting cubes, wherever a bit at the ith position of one cube is either 0 or 1, the bit in the ith position of the other cube should be identical, or 2.

The intersection operation can be defined by a coordinate table as shown in Table 4.10.1. Thus

$$0122 \wedge 0120 = 0120$$

$$1212 \wedge 0212 = \phi212 = \varnothing \quad \text{(null cube)}$$

2. *Inclusion:* The cube C_i will be included in cube C_j ($C_i \leqslant C_j$) when the intersection of C_i and C_j is C_i. That is, $C_i \leqslant C_j$ if $C_i \wedge C_j = C_i$. It can easily be verified that in such a situation the variables present in both C_i and C_j are in the same form. For example, 0102 is included in 0122, since $0102 \wedge 0122 = 0102$. Note that the variables a and b present in both cubes are in the same form.

TABLE 4.10.1

		\(a\)		
$\wedge$		0	1	2
	0	0	ϕ	0
b	1	ϕ	1	1
	2	0	1	2

3. *Disjunction:* Two cubes that do not intersect with each other will be called disjoint cubes. Obviously, the intersection of two disjoint cubes is a null cube. Hence in the ternary notation of the cube, if there is at least one position where there is 0 in one cube and 1 in the other, the two cubes are disjoint.

4. *Adjacency:* Two cubes are adjacent if they are disjoint and have one and only one variable as a 0 (complemented form) in one cube and as a 1 (true form) in the other cube, all other variables that are present in both cubes being identical. Thus the cube abc (1112) and the cube $a'bd$ (0121) in a four-variable function are adjacent. Note that 2's do not count, as these variables are not present in both cubes.

Quite often it may be necessary to "subtract" one cube from another. This operation is called *sharp operation*. Let us illustrate this with the help of a map. Let the two three-variable cubes a and b be as shown in the map of Fig. 4.10.1(a).

Then $a \, \# \, b$ (when cube b is subtracted from cube a) are the two cubes shown in the map of Fig. 4.10.1(b), where the two cubes are shown intersecting or joint. The result of this # operation can also be expressed as two disjoint cubes, as shown in the map of Fig. 4.10.1(c) and (d). When the result of the # operation is expressed as disjoint cubes, the sharp operation is called disjoint sharp and is denoted by the symbol $\circledast$. Note that sharp operation cannot be defined by a coordinate table as has been done for the intersection operation. For this reason an algorithm has to be followed to perform a sharp operation.

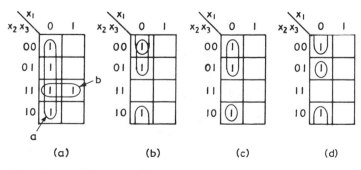

Figure 4.10.1 Sharp operation on map.

However, for functions up to six variables, sharp operation can be carried out on a map by observation. Also note that *unlike the intersection operation, sharp is not commutative*.

The sharp operation is a very useful operation in most cube-based algorithms. It is very useful to determine if a particular cube is totally within a given function. This is illustrated in the following example.

Example 4.10.1

Determine if the cubes 0221 and 2122 are wholly within the function

$$f = 0021 + 2201 + 2121 + 1210$$

Solution   From the map of Fig. 4.10.2, for 0221 the included or intersecting cubes are 0021, 2201, and 2121. Hence we must compute the results of the successive disjoint sharp operations.

$$((0221 \,\#\, 0021) \,\#\, 2201) \,\#\, 2121$$

Now

$$
\begin{aligned}
((0221 \,\#\, 0021) \,\#\, 2201) \,\#\, 2121 &= (0121 \,\#\, 2201) \,\#\, 2121 \\
&= 0111 \,\#\, 2121 \\
&= \varnothing \quad \text{(null cube)}
\end{aligned}
$$

Therefore, the cube 0221 is wholly in f. For 2122 the included and intersecting cubes are 2201, 2121, and 1210. Hence we must compute

$$((2122 \,\#\, 2201) \,\#\, 2121) \,\#\, 1210$$

Now

$$
\begin{aligned}
((2122 \,\#\, 2201) \,\#\, 2121) \,\#\, 1210 &= ((2100 + 2112) \,\#\, 2121) \,\#\, 1210 \\
&= (2100 \,\#\, 2121 + 2112 \,\#\, 2121) \,\#\, 1210 \\
&= ((2100) + (2110)) \,\#\, 1210 \\
&= 2100 \,\#\, 1210 + 2110 \,\#\, 1210 \\
&= 2100 + 0110
\end{aligned}
$$

Hence the cube 2122 is not wholly in f.

We must mention here that these are not the only cubical operations that may be performed. It is possible to define any number of new operations that

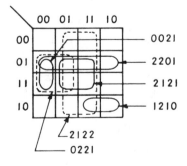

Figure 4.10.2   Map method of performing sharp operation. Example 4.10.1 solved on map.

may be necessary in developing an algorithm. In fact, it will be a good exercise to apply these basic cubical operations and define one or more new ones to develop a cubical CAMP algorithm. Such an algorithm will be able to minimize the 20-variable function f_8 as discussed in Section 4.8 in almost no time, since the required cubical operations have to be performed with only two cubes.

REFERENCES

BISWAS, N. N. Minimization of Boolean functions, *IEEE Trans. Comput.*, Vol. C-20, No. 8, August 1971, pp. 925–929.

BISWAS, N. N. Computer aided minimization procedure for Boolean functions, *Proc. 21st Design Automation Conference*, Albuquerque, N.Mex., June 1984, pp. 699–702.

BISWAS, N. N. Computer aided minimization procedure for Boolean functions, *IEEE Trans. Comput.-Aided Des. Integrated Circuits Syst.*, Vol. CAD-5, No. 2, April 1986, pp. 303–304.

BISWAS, N. N. On covering distant minterms by the CAMP algorithm, *IEEE Trans. Comput.-Aided Des. Integrated Circuits Syst.*, Vol. CAD-9, No. 7, July 1990, pp. 786–789.

BRAYTON, R. K., G. D. HACHTEL, C. T. McMULLEN, AND A. SANGIOVANNI-VINCENTELLI. *Logic Minimization Algorithms for VLSI Synthesis.* Norwell, Mass.: Kluwer Academic Publishers, 1984.

DIETMEYER, D. L. *Logic Design of Digital Systems,* 2nd ed. Boston: Allyn and Bacon Inc., 1978.

HONG, S. J., R. G. CAIN, AND D. L. OSTAPKO. MINI: a heuristic approach for logic minimization, *IBM J. Res. Dev.*, Vol. 18, No. 9, September 1974, pp. 443–458.

KOHAVI, Z. *Switching and Finite Automata Theory,* 2nd ed. New York: McGraw-Hill Book Company, 1978.

McCLUSKEY, E. J. Minimization of Boolean functions, *Bell Syst. Tech. J.,* Vol. 35, No. 11, November 1956, pp. 1417–1444.

McCLUSKEY, E. J. *Logic Design Principles.* Englewood Cliffs, N.J.: Prentice-Hall, 1986.

QUINE, W. V. The problem of simplifying truth functions, *Am. Math. Mon.*, Vol. 59, No. 10, October 1952, pp. 521–531.

RHYNE, V. T., P. S. NOE, M. H. McKINNEY, AND U. W. POOCH. A new technique for the fast minimization of switching functions, *IEEE Trans. Comput.*, Vol. C-26, No. 8, August 1977, pp. 757–764.

SURESHCHANDER. Minimization of switching functions: a fast technique, *IEEE Trans. Comput.*, Vol. C-24, No. 7, July 1975, pp. 753–756.

PROBLEMS

4.1. How is an essential prime cube (EPC) detected in **(a)** the Quine–McCluskey method; **(b)** the adjacency method; **(c)** the CAMP algorithm?

4.2. How is a redundant prime cube (RPC) detected in **(a)** the QM method; **(b)** the adjacency method; **(c)** the CAMP algorithm?

4.3. How is a selective prime cube (SPC) detected in **(a)** the QM method; **(b)** the adjacency method; **(c)** the CAMP algorithm?

4.4. Minimize the following functions by the QM method. For each function determine the number of (1) EPCs generated; (2) RPCs generated; (3) SPCs generated. If there is more than one solution, give all solutions.
(a) $f_1(abcd) = \Sigma(0,2,4,5,8,9,12,14)$
(b) $f_2(wxyz) = \Sigma(0-2,5,7,8,10,13,15) + \phi\Sigma(9)$
(c) $f_3(wxyz) = \Sigma(2-8,10-13,15)$
(d) $f_4(x_1x_2x_3x_4) = \Sigma(1,3,6,7-10,11,13-15)$

4.5. Minimize the following functions by the QM method.
(a) $f_1(abcde) = \Sigma(1-4,8,9,13,18,20-24,28)$
(b) $f_2(abcde) = \Sigma(0,3,7,10-16,19-21,23,28-30)$
(c) $f_3(x_1x_2x_3x_4x_5) = \Sigma(1-4,8-12,15-18,24-29)$

4.6. Minimize the following function by the QM method. Is the solution unique? How many EPCs, RPCs, and SPCs are generated?

$$f(abcde) = \Sigma(1-4,6-13,15,19,23,27,31)$$

4.7. Applying the dominance relation to columns of an SPC table, a pair of dominating and dominated columns can be defined as follows: If a column C_i has crosses in all rows where another column C_j has crosses, and in addition C_i has at least one more cross in a row where the column C_j does not, then column C_i is said to *dominate* column C_j. Among the pairs of columns C_i and C_j, C_i is the *dominating* and C_j is the *dominated* column. Now show that the minimum subset of the SPC is not affected by eliminating the dominating columns.

4.8. Try to solve the SPC table of the example function f_1 of Section 4.2 considering the dominance relation among columns.

4.9. Is the following statement true? "If an SPC table can be solved by applying the dominance relation among rows, then it can also be solved by applying the dominance relation among the columns." If true, furnish a proof; otherwise, give a counterexample.

4.10. Show that the number of wasteful computations to generate an α-cube in table T_α in the QM method is always greater than 2^α.

4.11. The PC and SPC tables used in the Quine–McCluskey method to determine the EPCs and SPCs are known as cover tables. Many problems in switching theory can be conveniently solved by the cover table approach. Solve the following problem by cover tables. A safe has five locks, 1, 2, 3, 4, and 5. To open the safe all five locks must be unlocked. Five officers, *A, B, C, D,* and *E,* have keys to these locks distributed in the following manner.

> *A* has keys for locks 1 and 2.
> *B* has keys for locks 3 and 5.
> *C* has keys for locks 2 and 3.
> *D* has keys for locks 2 and 4.
> *E* has keys for locks 1 and 5.

Identify the minimum number of officers required to open the safe. Is there any "essential" officer?
(*Hint:* To find "essential" officers construct a PC table with locks 1, 2, . . . , 5 as

columns and officers $A, B, \ldots, E$ as rows. Find the minimum number of "selective" officers by constructing an SPC table.)

4.12. Solve Example 3.6.1 by the cover table approach.

4.13. Calculate the degree of adjacency of all the minterms in the following functions.
   (a) $f_1 = \Sigma(2,5,8,10,12)$
   (b) $f_2 = \Sigma(1-3,6,8,13-15)$
   (c) $f_3 = \Sigma(2,8,10,11,13,15)$

4.14. With the help of a map, calculate the DA and SSM of minterms 2, 4, 12, and 15 in the following function:

$$f = \Sigma(2-4,6-8,12,15) + \phi\Sigma(5,11,13)$$

4.15. With the help of a map, find the EPCs as computed by the CAMP algorithm of the function of Problem 4.14. Identify the EPC- and SPC-generating minterms.

4.16. With the help of a map in computing the DA and SSMs of the minterms, determine the CAMP printout of the function of Problem 4.14.

4.17. With the help of maps for determining DAs and SSMs of minterms, find the CAMP printouts of the functions of Problem 4.4.

4.18. With the help of a map, find the CAMP printout of the following cyclic function. After branching, how many times, and at which minterms, will the program fail to get a VSPC and therefore skip the minterm? The function will be input in the same order as given in the function

$$f(abcd) = \Sigma(0,1,3,5-8,10-14)$$

4.19. Construct four-variable Boolean functions whose processing by the CAMP algorithm involves the following. If impossible, explain why.
   (a) Generation of a single-row MAM.
   (b) Generation of a single-row MUM.
   (c) Generation of a single-row MAM and a single-row MUM.
   (d) Branching twice.
   (e) Invocation of Theorem 4.6.5.

4.20. Repeat Problem 4.19 with five-variable functions.

4.21. The cubical form of a Boolean function is as follows:

$$f = 0112 + 1002 + 1221 + 2112$$

Find all the intersecting pairs of cubes without the help of a map.

4.22. With the help of maps, determine if the following cubes are wholly within the function of Problem 4.21. (a) 2122; (b) 1001; (c) 2221; (d) 1212

5

Logic Synthesis

5.1 INTRODUCTION

The various principles, algorithms, and techniques for logic synthesis are greatly influenced by the contemporary technology of logic devices. Again many new algorithms for design that appear purely theoretical have led to the invention or perfection of new devices. Thus the theoretical foundation and the practical implementation in the domain of logic synthesis and analysis are very much interdependent. This interdependence has resulted in evolving logic circuits from discrete to integrated circuits. Again integrated circuits (ICs) have moved from small-scale integration (SSI) to medium-scale integration (MSI), to large-scale integration (LSI), and currently to very large scale integration (VLSI). In this chapter we do not discuss the physics and electronics of devices. Readers interested in this aspect are referred to the many books devoted to this subject. We do, however, discuss the basic principles of designing the SSI and MSI building blocks used in the design of LSI and VLSI chips. We also introduce the new configurations of these components, which make the design in the VLSI domain feasible. Individual and random AND, OR, NOR, and NAND gate designs are good for small- and medium-scale integrated circuits but are not so efficient in the design of LSI or VLSI chips. It is very interesting and remarkable to note that when arranged in a regular structure such as programmable logic arrays, standard cells, or gate arrays, these gates suit LSI and VLSI circuits and perform very well.

The starting point of synthesis of any medium-scale circuit is a clear description of what the circuit is expected to do in words of any natural language. This is known as "word specification." From word specification the logic designer first determines if the circuit is combinational or sequential. If it is a combinational circuit, the designer constructs a truth table that depicts the objective and performance of the circuit expressed in words. If the circuit is sequential, instead of a truth table, a state table or state diagram is constructed. In this chapter we confine our attention to combinational circuits, which may be defined as follows.

Definition 5.1.1. A *combinational circuit* has n inputs and m outputs, and the values of all its outputs at any time depend only on the values of the inputs at that time.

For this reason it is possible to construct a truth table that describes precisely the behavior of the circuit for various combinations of inputs. In contrast to these, in a sequential circuit that also has n inputs and m outputs, the values of its outputs depend not only on the present input, but also on its past history, which is known as the *state* of the circuit. It is obvious that a sequential circuit must remember in what state it is. In other words, it must have a memory. Therefore, the fundamental difference between a combinational and a sequential circuit is that whereas the former is *memoryless*, the latter has a memory to remember its *state*. Hence a sequential circuit has to be described by a *state table* and cannot be described by a simple truth table.

5.2 AND, OR, AND INVERTER NETWORKS

From the truth table of a combinational circuit, all the outputs can be expressed as Boolean functions of the input variables. All functions are in their disjunctive canonical forms (DCFs). When minimized into their MSOP forms, the functions can be implemented by a two-level AND–OR network with a minimum number of gates if all the variables are available in both true and complemented forms (*double-rail logic*). If the variables are available only in the true form (*single-rail logic*), one more level is required to accommodate the inverters. While the MSOP form gives the minimum number of gates in a two-level realization of a Boolean function, sometimes the number of gates can be reduced further by increasing the number of levels.

5.3 NAND AND NOR NETWORKS

In Chapter 2 we introduced NAND and NOR as independent Boolean operations. Independent NAND and NOR gates are available where the inverter following the AND and OR gate is integrated with these gates by the circuit itself. From the basic definition of NAND (NOR) operation, it can be represented in two ways. One of them is recognized as its preferred symbol; the other, which is an equivalent form, is considered as an alternative symbol. These are shown in Fig. 5.3.1, where the inverters are shown by small circles or "bubbles." We have also discussed in Chapter 2 how two-level AND–OR (OR–AND) networks can easily be converted into two-level NAND(NOR) networks. If the input variables

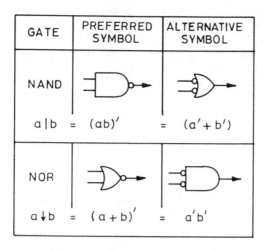

GATE	PREFERRED SYMBOL	ALTERNATIVE SYMBOL
NAND $a \mid b$ =	$(ab)'$	$(a' + b')$
NOR $a \downarrow b$ =	$(a + b)'$	$a'b'$

Figure 5.3.1 NAND- and NOR-gate symbols.

are not available in both the true and complemented forms (that is, the logic is single-rail), one more level may be required to provide the inverters. Take, for example, the simple circuit to perform the XOR (EXCLUSIVE-OR) operation. In the form of equation,

$$a \oplus b = a'b + ab' = (a' + b')(a + b)$$

With single-rail logic this equation leads to the NAND and NOR circuits shown in Fig. 5.3.2. A more general and powerful technique to convert an AND–OR network (not necessarily two-level) is to introduce two inverters in all the lines and then to identify the NAND or NOR gates that can be obtained by the

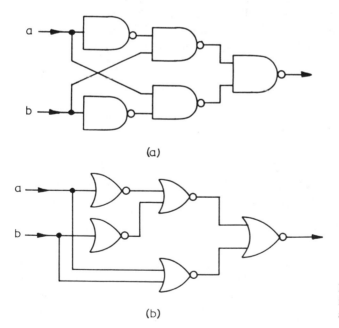

(a)

(b)

Figure 5.3.2 EXCLUSIVE-OR gate implementation by (a) NAND network and (b) NOR network.

Logic Synthesis   Chap. 5

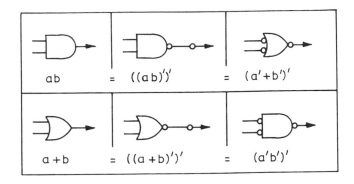

Figure 5.3.3 Equivalent configurations of AND, OR, NAND, and NOR gates by inverting inputs, output, or both.

combination of inverters with the AND and OR gates. However, for this it is necessary to know the various equivalent configurations of AND, OR, NAND, and NOR gates. Some of these follow from the well-known identities of the NAND–NOR operations. These have been shown in Fig. 5.3.3. From these figures it can be seen how when both the inputs and outputs of an AND–OR gate are inverted, the gate can be replaced by an OR–AND gate.

Now let us insert double inverters (shown only by circles or bubbles) in all lines of a simple two-level AND–OR network (see Figure 5.3.4). We see that ultimately the AND–OR network becomes an OR–AND network, provided that extra inverters are used in all inputs and also in the output. If the input variables are available in both the true and complemented forms, then instead of using inverters at the inputs, the other form of an input variable can be fed to each of the inputs of the gates. While converting a complex network of AND–OR gates into a network of NAND or NOR gates, extra inverters may have to be inserted in some lines (see Problem 5.9).

In the discussion above we find that the synthesis of NAND and NOR networks is done by first implementing the function by either an AND–OR or an

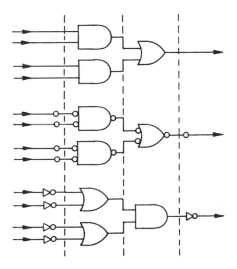

Figure 5.3.4 Transformation of an AND–OR network into an OR–AND network.

OR–AND network, and then converting the network into the required NAND or NOR network. Consider the implementation of the function $f = \Sigma(4\text{--}6,8\text{--}10,12\text{--}14)$ first by NAND gates and then by NOR gates. For NAND-gate synthesis, first minimize the function (in this case) on the map [Fig. 5.3.5(a)]. The MSOP form of the function turns out to be

$$f = x_1 x_3' + x_2 x_3' + x_2 x_4' + x_1 x_4'$$

This AND–OR form is then implemented in an all-NAND network as shown in Fig. 5.3.5(b). To synthesize in NOR gates, the minimum product-of-sums (MPOS) form of the function is found [in this case by minimizing the complementary function on the map, Fig. 5.3.5(c)]. Thus $f' = x_1' x_2' + x_3 x_4$. Therefore, $f = (x_1 + x_2)(x_3' + x_4')$. This OR–AND form is implemented by the all-NOR network as shown in Fig. 5.3.5(d). These implementations are due to Theorems 2.9.1 and 2.10.1.

It should be noted at this point that when a NAND(NOR) network is obtained from a minimum AND–OR (OR–AND) network, the resultant NAND(NOR) network is not necessarily minimum in number of NAND(NOR) gates. An excellent example of this is the five-gate implementation of the XOR function by this method, as shown in Fig. 5.3.2(a). The minimum NAND-gate realization of the XOR function needs only four gates (Fig. 5.3.6). The design of a minimum NAND- or NOR-gate network posed a formidable problem to computer scientists and engineers in the decade of the 1960s. Maley and Earle (1963) made

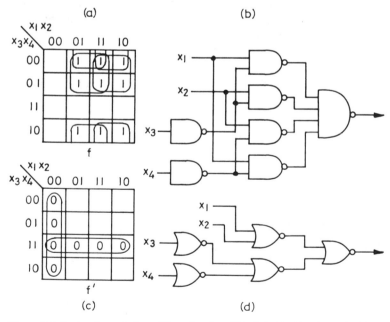

Figure 5.3.5 Implementation of function $f = \Sigma(4\text{--}6, 8\text{--}10, 12\text{--}14)$: (a) MSOP form of f on map; (b) all-NAND network; (c) MSOP form of f' on map; (d) all-NOR network.

Logic Synthesis   Chap. 5

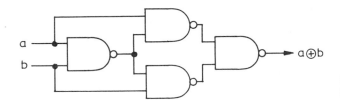

Figure 5.3.6 EXCLUSIVE-OR
function realized by four NAND gates.

a bold attempt to devise a map method to minimize NAND or NOR networks. But even for three-variable problems, rules were too cumbersome. McCluskey (1986) and Gimpel (1967) suggested many techniques, mostly algebraic "tricks." McCluskey (1986) even coined the name TANT (*t*hree-stage *A*ND–*N*OT with *t*rue inputs) to specify this class of networks. However, as far as three or fewer variable networks with only true inputs are concerned, the minimization problem was solved once and for all by Hellerman (1963). Hellerman used an exhaustive method that decides on the minimum network after trying every possible combinational interconnection. His catalog gives 80 circuits, from which all the 256 logic functions of three variables can be obtained by appropriate permutation. Of these 80 circuits, 68 are really of three variables; the other 12 are degenerate circuits. Among these, three are trivial functions ($f = 0, f = 1$, and $f = a$), one is a one-variable function INVERT ($f = a'$), and eight are functions of two variables: AND ($f = ab$), OR ($f = a + b$), NAND [$f = (ab)'$], NOR [$f = (a + b)'$], XOR ($f = a \oplus b$), XNOR [$f = (a \oplus b)'$], INHIBIT ($f = a'b$), and IMPLY ($f = a' + b$).

While many researchers were investigating various ways and means to develop minimum NOR or NAND networks, a revolution in the device area changed the picture completely. *Integrated circuits* (ICs) appeared on the scene, bringing tens and hundreds of NAND or NOR gates on a tiny wafer of silicon. Consequently, it hardly makes any difference in cost if one uses a few more gates here and there. The impact of ICs on logic synthesis is very well known and will be felt directly or indirectly on various topics in various ways. We have already seen some of these in the preceding chapters and will see more in subsequent chapters of this book.

5.4 EXCLUSIVE-OR NETWORKS

In Chapter 2 we discussed some basic concepts regarding EXCLUSIVE-OR (XOR) operation. Unfortunately, an independent single-level circuit cannot be designed to perform the XOR operation. For this reason an XOR gate is made out of several NOR or NAND gates. The circuit implemented on an IC chip is the one shown in Fig. 5.3.2(a), with inverters instead of NAND gates at the input stage. One drawback of the XOR gate that is immediately visible is that its delay is more than that of other gates. Another difficulty is that while any number of inputs can be parallelly fed to AND, OR, NAND, and NOR gates, this cannot be done in an XOR gate unless its complexity is increased. As an example, see the circuit of a three-input XOR gate realizing the function $a \oplus b \oplus c$, as obtained

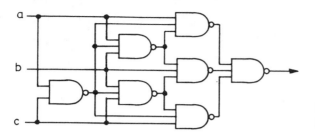

Figure 5.4.1 $f = a \oplus b \oplus c$ implementation by NAND gates.

by Hellerman (1963) using his exhaustive search method (Fig. 5.4.1). For this reason, XOR gates of only two inputs are usually used. For a multi-input realization of XOR gates, the two-input gates are used either in cascade or in the binary tree configuration. Figure 5.4.2 shows a four-input XOR gate with three two-input gates in cascade. Figure 5.4.3 shows an eight-input XOR gate with seven two-input gates in binary tree configuration. In both cases the delay by the circuit increases with the increase in number of inputs. It can also be seen that the cascade configuration is completely serial, whreas the binary tree configuration is parallel–serial. Therefore, if entirely parallel operation is desired, XOR gates cannot be used. Instead, the XOR operation has to be implemented by AND, OR, NAND, or NOR gates. Consider, for example, the design of a four-variable odd-parity function, which produces an output 1 whenever there are an odd number of 1's in a binary string of 4 bits. The four-input XOR circuit of Fig. 5.4.2 achieves this objective and will therefore act as an odd-parity generator/checker. However, this circuit is serial and will therefore have consequential delay. In case wholly parallel operation is desired, the parity function has to be implemented by two-level AND–OR or logically equivalent networks. For this the parity function must be expressed in the sum-of-minterms form and then mimimized. Unfortunately, a parity function cannot be minimized. Hence the MSOP form of an n-variable parity function will always have 2^{n-1} product terms, each of which is a minterm. Therefore, for an eight-variable parity function there will be 2^7, or 128, product terms. It will therefore require 128 AND gates, each of which must be capable of having a fan-in of eight inputs. Again, the OR gate should have the

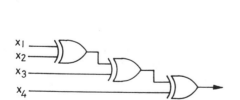

Figure 5.4.2 Four-input XOR gate realized by three two-input XOR gates in cascade.

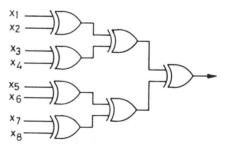

Figure 5.4.3 Eight-input XOR gate realized by seven two-input XOR gates in binary tree configuration.

capability of having a fan-in of 128 inputs. These are difficult requirements for the usual AND and OR gates. However, we shall see shortly that a different configuration of AND and OR gates (practically of NOR and NOR gates), known as programmable logic arrays (PLAs), satisfactorily overcomes these technical difficulties.

5.5 MULTIPLEXERS

An immediate benefit of the appearance of integrated circuits was the availability of a large number of gates without additional cost. In fact, at the present state of device technology, an IC chip is cheaper than a single gate, and although it may sound strange, a group of devices on a chip work more efficiently in many ways when they are placed in a smaller rather than in a larger area. Hence it is natural that the elementary building blocks of logic synthesis became different arrrangement or conglomeration of gates, which came to be known as circuit modules or arrays. We discuss some of these in this and subsequent sections.

The multiplexer is one such module. The circuit arrangement of a multiplexer having the capacity of connecting any one of four inputs (depending on a control code) to a single output is shown in Fig. 5.5.1. Here, depending on the control code set up by the two control bits c_1 and c_2, the appropriate AND gate is "on." For example, when $c_1 c_2 = 00$, only the gate G_0 is on; all other gates are off. The four AND-gate circuits with two control lines c_1 and c_2 act as a 2-to-4 binary-to-decimal decoder.* An enable lead, E, activates all the AND gates when $E = 0$. The I_0 input connected only to gate G_0 feeds the incoming data from the I_0 channel to the multiplexer. Similarly, the I_1, I_2, and I_3 feed the gates G_1, G_2, and G_3, respectively. It is easy to see that the data on the line I_1 only will appear at the output of the multiplexer if the control code is 01. The multiplexer made by the 2-to-4 decoder is called a 4-to-1 multiplexer (MUX). The same decoder can be so connected that the circuit module acts as a demultiplexer. The demultiplexer (DMUX) is then called a 1-to-4 demultiplexer (Fig. 5.5.2). Thus by using an n-to-2^n decoder, a 2^n-to-1 MUX or a 1-to-2^n DMUX can be made. It is now evident that if the output of an m-to-1 MUX is connected to the input of a 1-to-m DMUX, any data coming from a source I_i connected to the MUX can be channeled to any destination D_j connected to the DMUX by setting appropriate control codes at the MUX and DMUX. When a MUX works in this fashion it acts as a data selector.

Another interesting application of a multiplexer is that it can implement any arbitrary Boolean function. Consider the three-variable function f shown in the truth table of Table 5.5.1(a).

From the truth table when the combinations of $x_1 x_2 x_3$ are decimal 0, 1, 3, and 6, the function is 1. For other rows, $f = 0$. Hence if I_0, I_1, I_3, and I_6 are connected to logical 1 and the remaining input terminals to 0 [see Fig. 5.5.3(a)],

---

* If a circuit having n inputs and m ($m = 2^n$) outputs is such that for each combination of n input bits, only one of the m outputs is activated (one hot), it is called an n-to-m decoder.

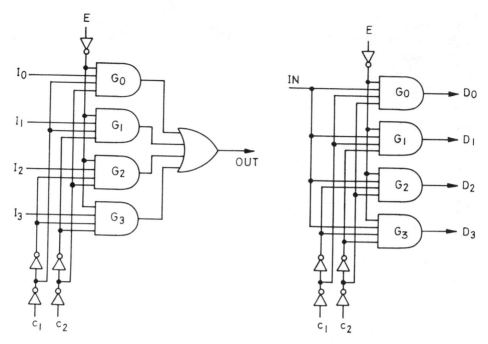

Figure 5.5.1 A 4-to-1 multiplexer circuit.

Figure 5.5.2 A 1-to-4 demultiplexer circuit.

the output of the MUX will satisfy the truth table of function f for various combinations of x_1, x_2, and x_3. Hence the 8-to-1 MUX implements the three variable function in a very straightforward way. In general, any 2^n-to-1 MUX can implement any n-variable function. In this respect it acts as a *universal logic*

TABLE 5.5.1 TRUTH TABLE OF A THREE-VARIABLE FUNCTION

(a)				(b)				
x_1	x_2	x_3	f	x_1	x_2	x_3	f	I
0	0	0	1	0	0	0	1	1
0	0	1	1	0	0	1	1	
0	1	0	0	0	1	0	0	x_3
0	1	1	1	0	1	1	1	
1	0	0	0	1	0	0	0	0
1	0	1	0	1	0	1	0	
1	1	0	1	1	1	0	1	x_3'
1	1	1	0	1	1	1	0	

Logic Synthesis   Chap. 5

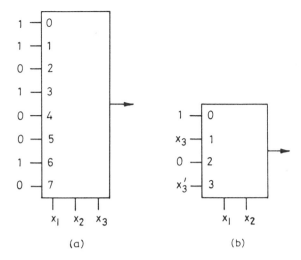

1	0		
1	1		
0	2		
1	3		
0	4		
0	5		
1	6		
0	7		

x_1 x_2 x_3

(a)

1	0
x_3	1
0	2
x_3'	3

x_1 x_2

(b)

Figure 5.5.3 Implementation of a three-variable function by (a) an 8-to-1 MUX and (b) a 4-to-1 MUX.

module. The capacity of a 2^n-to-1 MUX can be increased to realize any arbitrary $(n + 1)$-variable function, provided that we process the truth table to extract additional information. Let the procedure be described considering the three-variable function of Table 5.5.1. First, partition the eight rows of the truth table in four partitions as shown in Table 5.5.1(b). Now compare the values of f in each partition with those of column x_3. Note that there are only four possibilities for each partition. f may be 1, or 0, or the same as the value of x_3 or the complement of x_3. The result of the comparison of f with x_3 is shown in column I of Table 5.5.1(b). From this it is apparent that if we now use a 4-to-1 multiplexer and connect I_0 to 1, I_1 to x_3, I_2 to 0, and I_3 to x_3' [see Fig. 5.5.3(b)], the 4-to-1 MUX will realize the three-variable function of Table 5.5.1. A quicker way to find the logic to be connected to the four inputs of the 4-to-1 MUX is to convert the binary number expressing the function into a 4-ary (base 4) number as shown below.

$$f = (0\ 1,\ 0\ 0,\ 1\ 0,\ 1\ 1)_2$$
$$= (1\ 0\ 2\ 3)_4$$

It is now easy to see that the numerals of the 4-ary number tell us the logic values of the four inputs of the 4-to-1 MUX. These are: logic 0 for 0, x_3' for 1, x_3 for 2, and logic 1 for 3. Although we have explained the procedure for a 4-to-1 MUX realizing a three-variable Boolean function, it is a general procedure to realize an n-variable function with a 2^{n-1}-to-1 MUX.

Example 5.5.1

Implement the four-variable function $f = (x_1 x_2 x_3 x_4) = \Sigma(3,6\text{--}8,10,13\text{--}15)$ with a 8-to-1 multiplexer.

Solution Expressing the function in its binary designation, we have

$$f = (1\ 1\ 1\ 0\ 0\ 1\ 0\ 1\ 1\ 1\ 0\ 0\ 1\ 0\ 0\ 0)_2$$

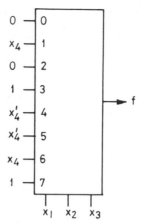

Figure 5.5.4 Implementation of $f(x_1 x_2 x_3 x_4) = \Sigma(3, 6\text{–}8, 10, 13\text{–}15)$ by a 8-to-1 multiplexer.

Converting f into a 4-ary number yields

$$f = (11,\ 10,\ 01,\ 01,\ 11,\ 00,\ 10,\ 00)_2$$
$$= (3\ 2\ 1\ 1\ 3\ 0\ 2\ 0)_4$$

Hence the input vector is given by

$$= I_7 I_6 I_5 I_4 I_3 I_2 I_1 I_0$$
$$= 1\ x_4\ x_4'\ x_4'\ 1\ 0\ x_4\ 0$$

The multiplexer diagram is shown in Fig. 5.5.4.

Although the procedure for implementing any arbitrary Boolean function by a MUX is very simple, it has a serious limitation. If the number of variables in the function increases by 1, the size of the MUX gets doubled. For this reason a MUX is seldom used for this purpose. Another limitation is that a MUX is not adequate for multiple-output functions.

5.6 READ-ONLY MEMORIES

A simple way to implement a multiple-output function is to use read-only memories (ROMs). Like the demultiplexer, a ROM has an n-to-2^n decoder. A close look at the 2^n outputs of a decoder will reveal that the 0th to the $(2^n - 1)$th output really generates the 0th to $(2^n - 1)$th minterms of the n-variable function. Thus in the demultiplexer of Fig. 5.5.2, the minterms m_0, m_1, m_2, and m_3 are available at D_0, D_1, D_2, and D_3, respectively. In a ROM each output is capable of being connected to several wires, as shown in Fig. 5.6.1. Each horizontal line generates a minterm and each vertical line is an output function as a sum of minterms. Thus it is easy to realize a multiple-output function by providing an appropriate number of vertical lines. At each crosspoint (intersection of a horizontal and a vertical line) there is a device acting as an OR gate. In Fig. 5.6.1, for the sake of simplicity, only diodes have been used as the ORing device. Also note that the devices at some of the crosspoints are not connected. Here the particular minterm line is

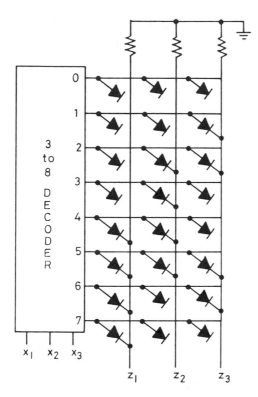

Figure 5.6.1 A ROM as a BCD-to-Gray code converter.

not connected to the relevant output line. The ROM of Fig. 5.6.1 acts as a binary coded decimal (BCD)-to-Gray code converter, whose truth table is shown in Table 5.6.1.

In the truth table, for $x_1 x_2 x_3 = 000$, $z_1 z_2 z_3 = 000$. Therefore, the 0-line is not connected to z_1, z_2, or z_3. Hence all three diodes have their connecting fuses burned out. Similarly, for the three-line of the decoder, since $z_1 z_2 z_3$ is 010, only the z_2-line remains connected to the three-line via the ORing diode. Thus it can be seen that the ROM circuit satisfies the truth table of Table 5.6.1, and therefore it acts as a BCD-to-Gray code converter. Since it remembers the Gray code corresponding to each binary number combination, it is a memory. The Gray code corresponding to any binary number can be read out by putting the appropriate bits at x_1, x_2, and x_3. However, nothing new can be written in the memory. Hence writing in the memory is done once and for all. But reading from the memory can be done any number of times without destroying the contents. Hence the circuit is known as a read-only memory (ROM). Following the terminology used in the memory circuits, each horizontal line of the ROM stores a 3-bit word corresponding to the values of z_1, z_2, and z_3. Again, each line storing a word has a 3-bit address corresponding to the values of x_1, x_2, and x_3. Thus if we want to know the word stored, say, on line 6 of the ROM, we will have to set the address of this line (that is, 110) to $x_1 x_2 x_3$, which will activate only line 6, and the values of z_1, z_2, and z_3 at this line will be available at the three output

TABLE 5.6.1 BINARY CODED DECIMAL-TO-GRAY CODE CONVERSION

BCD			Gray		
x_1	x_2	x_3	z_1	z_2	z_3
0	0	0	0	0	0
0	0	1	0	0	1
0	1	0	0	1	1
0	1	1	0	1	0
1	0	0	1	1	0
1	0	1	1	1	1
1	1	0	1	0	1
1	1	1	1	0	0

lines. Thus ROM is a very convenient device for storing tables whose values may have to be read many times. Thus it is very much used for code conversion and also as a generator of many arithmetic and trigonometric functions. The term "generator," although used extensively in the literature, is not a very precise term. A ROM acting as a sine generator really stores values of sin x for various values of x expressed in radians. Both x and sin x are coded in binary, and their accuracy depends on the number of bits used for encoding. The values of sin x versus x have already been computed; ROM simply stores the table. It is therefore the sine table found in any book on trigonometic function, implemented by hardware. In contrast, a software program that generates $y = \sin x$ really computes the value of y from the series

$$\sin x = x - (x^3/3!) + x^5/5!) - (x^7/7!) + \cdots$$

Any table stored or written in a ROM can be stored or written at two different times. It can be stored at the factory, and therefore need not have any active device at all at those crosspoints where they are not needed. On the other hand, a factory can produce a ROM provided with devices at all crosspoints, each, however, having its connection completed through a fuse. The user who buys such a ROM can write any table on the ROM by removing the fuses by burning. Such a ROM is called a field-programmable ROM (FPROM). There are many techniques available for writing, or even erasing and then writing again on a ROM. We shall not discuss these technological details, which are available in many books. Consider the implementation of a seven-segment display by a ROM. The circuit is shown in Fig. 5.6.2. Here a crosspoint shown by a $\times$ has a device acting as an OR gate. If a user buys a standard (4-to-16) ROM, all the crosspoints of lines 10 to 15 will remain unused. However, if a ROM is manfactured as a module for seven-segment display, the entire portion meant for lines 10 to 15 can be omitted. Note that in the truth table of the seven-segment display, all columns of rows 10 to 15 will have don't-care terms.

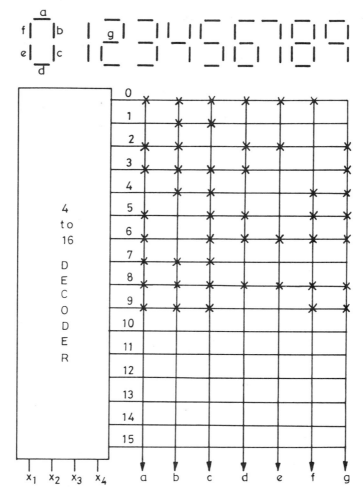

Figure 5.6.2 Seven-segment display stored in a ROM.

Let us discuss here the basic principle of how a ROM can act as a generator of the trigonometric sine function. We have already seen how ROM can store a truth table. Now consider the truth table shown in Table 5.6.2. The truth table has 3 address bits (and therefore eight rows) and 5 word bits (and therefore five columns). Each word at this address stores one decimal value, whose magnitude is given by the bits z_2 through z_5 and whose sign is given by bit z_1. A sign bit 0(1) means that the magnitude is positive (negative). The eight addresses divide the time period 2π or 360°, into eight equal intervals, each of which fixes the value to be stored at a particular address. Since the table must act as a look-up table for $y = \sin x$, the values at each address have been made sin x. For example, sin 45° = 0.707. So y has been made 7 by making $z_2 z_3 z_4 z_5 = 0111$. z_1 gives the sign, and we assume that there is a mechanism to read 7 as 0.7. The various values of $y = \sin x$ for eight values of x are shown graphically in Fig. 5.6.3. It can easily

TABLE 5.6.2 LOOK-UP TABLE FOR $y = $ SIN x

Input					Output					
					Sign bit	Magnitude				
x	θ	x_1	x_2	x_3	z_1	z_2	z_3	z_4	z_5	y
0	0	0	0	0	0	0	0	0	0	0
$\pi/4$	45	0	0	1	0	0	1	1	1	7
$\pi/2$	90	0	1	0	0	1	0	0	1	9
$3\pi/2$	135	0	1	1	0	0	1	1	1	7
π	180	1	0	0	1	0	0	0	0	-0
$5\pi/4$	225	1	0	1	1	0	1	1	1	-7
$3\pi/2$	270	1	1	0	1	1	0	0	1	-9
$7\pi/4$	315	1	1	1	1	0	1	1	1	-7

be seen that these values can be stored in a ROM having an eight-row, five-column matrix, and that the absence and presence of a device at a crosspoint is given by the output z matrix. Hence this matrix is known as the ROM program. Note that this program is a hardware program, not a software program. Also note that since we have only 4 bits to encode y, we can have only one-digit accuracy. It is now easy to see that if more values of y are to be stored, the program matrix must have more rows, and if the value of y is to be stored more accurately, the matrix must have more columns. To store the value of y with two-digit accuracy, we should be able to code in binary accurately all decimal numbers up to 99. Hence we must have 7 bits, since $2^6 < 99 < 2^7$. So the ROM must have 8 bits, as an extra bit is required for the sign. In general, to have n-digit accuracy, the number of coding bits required will be given by

$$n = \lceil \log_2 N \rceil$$

where N is the highest number in n digits. For example, for four-digit accuracy

$$n = \lceil \log_2 9999 \rceil = 14$$

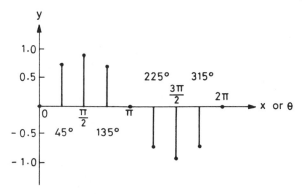

Figure 5.6.3 Eight samples of a ROM implementation of a sine generator by the ROM program of Table 5.6.2.

Logic Synthesis   Chap. 5

Again, if we activate the rows of the ROM of Table 5.6.2 one after another by a counter and read the values of y, we get a sine wave obtained from the eight digital samples as given in Fig. 5.6.3. When these samples are passsed through a digital-to-analog converter, we get an analog sine wave. The ROM then acts a sine-wave generator. However, such a sinewave, as given by the ROM of Table 5.6.2, will not be very good, as the number of samples per cycle as well as the accuracy of y are very low. It is now obvious that an increase in the number of rows and number of columns of the ROM program means an increase in sampling frequency and digital accuracy of y, respectively. This discussion will lead the reader to design a reasonably good sine-wave generator ROM with 32 rows and 15 columns to ensure 32 samples per cycle and a four-digit accuracy of each sample. This will require a memory space of 32×2^{15} or 1,048,576 bits. While such a ROM will work well, it will take an enormous amount of bit space. A very effective way to reduce the bit space is to use more smaller ROMs rather than a single ROM. An excellent discussion of the procedures and techniques needed to achieve this objective can be found in Chapter 7 of Muroga (1982). It is now apparent how ROMs can be used to generate any waveform. In fact, recorded speech waveforms can be stored in ROMs and played whenever necessary.

Another novel application of ROMs is in the generation of sequences of binary waveforms that can be used for various control signals. Consider the eight-row, four-column truth table of Table 5.6.3. It can easily be seen that if the outputs of z_1, z_2, z_3, and z_4 are scanned serially one after another, the sequence of binary waveforms shown in Fig. 5.6.4 will be generated. On the other hand, if the four outputs are scanned in parallel, the four waveforms are available simultaneously.

Whereas ROM is very convenient for storing tables that will be used repeatedly, it is very wasteful of space for logic synthesis. Although it has the capability of multiple-output synthesis, it is also minterm-based, like the multiplexers. Consequently, here also the size of the ROM gets doubled when the number of variables increases by 1. Like any other minterm-based system, it is inadequate for VLSI circuits and systems.

TABLE 5.6.3 ROM PROGRAM TO GENERATE A SEQUENCE OF FOUR BINARY WAVEFORMS

x_1	x_2	x_3	z_1	z_2	z_3	z_4
0	0	0	0	1	0	1
0	0	1	1	1	1	0
0	1	0	0	0	0	1
0	1	1	1	0	1	1
1	0	0	1	0	0	0
1	0	1	0	1	1	0
1	1	0	0	1	0	1
1	1	1	1	0	1	1

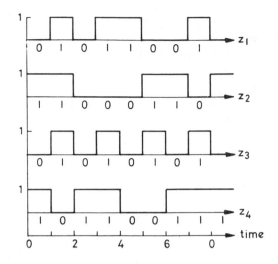

Figure 5.6.4 Sequence of binary waveforms generated by the ROM program of Table 5.6.3

5.7 PROGRAMMABLE LOGIC ARRAYS

A programmable logic array (PLA) can be thought of as a cube-based ROM. In a ROM each output function is implemented as a sum of minterms. In a PLA each output function is implemented as a sum of cubes, that is, products. Hence before implementing a multiple-output function, it is minimized so that the functions are expressed as sums of product terms, some of which may be shared by more than one output function. Let us illustrate the working of PLAs by implementing the BCD-to-Gray code converter of Table 5.6.1. Carrying out multiple-output minimization of z_1, z_2, and z_3 yields

$$z_1(x_1x_2x_3) = x_1 = 122$$

$$z_2(x_1x_2x_3) = x_1x_2' + x_1'x_2 = 102 + 012$$

$$z_3(x_1x_2x_3) = x_2'x_3 + x_2x_3' = 201 + 210$$

The PLA will therefore require five product terms. Its schematic diagram is shown in Fig. 5.7.1. In a PLA the (3-to-8) decoder used in ROM is not required. This is because all eight minterms or fundamental products need not be generated. Only each input line has a 1-to-2 decoder to generate both the true and complemented forms of each input variable. Here each output function is not a sum of minterms but a sum of specific product terms. These product terms are generated by an AND matrix fed by the double-rail input variables. A device acting as an AND gate at the appropriate crosspoints (shown by dots in Fig. 5.7.1) generate the product terms required. Generation of the five product terms required in the BCD-to-Gray code converter has been shown in Fig. 5.7.1. It also shows how the three output functions z_1, z_2, and z_3 are obtained as sums of product terms by an OR matrix, where devices acting as OR gates (shown by ×'s in Fig. 5.7.1) at appropriate crosspoints realize the output functions. Thus almost every PLA has a 1-to-2 decoder for each of its n input variables, an AND

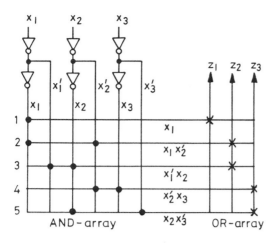

Figure 5.7.1 Schematic diagram of PLA P_1 as a BCD-to-Gray code converter.

array or matrix to generate the product terms, and an OR array or matrix to realize each output function as a sum of appropriate product terms. Like a PROM, a PLA having devices at every crosspoint of the AND and OR array can be bought, and then to realize a particular multiple-output function the devices at the required crosspoints can be disconnected: hence the name "programmable logic array." A PLA can be shown by its schematic diagram, as in Fig. 5.7.1. It can also be represented in the form of two arrays, the AND array and the OR array. The array form of the PLA of Fig. 5.7.1, which realizes a 3-bit BCD-to-Gray code converter, is shown in Table 5.7.1. A PLA realizing an n-variable, m-output function with p product terms is often referred to as a (p,n,m) PLA.

In the AND array a 1(0) means that the variable has been connected to the product line in its true (complemented) form. A 2 means that the variable is not connected. In the OR array, a 1(0) means that the output is connected (not connected) to the product line. Note that each row of the AND array depicts the product term in its cubical form with the ternary (0,1,2) notation. Each column of the OR array shows the constituents of the output function heading the column. A PLA can also be represented by listing the set of subsuming rows of each column, which is defined as follows.

TABLE 5.7.1 PLA P_1 IN ARRAY FORM

Product term	Inputs			Outputs		
	x_1	x_2	x_3	z_1	z_2	z_3
1	1	2	2	1	0	0
2	1	0	2	0	1	0
3	0	1	2	0	1	0
4	2	0	1	0	0	1
5	2	1	0	0	0	1

TABLE 5.7.2 PLA P_1
IN SSR NOTATION

Column	SSR
x_1	1,2
x_1'	3
x_2	3,5
x_2'	2,4
x_3	4
x_3'	5
z_1	1
z_2	2,3
z_3	4,5

Definition 5.7.1.   The rows that are connected to a column constitute the *set of subsuming rows* (SSR) of that column.

Following this notation, PLA P_1 can be written as in Table 5.7.2. However, here we must consider that each column of the AND array should be taken as two columns, as the cubical form indicates whether a row is connected to the true or the complemented form of the input variable.

In the actual device implementation of a PLA, how a transistor is connected at a crosspoint depends on the technology. In an NMOS implementation, the transistors are so connected in both the AND and OR planes that they act as NOR gates in both planes. Such an implementation is therefore called a NOR–NOR implementation. The NOR–NOR implementation of the (5,3,3) PLA P_1 is shown in Fig. 5.7.2. A close comparison of this NOR–NOR implementation with the AND–OR implementation of Fig. 5.7.1, where the AND and OR devices have been shown schematically by dots and crosses, will reveal a difference. Note that if in a product term p_i in the AND–OR array, there is a device on an input column x_j' (x_j), then in the NOR–NOR array, a device is connected on the $x_j(x_j')$ column. In the output column, however, devices are connected in the same crosspoints of both types of arrays. To explain this shift of devices in the input columns, convert an AND–OR network to its equivalent NOR–NOR network by introducing pairs of canceling inversion bubbles, as shown in Fig. 5.7.3. It can be seen that the input variables in the NOR–NOR circuit are complemented values of those of the AND–OR circuit, and the outputs of the NOR–NOR circuit have to be obtained via inverter gates. Thus the basic matrix structure of the PLA remains unchanged in both implementations. As it is more convenient to analyze Boolean functions in the AND–OR form rather than in the NOR–NOR form, various theoretical analysis and synthesis are done in the AND–OR form, although the circuit implementation of the same PLA is done in the NOR–NOR form.

As we have seen, a PLA saves lots of space compared to a ROM. Even then it still has lots of empty spaces. In the (5,3,3) PLA P_1, there are $5(2 \times 3 +$

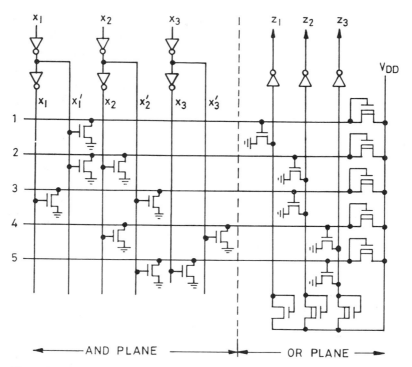

Figure 5.7.2 NMOS NOR–NOR implementation of PLA P_1.

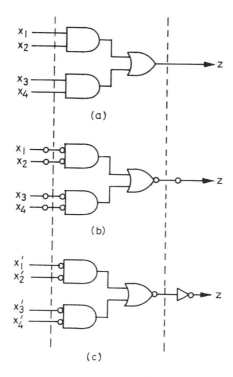

(a)

(b)

(c)

Figure 5.7.3 (a) An AND–OR circuit; (b) its conversion to NOR–NOR configuration; (c) NOR–NOR equivalent of the AND–OR circuit.

Sec. 5.7   Programmable Logic Arrays   **113**

3), or 45, crosspoints. Of these only 14 have active devices. An ingenious way for better utilization of the empty space is to allow two or more input lines to share the same column, or to let two product lines share the same row—and better still, to have a mixture of both these types of sharing. This sharing of columns (rows) by more than one input/output line (product line) is called folding. When only two input or output lines share a column, the folding is called *simple column folding* (SCF). Similarly, when two product terms share a row, it is called *simple row folding* (SRF). When a single column or a row is shared by more than two lines, we get *multiple folding*. When both columns and rows are folded, we get *mixed* or *composite* folding. Figure 5.7.4 shows a SCF of PLA P_1 of Fig. 5.7.1. Here the two columns of the x_1 input have been folded with two columns of the x_3 input, and output column z_1 has been folded with output column z_3. As a result of this folding, the total area occupied by the crosspoints has been reduced from 45 to 30. Hence the 14 devices have now been accommodated within the 30-crosspoint area. Due to the restrictions imposed by the technology, an SCF has to obey two constraints. First, both the true and complemented columns of an input variable must always appear at either the top or bottom of a PLA layout. Hence, for the purpose of folding, an input variable is treated as a single column. The SSR specification for the purpose of folding can be written as given in Table 5.7.3. The second constraint for folding is that an input column cannot be folded with an output column.

Thus the two operations—minimization, which reduces the number of product terms, and folding, which further reduces the area occupied by crosspoints—are very important for better utilization of the silicon area of a chip. These two topics are discussed in detail in Chapter 7.

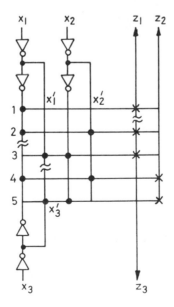

Figure 5.7.4 Simple column folding of PLA P_1.

TABLE 5.7.3 SSR
SPECIFICATION OF
PLA P_1 FOR THE
FOLDING OPERATION

Column		SSR
(x_1, x_1')	A	1,2,3
(x_2, x_2')	B	2,3,4,5
(x_3, x_3')	C	4,5
	z_1	1
	z_2	2,3
	z_3	4,5

5.8 SYSTEM-LEVEL LOGIC SYNTHESIS: THE SEMICUSTOM DESIGN APPROACH

The various circuits and modules that we have discussed so far are available in standard SSI (small-scale integration) or MSI (medium-scale integration) parts. IC chips with fewer than 10 gates are called SSI, whereas those having 10 to 100 gates are MSI. Chips having more than 100 to 10,000 gates are called LSI (large-scale integration), whereas those having more than 10,000 gates are known as VLSI (very-large-scale integration) chips. Typical examples of SSI packages are chips having a few INVERTER gates, AND–OR gates, NOR, NAND gates, a couple of flip-flops, and so on. Typical MSI circuits are multiplexers, demultiplexers, decoders, encoders, code converters, parity checkers/generators, counters, shift registers, and so on. When chips are designed with individual gates, the design is called a *full custom design*. Thus the SSI and MSI parts are examples of full custom design. When a more complex circuit is to be designed, it is much more convenient to design them not in terms of individual gates, but in terms of SSI and/or MSI building blocks. This approach is known as *semicustom design*.

When various building blocks are to be brought together, that is, laid out on a single chip, the various blocks must be compatible. For this purpose they must belong to a single family. Currently, most MSI parts are available in TTL (transistor–transistor logic), CMOS (complementary metal–oxide semiconductor), and ECL (emitter-coupled logic) families. To design an LSI or a VLSI chip, our objective shifts from the design of small circuits to large systems. While designing such a system, the available SSI and/or MSI parts may not be adequate. To overcome this limitation, various gate networks, each consisting of different types of configurations, different combinations of inputs, and so on, are made available in a library of cells, usually known as standard cells or polycells. To enhance the capability of the cell library, the standard cells also store the circuits of all the SSI and MSI parts as well. The designer has to pick up the appropriate cells and then draw up an appropriate interconnection between them, more commonly

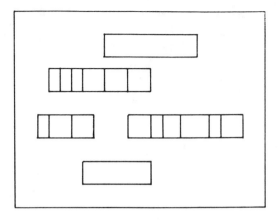

Figure 5.8.1 Standard cells on an LSI chip.

known as layout or routing. Another more powerful and versatile arrangement of cells is the gate array. In a standard cell layout, the cells are placed side by side, and the interconnection or routing channels are on the top and bottom of the cells (Fig. 5.8.1). In a gate array, a number of gates are arranged in the form of a matrix (Fig. 5.8.2). Each gate in the matrix is separate and has routing channels on all four sides. Another, important difference is that a "gate" in a gate array is not one that is already wired to perform a predetermined function. It is, on the other hand, a cell having all the ingredients of a gate without any interconnection between them. As an example, in the Motorola 112-gate array, based on TTL, each cell has three bipolar transistors and five resistors. These components can therefore be connected to realize any one of certain types of gates. For this reason gate arrays are also called *master slices* or *uncommitted logic arrays*. An excellent discussion and statistics about various aspects and features of gate arrays appears in Muroga (1982).

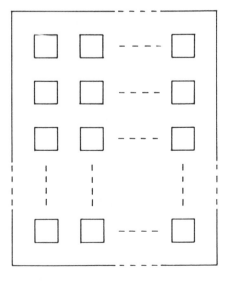

Figure 5.8.2 Uncommitted logic cells in a gate array.

Over the years the cells in gate arrays have increased both in number and in their capabilities to realize bigger and more complex systems. According to the statistics given by Muroga (1982), the 112-gate TTL array was offered by Motorola in 1972. In 1978 a gate array of 704 Schottky TTL gates was adopted by IBM for their system/38 and 4300 series computers. In 1980 IBM announced a gate array for 7640 TTL gates on a chip of size 7 by 7 mm for their 370/138 central processor unit (CPU).

As the system becomes larger and larger the layout problem becomes more and more complex. An efficient layout of a VLSI chip can pack many more devices in a small area, make it easily testable, and increase the yield. A combination of many such good points also speeds up the design time, an important consideration of competing industries. It is obvious that proper placement and routing of cells on a VLSI chip are not possible by manual synthesis. Hence many automated design procedures have been developed. For this, many hardware description languages (HDLs) have been developed. Again, each design tool has its own FPDL (function primitive description language). It must be evident by now that system-level design techniques, languages, and so on, have grown so vast that they have become a subject by themselves and are discussed in many books on VLSI system design. Interested readers may refer to many articles and books on the subject, a few of which are included in the references.

REFERENCES

DeGeus, A. J. Logic synthesis speeds ASIC design, *IEEE Spectrum,* Vol. 27, No. 8, August 1989, pp. 27–31.

DeMicheli, G., A. Sangiovanni-Vincentelli, and P. Antognetti (Eds.). *Design Systems for VLSI Circuits: Logic Synthesis and Silicon Compilation.* Dordrecht, The Netherlands: Martinus Nijhoff, 1987.

Dunlop, A. E., and B. W. Kernighan. A procedure for placement of standard cell VLSI circuits, *IEEE Trans. Comput.-Aided Des.,* Vol. CAD-4, No. 1, January 1985, pp. 92–98.

Dussault, J., C.-C. Liaw, and M. M. Tong. A high level synthesis tool for MOS chip design, *Proc. 21st Design Automation Conference.* Albuquerque, N.Mex., 1984, pp. 308–314.

Gimpel, J. F. The minimization of TANT networks, *IEEE Trans. Electron. Comput.,* Vol. EC-16, No. 2, February 1967, pp. 18–38.

Hellerman, L. A catalog of three-variable OR–INVERT and AND–INVERT logic circuits, *IEEE Trans. Electron. Comput.,* Vol. EC-12, No. 6, June 1963, pp. 198–223.

Maley, G. A., and J. Earle. *The Logic Design of Transistor Digital Circuits.* Englewood Cliffs, N.J.: Prentice Hall, 1963.

Marek-Sadowska, Global router for gate array, *Proc. IEEE International Conference on Computer Design,* 1984, pp. 298–307.

McCluskey, E. J. *Logic Design Principles.* Englewood Cliffs, N.J.: Prentice Hall, 1986.

Mead, C., and L. Conway. *Introduction to VLSI Systems.* Reading, Mass.: Addison-Wesley Publishing Co., Inc., 1980.

Muroga, S. *VLSI System Design*. New York: John Wiley & Sons, Inc., 1982.

Smith, R. A. Minimal-variable NOR and NAND logic circuits, *IEEE Trans. Electron. Comput.*, Vol. EC-14, No. 2, February 1965, pp. 79–81.

Vecchi, M. P., and S. Kirkpatrick. Global wiring by simulated annealing, *IEEE Trans. Comput.-Aided Des.*, Vol. CAD-2, No. 4, October 1983, pp. 215–222.

PROBLEMS

5.1. Implement the following functions with all NAND networks. Assume single-rail logic.
   (a) $f_1(abcd) = \Sigma(1-6,8,10,13,15)$
   (b) $f_2(abcd) = \Sigma(2,9,10,12,14,15)$
   (c) $f_3(x_1x_2x_3x_4) = x_1x_2'x_3 + x_3x_4' + x_1'x_2x_3$
   (d) $f_4(x_1x_2x_3x_4) = x_1x_2(x_3'(x_2' + x_4))$
   (e) $f_5(abcde) = (a + b)(c + d')(b' + d' + e')$

5.2. Implement the functions of Problem 5.1 with all-NOR networks. Assume single-rail logic.

5.3. A half-adder circuit has two inputs x_1 and x_2, representing the bits to be added, and two ouputs S and C as the sum and carry functions. Write its truth table and then implement it with **(a)** an all-NAND network; **(b)** an all-NOR network.

5.4. A full-adder circuit has three inputs, x_1 and x_2, the two bits to be added, and c, the carry bit from the previous adder. It has two outputs, S and C, the sum and carry functions, respectively. Write its truth table and then implement it with **(a)** two half-adders, **(b)** an all-NAND network, and **(c)** an all-NOR network.

5.5. Show that if in an all-NAND(NOR) network realizing f, all NAND(NOR) gates are replaced by NOR(NAND) gates, then the network realizes the dual of function f.

5.6. A NAND–NAND network realizes the three-variable function $f(x_1x_2x_3) = \Sigma(0,3,6,x)$. When all the NAND gates are replaced by NOR gates, the NOR–NOR network realizes the same function. What is the value of x?

5.7. Show that the all-NAND network realizing the function $f = a \oplus b \oplus c$ of Fig. 5.4.1 will realize the same function if all its NAND gates are replaced by NOR gates.

5.8. Convert the circuit of Fig. 5.4.1 into an AND–OR circuit by inserting inversion bubbles. Find the truth table of the resulting AND–OR circuit. Determine if it is the same as $a \oplus b \oplus c$. Now implement the truth table by a PLA having the minimum number of product terms.

5.9. Convert the circuit of Fig. P.5.9 into **(a)** an all-NAND network, and **(b)** an all-NOR network.

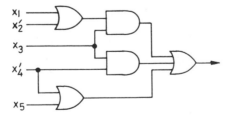

Figure P.5.9

5.10. It was shown in Table 2.12.1 that the set of XOR and AND operations form a functionally complete set because of the two identities

$$a + b = a \oplus b \oplus ab$$
$$a' = a \oplus 1$$

Prove these identities algebraically, and not by means of a truth table.

5.11. Whenever a Boolean function is expressed in XOR and AND operators only, it is said to be expressed in Reed–Muller canonical form. With the help of the identities of Problem 5.10, express the following functions in RM canonical form:

(a) $f_1 = xy + x'z + y'z$
(b) $f_2(x_1x_2x_3) = \Sigma(1,4,6,7)$
(c) $f_3(abcd) = \Sigma(2-6,9-12,15)$

5.12. Implement the following multiple-output circuit with standard cells. The library of standard cells made of CMOS logic gates has NOR, NAND, INVERTER, AND–OR–INVERT, OR–AND–INVERT, and two- and three-input EXNOR gates. The maximum number of gate in a cell is five, and the maximum number of inputs (fan-in) to a gate is four. Make the implementation as much chip-area efficient as possible.

(a) $y_1 = x'_4$, $y_2 = x_1x_3 + x'_2x_4$, $y_3 = x'x_2 + x_2x'_3$, $y_4 = x_1x_2x_3x_4 + x'_2x'_4$
(b) $y_1 = \text{DA57}$, $y_2 = \text{E1DE}$, $y_3 = \text{3B89}$, $y_4 = \text{1A01}$

5.13. Implement the following four-variable functions with 3-to-1 multiplexers. How many of the four functions will require an extra inverter?

(a) $f_1 = x_1x_2x_3 + x'_3x'_4$
(b) $f_2 = x'_1(x_2 + x'_3) + x'_2x_4$
(c) $f_3(x_1x_2x_3x_4) = \Sigma(3-6,8-10,13-15)$
(d) $f_4(abcd) = \Sigma(1,3,8,10-13)$

5.14. Can you so select the control variables that the functions of Problem 5.13 that require an extra inverter will no longer need it? Is it always possible to implement any arbitrary function without any inverter?

5.15. Can you find a simple algorithm that will detect a given Boolean function of n-variable that can be implemented without any extra inverter by a 1-to-$(n - 1)$ MUX? The algorithm should also identify the control variables needed for such an implementation.

5.16. Find the value of f realized by the circuit of Fig. P.5.16. Express f as a sum of minterms and realize it with a 1-to-5 MUX. Which of the two realizations requires less hardware?

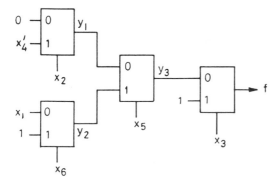

Figure P.5.16 A six-variable function realized by four 2-to-1 multiplexers.

5.17. Implement a BCD-to-excess-three code converter by ROM. Calculate the crosspoint density (the ratio of crosspoints with device to the total number of crosspoints) of the implementation.

5.18. Write a ROM program for a sine-wave generator with a sampling rate of 16 per cycle and a three-digit accuracy for the samples.

5.19. Write a ROM program to generate the character B whose encoding in a 5×7 dot matrix is as follows:

$$
\begin{array}{ccccc}
1 & 1 & 1 & 1 & 0 \\
1 & 0 & 0 & 0 & 1 \\
1 & 0 & 0 & 0 & 1 \\
1 & 1 & 1 & 1 & 0 \\
1 & 0 & 0 & 0 & 1 \\
1 & 0 & 0 & 0 & 1 \\
1 & 1 & 1 & 1 & 0
\end{array}
$$

5.20. Implement the multiple-output functions of Problem 5.12 by ROMs.

5.21. Implement the multiple-output functions of Problem 5.12 by PLAs. Compare the crosspoint densities of the ROM implementations of Problem 5.20 with those of the PLA implementations.

5.22. Find by observation the SCF implementations of PLAs of the unfolded implementations of Problem 5.21.

5.23. Draw the NMOS NOR–NOR circuit of the folded PLA of Fig. 5.7.4.

6

Fault Diagnosis and Tolerance

6.1 INTRODUCTION

The subject of fault modeling, diagnosis, testing, and fault tolerance of digital circuits is of crucial importance to the logic designer. The advent of VLSI circuits has resulted in a dramatic increase in the number of components on a single chip. As a consequence of the large circuit density, the probability of a fault occurring in the circuit also increases. Basically, the logic designer is confronted with two problems. First, it should be determined whether a digital circuit operates correctly and is free from faults. This involves the process of fault diagnosis and testing and is a necessary part of the manufacturing process. Second, its correct operation should be ensured even in the presence of faults. This is the topic of fault tolerance. In general, fault tolerance is obtained by introducing redundancy in the circuit. As the number of components on a chip increases, the fault detection and testing problem becomes more difficult and the techniques for fault tolerance become more expensive. Hence research on new and efficient techniques to handle the problem of faults has received considerable interest. In this chapter we discuss some basic concepts regarding faults in logic circuits, their diagnosis, testing, and techniques for fault tolerance.

6.2 FAULT CLASSES AND MODELS

We first discuss the different types of faults in a digital circuit and define the various terms used. A *fault* of a circuit is the physical defect of one or more components or connections of the circuit. Faults can be either permanent or temporary. *Permanent faults* are typically caused by the breaking or wearing out of a component. Such faults are always present and do not appear, disappear, or change their nature during operation. Permanent faults are also called *hard* and *solid faults. Temporary faults,* also known as *soft faults,* are those that occur only during certain intervals of time. These faults can be either transient or intermittent. A *transient fault* is usually caused by some externally induced signal perturbation, such as power-supply fluctuations. An *intermittent fault* is one that often occurs when a component is in the process of developing a permanent fault.

Another approach to classification is to classify a fault as logical or parametric, depending on its effect. A *logical fault* changes the Boolean function realized by the digital circuit, while a *parametric fault* alters the magnitude of a circuit parameter, causing a change in a factor, such as circuit speed, current, or voltage. An important type of parametric fault is the delay fault, which is caused by slow gates. This type of fault usually leads to problems of hazards or *critical races* (this topic is dealt with in Chapter 12).

Stuck-at, bridging, and crosspoint faults are three important types of logical faults.

Definition 6.2.1. A *stuck-at fault* is said to have occurred if a signal line appears to have its value fixed at either a logical 1 or a logical 0, irrespective of the input signals applied to the circuit. When the signal line is always at logical 1(0), the fault is known as a *stuck-at-one* or SA1 (*stuck-at-zero* or SA0) *fault.*

Stuck-at faults are one of the simplest faults to analyze. Further, they are proved to be very effective in modeling the fault behavior of actual devices since they represent the most commonly occurring circuit faults. Hence most of the proposed testing techniques cater to this type of fault. A stuck-at fault model generally assumes that the faults affect only the interconnections, especially inputs and outputs of the logic gates.

A *bridging fault* is said to have occurred if two signal lines are shorted together. It may be either an AND- or an OR-type of bridging fault.

Faults that occur in programmable logic arrays due to extra or missing devices (such as a diode or a transistor) are called *crosspoint faults.* Depending on their effect, crosspoint faults are classified as growth (G) faults, shrinkage (S) faults, appearance (A) faults, and disappearance (D) faults. Crosspoint faults are discussed in detail in Chapter 8.

Definition 6.2.2. If a circuit has only one fault at any given time, it is said to have a *single fault.* If there are two or more faults in the circuit, the circuit is said to have *multiple faults.*

Definition 6.2.3. Two faults are said to be *equivalent* or *indistinguishable* if they cause the circuit to malfunction in exactly the same way.

Definition 6.2.4. A fault is said to be *redundant* if the function realized by the circuit with the fault is exactly the same as that of a fault-free circuit.

In addition to the foregoing types, there are other faults that occur in specific devices. For example, *pattern-sensitive faults* occur in random-access memories (RAMs), and their effect is dependent on the particular input pattern applied to the RAM.

Throughout this chapter we assume the stuck-at fault model for presenting all testing and diagnosis techniques. Further, the fault is assumed to be logical and permanent.

6.3 FAULT DIAGNOSIS AND TESTING

An important task during the manufacturing process is to determine whether the circuit contains a fault, and if so, to locate it so that the faulty components can be replaced. The task of determining whether a fault is present or not is called *fault detection,* and the task of isolating the fault is *fault location.* The combined task of fault detection and location is referred to as *fault diagnosis.*

The technique adopted to diagnose faults is *testing.* Generally, testing of logical circuits consists of applying a set of input combinations to the *primary inputs* of the circuit (the primary inputs or outputs of a circuit are those that are externally accessible).

Definition 6.3.1. An input combination which in the presence of a fault produces an output different from the fault-free output is known as a *test vector* (TV).

Definition 6.3.2. The set of test vectors used for testing the circuit is called the *test set.*

Depending on whether the testing process results in detection or detection and location, the test set is classified as a *fault detection test set* or a *fault diagnostic test set. Test generation* is the process of finding the set of test vectors that can detect (or detect and locate) faults in a circuit.

Figure 6.3.1 shows the typical stages of the testing process. The first step is *fault modeling,* which consists of developing a fault dictionary, or list of possible faults, based on the assumed fault model. The next step is to generate the test vectors for the set of faults. The methods for *test generation* are described in the following sections. *Fault simulation* is the process of verifying the test set. A fault simulator computes the output of the circuit in the presence of various faults and verifies the detectability of the faults by the test set.

The increasing complexity of LSI and VLSI circuits has made it extremely difficult to detect all faults in a circuit. Hence the testing process usually aims at detecting or diagnosing only a fraction of the faults modeled. The *fault coverage* of the test set refers to the percentage of faults that can be detected by the test set. *Evaluation of the fault coverage* is the next important step in the testing process. If the coverage is inadequate, the test generation and fault simulation process is repeated until an adequate percentage of fault coverage is obtained. *Test application* forms the last stage, in which the test vectors are applied to the

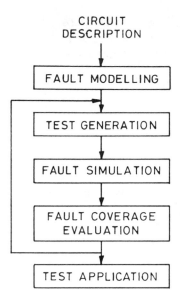

CIRCUIT
DESCRIPTION

FAULT MODELLING

TEST GENERATION

FAULT SIMULATION

FAULT COVERAGE
EVALUATION

TEST APPLICATION

Figure 6.3.1 Testing process.

actual circuit and the responses are checked for correctness. An incorrect response implies the presence of a fault in the circuit. Further test vectors may need to be applied to locate the fault.

6.4 TEST GENERATION

The generation of test vectors forms one of the most important and difficult tasks in the testing process. The complexity arises mainly due to the reduction in the ratio of the number of primary inputs and outputs to the number of internal inaccessible points in the circuit. Consider a circuit with n signal lines. Then under the assumption of a multiple-stuck-at-fault model, the total number of possible states is 3^n, since each line can be fault-free, stuck-at-0, or stuck-at-1. It can now be computed easily that even for a circuit with about 20 lines, this gives rise to an astronomical number of possible states. Generating the test set for checking such an enormous number of states is infeasible. However, it has been found that the assumption of a single stuck-at-fault model provides a good practical basis for testing most circuits. For the circuit with n lines, there are at most $2n$ possible single stuck-at faults. However, even for the single-stuck-at-fault model, there is a need for good techniques for efficient test generation. The objective of test generation is to obtain a *minimal complete test set*.

Definition 6.4.1. A test set of a circuit is *complete* if it detects every fault (of the assumed fault model) in the circuit under consideration.

Definition 6.4.2. A *minimal complete test set* is a complete test set that contains the minimum number of test vectors.

To illustrate the principles involved in test set generation, we describe below a technique called the fault-table method that gives the minimal complete test set.

6.5 FAULT-TABLE METHOD

Consider the circuit of Fig. 6.5.1, consisting of an AND and an OR gate. The primary inputs to the circuit are x_1', x_2, and x_3, while the primary output is z. Table 6.5.1 illustrates a fault table listing the outputs for each input pattern under fault-free and faulty conditions. The single-stuck-at-fault model is assumed. A stuck-at-0 fault on line a, for example, is denoted as a_0. The column under a_0 gives the output of the circuit for each input in the presence of this fault. Similarly, each of the other columns gives the response when a fault on the corresponding line is present. Now, a close look at the eight columns of the faulty outputs will reveal that the columns for faults a_0, b_0, and c_0 have identical responses. Hence these three SA0 faults are indistinguishable or equivalent faults. Similarly, the two SA1 faults c_1 and d_1 are also equivalent. The equivalence of faults may be ascertained by another observation. Note that a_0 and b_0 are the SA0 faults at the two inputs of the AND gate. When a SA0 fault occurs at the input of an AND gate, it forces the output of the gate to 0 irrespective of what happens at other inputs. Hence a SA0 fault at the input of an AND gate is classified as a *dominant* or *strong* fault. On the other hand, a SA1 fault at one of the inputs alone of an AND gate cannot force the output of the gate to 1. Hence a SA1 fault at the input of an AND gate is a *weak* fault. For similar reasons, a SA1 fault at the input of an OR gate is a dominant or strong fault, whereas an SA0 fault at the input of an OR gate is a weak fault. It is also obvious that either the SA0 or the SA1 fault at the output of any gate will belong to the dominant class of faults of that gate. It is now easy to see that all dominant faults pertaining to a gate will be indistinguishable and therefore equivalent.

The next step is to obtain a fault cover table that gives the test set for detecting each fault. In this table (Table 6.5.2) all the equivalent faults are grouped together and are treated as a single column. The test vectors for detecting each fault is determined by comparing the fault-free output with the faulty output of the fault.

Consider the first input pattern ($x_1 x_2 x_3 = 000$). The fault-free output z for this input is 0. All single stuck-at faults in the circuit except the faults b_1, c_1, and d_1 result in an output 0. The presence of any one of the faults b_1, c_1, or d_1 produces an output 1 that differs from the fault-free output. This implies that these faults can be detected by the test vector 000. Thus a $\times$ is placed under columns b_1 and $(c_1 d_1)$ in the first row corresponding to input 000. Considering another example,

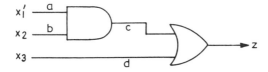

Figure 6.5.1 A circuit under test.

TABLE 6.5.1 SET OF ALL POSSIBLE SINGLE STUCK-AT-FAULTS AND THE FAULT-FREE AND FAULTY RESPONSES

				Faulty outputs							
			Fault-free output z	SA0 faults				SA1 faults			
x_1	x_2	x_3		a_0	b_0	c_0	d_0	a_1	b_1	c_1	d_1
0	0	0	0	0	0	0	0	0	1	1	1
0	0	1	1	1	1	1	0	1	1	1	1
0	1	0	1	0	0	0	1	1	1	1	1
0	1	1	1	1	1	1	1	1	1	1	1
1	0	0	0	0	0	0	0	0	0	1	1
1	0	1	1	1	1	1	0	1	1	1	1
1	1	0	0	0	0	0	0	1	0	1	1
1	1	1	1	1	1	1	0	1	1	1	1

input vector 001 gives a fault-free output of 1. The presence of fault d_0 gives an output 0. This means that test vector 010 is able to detect fault d_0. Hence a $\times$ is placed under column d_0 in row 001. The other rows are completed in a similar manner. It can also be observed from Table 6.5.1 that input vector 011 is not able to detect any fault.

Now the problem of obtaining a minimal complete test set is that of finding the smallest number of rows in the fault table such that all faults are detected. This is very similar to the problem of obtaining the minimum number of rows to cover all the minterms of a prime implicant table of the Quine–McCluskey algorithm for minimization of Boolean functions. Here also we can define three types of test vectors: essential, redundant, and selective. We define only the

TABLE 6.5.2 FAULT COVER TABLE

TVs			Faults				
x_1	x_2	x_3	$(a_0 b_0 c_0)$	d_0	a_1	b_1	$(c_1 d_1)$
*0	0	0				$\times$	$\times$
0	0	1		$\times$			
*0	1	0	$\times$				
1	0	0					$\times$
1	0	1		$\times$			
*1	1	0			$\times$		$\times$
1	1	1		$\times$			

essential test vector below. The definitions of the other two types are similar to those of the redundant and selective prime cubes of Chapter 3.

Definition 6.5.1. If a fault is detected by one and only one test vector, this test vector is an *essential test vector* (ETV).

It is obvious that an ETV can be identified on the fault cover table (Table 6.5.2) by observing single-cross columns. Thus the ETVs 000, 010, and 110 (marked by an * in Table 6.5.2) are ETVs. The other faults covered by the ETVs are now checked ($\sqrt{}$) off. The remaining columns are to be covered by STVs. In this case, only fault d_0 remains to be covered. As can be seen from the table, it can be tested by any one of the TVs 001 or 101 or 111. Thus the minimum test set to test all SA0 and SA1 faults of the circuit is

$$\{000, 010, 110, (001 \text{ or } 101 \text{ or } 111)\}$$

Note that in Table 6.5.2, TV 100 is a redundant TV.

For larger cover tables, after ETVs have been chosen, a selective test vector (STV) table is derived from the fault cover table. In this table all rows that are ETVs and all columns that have been checked off are not included. This table is reduced either by deleting all dominated rows or by deleting all dominating columns (see the reduction of the SPC table of Chapter 4). Dominating and dominated rows and columns are defined in the same way as has been done in Chapter 4. The minimal subset of STVs to detect all faults is now determined from the reduced STV table.

It should be mentioned here that although the problem of determining a minimum cover from the fault cover table is very similar to the problem of determining a minimum cover of the prime implicant cover table, it is definitely not identical. In fact, there is an important difference between the two. In the rows of a prime implicant table, all the cubes may not be of the same dimension but may vary from a 0-cube to an $(n - 1)$-cube in an n-variable Boolean function. On the other hand, the rows, that is, TVs of a fault cover table, are of the same dimension, each being a minterm or a 0-cube. For this reason any one of the STVs covering a fault is a valid solution, whereas any one of the SPCs covering a minterm may not be a valid cover.

The test application process that follows test set generation consists of applying the four test vectors in sequence to the circuit and observing the output z. For example, if 000 results in output 0, we know that the circuit is free of faults b_1, c_1, and d_1, but other faults might be present. Hence the second test vector 001 needs to be applied. If the output z is 1, the circuit can immediately be declared as faulty. This process is repeated with other test vectors to diagnose other faults.

The foregoing method, although simple, becomes infeasible for large circuits, due to excessive time complexity and memory storage requirements. Hence many other efficient approaches to test generation have been developed over the years. We discuss three such algorithms: path sensitization, Boolean difference, and Kohavis's a and b test methods.

6.6 PATH-SENSITIZATION METHOD

The main idea behind this approach is to create a sensitized path in order to move the effect of the fault at any line in the circuit to primary output. Suppose that it is required to detect a SA0 fault on a line. Then it is essential that a test vector create a change on that line and ensure that the change can be seen at a primary output. In other words, the test vector must produce a 1 on that line, and the path from the line to the output must be sensitized so that the output clearly shows whether the signal on the line under consideration is 0 or 1. Then the fault can be detected. This is the principle of the path-sensitization method.

To illustrate the approach, consider Fig. 6.6.1, which shows a two-level circuit with four inputs, x_1, x_2, x_3, and x_4, and a single output, z. Suppose that it is required to detect if any fault is present on the input line a. Then we sensitize the path from a to the output in order to propagate its effect to the output. If the path from a is traced, the first condition we get is $x_2 = 1$. This is so because if x_2 is 0, the output y_1 of the NAND gate will be 1 irrespective of the signal on line a. Following a similar reasoning, the input y_2 to the NOR gate must be 0. This in turn gives the condition $x_3 = 1$ and $x_4 = 1$. Thus, to detect the fault SA0 on line a, the test vector 1111 is applied. If the output z is 1, the line a is free of an SA0 fault. If z is 0, line a has an SA0 fault. To detect fault SA1 on line a, the test vector 0111 is applied. If z is 0, a does not have an SA1 fault; if z is 1, a has the fault.

As another example, consider the three-level circuit of Fig. 6.6.2. Suppose that it is required to check if line g (shown by a $\times$) has an SA0 fault. Now it is required to form a test vector so that a 1 is produced on g. This gives $x_1 = 1$ and $x_2 = 1$. Next, the path $G_1 G_4 G_6$ from g to the output has to be sensitized. This

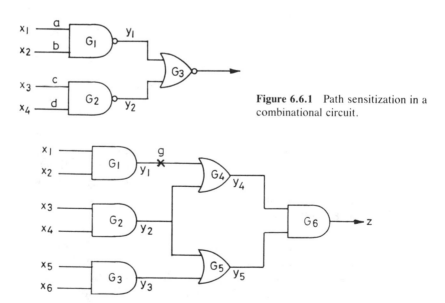

Figure 6.6.1 Path sensitization in a combinational circuit.

Figure 6.6.2 Path sensitization in a three-level combinational circuit.

Fault Diagnosis and Tolerance   Chap. 6

immediately requires that y_2 be 0, since if y_2 is 1, y_4 will be 1 irrespective of g being 0 or 1, and thus the path would be desensitized. The condition $y_2 = 0$ requires that $x_3 = 0$ and $x_4 = 2$ ("don't care") (alternatively, $x_3 = 2$ and $x_4 = 0$). Proceeding in a similar fashion, the next condition for path sensitization is $y_5 = 1$, which in turn gives $x_5 = 1$ and $x_6 = 1$. Thus any of the two test vectors within the cube 110211 detects the SA0 fault on g. If, on the application of the test vector, the output $z = 1$, the fault is not present; if $z = 0$, g has a SA0 fault.

In summary, the path-sensitization approach to test generation has the following steps (suppose that the test vector for a fault on line g is to be found).

1. A path is found from g to the output.
2. The input signals necessary to produce the appropriate signal at g (opposite the fault value) are determined.
3. The path from g to the output is sensitized and other inputs are determined by back propagation.

A general rule for path sensitization can be stated as follows: The output of an AND (NAND) gate is sensitized to one of its inputs (complement of the input) by placing a 1 on all other inputs. Similarly, the output of an OR (NOR) gate is sensitized to one of its inputs (complement of the input) by placing a 0 on all other inputs.

The single-path sensitization method, although simple and straightforward, has one major drawback. Although it works well for fanout-free circuits, it can sometimes fail in circuits with reconvergent fanout, as the following example demonstrates.

Consider the circuit shown in Fig. 6.6.3, which realizes the XOR function of variables x_1 and x_2. Let us try to derive a test vector for the SA1 fault on line y_1. There are two possible paths, $G_1G_2G_4$ and $G_1G_3G_4$, from the fault site to the primary output z. Let us first try to sensitize the path $G_1G_2G_4$. To excite the fault, we must set $y_1 = 0$, which implies that $x_1 = x_2 = 1$. Gate G_2 is already sensitized since $x_1 = 1$ and the fault effect reaches y_2. To sensitize gate G_4, we have to set $y_3 = 1$, and this in turn requires that $x_2 = 0$, leading to a contradiction, since the value of x_2 was determined earlier to be 1. Note that the logic value 0 on y_1 in the fault-free circuit cannot be used to justify the 1 required on y_3, as y_1 will change to 1 in the presence of the fault. Thus the path $G_1G_2G_4$ cannot be sensitized

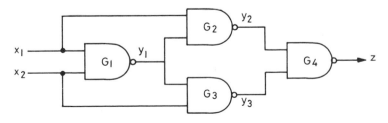

Figure 6.6.3 A reconvergent combinational circuit.

to detect the SA1 on y_1. Similarly, it can easily be verified that sensitizing the path $G_1 G_3 G_4$ will require setting x_1 to 0, which again leads to a contradiction. Thus single-path sensitization will fail to generate a test for y_1 SA1.

However, the fault above can be detected if we sensitize both paths from y_1 to the output simultaneously. If we set $x_1 = x_2 = 1$, the fault effect will propagate through gates G_2 and G_3, as both of these gates are sensitized. Under this condition, if the fault is present in the circuit, $y_2 = y_3 = 0$ and we get $z = 1$. However, if the circuit is fault-free, $y_2 = y_3 = 1$ and $z = 0$. Thus the fault is detected by the vector 11, through multiple-path sensitization, even though it is not possible to detect this fault via single-path sensitization. Thus any complete test generation algorithm should be capable of sensitizing all possible combinations of paths from the fault site to the primary output, so as to ensure detection of the fault. The D-algorithm developed by Roth (1966) is one such algorithm and guarantees to generate a test if a test exists for any given fault. The D-algorithm is a fairly complex algorithm and is not discussed in this book.

6.7 BOOLEAN DIFFERENCE METHOD

The Boolean difference method is an algebraic technique for test generation in which the test vectors are generated by utilizing the properties of Boolean algebra. Consider a logic circuit that realizes, under fault-free conditions, the Boolean function $F(X) = F(x_1 x_2, \ldots, x_n)$ of n input variables, namely, $x_1, x_2, \ldots, x_n$. Suppose that a fault is present in the circuit. Let $F'(X)$ be the function realized by the circuit in the presence of the fault. Then the underlying basis for the Boolean difference method is stated in the following theorem.

Theorem 6.7.1. The complete set of test vectors for the fault is the set

$$\{X \mid F(X) \oplus F'(X) = 1\}$$

It is easy to see that any input vector $X = x_1 x_2 \cdots x_n$, that satisfies the equation $F(X) \oplus F'(X) = 1$ distinguishes between the two functions. Hence X is a test vector—hence the theorem.

The algebra of *Boolean differences* provides an elegant method for determining the set above. The Boolean difference of a logic function is defined as follows:

Definition 6.7.1. The *Boolean difference* of a logic function $F(X)$ with respect to an input variable x_i is defined as

$$\frac{dF(X)}{dx_i} = F(x_1, \ldots, x_i, \ldots, x_n) \oplus F(x_1, \ldots, x_i', \ldots, x_n)$$

Let us denote the values of the function $F(X)$ when x_i assumes the values 0 and 1, respectively, as $F_i(0)$ and $F_i(1)$, that is,

$$F_i(0) = F(x_1, \ldots, x_{i-1}, 0, x_{i+1}, \ldots, x_n)$$

$$F_i(1) = F(x_1, \ldots, x_{i-1}, 1, x_{i+1}, \ldots, x_n)$$

Then it is easy to see that

$$\frac{dF(X)}{dx_i} = F_i(0) \oplus F_i(1) \tag{1}$$

First, we describe the method of test generation assuming a fault in one of the input lines. Later this result is generalized to a fault in any line. Consider a stuck-at-0 fault on an input line, say x_i. Then the function realized in the presence of the fault is $F'(X) = F_i(0)$. Hence, by Theorem 6.7.1, the test set for the fault can be obtained by solving the equation

$$F(X) \oplus F_i(0) = 1 \tag{2}$$

Similarly, it can be seen that the test set for a stuck-at-1 fault on input line x_i can be obtained by solving

$$F(X) \oplus F_i(1) = 1 \tag{3}$$

Now we state a theorem that provides a method for solving the equations above using Boolean differences.

Theorem 6.7.2. Equations (2) and (3) can be expressed, respectively, as

$$x_i \frac{dF(X)}{dx_i} = 1 \tag{4}$$

and

$$x_i' \frac{dF(X)}{dx_i} = 1 \tag{5}$$

Hence, the test sets for the faults SA0 and SA1 on input x_i are, respectively,

$$\left\{ X \mid x_i \frac{dF(X)}{dx_i} = 1 \right\}$$

and

$$\left\{ X \mid x_i' \frac{dF(X)}{dx_i} = 1 \right\}$$

The derivations of (4) and (5) are left as exercises (see Problem 6.6).

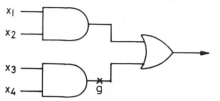

Figure 6.7.1 AND–OR circuit realizing $F(x) = x_1 x_2 + x_3 x_4$.

Example 6.7.1

In the circuit of Fig. 6.7.1, which realizes the function $F(X) = x_1 x_2 + x_3 x_4$ under fault-free conditions, find the test set for a SA0 fault at input line x_1 of the circuit.

Solution From Theorem 6.7.2 the test is

$$\left\{ X \mid x_i \frac{dF(X)}{dx_i} = 1 \right\}$$

Now

$$
\begin{aligned}
x_1 \frac{dF(X)}{dx_1} &= x_1(F_1(0) \oplus F_1(1)) && \text{from (1)} \\
&= x_1(x_3 x_4 \oplus (x_2 + x_3 x_4)) && \text{by substitution} \\
&= x_1 x_2 x_3' + x_1 x_2 x_4' && \text{after simplification}
\end{aligned}
$$

The equation $x_1 x_2 x_3' + x_1 x_2 x_4' = 1$ yields the two cubes 1102 and 1120 as solutions. Hence the test set is (1102, 1120) where the 2 represents a don't care; that is, the corresponding variable can be either 0 or 1.

The following theorem, which is an extension of Theorem 6.7.2, is used to obtain the test set for a fault in an internal signal line of the circuit.

Theorem 6.7.3. Let g be any signal line in the circuit. Let $G(x_1, x_2, \ldots, x_n)$ be the logic function giving the dependence of the value of the signal on g to the values of the input variables. Let $F(G, x_1, x_2, \ldots, x_n)$ be the function realized by the circuit as a function of G and the input variables. Then the test vectors for a SA0 on g are obtained by solving the equation

$$G = \frac{dF}{dG} = 1 \tag{6a}$$

and those for SA1 on g are obtained by the solution of

$$G' \frac{dF}{dG} = 1 \tag{6b}$$

The proof of this theorem is left as an exercise for the reader (see Problem 6.7).

Example 6.7.2

Find the test vectors for a SA0 fault on line g of the circuit of Fig. 6.7.1.

Solution The signal on line g can be expressed as $G = x_3 x_4$ and the output of the circuit is $F(G, x_1, x_2) = G + x_1 x_2$. By Theorem 6.7.3 the test vectors for a SA0 fault on g are obtained by solving

$$G = \frac{dF}{dG} = 1$$

The left-hand side of the equation above is

$$x_3 x_4 (F_G(0) \oplus F_G(1)) = x_3 x_4 (x_1 x_2 \oplus 1)$$
$$= x_1' x_3 x_4 + x_2' x_3 x_4$$

Thus the test vectors are (0211, 2011).

6.8 THE KOHAVI ALGORITHM

The path sensitization and the Boolean difference methods become practically infeasible for multiple faults, even for circuits of moderate size. This is because both methods consider only one fault at a time, and the total number of states to be tested in a circuit with n lines becomes $3^n - 1$ if multiple faults are allowed. Kohavi and Kohavi (1972) have proposed a method that overcomes this difficulty for test generation for multiple faults in two-level networks. The technique, which consists of determining two sets of tests, the a-tests and b-tests, considers the altered Boolean function realized by the circuit due to the presence of a single fault rather than considering the faults themselves. Kohavi and Kohavi have then proved that this single fault test set detects all multiple faults (see Theorem 6.8.1). However, to achieve the objective of providing a single fault test set with the capability of detecting all multiple stuck-at faults, Kohavi and Kohavi have put three severe restrictions on the networks, where alone the algorithm has to be applied. First, the network must be a two-level AND–OR or (OR–AND) network. Second, each AND gate must realize a prime cube. Third, the AND–OR network must implement a Boolean function which is a sum of irredundant prime implicants.* The Kohavi algorithm is quite simple and straightforward. But as we discussed in Chapter 5, the programmable logic arrays (PLAs) are two-level AND–OR networks, and extensive research has been done in finding efficient algorithms for PLA test generation. Consequently, quite a few excellent CAD packages are available to test PLAs. These are discussed in Chapter 8. It will then be apparent that Kohavis's a and b test set becomes a subset of the PLA test set. Hence this algorithm has lost much of its practical importance. Nevertheless, we shall discuss this algorithm, as it clearly brings out some of the fundamental concepts, which will be very useful in understanding faults in PLAs.

We first describe the algorithm for a two-level AND–OR circuit. As mentioned earlier, it is assumed that each AND gate of the circuit realizes an

---

*By "a sum of irredundant prime implicants," Kohavi and Kohavi (1972) mean a sum that does not contain either a redundant prime implicant or a redundant literal. However, it is not equivalent to the term "minimum sum of product" (MSOP), as we discussed in Chapter 3. For example, the function $f = \Sigma \, (0,1,3,5,7,8,12,13)$ has two irredundant sum forms, $f_1 = 0221 + 2000 + 1102$ and $f_2 = 0221 + 0002 + 2101 + 1200$. But only one of these, f_1, is the MSOP form.

irredundant prime implicant. Thus the output function of the circuit can be expressed as a sum of irredundant prime implicants or cubes. Consider a SA0 fault on any of the inputs of an AND gate. The effect of this fault on the output function is the elimination of the prime implicant realized by the AND gate. This can be checked by any one of the distinguished minterms of the prime cube (see Definition 3.4.3).

Definition 6.8.1. The set of distinguished minterms that tests each AND gate for SA0 faults is called the *set of a-tests*.

Consider a SA1 fault on any of the inputs of an AND gate. To illustrate the effect of such a fault, consider the circuit of Fig. 6.8.1(a), which realizes the function $f = x_1 x_2' + x_3 x_4$. The prime implicants of the function are $x_1 x_2' = 1022$ and $x_3 x_4 = 2211$, which are shown in the Karnaugh map of Fig. 6.8.1(b). Suppose that there is an SA1 fault on the input line x_2'. The effect of this fault is to change the prime implicant $x_1 x_2'$ to x_1. In other words, the cube 1022 expands to the cube 1222 (shown by the dashed line in the figure). Thus the fault can be detected choosing, as a test vector, a minterm that is in the subcube 1122, which is adjacent to the original cube. Another important consideration is that the minterm should be in the offset of the function. To test an SA1 fault in *any* input of an AND gate, it is necessary to select a test minterm in *each* of the adjacent subcubes of the prime implicant realized by the AND gate. The set of all such minterms constitutes the set of *b*-tests.

Definition 6.8.2. The set of minterms that test each AND gate for SA1 faults is called the set of *b*-tests.

The following theorem can now be stated.

Theorem 6.8.1. (Kohavi and Kohavi, 1972). The set of *a*- and *b*-tests detects all multiple faults in the two-level AND–OR network.

For proof, see Theorem 2 of Kohavi and Kohavi (1972) or Theorem 8-1 of Kohavi (1978).

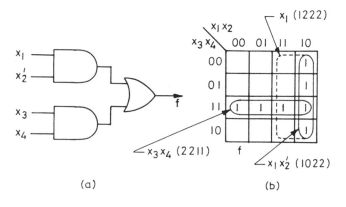

Figure 6.8.1 (a) AND–OR network realizing the function $f = x_1 x_2' + x_3 x_4$; (b) generation of *a*-tests and *b*-tests on the map.

Fault Diagnosis and Tolerance   Chap. 6

Example 6.8.1

Figure 6.8.2(a) shows a two-level AND–OR circuit that realizes the function $f = x_1x_2 + x_1x_3'x_4' + x_2x_4$. Find a minimum test set for this network.

Solution The prime implicants of the function x_1x_2 (1122), $x_1x_3'x_4'$ (1200), and x_2x_4 (2121) are shown in the map in Fig. 6.8.2(b). To derive the a-tests, consider each cube and mark a minterm that belongs to that and only that cube. Thus minterm 14 is chosen for 1122, minterm 8 for 1200, and either of minterms 5 or 7 can be chosen for 2121; these minterms are marked * in Fig. 6.8.2(b). Thus the set of a-tests is {14,8,5 or 7}.

Next we consider the derivation of b-tests. Figure 6.8.2(c) shows the subcubes that are adjacent to each of the prime implicants. The adjacent subcubes are 0122 and 1022 (adjacent to 1122), 0200, 1210, 1201 (adjacent to 1200), 2021, and 2120 (adjacent to 2121). Now we choose a set of minterms that are present in each of these adjacent subcubes but not present in the function. One such selection is shown in the figure (hatched circles). Minterm 9 covers 1022, 1201, and 2021. Minterm 4 covers 0122, 2120, and 0200. Next, minterm 10 is chosen to cover the remaining

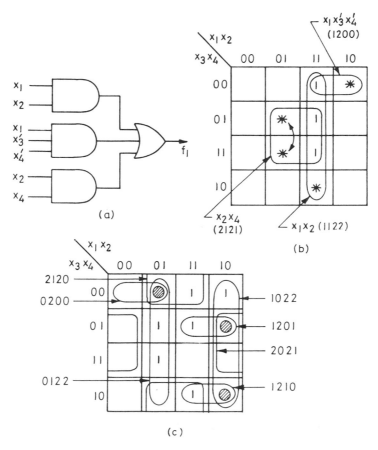

(a)

(b)

(c)

Figure 6.8.2 (a) AND–OR network realizing $f = x_1x_2 + x_1x_3'x_4' + x_2x_4$; (b) derivations of a-tests for f; (c) derivation of b-tests for f.

subcube 1210. Thus the set of b-tests is {4,9,10}. Thus the set {14,8,5 or 7,4,9,10} is the test set for the circuit of Fig. 6.8.2(a).

Now let us consider the derivation of a- and b-tests for a two-level OR–AND circuit. The basic strategy of the Kohavi algorithm in this case is to find a test equivalent AND–OR circuit for the given OR–AND network. For the sake of illustration, consider the two-level OR–AND circuit of Fig. 6.8.3(a). Let us find the test vectors for a SA1 fault on an input line of the OR gate G_1. Then, from the path-sensitization principle, it is easy to see that this requires $x_1 = 0$, $x_2 = 0$, and among x_3 and x_4, at least one of them must be 1. Thus the test vector is within the cube 0021 or 0012, and we can choose any of the minterms 1, 2, and

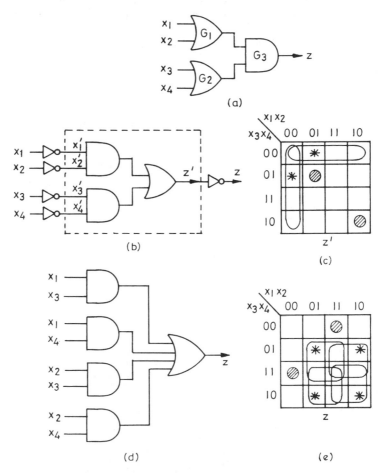

Figure 6.8.3 (a) OR–AND network for $z = (x_1 + x_2)(x_3 + x_4)$; (b) test-equivalent AND–OR circuit for z; (c) derivation of a- and b-tests for z'; (d) equivalent AND–OR circuit for z; (e) derivation of a- and b-tests for circuit (d).

3 to detect the SA1 fault. By following a similar procedure for G_2, we find that any of the minterms 4, 8, and 12 can detect a SA1 fault on the input line of G_2. Now if we consider both gates G_1 and G_2, the SA1 fault can be detected by minterms 1 or 2 or 3 (for G_1) and 4 or 8 or 12 (for G_2). An interesting observation can be made by comparing this result with the Kohavi algorithm for an AND–OR network. Convert the OR–AND network into an AND–OR network with inverters as discussed in Section 5.3. This is shown in Fig. 6.8.3(b). Now find the a-tests for the AND–OR network of the equivalent circuit shown in the dashed box of Fig. 6.8.3(b). This AND–OR circuit realizes the sum of the two cubes 0022 and 2200. It can be seen from Fig. 6.8.3(c) that the a-test vectors are the same as those obtained by the path-sensitization method.

Now the algorithm to find the test vectors for any SA1 fault in a two-level OR–AND circuit can be written as follows:

1. Replace all OR gates in the OR–AND circuit by AND gates, and vice versa. Replace all primary inputs and the outputs by their respective complements. This gives the test-equivalent AND–OR circuit.
2. Determine the a-tests for the equivalent AND–OR circuit.
3. The a-tests are the test vectors for any SA1 fault in the OR–AND circuit. The fault-free output for the OR–AND circuit should be taken as 0 and not 1.

Following a similar analysis, we can prove that the b-tests for the test-equivalent AND–OR circuit give the test vectors for any SA0 fault in the OR–AND circuit. In this case, its fault-free output will be 1.

Thus the minimum test set for testing all stuck faults of the OR–AND network of Fig. 6.8.3(a) as obtained on the map Fig. 6.8.3(c) is {1,4,5,10}. The function-equivalent circuit of the OR–AND network is shown in Fig. 6.8.3(d). The a and b tests of this AND–OR network are shown in the map of Fig. 6.8.3(e). Note that the test set obtained by this method is not the same as obtained by the path-sensitization method, and may sometimes fail to detect all stuck faults of the OR–AND network.

Consider the OR–AND circuit shown in Fig. 6.8.4(a). A possible test set for all single stuck faults in this circuit as can be obtained from the test-equivalent circuit of Fig. 6.8.4(b) is $T = \{0,2,5,7\}$ [shown by stars and shaded circles in Fig. 6.8.4(c)].

Now consider the function-equivalent AND–OR circuit of the above OR–AND circuit [Fig. 6.8.4(d)]. A test set for all single stuck faults in this circuit is $T = \{0,4,6,7\}$ [shown by stars and shaded circles of Fig. 6.8.4(e)]. Note that these test vectors will not detect all SA0/SA1 faults of the test-equivalent AND–OR implementation of the OR–AND network, and it can be verified that these will fail to detect some faults in the original OR–AND network. For example, the SA0 faults for G_1 and G_2 cannot be detected without the test vectors 2(010) and 5(101). But these are not included in T for the AND–OR network of Fig. 6.8.4(d).

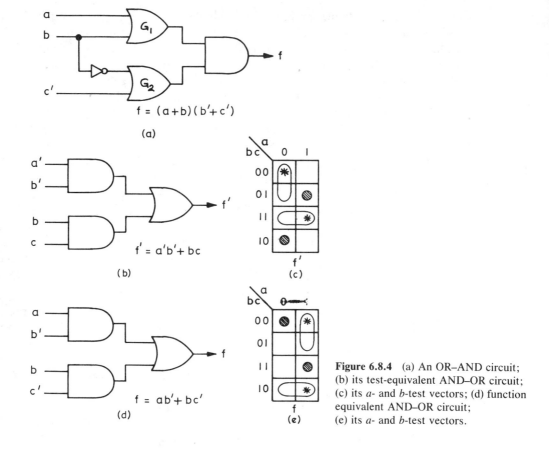

$$f = (a+b)(b'+c')$$

(a)

$$f' = a'b' + bc$$

(b)

$$f'$$

(c)

$$f = ab' + bc'$$

(d)

$$f$$

(e)

Figure 6.8.4 (a) An OR–AND circuit; (b) its test-equivalent AND–OR circuit; (c) its a- and b-test vectors; (d) function equivalent AND–OR circuit; (e) its a- and b-test vectors.

6.9 FAULT-TOLERANCE TECHNIQUES

Fault tolerance can be defined as the ability of the circuit to function correctly despite the presence of faults. This is in contrast to the fault-avoidance or fault-prevention methods discussed thus far, which are used to detect and locate faults during the manufacturing process. The increasing use of VLSI circuits in critical applications such as computer-controlled aircraft, spacecraft, medical electronics, and traffic control has called for consideration of providing fault tolerance as one of the important issues in the design of systems for such applications.

The underlying basis for obtaining fault tolerance in logic circuits is *hardware redundancy*, that is, the utilization of extra hardware. This can be of two types:

1. Static redundancy techniques
2. Dynamic redundancy techniques

Fault tolerance through static redundancy is achieved by replicating the circuit modules. Each circuit module takes the same input (or set of inputs) and feeds a voter circuit, which votes the majority of the outputs as the output of the

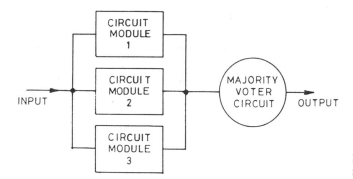

Figure 6.9.1 Triple modular redundancy (TMR) scheme.

circuit. Thus faults in up to a certain number of modules are, in effect, masked by this method. A popular scheme used is the triple modular redundancy (TMR) scheme shown in Fig. 6.9.1. Here three identical circuit modules take the same input and feed a common voter. The voter takes a majority vote to provide the correct output when a major number of modules (two, in this case) are fault-free. Thus it is seen that the TMR scheme can mask faults in any one of the circuit modules.

The TMR scheme can be extended to the NMR (N modular redundancy) scheme, where N identical modules feed a common voter. Since the voter has to take a majority decision, the number of modules N should be odd. In this case, faults in up to $(N - 1)/2$ modules can be tolerated.

The main advantage of the TMR/NMR scheme is that it can mask faults instantaneously allowing correct functioning of the circuit without interruption, since there is no need for any fault detection or recovery procedure. Hence it is used in systems employed for critical applications where even a small delay due to the occurrence of a fault can jeopardize the entire operation. However, the scheme is a rigid and expensive way of achieving fault tolerance. The power consumption is considerable since all the redundant modules need to be powered. Further, the voter circuit has to be designed to provide very high reliability, since a fault in the voter can cause system failure. To overcome this problem, a redundant voter scheme is sometimes adopted, in which the voter is also replicated.

Many variations to the TMR/NMR scheme have been suggested to suit specific fault-tolerant requirements. One such scheme makes use of a threshold voter in place of the majority voter. The voter output is 1 only if the weighted sum of its inputs is equal to or greater than its threshold M. Thus up to M faulty modules can be tolerated. Another method utilizes the TMR scheme with bidirectional voters.

In contrast to the static redundancy technique, the dynamic redundancy scheme achieves fault tolerance by automatic diagnosis of the faulty units, followed by reconfiguration and recovery, thus providing safe operation. This scheme removes the inflexibility of the static redundancy scheme, inasmuch as it makes possible the repair or replacement of the faulty units or allows the system to work in a gracefully degraded fashion. But the trade-off for this advantage is the requirement of techniques for rapidly detecting and locating the faults and recovery to the fault-free state.

The practical implementation of a dynamic redundancy scheme typically consists of an ideal spare circuit module along with the module under operation. A checking circuit monitors the output of the operating module, and when a fault is detected, a switch is made to bring the spare into operation and the faulty module is disconnected.

6.10 FAULT-TOLERANT VLSI PROCESSOR ARRAYS

Although this topic is not strictly within the purview of this book, this section has been added mainly for two reasons. First, it will show how the basic concepts of fault tolerance are utilized even when the operation is shifted from the domain of logic modules to that of processors. Second, it will introduce the reader to some special phenomena while dealing with very-large- and wafer-scale integrations.

Fault-tolerance consideration in multiprocessor systems have received a lot of attention lately. Processor arrays that afford high parallelism are well suited to VLSI implementation because of the regularity of their architecture and the locality of their interconnection structure. When a processor array is implemented on a single chip, the provision of fault tolerance poses many extra problems not encountered in multichip systems. First, the chip area should be utilized very efficiently. It has been found that the probability of finding a fault-free circuit on chip decreases exponentially with the chip area. Hence excessive increase in chip area due to the introduction of fault-tolerance circuits may actually decrease the reliability of the system rather than enhancing it. Another consequence of an increase in area is a possible reduction in wafer yield. Hence the fault-tolerance circuits should be simple and regular and should occupy less area, but at the same time, should support a variety of fault-tolerance algorithms. The importance of maintaining a small chip area is evidenced by the fact that many fault-tolerance models measure the suitability of the design in terms of the area occupied. Second, ordinary fault models do not suffice in the VLSI environment. A physical defect, which may have occurred at production time, may render a large block of logic as faulty. Hence the fault model should be able to take care of such cluster distribution of faults also. Third, faulty processors on chips cannot be repaired or replaced. The alternative is to utilize spare processors and dynamically reconfigure the array to bring in the spares and purge out the faulty modules or allow for graceful degradation of the system. In the case of reconfiguration, the locality of the interconnections should be maintained and simple routing techniques should be adopted. Further, each processor should have self-testing circuits and should be able to transmit its state (faulty or fault-free) to its neighboring processors by a single-bit code.

A number of configuration algorithms for two-dimensional VLSI processor arrays have been proposed, which vary in terms of the probability of survival to a given number of processor faults and the complexity of the reconfiguration-controlling circuits (*Proc. IEEE,* 1986). To understand the basic principles involved in such algorithms, consider the 5 × 5 VLSI processor array shown in Fig. 6.10.1(a). In addition to the 16 processors active under fault-free conditions, it has an extra row and an extra column of processors. In the event of multiple faults occurring in the array [Fig. 6.10.1(b)], the reconfiguration algorithm restructures the array into the fault-free array with the faulty cells bypassed. Variations to the straightforward reconstructing in the example above include the "fixed fault stealing" and "variable fault stealing" algorithms (Sami and Stefanelli, 1986; Negrini et al., 1986), which are more complex but show an increased probability of tolerance to faults,

Many fault-tolerant array architectures, in addition to the one discussed above, have internal switching mechanisms to establish connections on the occurrence of a fault. The CHiP (configurable, high parallel) computer (Snyder, 1982) is one architecture in which the switches are segregated from the processors. The CHiP architecture consists of a collection of processors, a switching lattice, and a controller. Each switch contains memory that stores several configuration settings which enable it to establish connections among its incident data paths. The controller loads the switch memory with the configuration codes. In the event of a faulty processor being detected, a configuration code is broadcast to route around the faulty processor. This scheme utilizes the fault-free processors adequately, but the reconfiguration algorithm is complex. Readers desirous to know more about this topic are referred to books and papers on this subject, some of which are included in the references.

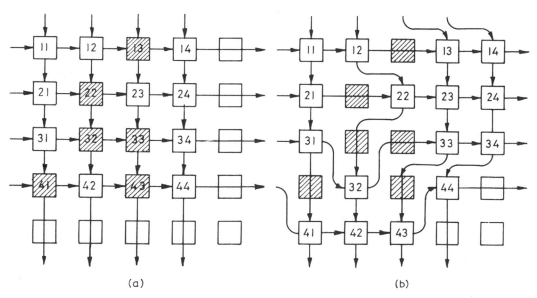

(a) (b)

Figure 6.10.1 (a) A VLSI array with faulty processors (shaded cells are faulty); (b) reconfiguration of (a) to a fault-free array by bringing in spare processors.

REFERENCES

On Combinational Logic

ABRAMOVICI, M., M. A. BREUER, AND A. D. FRIEDMAN, *Digital Systems Testing and Testable Design*. Rockville, Md.: Computer Science Press, Inc., 1990.

ARMSTRONG, D. B. On finding a nearly minimal set of fault detection tests for combinational logic nets, *IEEE Trans. Electron. Comput.*, Vol. EC-15, No. 2, February 1966, pp. 66–73.

CHENG, K. T., AND V. D. AGRAWAL. *Unified Methods for VLSI Simulation and Test Generation*. Norwell, Mass.: Kluwer Academic Publishers, 1989.

FUJIWARA, H. *Logic Testing and Design for Testability*. Cambridge, Mass.: The MIT Press, 1985.

KAUTZ, W. H. Fault testing and diagnosis in combinational digital circuits, *IEEE Trans. Comput.*, Vol. C-17, No. 4, April 1968, pp. 352–366.

KOHAVI, Z. *Switching and Finite Automata Theory*, 2nd ed. New York: McGraw-Hill Book Company, 1978.

KOHAVI, I., AND Z. KOHAVI. Detection of multiple faults in combinational logic networks, *IEEE Trans. Comput.*, Vol. C-21, No. 6, June 1972, pp. 556–568.

LEE, S. C. *Digital Circuits and Logic Design*. Englewood Cliffs, N.J.: Prentice Hall, 1987.

MCCLUSKEY, E. J. *Logic Design Principles*. Englewood Cliffs, N.J.: Prentice Hall, 1986.

PRADHAN, D. K. (Ed.). *Fault-Tolerant Computing Theory and Techniques*. Englewood Cliffs, N.J.: Prentice Hall, 1986.

ROTH, J. P. Diagnosis of automata failures: a calculus and a method, *IBM J. Res. Dev.*, Vol. 10, No. 7, July 1966, pp. 278–291.

SELLERS, F. F., M. Y. HSIAO, AND C. L. BEARSON. Analyzing errors with the Boolean difference, *IEEE Trans. Comput.*, Vol. C-17, No. 7, July 1968, pp. 676–683.

SU, S. Y. H., AND Y. C. CHO. A new approach to the fault location of combinational circuits, *IEEE Trans. Comput.*, Vol. C-21, No. 1, January 1972, pp. 21–30.

YAU, S. S., AND Y. S. TANG. An efficient algorithm for generating complete test sets for combinational logic circuits, *IEEE Trans. Comput.*, Vol. C-10, No. 11, November 1971, pp. 1245–1251.

On Fault-Tolerant VLSI Processor Arrays

BISWAS, N. N., AND S. SRINIVAS. Fault tolerance in multiprocessor systems, *Sadhana, Indian Acad. Sci. Proc. Eng. Sci.*, Vol. 11, Parts 1 and 2, October 1987, pp. 93–110.

IEEE. Special issue on fault-tolerance in VLSI, *Proc. IEEE*, Vol. 74, No. 5, May 1986.

KOREN, I. A reconfigurable and fault-tolerant VLSI multiprocessor array, *Proc. 8th IEEE Annual Symposium on Computer Architecture*, 1981, pp. 425–442.

KUHL, J. G., AND S. M. REDDY. Fault-tolerance considerations in a large, multiprocessor system, *IEEE Comput.*, Vol. 19, No. 3, March 1986, pp. 56–57.

NEGRINI, R., M. SAMI, AND R. STEFANELLI. Fault-tolerance techniques for array structures used in supercomputing, *IEEE Comput.*, Vol. 19, No. 2, Febuary 1986, pp. 78–87.

SAMI, M., AND R. STEFANELLI. Reconfigurable architectures for VLSI processing arrays, *Proc. IEEE*, Vol. 74, No. 5, May 1986, pp. 712–722.

SNYDER, L. Introduction to the configurable, highly parallel computer, *IEEE Comput.*, Vol. 15, No. 1, January 1982, pp. 47–56.

PROBLEMS

6.1. For the three-input circuit shown in Fig. P.6.1:
   (a) Draw the table giving the set of all possible single stuck faults and the faulty and fault-free responses.
   (b) With the help of the above table prepared in part (a), construct the fault cover table and derive the minimum complete test set.

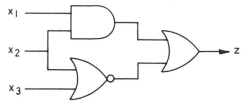

Figure P.6.1

6.2. For the circuit in Fig. P.6.2, find a minimum test set for all stuck-at faults by the fault table method. Assume that faults can occur only on lines a, b, c, d, and e. All other lines are fault safe. Find those input vectors that cannot test any fault, and those faults for which there does not exist any test vector. Such faults are called *undetectable faults*.

Figure P.6.2

6.3. Figure P.6.3 shows a 3-bit parity checker circuit. Using the path-sensitization method, find the test vectors for SA0 and SA1 faults on each line of the circuit.

Figure P.6.3 Three-bit parity checker.

6.4. Derive by the path-sensitization method the test vectors for the SA0 and SA1 faults at g and h in the network of Fig. P.6.4.

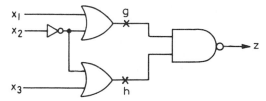

Figure P.6.4

6.5. A circuit realizes the function $z = x_1'x_4 + x_2'x_3 + x_1x_4'$. Using the Boolean difference method, find the test vectors for SA0 faults and SA1 faults on all input lines of the circuit.

6.6. Derive equations (4) and (5) of Section 6.7.

6.7. Using the result of Problem 6.6, prove Theorem 6.7.3.

6.8. Using the Boolean difference method, find the test vectors for SA0 fault on input line 1 and SA1 fault on the internal line 2 of the circuit of Fig. P.6.8.

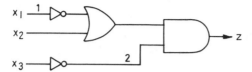

Figure P.6.8

6.9. A two-level AND–OR circuit has four AND gates feeding one OR gate. The four AND gates realize the product terms $x_1 x_3' x_4$, $x_2 x_4$, $x_1' x_3' x_4'$, and $x_1 x_2 x_3$, respectively. Derive the a- and b-tests for detecting multiple stuck-at faults.

6.10. Two-level AND–OR networks realize the following Boolean functions expressed as an irredundant sum of cubes. Each cube is realized by an AND gate. Derive on the map the minimum test set along with fault-free outputs using Kohavi algorithm for each of the networks.
   (a) $f_1 = 0201 + 1102 + 1211 + 0112$
   (b) $f_2 = 0200 + 1002 + 2121$
   (c) $f_3 = 1220 + 2201 + 0212$

6.11. In the AND–OR network realizing the function f_1 of Problem 6.10, add one more AND gate realizing the redundant cube 0221. Determine which single and double faults, if any, become undetectable as a result of this cube.

6.12. Find the undetectable faults, if any, of the circuit of Problem 6.2 by the Kohavi algorithm.

6.13. Find the test vectors of all SA0 and SA1 faults of the circuit of Problem 6.1 by the Kohavi algorithm.

6.14. Let the function f_2 of Problem 6.10 be realized by four AND gates (instead of three) as given below. Determine which single and double faults, if any, become undetectable due to this modification.

$$f_2 = 2000 + 0102 + 1201 + 2121$$

6.15. Two-level OR–AND networks realize the following functions. For each network find a minimum set of a and b tests.
   (a) $f_1 = (x_1 + x_2)(x_2' + x_4')(x_1' + x_2' + x_3')$
   (b) $f_2 = (x_1' + x_2' + x_3 + x_4)(x_1 + x_2 + x_3' + x_4')(x_1' + x_3')$
   (c) $f_3 = (x_1' + x_2' + x_3)(x_3' + x_4')(x_1 + x_2' + x_3')$

6.16. From first principles, derive a test-equivalent circuit of a two-level NAND–NAND network.

6.17. From the first principles, derive a test-equivalent circuit of a two-level NOR–NOR network.

6.18. In the multiprocessor array of Fig. 6.10.1(a) processors 12, 23, 33, 42, and 44 are faulty. Show by a diagram similar to Fig. 6.10.1(b) how these faulty processors can be taken out of the array that will still function correctly.

7

Programmable Logic Arrays

7.1 INTRODUCTION

In Chapter 5 we discussed how programmable logic arrays (PLAs) can be used very conveniently for the synthesis of combinational logic circuits. The most important feature that makes a PLA so attractive to a logic designer is its matrix-like regular structure. However, this regular structure also makes it quite sparse as far as the distribution of active devices is concerned. Thus a PLA will obviously take more space or area when implemented in a VLSI chip than, say, the gate or standard cell circuits. To accommodate all the components and modules within as small an area as possible is an important objective of a logic designer. Two operations that help to achieve this objective of area-efficient design are the minimization and folding of PLAs. A PLA is effectively a multiple-output two-level AND–OR circuit in the form of a regular structure of an array. It has a number of product lines connected by the input and output lines. While the number of input and output lines are fixed, the number of product lines or terms can be reduced, sometimes substantially, by an efficient minimization algorithm. PLAs, especially those used in a VLSI circuit, have invariably a large number of inputs and outputs. The minimization algorithm should therefore be a computer-

Some materials in this chapter are reproduced by permission of the IEEE, New York, USA, from author's paper mentioned at Reference, Gurunath and Biswas (1989), from their publication, *IEEE Trans on Computer-aided Design of Integrated Circuits and Systems*; and of Taylor & Francis Ltd., London, UK from author's paper mentioned at Reference, Biswas (1990), from their publication *International Journal of Systems Science*.

aided design (CAD) package capable of handling very large PLAs. Such packages are often called *PLA minimizers*. In effect, a PLA minimizer is a multiple-output minimization algorithm that can be applied in all cases involving minimization of single- or multiple-output Boolean functions.

The other operation that reduces the chip area further is the folding. This is done after the PLA has been minimized; that is, the number of product terms has been reduced to an extent possible by a PLA minimizer. In a matrix representing a PLA, the inputs and outputs appear as columns and the product terms as rows. Normally, all inputs and outputs appear as distinct and separate lines on a chip. It may be possible to find one or more pairs of inputs and also of outputs, where a pair of inputs or outputs will share a line. In the matrix representation this will appear as two columns sharing one line. This is the case of *column folding*. Similarly, when pairs of product terms share the same line, we get *row folding*. When both the columns and rows are folded, we get column and row folding. Clearly, the folding reduces the chip area of a PLA to a great extent. Considering an ideal case, where all the columns and rows of a PLA get folded, the area of the PLA reduces to 25%.

In this chapter we discuss these two operations. Although PLA is not the only module to synthesize a combinational logic circuit, it is an excellent medium to introduce many fundamental principles of logic synthesis which may be applied to even other ways of designing VLSI systems. Once these basic principles and concepts are understood with respect to PLAs, the reader will find it easier to extend these concepts to other devices and also will be able to develop new concepts and algorithms to suit an entirely new system.

7.2 PLA MINIMIZATION

Like many other problems in switching theory, the problem of Boolean function minimization is also NP-complete. As such, it is a very difficult problem to solve. Although for many years many researchers from both industries and universities have contributed in this area, a universally accepted solution is perhaps yet to come. The advent of very-large-scale integration has added two more dimensions of difficulties to the problem, one a steep rise in the number of variables, and the other, the multiple nature of outputs. The latter phenomenon makes even some of the classical methods obsolete, as it fails to produce a minimum solution even for small problems. Consider a four-input, three-output function where the three functions are

$$f_1 = \Sigma(1,3,4,5,8\text{--}13)$$

$$f_2 = \Sigma(1,3,4,5,7,9,11,13,15)$$

$$f_3 = \Sigma(5,7,8,10,12,13,15)$$

When solved by the classical *multiple-output prime implicant* method (for a detailed exposition of this method, see McCluskey, 1986) yields a six-product term solution as shown in the maps of Fig. 7.2.1. By observing the map a little more carefully, the reader can see that the product term 5 is superfluous. It should

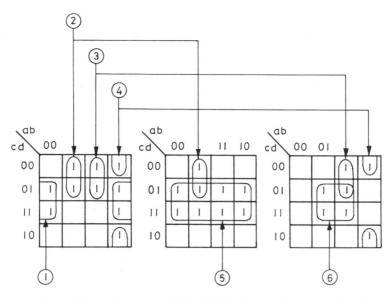

Figure 7.2.1 Six product term solution of a four-input, three-output function obtained by the multiple-output prime implicant method.

be split into two, one of which is shared with product term 1 and the other with 6. Thus even the classical method that carries out exhaustive computations fails to produce a minimum solution in multiple-output cases. Another reason why the multiple-output functions become difficult is that many times the essential prime cubes (EPCs) of an individual function have to be split to increase sharing, thereby reducing the number of product terms. Multiple-output functions of Fig. 7.2.1 and also of Fig. 3.9.1 are good illustrations of this phenomenon. The effect of increase in the number of variables, that is, the number of inputs and outputs, is more sweeping, as it takes all the minterm-based algorithms out of reckoning. Thus when we step into the domain of VLSI PLA minimization, we face a very difficult proposition. Due to the reasons explained in Section 4.8, all PLA minimization algorithms must be cube-based. The first cube-based algorithm MINI was developed at IBM by Hong et al. (1974). It has many heuristic procedures to compute the final solution by the iterative improvement of an initial solution. However, by far the most extensively used PLA minimizer currently available is ESPRESSO II, developed at the University of California–Berkeley by Brayton et al. (1984). It is also another heuristic algorithm based on the philosophy of MINI. The McBOOLE logic minimizer developed at McGill University by Dagenais et al. (1986) is based on the Quine–McCluskey philosophy and generates all the prime cubes. Since it uses some very efficient graph and partioning techniques, it can find minimal cover for very large functions. It has reported CPU time better than ESPRESSO II in many PLAs. However, as has been mentioned by the authors of McBOOLE, the very high number of prime cubes was the limitation in most of the examples that McBOOLE could not handle. Another multiple-output minimization algorithm that performs better than

ESPRESSO II and McBOOLE in many PLAs has been developed at the Indian Institute of Science, Bangalore, India, by Gurunath and Biswas (1989). This algorithm based on switching theoretic concepts has a fast technique for the determination of essential prime cubes without generating all the prime cubes. Unlike ESPRESSO II, it does not require the generation of the complement of the function either.

7.3 ESSENTIAL PRIME CUBE THEOREMS

A discussion of the various features and procedures of cube-based algorithms is beyond the scope of this book. Readers desirous to know more of these are referred to Brayton et al. (1984), which gives an excellent exposition of the various procedures of ESPRESSO II. However, to introduce the reader to the nature of operations that are done, the procedures to find the essential prime cubes of the algorithm developed at the Indian Institute of Science (IISc), Bangalore, India, are described in this section.

Let the procedure of the IISc algorithm to determine the essential prime cubes (EPCs) be explained by working them out on the following four-variable single-output function,

$$f = 0200 + 1102 + 2201 + 0011 + 0010$$
$$= C_1 + C_2 + C_3 + C_4 + C_5, \text{ say}$$

The cubes are shown on a Karnaugh map in Fig. 7.3.1(a). Take up the cubes in descending order of their dimensions. Therefore, first consider C_3. Find all the adjacent and properly intersecting cubes of C_3. Let these cubes form the adjacent and intersecting matrix (AIM) of the generating cube (GC). These are shown in Table 7.3.1. Directions covered by each cube of AIM(GC) are shown in parentheses.

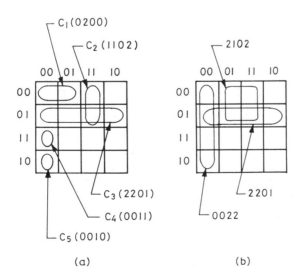

(a)   (b)

Figure 7.3.1 (a) Given four-variable function; (b) three EPCs of the given function as obtained by the IISc algorithm.

TABLE 7.3.1 EPC PROCEDURES FOR C_3

Variables or directions	1 2 3 4
Cube C_3	2 2 0 1
AIM (GC) C_1 C_2 C_4	0 2 0 0 (4) 1 1 0 2 (4) 0 0 1 1 (3)
All expandable directions covered, EPC test 1	Yes
Directions cube expands	$-\ -\ \times\ \times$
CSC	2 2 0 1
AIM (CSC)	Same as (AIM GC)
All expandable directions covered, EPC test 2	Yes
EPC test combinations	0 2 1 1 0 0
All combinations present, EPC test 3	No
CSC $\leq$ F	Test not required
An EPC as SC	2 2 0 1

From AIM we can find the directions in which C_3 can expand, that is, the variables that can be eliminated by combining with one or more cubes of AIM. As C_3 has 2's in directions 1 and 2, it cannot expand in these two directions. These are therefore not expandable directions. There are only two expandable directions (directions where there is either a 0 or a 1) for this cube, 3 and 4, where the cube can expand. Hence consider direction 3. If cube C_3 can expand in this direction, the cube 2211 must be contained in the cubes of AIM. This can be found by sharping 2211 from those cubes of AIM that cover direction 3, that is, only the cube C_4, 0011. Performing these operations with the help of a map (in this example), it can be seen that the cube 2211 does not exist, and therefore cube C_3 cannot expand in direction 3. Similarly, it can be ascertained that cube C_3 cannot expand in direction 4 also. Hence the candidate solution cube (CSC) is the same as the generating cube: 2201. Note that if a cube can really expand or not in a certain direction is ascertained only when there is at least one cube in AIM covering this direction. In the CAMP algorithm, as soon as we get a CSC, we test if it is within the function. If "Yes," we say that it is an EPC and is a solution cube (SC) (Theorem 4.6.1). In a cube-based algorithm, the condition of Theorem 4.6.1 is only a necessary but not a sufficient one. Here an EPC must satisfy an additional criterion stated in the following theorem.

Theorem 7.3.1 Essential Prime Cube Theorem. A candidate solution cube C is an essential prime cube of function F if:

(a) There exists at least one subcube (may be an elementary cube) within C that does not have any cube adjacent to it outside C.

(b) $C < F$; here $F = F_{ON} + F_{DC}$, where F_{ON} is the sum of all true cubes and F_{DC} is the sum of all don't-care cubes.

Corollary 7.3.1A. A candidate solution cube of dimension α generated by a cube of dimension α or $\alpha - 1$ is completely present in the given function.

Proofs of the theorem and corollary are given in (Gurunath and Biswas, 1989). To ascertain if a cube satisfies condition (a) of the EPC theorem, we find the adjacent and properly intersecting cubes of the CSC. These have been shown in AIM(CSC) in Table 7.3.1. The directions of the CSC covered by each cube of AIM(GC) are also shown in parentheses. If a single expandable direction remains uncovered, there is at least one subcube that is covered by only the CSC. Therefore, the CSC satisfies condition (a) of the EPC theorem and is a potential EPC. One can now proceed to test if the CSC is within F. For cube C_3, both expandable directions of CSC are covered by the cubes of AIM. So we find all combinations present in each cube of AIM under the 2's of the CSC. These are shown in the subtable and are called EPC test combinations. If these combinations have all the binary combinations, then all the subsuming minterms of the CSC have a cube adjacent to it outside C. Therefore, the CSC cannot be an EPC and is stored as a potential RPC or SPC. If, on the other hand, all combinations are not present, we must proceed to test if the CSC is within the function. If it is within the function, the CSC is an EPC among the solution cubes (SCs). When the CSC has been generated by a cube either by not expanding in any direction, or by expanding in only one direction, the (CSC $\leq F$) test need not be done (see Corollary 7.3.1A). For the cube that is under consideration, C_3, the EPC test combinations are shown in Table 7.3.1. Note that the combination 02 means the combinations 00 and 01. Now, scanning through the combinations, we find that the combination 10 is not present. Therefore, the CSC can be an EPC if it is in F. By Corollary 7.3.1A it is in F, and no further test is required. It is therefore stored as an EPC and a solution cube (SC).

There are two simpler ways of testing condition (a) of the EPC theorem. When the AIM(GC) of the generating cube is formed, it is checked if the cubes of AIM covers all expandable directions of the GC. Even if a single direction remains uncovered, then there is at least one subcube that is covered by only the GC. Therefore, the CSC generated by the GC satisfies condition (a) of the EPC theroem. In such a case the AIM of the CSC need not be formed at all. In case all directions of the GC are covered by its AIM, the AIM of the CSC is formed. Again it is checked if the cubes of AIM(CSC) cover all expandable directions of the CSC. If not, the CSC satisfies condition (a) and the EPC test combinations need not be computed.

The procedures* are now applied to the remainder of the cubes. The computations and results are shown in Table 7.3.2.

*The EPC procedures described in this book are improved versions of those reported in (Gurunath and Biswas, 1989).

TABLE 7.3.2 EPC PROCEDURES FOR C_1, C_2, AND C_4

Variables or directions	C_1	C_2	C_4
	1 2 3 4	1 2 3 4	1 2 3 4
Cube	0 2 0 0	1 1 0 2	0 0 1 1
AIM (GC)	C_2 1 1 0 2 (1) C_3 2 2 0 1 (4) C_4 0 0 2 1 (4) C_5 0 0 1 0 (3)	C_1 0 2 0 0 (1) C_3 2 2 0 1 (1,2)	C_3 2 2 0 1 (3) C_5 0 0 1 0 (4)
All expandable directions covered, EPC test 1	Yes	No	No
Directions cube expands	× – × √	√ × – ×	× × √ √
CSC	0 2 0 2	2 1 0 2	0 0 2 2
AIM (CSC)	C_2 1 1 0 2 (1) C_3 2 2 0 1 (1) C_4 0 0 2 1 (3) C_5 0 0 1 0 (3)	Not required	Not required
All expandable directions covered, EPC test 2	Yes		
EPC test combinations	1 2 2 1 0 1 0 0	Not required	Not required
All combinations present, EPC test 3	Yes	Test not required	
CSC ≤ F	Test not required	Test not required	Yes
An EPC as SC	No	2 1 0 2	0 0 2 2

The program also has a bookkeeping register that keeps an account of partial coverage of all adjacent cubes whenever a solution cube (SC) is generated. Thus when C_3 is "generated" as an SC, the bookkeeping register stores the information that the subcube 1101 of C_2 has been covered by the SC 2201. Note, however, that the partially covered cubes are not shrunk but kept as they are. When the entire cube becomes covered by one or more SCs, it is deleted from the list of cubes awaiting to be processed. In this example, after SCs 2102 and 0022 are generated, the cubes C_1 and C_5 get fully covered, and are therefore deleted. Hence the algorithm does not process C_5 any more. However, C_1 had been processed before the two SCs were generated. As can be seen from Table 7.3.2, it failed the EPC test and was therefore kept stored as a potential redundant or selective prime cube. In this case its deletion from the list shows that it is an RPC. After all EPCs are selected, still uncovered (partially or wholly) cubes are to be processed to generate the best set of SPCs.

Now, consider the 20-variable function discussed in Section 4.8. The function can be rewritten as a sum of two cubes:

$$f = C_1 + C_2$$

where

$$C_1 = 1\ 1\ 2\ 2\ 2\ 2\ 2\ 2\ 2\ 2\ 2\ 2\ 2\ 2\ 2\ 2\ 2\ 2\ 2\ 2$$
$$C_2 = 2\ 2\ 1\ 1\ 1\ 1\ 1\ 1\ 1\ 1\ 1\ 1\ 1\ 1\ 1\ 1\ 1\ 1\ 1\ 1$$

It can be seen that the two cubes intersect each other and none of them has an adjacent cube. Therefore, the AIM of each of these cubes will consist of only one cube. No cube can expand in any direction. Hence the CSC of each cube will be the cube itself, and it will also pass the EPC test 3. Consequently, each of the two cubes will be selected as an EPC and a solution cube. Thus the problem that appeared quite formidable in a minterm-based algorithm becomes almost trivial in a cube-based algorithm.

7.4 PLA FOLDING

Most of the existing PLA folding algorithms (Suwa and Kubitz, 1981; Luby et al., 1982; Hachtel et al., 1982; Grass, 1982; Lewandowski and Liu, 1984; Makarenko and Tartar, 1985) are graph and set theoretic. A CAD package named PLEASURE (Micheli and Sangiovanni-Vincentelli, 1983a) has been developed at the University of California–Berkeley. It is based on the graph-theoretic algorithm of Hachtel et al. (1982), whose aim it is to produce an optimal folding. It may not, therefore, produce the maximum folding even when one exists. Consider the 10-column $(A, B, \ldots, J)$ and 16-row $(1, 2, \ldots, 16)$ PLA P_1 shown in Fig. 7.4.1. When fed to PLEASURE it produces four pairs of foldable columns. The ordered foldable pairs are (D, A) (F, C) (G, B), and (H, J). The columns E and I are not folded. The reordered rows are given as follows:

2 6 7 8 10 11 13 1 15 3 5 12 14 4 9 16

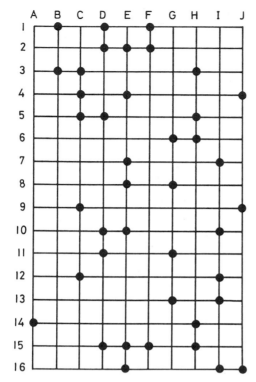

Figure 7.4.1 PLA P_1.

The folded PLA is shown in Fig. 7.4.2(a). It can be seen that the folding obtained by PLEASURE has left two columns unfolded. Hence if a solution exists where all the 10 columns can be folded, yielding five foldable pairs, the five-pair folding is the maximum folding. In the case of this PLA a five-pair folding exists and is shown in Fig. 7.4.2(b). Here the ordered foldable pairs are (A,C), (B,E), (F,G), (H,I), and (D,J). The reordered rows are

$$14 \quad 1 \quad 3 \quad 2 \quad 15 \quad 5 \quad 6 \quad 10 \quad 11 \quad 4 \quad 7 \quad 8 \quad 9 \quad 12 \quad 13 \quad 16$$

This maximum folding is obtained by the COMPACT algorithm, which is described in the next few sections. This algorithm is based on the concept of a foldable compatibility matrix (FCM).

7.5 FOLDABLE COMPATIBILITY MATRIX

The foldable compatibility matrix (FCM) is similar to the upper triangular matrix introduced by Luby et al. to prove that the problem of PLA folding is NP-complete (Luby et al., 1982). In their paper Luby et al. have also shown rigorously the equivalence between the folding problem and the bandwidth problem on undirected graphs and have introduced a fast heuristic algorithm to obtain nearly optimal folding from the bandwidth problem solution. In a communication to

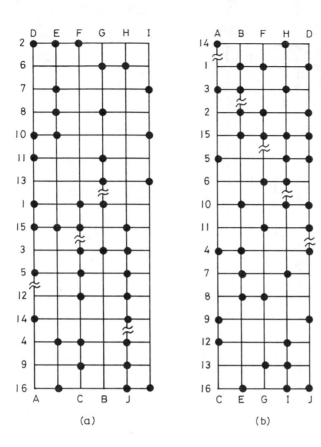

Figure 7.4.2 (a) Four-pair simple column folding obtained by PLEASURE; (b) five-pair (maximum) simple column folding obtained by COMPACT algorithm.

Electronics Letters (Biswas, 1985), the author developed the FCM independently and directly from the first principles and conjectured how with the help of the FCM concept, a maximum PLA folding algorithm can be obtained.

The PLA of Fig. 7.4.1 has the structure of a matrix with 10 columns ($A, B, \ldots, J$) and 16 rows ($1, 2, \ldots, 16$). As already mentioned in Chapter 5, the dots represent the presence of a device and are known as the crosspoints, and the particular configuration is known as the personality matrix of the PLA. Using the SSR notation (Definition 5.7.1) to describe the personality matrix of a PLA, the SSRs of the PLA of Fig. 7.4.1 are given in Table 7.5.1.

Definition 7.5.1. Two columns of a PLA are said to be *compatible* (*incompatible*) if their SSRs are disjoint (joint).

Definition 7.5.2. A square matrix that depicts the compatibility relation among all pairs of the columns of a PLA will be called a *compatibility matrix* (CM) of the given PLA.

In the compatibility matrix every column of the PLA appears as both a column and a row. A 1(0) will be entered into the (i, j)th cell of the CM if the column C_i and C_j of the PLA are compatible (incompatible). The compatibility

TABLE 7.5.1 SSRs OF PLA P_1

Column	SSR
A	14
B	1, 3
C	3, 4, 5, 9, 12
D	1, 2, 5, 10, 11, 15
E	2, 4, 7, 8, 10, 15, 16
F	1, 2, 15
G	6, 8, 11, 13
H	3, 5, 6, 14, 15
I	7, 10, 12, 13, 16
J	4, 19, 16

matrix (CM) for the example PLA P_1 is shown in Fig. 7.5.1. For the sake of visual clarity, 0's have not been shown. Hence a blank cell implies a 0 in it.

Consider now a folded PLA, shown in Fig. 7.5.2(a). The folded PLA has eight columns, of which $T_1, T_2, \ldots, T_4$ are at the top and $B_1, B_2, \ldots, B_4$ are at the bottom. The column T_i has been folded with column B_i. The pairs of folded columns have been so arranged that the gaps $g_1, g_2, \ldots, g_4$ satisfy the following relation. The level of g_i is higher than or equal to that of g_j if $i < j$. When the gaps are so arranged, they are said to be arranged in descending order.

It is now significant to note that the compatibility matrix of this folded PLA will always exhibit the pattern shown in Fig. 7.5.2(b). A cell with a "1" in it represents a compatible pair, whereas a cell with a "ϕ" in it represents a pair of columns that may or may not be compatible. The lower triangle about the leading diagonal has 1's in all the cells. It can be proved that the existence of such an

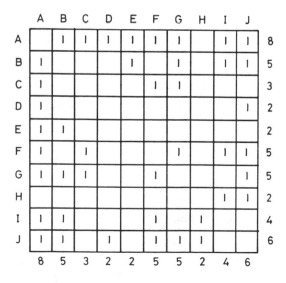

Figure 7.5.1 Compatibility matrix CM_1 of PLA P_1.

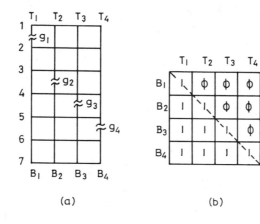

(a)

Figure 7.5.2 (a) A folded PLA; (b) foldable compatibility matrix of the PLA.

(b)

all-1 triangle is both necessary and sufficient for folding a PLA where the column T_i is folded with the column B_i. The T columns will appear at the top and the B columns at the bottom and the gaps in the columns will be in descending order.

Definition 7.5.3. A reduced compatibility matrix as shown in Fig. 7.5.3 is called a *foldable compatibility matrix* (FCM). It exhibits the following properties:

(a) Its columns and rows are two disjoint subsets of the set of columns of the PLA.

(b) It is an $m \times m$ matrix where $2m \leqslant n$, n being the total number of columns of the PLA. *The FCM is said to have order m.*

(c) It has the all-1 lower triangle about the leading diagonal.

(d) The columns (rows) of the FCM are the top (bottom) columns of the folded PLA. The PLA column denoted by column C_i of the FCM folds with the PLA column denoted by row R_i in the FCM. The gap g_i between C_i and R_i is at a level not higher than that of the gap g_{i-1} between C_{i-1} and R_{i-1}.

We now state a significant theorem and its corollary, which are at the heart of the folding algorithm. We shall call this theorem the folding theorem.

Theorem 7.5.1 The Folding Theorem. The $2m$ columns of an n-column PLA ($2m \leqslant n$) can be folded if and only if an $m \times m$ foldable compatibility matrix (FCM) can be derived from the $n \times n$ compatibility matrix of the PLA.

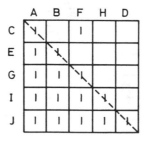

Figure 7.5.3 FCM of PLA P_1.

Corollary 7.5.1A. The ordering of the rows in the folded PLA is determined by the SSRs of the top columns $T_1, \ldots, T_m$ arranged in that order.

Proofs of the theorem and its corollary are given in (Biswas, 1986).

The FCM for the example PLA P_1 of Fig. 7.4.1 as derived from its CM of Fig. 7.5.1 is shown in Fig. 7.5.3. The ordered foldable pairs as given by the FCM are (A,C), (B,E), (F,G), (H,I), and (D,J). The reordering of rows as given by Corollary 7.5.1A are as follows: $(14)/(1,3)/(2,15)/(5,6)/(10,11)/$(remainder of the rows). Figure 7.4.2(b) shows the folded PLA.

7.6 THE COMPACT ALGORITHM

The COMPACT algorithm derives an FCM that gives all the information required to fold a given PLA.

Definition 7.6.1. If $2m$ ($2m \leq n$) columns of a PLA having n columns are folded, the folding is said to have *order m*. For a PLA to have a folding of order m, it must have an FCM of order m.

It is also obvious that the maximum value that m can have is given by

$$m_{\max} = \lfloor n/2 \rfloor$$

Definition 7.6.2. The number of 1's in any column (or row) of a CM or an FCM will be called its *weight*.

Definition 7.6.3. The columns and the rows of an FCM are two disjoint subsets of the entire set of the columns of the PLA. These two subsets will be called the *FCM columnset* (FCMCS) and the *FCM rowset* (FCMRS), respectively. The columnset (and rowset) of an FCM of order m will have m elements in it.

We shall now describe a procedure to determine the columnset and rowset of the FCM. To achieve this objective, the following properties of an FCM are utilized.

1. An FCM of order m has m columns and m rows. The m columns will be designated as $C_1, C_2, \ldots, C_m$, and the m rows as $R_1, R_2, \ldots, R_m$. The rows will also have an alternative designation. This will be $R'_1, R'_2, \ldots, R'_m$, where the subscripts are in the reverse order, that is,

$$R'_i = R_{m-i+1} \qquad (1 \leq i \leq m)$$

2. For every FCM a first column (FC) and a last row (LR) can be identified. According to our notation, the first column is C_1 and the last row is R'_1.

3. For an $m \times m$ FCM both the FC, C_1, and the LR, R'_1, have m 1's. Therefore, a column C_i of the PLA that becomes either the FC or the LR of the FCM must have a weight $W(C_i)$, such that

$$W(C_i) \geq m$$

Definition 7.6.4. The *set of compatible columns* of a PLA column C_i, SCC(C_i), is the set of columns of the PLA that are compatible with the column C_i.

Obviously, these PLA columns are the rows of the CM having 1's under the column C_i. For example, in the CM of Fig. 7.5.1,

$$SCC(A) = \{B,C,D,E,F,G,I,J\}$$

$$SCC(G) = \{A,B,C,F,J\}$$

Definition 7.6.5. The number of members in SCC(C_i) will be called the *cardinality* of SCC(C_i) and will be denoted by $|SCC(C_i)|$. Thus $|SCC(A)| = 8$ and $|SCC(G)| = 5$.

Definition 7.6.6. A column C_i and row R_j of the compatibility matrix that satisfy the following three relations will be called a *companion pair* (CP) or order m.
(a) $W(C_i) \geqslant m$ and $W(R_j) \geqslant m$.
(b) C_i and R_j are compatible.
(c) $|SCC(C_i) \cup SCC(R_j)| \geqslant 2m$, where m is the order of the FCM.

These three relations will be referred to as the *qualifying relations* for a companion pair.

We can now state the following theorem, which is obvious.

Theorem 7.6.1. Every foldable compatibility matrix (FCM) has a companion pair as its first column and last row.

It can easily be verified that the first column and last row of an FCM are interchangeable. Now proceed to determine a companion pair from the CM of the PLA to be folded. First determine the weights of all the rows of the CM. Then find a CP by checking each row with the rest, to see which pairs satisfy the three qualifying relations of a CP. Choose the row with the least weight as row R_j and the row with higher weight as column C_i of the companion pair.

It may happen that no CP of order m can be found. Then reduce m by 1 and repeat the procedure. If no companion pair is still available, further reduce m by 1 and repeat the procedure, and so on, until a CP with the highest value of m that is possible is found.

Applying this procedure to the example PLA P_1, that is, to the CM of Fig. 7.5.1, for which $m = \lfloor 10/2 \rfloor = 5$, it is seen that the pair of rows A and J form a companion pair. In fact, for this PLA, this is the only CP available. Here $W(J) = 6$ and $W(A) = 8$. Hence column A is taken as C_i and column J as the R_j of the companion pair. Let us now take a second look at the FCM of the example PLA P_1 as given in Fig. 7.5.3. The FCM is bounded by the two columns of the companion pair; column A is the first column C_1 of the FCM, whereas column J has become the last row R_1' of the FCM. If column A and row J are deleted from the FCM, another FCM of order $m - 2$, bounded by its companion pair B and I, is obtained. Arguing in this manner, we arrive at the following significant conclusion: *An FCM is constituted by a series of nested companion pairs whose order progressively descreases by 2.*

It can also easily be verified that the orders of the successive companion pairs are given by

$$m, m - 2, m - 4, \ldots, 1 \text{ when } m \text{ is odd}$$
$$m, m - 2, m - 4, \ldots, 2 \text{ when } m \text{ is even}$$

Two more theorems that are also obvious from the construction of the FCM are stated below.

Theorem 7.6.2. The necessary conditions for an $m \times m$ matrix to become an FCM of order m are given by the following relation:

$$W(C_i) \geq m - i + 1 \quad \text{and} \quad W(R_i) \geq i \tag{1}$$

where $W(C_i)$ and $W(R_i)$ are the weights of columns C_i and row R_i, respectively, of the FCM.

Theorem 7.6.3. The sufficient condition for an $m \times m$ matrix to become an FCM of order m is given by any one of the following two relations:
(a) $W(C_i) = m - i + 1$ and $W(R_i) = i$.
(b) $W(C_i) = W(R_i) = m$.

The algorithm for the derivation of the FCM of the highest order is based on the three theorems above. Let this be illustrated by working out two example PLAs.

For any PLA, first the compatibility matrix CM_1 is determined from the personality matrix of the PLA. Then the first companion pair, CP_1, is determined. For the PLA P_1, we have already seen that the CP_1

$$(C_1, R_1') = (\text{column } A, \text{ row } J)$$

Now derive CM_2 whose column and row sets are given by

$$CM_2CS = SCC(R_1') \sim C_1$$

$$CM_2RS = SCC(C_1) \sim R_1'$$

For the PLA P_1,

$$CM_2CS = SCC(J) \sim A$$
$$= \{B, D, F, G, H\}$$
$$CM_2RS = SCC(A) \sim J$$
$$= \{B, C, D, E, F, G, I\}$$

The columns and rows of CM_2 are also ordered according to their weights. The CM_2 of PLA P_1 is shown in Fig. 7.6.1(a).

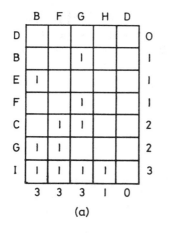

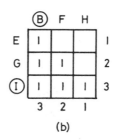

(a)

(b)

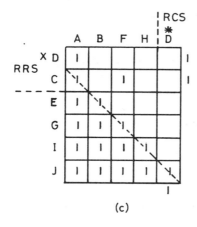

(c)

Figure 7.6.1 (a) CM$_2$ of PLA P_1; (b) CM$_2$ (CP$_2$) of PLA P_1; (c) pre-FCM of PLA P_1. Shows RCS and RRS with significant weights of columns and rows. Column D becomes an essential column.

In the CM$_2$ of PLA P_1 of Fig. 7.6.1(a) the column and row sets are not disjoint. Therefore, the necessary condition for the existence of an FCM of order 5 cannot be ascertained from the column and row weights (Theorem 7.6.2). Hence determine CP$_2$, (C_2, R_2'). A CP$_2$ is given by column B and row I. Derive another CM, called CM$_2$(CP$_2$) from CM$_2$ bounded by C_2 and R_2'. This is shown in Fig. 7.6.1(b). In this case CM$_2$(CP$_2$) shows that both the necessary and sufficient conditions for the existence of the nested FCM of order 3 are satisfied. Hence for this PLA an FCM of order 5 exists whose first column and last row are given by the CP$_1$, (C_1, R_1'). Figure 7.6.1(b) also gives the columns C_2, C_3, C_4 and rows R_2', R_3', R_4', which are columns B, F, H, and rows I, G, E, respectively. C_1 and R_1' are A and J, respectively. These sets of columns and rows will be called the *ordered selected column set* (OSCS) and *ordered selected row set* (OSRS). For PLA P_1,

$$OSCS = \{A, B, F, H\}$$

$$OSRS = \{J, I, G, E\}$$

The remaining sets of columns and rows (RCS) and (RRS) can be shown to be

$$RCS = SCC(R_1') \sim \{OSCS \cup OSRS\}$$

$$RRS = SCC(C_1) \sim \{OSCS \cup OSRS\}$$

For PLA P_1,

$$RCS = \{A,B,D,F,G,H\} \sim \{A,B,F,H,J,I,G,E\}$$
$$= \{D\}$$
$$RRS = \{B,C,D,E,F,G,I,J\} \sim \{A,B,F,H,J,I,G,E\}$$
$$= \{C,D\}$$

Now construct another compatibility matrix called pre-FCM (PFCM), whose columns and rows are given by

$$PFCMCS = OSCS \cup RCS$$

$$PFCMRS = OSRS \cup RRS$$

The columns and rows of the RCS and RRS are also ordered among themselves according to their significant weight, as defined below.

Definition 7.6.7. In a column or a row of the RCS and RRS, the number of 1's in the first string of consecutive 1's is called the *significant weight* of the column or row. In the RCS the bottommost string is the first string, whereas in the RRS it is the leftmost string.

Thus the PFCM of PLA P_1 is as shown in Fig. 7.6.1(c). If a PLA column appears both in the RCS and RRS, then retain it in the set where it is "essential" and delete it from the other. In Fig. 7.6.1(c), D is retained as a column and deleted from the rows. From this the FCM of Fig. 7.5.3 having an order 5 is easily obtained.

Note that the $CM_2(CP_2)$ shown in Fig. 7.6.1(b) is constructed with the companion pair (B,I). If this matrix would have failed to produce a necessary condition for the existence of an FCM of order 3, the other companion pair, (F,I), would have been tried. Such a situation is encountered in example PLA P_2, whose CM_1 is shown in Fig. 7.6.2.

PLA P_2 has 12 columns, and the CM_1 of PLA P_2 produces CP_1 to be (A,L) of order 6. This is the only CP of order 6. CM_2 derived from CM_1 amd CP_1 [Fig. 7.6.3(a)] does not satisfy the necessary condition for the existence of an FCM of order $(6 - 2)$, or 4, as there is no row (or column) of weight 4. Hence since there is no other CP_1 of order 6 in CM_1, the PLA does not have a folding of order 6. It may have a folding of order 5. So a CP_2 of order $(5 - 2)$ or 3 is found from CM_2. The CP_2 (D,I) is such a CP. But $CM_2(CP_2)$ with (D,I) as CP_2 does not satisfy the necessary condition for an FCM of order 3 [Fig. 7.6.3(b)]. So compute another CP_2. (D,K) is another CP_2 of order 3. But this too will not satisfy Theorem 7.6.2 for an FCM of order 3. The other CP_2 (B,I), however, satisfies the necessary (and

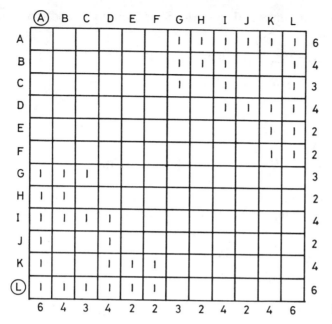

Figure 7.6.2 CM₁ of PLA P_2.

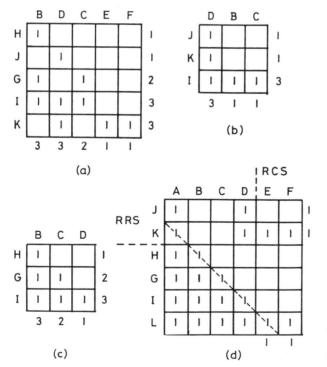

Figure 7.6.3 (a) CM₂ of PLA P_2; (b) CM₂ (CP₂) with (D, I) as CP₂; (c) CM₂ (CP₂) with (B, I) as CP₂; (d) pre-FCM of PLA P_2. Shows RCS and RRS with significant weights of columns and rows.

also the sufficient) condition for the existence of an FCM of order 3 [Fig. 7.6.3(c)]. Hence for this PLA

$$OSCS = \{A,B,C,D\}$$

$$OSRS = \{L,I,G,H\}$$

With these the PFCM can be constructed from which the FCM can be determined [Fig. 7.6.3(d)].

The PLA P_2 also shows how the order of an FCM gets reduced in an intermediate CM. *It is important to note that the algorithm proceeds to process the* CM$_p$ *only after making sure that the* CP$_{p-1}$ *has been so chosen as to produce the maximum folding that may exist.*

7.7 THE MAXIMUM FOLDING

Definition 7.7.1. Let n be the number of columns of a PLA. Let M be such that $M \leq \lfloor n/2 \rfloor$. Now if there exists a folding of order, M, but there does not exist any folding of order $(M + 1)$, the folding of order M will be called the *maximum folding*.

Note that the maximum folding does not always mean that all the columns are folded. For example, in a 10-column PLA, it may be possible to fold only eight columns, and not all the 10 columns. Then the eight-column folding of order 4 is the maximum folding.

As the PLA folding problem has been proved to be NP-complete (Luby et al., 1982), no nonexhaustive algorithm, including the compatibility relation algorithm discussed here, can guarantee that it will always produce maximum folding. However, because of the concept of the nested companion pairs and a limited number of backtracking, the COMPACT algorithm has a built-in tendency to obtain the maximum folding. This is supported by the fact that in all the problems solved by us the algorithm produced the maximum folding.

Some of the existing methods (Lewandowski and Liu, 1984; Makarenko and Tartar, 1985) which yield the maximum folding exhaustively search out all possible foldings and then select the maximum one. On the other hand, the COMPACT algorithm may lead to the maximum folding without much wasteful computation in most cases. In a few cases it may yield an optimal folding. At first sight it may appear that the search for appropriate companion pairs at various stages may require elaborate computation and in some cases may even lead to what is known as "combinatorial explosion." But we are yet to come across such a case. This is due to the fact that when the PLA is very dense there exists only one CP in almost all stages. On the other hand, when the PLA is very sparse, there are a number of CPs, and any one of them that is first computed yields the maximum folding. Thus the personality matrix of the PLA itself extends excellent cooperation to the algorithm for finding the maximum folding.

7.8 PRACTICAL PLAS

The PLA P_1 of Fig. 7.4.1, which has been used as the running example PLA to explain simple column folding, has only 10 columns, each showing the connection of the 10 input variables $A, B, \ldots, J$ to 16 product terms, $1, 2, \ldots, 16$. In a practical PLA each input variable has two lines, that is, columns, one for the complemented and the other for the true form of the variable. However, for the purpose of simple column folding the two lines are treated as one whose SSR is the union of the SSRs of the true and complemented forms of the variable. The actual SSRs of the 20 columns of PLA P_1 are as given in Table 7.8.1.

For the purpose of economical and technologically feasible implementation of the PLA on a VLSI chip, the true and complemented lines of an input variable are kept only on one side of the PLA, so that if, for example, A' is a top column, A cannot be a bottom column. Hence for the purpose of folding, A and A' are treated as a single column having the SSR given by SSR = {SSR of A'} $\cup$ {SSR of A}. These have been shown in Table 7.5.1.

TABLE 7.8.1 SSRs OF INPUT VARIABLES OF PLA P_1

Column	SSR
A	14
A'	Φ
B	Φ
B'	1, 3
C	3, 5, 12
C'	4, 9
D	5, 10
D'	1, 2, 11, 15
E	10, 15, 16
E'	2, 4, 7, 8
F	1, 2
F'	15
G	6, 8, 11
G'	13
H	5, 6, 14
H'	3, 15
I	12, 13, 16
I'	7, 10
J	4
J'	9, 16

TABLE 7.8.2 SSRs OF THE
OUTPUT COLUMNS OF PLA P_1

Column	SSR
Z_1	1, 2, 3, 6, 14
Z_2	5, 6, 8–13, 16
Z_3	3, 15
Z_4	4, 5, 7, 11

Another integral part of a PLA are the output columns or the OR matrix. These have also been omitted in the example PLA P_1. The PLA P_1 complete with both the input columns (AND matrix) and the output columns (OR matrix) has four outputs Z_1, Z_2, Z_3, and Z_4. The SSRs of these columns are given in Table 7.8.2.

To complete the SCF we must also fold the output columns. For this the FCM of the output columns must be determined. This can be done by the COMPACT algorithm applied to the output columns. However, an important point must be considered at this stage. Note that the input FCM requires a definite reordering of rows. Since the rows for the input and the output columns are the same, the reordering of rows demanded by the input FCM must not be in conflict with the reordering demanded by the output FCM. This can be achieved only if the output FCM can be nested in the input FCM. In other words, the first companion pair of the input column must also be the first companion pair of the output FCM. (Note that the situation will be reversed if the PLA has more output columns than the input columns and the output FCM has been determined first.) Hence, while computing the compatibility matrix of the output columns, their compatibilities with the first column and the last row are also determined. For our PLA P_1, these are shown in Fig. 7.8.1(a). Let us call this CM_0. Note that the CM_0 also has the last column and first row of the input FCM. CM_0 shows that Z_1 and Z_3 are compatible with row J. Therefore, they are the prospective columns of the output FCM. Similarly, since Z_2, Z_3, and Z_4 are compatible with A, they are the prospective rows of the output FCM. The compatibility matrix CM_1, from which the CP_1 for the output FCM are to be chosen, is now formed [Fig. 7.8.1(b)]. As the number of output columns is 4, we must look for an FCM of order 2. In this case only one companion pair of order 2 is required. Obviously, (Z_3, Z_4) is the only companion pair. This yields the output FCM as shown in Fig. 7.8.1(c). From this the ordered foldable pairs are (Z_3, Z_2), and (Z_1, Z_4). The simple column folding of PLA P_1 with both the input columns (with two lines for each input variable) and the output columns are shown in Fig. 7.8.2.

Example 7.8.1

Find a simple column folding of the PLA shown in Table 7.8.3. Draw the folded PLA.

Solution The PLA has six input columns, $x_1, x_2, \ldots, x_6$; two output columns, z_1 and z_2; and nine rows, as shown. The SSRs of the eight columns are tabulated in Table 7.8.4.

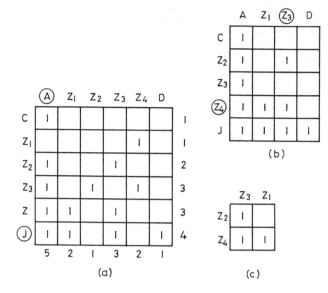

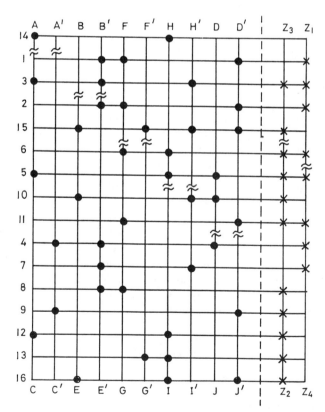

Figure 7.8.1 (a) Output CM_0; (b) output CM_1 for computing CP_1; (c) output FCM.

Figure 7.8.2 Simple column folding of both input and output columns of PLA P_1.

TABLE 7.8.3 PLA P_3

	x_1	x_2	x_3	x_4	x_5	x_6	z_1	z_2
1	1	1	2	2	2	2	2	1
2	0	2	1	2	0	2	1	2
3	2	2	0	0	0	2	1	2
4	2	2	2	1	1	2	1	2
5	2	0	1	2	2	2	2	1
6	1	2	0	2	2	2	1	2
7	2	2	2	1	2	1	2	1
8	2	2	2	2	0	0	1	2
9	2	2	2	1	0	1	1	2

TABLE 7.8.4 SSRs OF PLA P_3

Column	SSR
x_1	1, 2, 6
x_2	1, 5
x_3	2, 3, 5, 6
x_4	3, 4, 7, 9
x_5	2, 3, 4, 8, 9
x_6	7, 8, 9
z_1	2, 3, 4, 6, 8, 9
z_2	1, 5, 7

First determine the input FCM and then the output FCM. So, first the compatibility matrix CM_1 of the input columns is computed. This will be as given in Fig. 7.8.3(a). Here the number of input columns, $n = 6$. Therefore, we must look for an FCM of order $\lfloor 6/2 \rfloor$, or 3. From this the first companion pair, CP_1, is determined. CP_1 is (x_2, x_6) since

$$SCC(x_2) = \{x_4, x_5, x_6\}$$

$$SCC(x_6) = \{x_1, x_2, x_3\}$$

$$|SCC(x_2)| = 3 \quad \text{and} \quad |SCC(x_6)| = 3$$

and

$$|SCC(x_2) \cup SCC(x_6)| = 6$$

With (x_2, x_6) as CP_1, the $CM_1(CP_1)$ is shown in Fig. 7.8.3(b). As the weights of the rows and columns are 3, 2, 1, an FCM of order 3 exists. The next companion pair

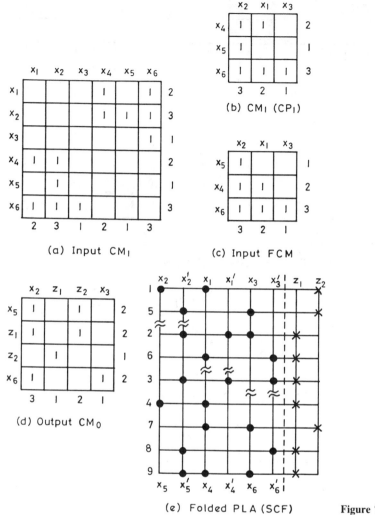

(a) Input CM$_I$

(b) CM$_I$ (CP$_I$)

(c) Input FCM

(d) Output CM$_O$

(e) Folded PLA (SCF)   **Figure 7.8.3** SCF of PLA P_3.

of order 1 is seen to be (x_1, x_4). Hence the input FCM is as shown in Fig. 7.8.3(c). From this the ordered foldable pairs are

$$(x_2, x_5), \quad (x_1, x_4), \quad \text{and} \quad (x_3, x_6)$$

The reordered rows are

$$1, 5/2, 6/3/\text{remainder of the rows}$$

Next determine CM$_0$ for the output columns with x_2 and x_6 as the first column and last row, and also with x_3 and x_5 as the last column and first row. This is shown in Fig. 7.8.3(d). As no output column is compatible with x_6, CM$_1$ for output columns cannot be formed. Therefore, no output FCM exists and the output columns cannot be folded. The folded PLA is shown in Fig. 7.8.3(e). It is interesting to note here that although z_1 and z_2 are compatible to each other, they cannot be folded. This is because the reordering of rows required for folding z_1 with z_2 will be in conflict with the reordering of rows demanded by the input FCM. This can be easily verified from the folded PLA diagram of Fig. 7.8.3(e).

So far we have discussed only simple column folding. As has been mentioned earlier, the COMPACT algorithm will also find simple row folding (SRF). However, unlike SCF, SRF can be implemented in two alternative architectures. In one of them all the output columns are placed in the middle of two groups of input columns. This is known as the AND–OR–AND architecture [Fig. 7.8.4(a)]. In the other, the output columns are split into groups and are placed in two sides of the PLA. This is known as the OR–AND–OR architecture [Fig. 7.8.4(b)].

To derive ample advantage from folding, quite often, both the columns and rows of a PLA are folded. For this first an SCF (or an SRF) is obtained, and then the SRF (or an SCF) is carried out. This way we get SCRF or SRCF. However, to reduce the area of the PLA still further, instead of simple folding, multiple folding may also be attempted. In multiple folding, a column (or a row) may be shared by more than two columns (or rows). These and various other types of folding, such as bipartite folding, are not discussed in this book. Interested readers are referred to the references at the end of the chapter. It should be mentioned here that although folding saves very valuable chip areas, it creates additional problems for layout designers, as the inputs and outputs are to be fed to the PLA from more than one direction, resulting in crisscrossing of many lines. This makes

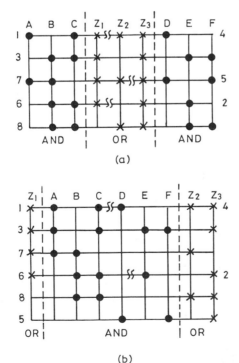

Figure 7.8.4 Simple row folding architectures: (a) AND–OR–AND; (b) OR–AND–OR.

the PLA layout more fault-prone and reduces the yield of the chip. For all these reasons, there may be many situations where it may be more advantageous to fold only the columns or only the rows of a PLA. There are also situations where a straightforward layout of an unfolded PLA is preferable to a more complex layout of a folded PLA.

REFERENCES

On PLA Minimization

BISWAS, N. N., AND B. GURUNATH. BANGALORE: an algorithm for the optimal minimization of programmable logic arrays, *Int. J. Electron.*, Vol. 60, No. 6, June 1986, pp. 709–725.

BRAYTON, R. K., G. D. HACHTEL, C. T. MCMULLEN, AND A. L. SANGIOVANNI-VINCENTELLI. *Logic Minimization Algorithm for VLSI Synthesis*. Norwell, Mass.: Kluwer Academic Publishers, 1984.

DAGENAIS, M. R., V. K. AGARWAL, AND N. C. RUMIN. McBOOLE: a new procedure for exact logic minimization, *IEEE Trans. Comput.-Aided Des.*, Vol. CAD-5, No. 1, Jan. 1986, pp. 229–238.

GURUNATH, B., AND N. N. BISWAS. An algorithm for multiple output minimiztion, *IEEE Trans. Comput.-Aided Des.*, Vol. CAD-8, No. 9, September 1989, pp. 1007–1013.

HONG, S. J., R. G. CAIN, AND D. L. OSTAPKO. MINI: a heuristic approach for logic minimization, *IBM J. Res. Dev.*, Vol. 18, Sept. 1974, pp. 443–458.

McCLUSKEY, E. J. *Logic Design Principles*. Englewood Cliffs, N.J.: Prentice-Hall, 1986.

On PLA Folding

BHAT, C., AND N. N. BISWAS. Transverse folding algorithm for PLAs, *Electron. Lett.*, Vol. 24, No. 6, 1988, pp. 306–308.

BISWAS, N. N. PLA folding algorithm from compatibility relations, *Electron. Lett.*, Vol. 21, No. 21, 1985, pp. 984–986.

BISWAS, N. N. A foldable compatibility matrix for the folding of programmable logic arrays, *Int. J. of Electronics*, Vol. 61, July 1986, pp. 709–725.

BISWAS, N. N. A compatibility relation algorithm for the folding of programmable logic arrays, *Int. J. Syst. Sci.*, Vol. 21, No. 8, September, 1990, pp. 1589–1601.

BISWAS, N. N., AND C. BHAT. A maximum PLA folding algorithm, *Proc. IEEE International Conference on Computer Design: VLSI in Computers and Processors*, 1987, pp. 686–689.

EGAN, J. R., AND C. L. LIU. Bipartite folding and partitioning of a PLA, *IEEE Trans. Comput.-Aided Des.*, Vol. CAD-3, No. 3, July 1984, pp. 191–199.

GAREY, M. R., AND D. S. JOHNSON. *Computers and Intractability: A Guide to the Theory of NP-Completeness*. San Francisco: W.H. Freeman and Company, Publishers, 1979.

GRASS, W. A depth-first branch and bound algorithm for optimal PLA folding, *Proc. 19th Design Automation Conference*, 1982, pp. 133–140.

HACHTEL, G. D., A. L. SANGIOVANNI-VINCENTELLI, AND A. R. NEWTON. Some results in optimal PLA folding, *Proc. International Conference on Circuits and Computers*, October, 1980, pp. 1023–1027.

HACHTEL, G. D., A. R. NEWTON, AND A. L. SANGIOVANNI-VINCENTELLI. An algorithm for optimal PLA folding, *IEEE Trans. Comput.-Aided Des. Integrated Circuits Syst.*, Vol. CAD-1, No. 2, April 1982, pp. 63–77.

HWANG, S. Y., R. W. DUTTON, AND T. BLANK. A best-first search algorithm for optimal PLA folding, *IEEE Trans. Comput.-Aided Des.*, Vol. CAD-5, No. 3, July 1986, pp. 433–442.

LECKY, J. E., O. J. MURPHY, AND R. G. ABSHER. Graph theoretic algorithms for the PLA folding problem, *IEEE Trans. Comput.-Aided Des.*, Vol. CAD-8, No. 9, September, 1989, pp. 1014–1021.

LEWANDOWSKI, J. L., AND C. L. LIU. A branch and bound algorithm for optimal PLA folding, *Proc. 21st Design Automation Conference*, 1984, pp. 426–433.

LUBY, M., U. VAZIRANI, V. VAZIRANI, AND A. SANGIOVANNI-VINCENTELLI. Some theoretical results in optimal PLA folding problem, *Proc. IEEE International Conference on Circuits and Computers*, 1982, pp. 165–170.

MAKARENKO, D., AND J. TARTAR. An efficient algorithm for the optimal folding of PLA's, *Proc. IEEE International Conference on Computer Design: VLSI in Computers*, 1985, pp. 57–60.

MICHELI, G. D., AND A. L. SANGIOVANNI-VINCENTELLI. PLEASURE: a computer program for simple/multiple constrained/unconstrained folding of programmable logic arrays, *Proc. 20th Design Automation Conference*, June, 1983a, pp. 530–537.

MICHELI, G. D., AND A. SANGIOVANNI-VINCENTELLI. Multiple constrained folding of programmable logic arrays: theory and applications, *IEEE Trans. Comput.-Aided Des. Integrated Circuits Syst.*, Vol. CAD-2, No. 3, July 1983b, pp. 151–167.

SUWA, I., AND W. J. KUBITZ. A computer-aided design system for segmented-folded PLA macro-cells, *Proc. 18th Design Automation Conference*, 1981, pp. 398–405.

PROBLEMS

7.1. Draw an all-NOR-gate circuit and a NOR–NOR PLA implementation of the following four-input, three-output Boolean function. Find the number of active devices in both types of implementations.

x_1	x_2	x_3	x_4	y_1	y_2	y_3
0	2	0	1	1	1	0
1	2	0	1	1	0	1
2	1	1	1	1	1	1
0	0	2	2	0	1	0
1	0	2	2	0	0	1

7.2. Check on map if in the following PLA every output function is individually fully minimized. Can it be further minimized? If yes, determine on the map the minimized PLA. Calculate the area and number of crosspoints in the given and minimized PLA. Hence calculate the improvement in area reduction and crosspoint compaction.

x_1	x_2	x_3	x_4	y_1	y_2	y_3
2	0	1	1	1	0	0
0	2	0	1	1	1	0
1	0	0	2	1	1	0
1	1	1	2	1	1	0
1	2	2	1	0	1	0
0	0	1	1	0	0	1
0	1	0	1	0	0	1
1	0	0	0	0	0	1
1	1	1	0	0	0	1

7.3. Find a minimized PLA of the following multiple-output Boolean functions either on a map, or better, by a PLA minimizer, in case there is one in your CAD center. Calculate the area and crosspoint densities of the unminimized and minimized PLAs. Also calculate the ratio of improvement in area reduction and crosspoint compaction.

(a) $f_1 = \Sigma(2,4,5,6,7,10,14,15)$
$f_2 = \Sigma(4,5,7,11,15)$

(b) $f_1 = \Sigma(1,4,5,7,13) + \phi\Sigma(3,6)$
$f_2 = \Sigma(3,5,7) + \phi\Sigma(6)$
$f_3 = \Sigma(3,4,11,13,15) + \phi\Sigma(9,14)$

(c) $f_1 = \Sigma(2,3,5,7,8,9,10,11,13,15)$
$f_2 = \Sigma(2,3,5,6,7,10,11,14,15)$
$f_3 = \Sigma(6,7,8,9,13,14,15)$

7.4. In the minterm-based CAMP algorithm, if a CSC is within the function, it is an EPC. On the other hand, in the cube-based IISc algorithm, a CSC becomes an EPC only when it is not only within the function but also passses the additional EPC test. Explain.

7.5. State the EPC test criteria as a theorem, and then furnish a proof.

7.6. Find the EPCs and the SPC-generating cubes of the following single-output functions by the EPC procedures of the IISc algorithm. Whenever necessary, perform the sharp operations on the map.

(a) $f_1 = 1100 + 1211 + 0110 + 0001 + 2121$
(b) $f_2 = 2102 + 0021 + 1112 + 2121 + 1010$
(c) $f_3 = 1220 + 2201 + 0212$
(d) $f_4 = 02222 + 10222 + 12120$

7.7. Minimize the following function by the IISC algorithm.

$f = 001210 + 001121 + 001200 + 001001 + 001011 + 011122 + 011221 + 101000$
$\quad + 101010$

How many cubes have been processed to get the final result?

7.8. Show that a generating cube having no AIM is an EPC of the solution. Hence explain why the IISc algorithm takes only 9.9 seconds compared to 4467.2 seconds of ESPRESSO II in minimizing the XOR12 PLA.

7.9. Work out in detail the EPC procedures of cubes C_1 and C_2 of the 20-variable function discussed in Section 7.3.

7.10. Determine from the following FCMs if there are any interchangeable columns or rows. Also determine if the permutations are dependent or independent.

(a)

	a	b	c	d
e	1	0	0	1
f	1	1	0	0
g	1	1	1	0
h	1	1	1	1

(b)

	a	b	c	d
e	1	0	0	1
f	1	1	1	0
g	1	1	1	0
h	1	1	1	1

(c)

	a	b	c	d	e
f	1	0	0	0	0
g	1	1	0	0	0
h	1	1	1	1	0
i	1	1	1	1	0
j	1	1	1	1	1

(d)

	a	b	c	d	e
f	1	0	1	0	0
g	1	1	0	0	0
h	1	1	1	0	0
i	1	1	1	1	0
j	1	1	1	1	1

7.11. When columns a and b of an FCM can be permuted if and only if rows c and d are also permuted, we get interdependent permutability. That is, permutability is bidirectional. If, however, the permutability of columns a and b depends on the permutation of rows c and d, but rows c and d can be permuted independently, we get a unidirectional permutability. Now, is the following statement true? All interdependent permutability is bidirectional. If yes, prove it as a theorem; otherwise, give a counterexample.

7.12. The compatibility matrix of the input part of a PLA having eight columns $(a, b, \ldots, h)$ is given below. Find the ordered foldable pairs for maximum folding by the FCM method. From the FCM, determine if there are interchangeable columns or rows. Is the interchangeability dependent or independent?

	a	b	c	d	e	f	g	h
a	0	0	0	1	1	0	1	0
b	0	0	1	0	1	1	0	1
c	0	1	0	0	1	1	1	0
d	1	0	0	0	1	1	1	0
e	1	1	1	1	0	0	1	0
f	0	1	1	1	0	0	1	0
g	1	0	1	1	1	1	0	1
h	0	1	0	0	0	0	1	0

7.13. The input columns of a PLA have the following compatibility matrix. Find the FCM for maximum folding of the PLA. Is the folding you obtain unique?

	a	b	c	d	e	f	g	h
a	0	0	1	0	0	0	0	0
b	0	0	1	0	0	1	1	0
c	1	1	0	0	0	1	1	0
d	0	0	0	0	0	0	1	0
e	0	0	0	0	0	0	1	0
f	0	1	1	0	0	0	0	0
g	0	1	1	1	1	0	0	1
h	0	0	0	0	0	0	1	0

7.14. In case you have PLEASURE or any other CAD tool for PLA folding, fold the PLAs of Problems 7.12 and 7.13 with the CAD package and compare the order of folding obtained using the COMPACT algorithm.

7.15. All columns of the following PLA can be folded. Find the SCF by the FCM method. Draw the folded PLA.

	A	B	C	D	E	F	Z_1	Z_2
1	1	1	2	2	2	2	0	1
2	1	2	1	2	1	2	0	1
3	2	2	1	1	1	2	1	0
4	2	2	2	1	1	2	1	0
5	2	1	1	2	2	2	0	1
6	1	2	1	2	2	2	1	0
7	2	2	2	1	2	1	1	0
8	2	2	2	2	1	1	1	0
9	2	2	2	1	1	1	1	0

7.16. All the columns of the following PLA can be folded. If there is more than one solution, find at least two FCMs of the maximum order. Draw both folded PLAs.

	A	B	C	D	E	F	Z_1	Z_2	Z_3	Z_4
1	2	1	2	1	2	1	0	1	0	0
2	2	2	2	1	1	1	0	1	0	1
3	2	1	2	2	2	2	0	0	1	0
4	1	2	1	2	1	2	0	1	0	1
5	1	1	2	2	1	2	1	0	0	1
6	2	2	2	1	2	2	0	0	1	0
7	2	1	2	2	2	1	0	0	0	1
8	2	2	1	2	1	1	0	1	0	1
9	1	2	1	2	2	2	1	0	1	0

7.17. Find the SCF of maximum order of the following PLA. How many CPs have you computed at each stage?

	a	b	c	d	e	f	z_1	z_2	z_3	z_4
1	2	2	1	2	0	2	1	0	0	0
2	0	2	2	1	2	2	0	1	0	0
3	2	2	0	2	1	2	1	0	0	0
4	2	0	2	2	2	1	0	0	1	0
5	2	2	2	0	2	2	0	1	0	0
6	2	2	2	2	0	2	0	0	0	1
7	2	2	1	2	2	2	0	0	0	1
8	2	1	2	2	2	2	0	0	1	0
9	2	0	0	1	0	0	1	0	0	0
10	2	2	2	2	2	0	0	0	1	0
11	2	2	1	2	2	2	0	0	0	1

7.18. Derive FCMs from the PFCMs of Fig. P.7.18.

	C	B	D	L	N	F	E	H
F	I							
E	I	I	I	I				
G	I	I						
A	I		I				I	
I	I	I	I	I				
J	I	I	I	I				I
K	I	I	I	I	I			I
M	I	I	I	I	I	I	I	I

Figure P.7.18

7.19. A PLA has the following SSR specifications. Find the maximum SCF for (a) only the input part; (b) only the output part; and (c) the entire PLA. If m_1, m_2, and m_3 are the order of folding found for (a), (b), and (c), respectively, does it turn out that $m_3 = m_1 + m_2$? Explain your results and conclusion.

$$A = \{1,2,6\}, \quad B = \{1,5\}, \quad C = \{2,3,5,6\}, \quad D = \{3,4,7,9\}$$
$$E = \{2,3,4,8,9\}, \quad F = \{7,8,9\}, \quad Z_1 = \{2,3,6,7,8,9\}, \quad Z_2 = \{1,4,5\}$$

7.20. Modify the COMPACT algorithm or develop your own algorithm so that a single FCM will produce the ordered foldable pairs for both the input and output columns, maintaining the constraint that an input (output) column can be folded with only another input (output) column. For example, a single FCM for the practical PLA P_1 of Fig. 7.8.2 will be as shown in Fig. P.7.20. Will such an algorithm be more efficient than the one presented in this chapter? Discuss.

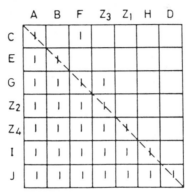

Figure P.7.20

7.21. Find a simple column folding of the following PLA having eight input and eight output columns, by first finding the SCF of the input columns and then finding the matching SCF of the output columns. Next find the SCF of the output columns and the matching SCF of the input columns. Do you get SCF of the complete PLA to be of the same order in both ways? If not, explain why.

Column	SSR	Column	SSR
x_1	4,5,10	z_1	5,10,11
x_2	1,2,3,6,11,12	z_2	3,9,11,12
x_3	2,9	z_3	2,9
x_4	4,7,8,9,10	z_4	1
x_5	3,5,6,10,11	z_5	7
x_6	1,5,7,8,12	z_6	2,6,8
x_7	1,2,3,7,9,12	z_7	5,6,9,12
x_8	3,9	z_8	1,4,7,10

7.22. Repeat the computations of Problem 7.21 with the following eight-input, six-output PLA.

Column	SSR		Column	SSR
x_1	4,8		z_1	1,4
x_2	2,3		z_2	8
x_3	1,3,7		z_3	2,3
x_4	5		z_4	5,7
x_5	7,8		z_5	2
x_6	1,4		z_6	6
x_7	4,5,6			
x_8	2,3			

7.23. Find a simple row folding (SRF) of the PLA of Problem 7.21 with both AND–OR–AND and OR–AND–OR architectures. Compare the area reduction of the PLA with the best SRF obtained in this problem with the best SCF obtained in Problem 7.21.

8

Design for Testability

8.1 INTRODUCTION

The advent of very-large-scale-integration is again responsible for the introduction of a new subject, design for testability, into the domain of switching theory and logical design. In this chapter we discuss some basic concepts about this with programmable logic arrays as the vehicle. The design of an area-efficient PLA becomes complete after PLA minimization and folding. This PLA is then manufactured. It now becomes necessary to test if the manufactured PLA really has all the devices, interconnections, and so on, exactly according to the theoretical specifications. For this purpose a number of input combinations known as test vectors are applied at the input, and their responses are observed at the output. However, when the PLA becomes very large, the generation of the set of test vectors to test various types of faults becomes very formidable. Also, the actual process of carrying out the test becomes very time consuming and sometimes has other difficulties. For this reason it becomes much simpler if some additional hardware is incorporated permanently into the PLA to make the testing process easier and more efficient to detect all types of faults. Some faults may remain so hidden that the usual test generation method will not be able to detect them within a reasonable computer time. These faults can be dealt with successfully by various techniques of design for testability.

Some materials in this chapter are reproduced by permission of the IEEE, New York, USA, from author's paper mentioned at reference, Biswas and Jacob (1985), from their publication, *Proceedings, Int. Test Conference,* 1985.

8.2 FAULTS IN PLAs

Due to the regular, memory-like structure of the PLA's layout, faults other than the traditional single stuck faults need to be considered for testing these devices. The spurious presence or absence of a device at crosspoints of a PLA cannot be modeled directly by the stuck-fault model. Hence the crosspoint fault model has been proposed (Smith, 1979). The major advantage of this fault model is that it is technology invariant and inherently models most of the frequently occurring physical failures, including shorts between lines (Wei and Sangiovanni Vincentelli, 1986). It can be shown that most of the stuck faults and bridging faults in a PLA are equivalent to multiple crosspoint faults. Since a test set for all crosspoint faults in a PLA will detect most of the physical defects in a PLA, the crosspoint fault model has emerged as the most popular fault model for testing PLAs.

The representation of PLA functions in terms of cubes was discussed in Chapter 5. Table 8.2.1 shows the personality matrix of a PLA having four inputs, two outputs, and five product terms. The functions realized are

$$z_1 = p_1 + p_2 + p_3 = x_1'x_3' + x_3'x_4 + x_1x_3$$

$$z_2 = p_2 + p_4 + p_5 = x_3'x_4 + x_2x_3x_4' + x_1x_2x_3$$

The two output functions z_1 and z_2 are plotted on a map in Fig. 8.2.1, which also shows the five product terms. This representation of a PLA on the Karnaugh map is quite convenient, and we shall use it frequently to explain the test generation for crosspoint faults.

Essentially, two types of crosspoint faults can occur: the extra crosspoint fault and the missing crosspoint fault. They produce four different types of faults based on their effect on the functions realized by the PLA (Smith, 1979).

1. *Growth (G) faults:* A missing crosspoint in the AND array at the intersection of product line p_i and input line x_j or x_j' is denoted $G(i, j)$. As a result of this missing crosspoint the variable x_j gets eliminated from the product term p_i. Consequently, the product term p_i that was an α-cube on the map now becomes

TABLE 8.2.1 PERSONALITY MATRIX
OF PLA P_1

	PT				OV	
	x_1	x_2	x_3	x_4	z_1	z_2
p_1	0	2	0	2	1	0
p_2	2	2	0	1	1	1
p_3	1	2	1	2	1	0
p_4	2	1	1	0	0	1
p_5	1	1	1	2	0	1

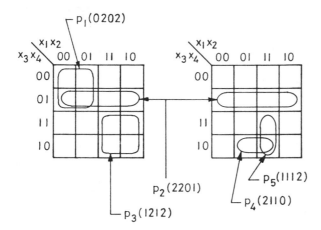

Figure 8.2.1 PLA P_1 on Karnaugh map.

an $(\alpha + 1)$-cube. Thus the cube grows into a larger cube due to a missing crosspoint in the AND array. Hence this type of fault is called a growth (G) fault.

2. *Shrinkage (S) faults:* An extra crosspoint fault in the AND array at the intersection of p_i and input line x_j (x_j') is denoted $S(i, j)$ [or $S(i, -j)$]. As a result of this extra crosspoint the variable x_j or x_j' gets ANDed with the product term p_i. Hence cube p_i (of dimension α now becomes a cube of dimension $\alpha - 1$. Therefore, the cube shrinks and this type of fault is called a shrinkage fault.

3. *Appearance (A) faults:* An extra crosspoint fault at the intersection of product term p_i and output line z_k is denoted by $A(i,k)$. Such a fault is called an appearance fault since product term p_i now newly appears on output function z_k as seen on a map.

4. *Disappearance (D) faults:* A missing crosspoint at the intersection of p_i and z_k is denoted by $D(i,k)$. This fault is called a disappearance fault since product term p_i now disappears from function z_k as seen on a map.

There is yet another type of crosspoint fault which is not explicitly included in the four types G, S, A, and D mentioned above. These are the *vanishing faults* (V-faults) in the AND array. A V-fault $(V(i, j), (V(i, -j))$ is said to occur if x_j' (x_j) is already connected to p_i and an extra crosspoint fault occurs on P_i with respect to x_j (x_j'). This fault introduces the term $x_j x_j'$ into the product term p_i, thereby making its value 0. Consequently, the product term p_i vanishes from each output function. It is easy to see that a V-fault is equivalent to a multiple D-fault on P_i and can be tested by any test vector for a detectable D-fault on P_i. Of course, if P_i is redundant with respect to every output function in the PLA, then all D-faults on p_i, and consequently the V-faults on it will be undetectable. However, such a situation will not occur in practical PLAs, since all redundant product terms will be identified and removed during PLA synthesis. Therefore, at least one D-fault on each p_i in a PLA will be detectable. For this reason V-faults will not be considered separately hereafter.

Design for Testability   Chap. 8

8.3 TEST GENERATION

In the single-crosspoint fault model, we assume that at a given time, only one crosspoint may exist in the faulty state. In an (n,m,q) PLA (a PLA having n input variables, m product lines, and q output lines) there are $m(2n + q)$ crosspoints and hence at most this number of single-crosspoint faults. However, if we consider multiple-crosspoint faults, since each crosspoint may exist either in its fault-free or faulty states, there can be $2^{m(2n+q)} - 1$ multiple-crosspoint faults. For example, for a small (16,48,8) PLA there are only 48 (16 $\times$ 2 + 8) or 1920 single-crosspoint faults, but an extremely large number ($2^{1920} - 1$) of multiple-crosspoint faults! Hence explicit consideration of anything other than single-crosspoint faults is impractical from the test generation point of view. We will stick to the single-crosspoint fault assumption for the rest of this chapter and now discuss the method of deriving tests for these faults, which is rather straightforward, since PLA is a two-level logic circuit.

Definition 8.3.1. The *distance* between two cubes a and b denoted $d(a,b)$ is the number of corresponding coordinates, where a and b have opposite logic values. In other words, $d(a,b)$ is the number of 0–1 (1–0) conflicts among the two cubes. Example: Let $a = 02012$, $b = 12001$; then $d(a,b) = 2$. Let $a = 1000$, $b = 1202$; then $d(a,b) = 0$.

Definition 8.3.2. A *test vector* or simply a *test* (TV or T) for a fault is any input vector for which the output of the circuit in the presence of the fault is different from the fault-free output.

Definition 8.3.3. A fault f in a logic circuit is said to be *undetectable* if the response of the circuit in its presence is identical to the fault-free response for all possible input combinations.

Undetectable faults cannot be detected since they do not alter the logical behavior of a circuit. However, undetectable faults are not quite desirable from a test generation point of view. The problems due to undetectable crosspoint faults are discussed in a later section. Our present aim is to obtain a test for each detetable single-crosspoint fault in a given PLA.

Consider a product term p_i $x_2 x_4' x_5$ or the cube 212012 in a PLA with six input variables, $x_1, x_2, \ldots, x_6$. Due to missing crosspoints in the line x_2 in this product line, the cube will have a growth fault as the cube will grow into the larger cube 222012. In so doing the cube 212012 adds to it the unwanted cube 202012. Hence any minterm within this cube that has a fault-free output 0 will now produce an output 1. Hence such a minterm will be a test vector for the growth fault $G(i,2)$. It is, however, important to note that if a minterm which is within the cube 202012 but is covered by another cube of the function will not qualify to be a test vector. The reason is that the fault-free output of such a minterm is also 1. The cube may have two other growth faults, $G(i,4)$ and $G(i,5)$.

$G(i,4)$ can be detected by a minterm within the cube 212112 and having a fault-free output 0. The growth fault $G(1,5)$ can be detected by a minterm within the cube 212002 and having a fault-free output 0. Thus the candidate test vectors of the three growth faults are within the three cubes 202012, 212112, and 212002. Note that these three cubes are disjoint from one another. This result can be stated as a theorem as follows.

Theorem 8.3.1. A product term (or a line) of a PLA that is an α-cube can develop $(n - \alpha)$ number of growth faults, which require $(n - \alpha)$ number of distinct test vectors for their detection.

Now consider the occurrence and detection of shrinkage faults in the same product line of the PLA. If an extra crosspoint appears in the x_1 line, the cube shrinks into a new one, 112012. In so doing, the cube 012012 gets "subtracted" from the original cube 212012. Therefore, any minterm within this subtracted cube 012012, which has a fault-free output 1 and which is not covered by any other product term, will now produce an output 0 and therefore can be a test vector for the shrink fault. If the extra crosspoint would have appeared in the x_1' line, the candidate test vector will be in the cube 112012. Note that this cube is disjoint from the cube 012012. Hence two distinct test vectors are required to test the shrink faults $S(i,1)$ and $S(i,-1)$. Similarly, two distinct test vectors within the cubes 210012 and 211012 are required to test the shrink faults $S(i,3)$ and $S(i,-3)$; and two distinct test vectors within the cubes 212010 and 212011 are needed to test the shrink faults $S(i,6)$ and $S(i,-6)$. At this point it may seem that we shall require six distinct test vectors to test the six different S-faults. Now, observe a significant thing. Take any three shrink faults on the three input variables, say $S(i,1)$, $S(i,-3)$, and $S(i,-6)$. The test vectors for these three tests are within the cubes 012012, 211012, and 212011, respectively. Now, there exists a single minterm that is within all these cubes and therefore can be a common test vector for these three S-faults. The test vector is the minterm 011011. Arguing in the same manner, it can be established that the minterm 110010 is the common test vectors for the three other S-faults, $S(i,-1)$, $S(i,3)$, and $S(i,6)$. Thus only two test vectors are required to test all the six S-faults. It can now easily be verified that these two test vectors are opposite minterms within the cube under test. This very important result was first observed by Bose and Abraham (1982) for an isolated product term. With necessary modification that is applicable for all product terms, we now get the following theorem.

Theorem 8.3.2 (Bose and Abraham, 1982). Two and only two test vectors that are opposite and distinguished minterms within the cube under test are sufficient to test all the 2α S-faults occurring in a product line that is an α cube $(\alpha > 0)$. For a product line that is a 0-cube, only one test vector, which is the cube itself, is required to test any S-fault.

Note that an S-fault in a 0-cube is really a vanishing (V) fault.

As there are $2^{\alpha-1}$ pairs of opposite minterms in a α-cube, the following corollary is obvious.

Corollary 8.3.2A. There are $2^{\alpha-1}$ pairs of candidate test vectors for the detection of all S-faults in a product line that is an α-cube ($\alpha > 0$).

It is obvious that a test vector for an S-fault will also detect a (vanishing) V-fault. It will also detect an (appearance) A-fault, on an output line z_k, provided that the TV has a fault-free output of 0 for the output function z_k. Thus most of the time it is possible to select a set of S-fault detecting TVs which will also detect all A- and D-faults. Thus in most cases the test generation problem reduces to the generation of TVs for the G- and S-faults only. Hence for an α-cube product line of an n-input variable PLA, we must find $(n - \alpha)$ TVs for $(n - \alpha)$ G-faults, and two or more TVs for all the S-, A-, and D-faults for α-cubes ($\alpha > 0$). For a 0-cube, only one TV is sufficient. This is a simple task for any PLA. But if we find all the TVs, their number so increases that the cost of testing the PLA becomes very high. Therefore, there is a need to find a minimal set. A minimal set is possible by judicious choice of TVs, as many a TV may detect faults in more than one product line. Let us illustrate this fact by finding a minimal test set for the PLA P_1 shown on the map of Fig. 8.3.1. We shall determine the minimal set by observation on the map. Here, there are nine TVs to detect all detectable single faults. Note that we have used the term "single fault" only for the detectable single faults. This is because there are some faults that cannot be detected. For example, for the product line p_1, the S-fault $S(1,-4)$ cannot be detected. The reader can easily find out the reason. Also note that the two TVs T_1 and T_2 which detect other S-faults on p_1 are not opposite minterms within the cube. The other undetectable faults in this PLA are the S-faults $S(5,4)$ and $S(4,-1)$ on p_5 and p_4, respectively, as also the A fault $A(5,1)$. The various faults detected by the nine TVs are listed in Table 8.3.1.

If we would have computed all the TVs for all the product lines of the PLA, we would have obtained 38 TVs, with some of them repeating, whereas only nine TVs are adequate. For larger PLAs, especially those encountered in a VLSI system, determination of the minimal set assumes greater importance. But this problem is also NP-complete. Hence any practical test generation algorithm must employ powerful heuristics aimed at obtaining a nearly minimal test set within

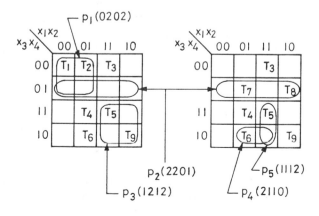

Figure 8.3.1 Generation of minimal test sets of PLA P_1 on map.

TABLE 8.3.1 TEST VECTORS AND FAULTS DETECTED

TV	m_i	Fault-free output		Faults detected
		z_1	z_2	
T_1	0	1	0	$G(2,4), S(1,2), S(1,4), A(1,2), D(1,1)$
T_2	4	1	0	$G(2,4), G(4,3), S(1,-2), S(1,4), A(1,2), D(1,1)$
T_3	12	0	0	$G(1,1), G(2,4), G(3,3), G(4,3), G(5,3)$
T_4	7	0	0	$G(1,3), G(2,3), G(3,1), G(4,4), G(5,1)$
T_5	15	1	1	$S(3,-2), S(3,-4), S(5,-4), D(3,1), D(5,2)$
T_6	6	0	1	$G(1,3), G(3,1), S(4,1), A(4,1), D(4,2)$
T_7	5	1	1	$S(2,1), S(2,-2), D(2,2)$
T_8	9	1	1	$S(2,-1), S(2,2), D(2,1), D(2,2)$
T_9	10	1	0	$G(4,2), G(5,2), S(3,2), S(3,4), A(3,2), D(3,1)$

reasonable computation time and memory requirements. Some of the more recent PLA test generation algorithms available as software packages, are PLATYPUS (Wei and Sangiovanni Vincentelli, 1986), developed at University of California–Berkeley and PLANET (Robinson and Rajski, 1988), developed at McGill University. The details of these algorithms are beyond the scope of our discussion. Reported performance results of these algorithms on 55 benchmark PLAs show that they can efficiently generate compact test sets even for very large PLAs. However, the usefulness of these packages are limited by the fact that they can handle only stand-alone PLAs and cannot handle embedded PLAs which are often encountered in practical VLSI chips.

8.4 UNDETECTABLE FAULTS

For the purpose of testing, the single-crosspoint fault model is favored because of its inherent simplicity. However, the occurrence of multiple-crosspoint faults cannot be ruled out in practice. Hence the use of a single fault test set (SFTS) derived under the single-crosspoint fault assumption can be justified only if it can be shown that such an SFTS will also detect most of the multiple-crosspoint faults. This can be shown to be true for crosspoint irredundant PLAs, that is, PLAs in which all single-crosspoint faults are detectable. Agarwal (1980) has shown that in a *crosspoint irredundant* PLA, a test set for all single-crosspoint faults will detect at least 98% of all multiple-crosspoint faults of size 8 (eight single-crosspoint faults occur simultaneously) or less. However, the problem is that most practical PLAs are not crosspoint irredundant, which means that they contain undetectable crosspoint faults.

Undetectable faults are undesirable from the test point of view. Although an undetectable fault occurring singly does not alter the function realized by a logic circuit, it may alter the function if two of them occur simultaneously. Again, a test set derived on single fault assumption can become invalid in the presence of undetectable faults. In other words, an SFTS capable of detecting all detectable single faults may fail to detect some of these faults if one or more undetectable faults actually occur in the circuit. To illustrate, let us consider PLA P_2 of Fig. 8.4.1(a). A test set for all detectable single-crosspoint faults is given by $T = \{3,4,6,7,11,13,14\}$. These minterms are shown by shaded circles on the map. It can be seen that the PLA has two undetectable faults; when p_4 appears on z_1, that is, $A(4,1)$ (an extra crosspoint ORs product term p_4 to the z_1 output), and when p_4 (2111) shrinks to the subcube 0111, that is, $S(4,-1)$ (an extra crosspoint comes on the x_1' line of product term p_4).

Consider the fault $S(1,-4)$ on p_1 (0122). This fault makes p_1 shrink to the subcube 0120. It is testable by minterm 7 in T. Now assume that the undetectable A-fault, $A(4,1)$, occurred first and then $S(1,-4)$ occurs. The output function z_1 now becomes as shown in Fig. 8.4.1(b). It is easy to see now that T fails to detect the detectable fault $S(1,-4)$ in the presence of the undetectable fault $A(4,1)$. $S(1,-4)$ could still be tested via z_1 using minterm 5, but 5 is not in T. So we see that the test set T becomes incapable of detecting all detectable faults, or is invalidated, in the presence of this undetectable fault.

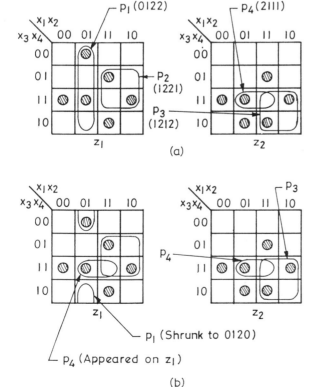

(a)

(b)

p_1 (Shrunk to 0120)

p_4 (Appeared on z_1)

Figure 8.4.1 (a) PLA P_2 (4,4,2) on map with an SFTS; (b) after faults $A(4,1)$ and $S(1,-4)$ occur. Shows how the SFTS is invalidated by the double fault.

The phenomenon above is known as masking. Here the undetectable fault $A(4,1)$ masks the detectable fault $S(1,-4)$ with respect to T. A formal definition for masking can now be given.

Definition 8.4.1. A detectable fault f_1 is said to be *masked* by another fault f_2, with respect to a test set T, if T can (cannot) detect f_1 in the absence (presence) of f_2.

The masking of detectable faults by undetectable faults is responsible for the invalidation of test sets derived under single-fault assumption. This is why undetectable faults were mentioned to be undesirable from the test point of view. There are yet other undesirable effects caused by undetectable faults. They are:

1. Two individually undetectable faults occurring in combination may alter the function and become detectable.
2. Occurrence of one undetectable fault may cause a detectable fault to become undetectable [this phenomenon is known as second-generation redundancy (Dandapani, 1974)].

We shall illustrate both these effects with a simple example on a map. Consider the single-output PLA function whose personality matrix is shown in Table 8.4.1 and whose map appears in Fig. 8.4.2(a).

The S-faults $S(1,-2)$ and $S(2,1)$ are individually undetectable. But the double fault $\{S(1,-2), S(2,1)\}$ alters the function and becomes detectable, as may be

TABLE 8.4.1 PLA P_3

	x_1	x_2	x_3	z_1
p_1	0	2	1	1
p_2	2	1	1	1
p_3	1	2	0	1

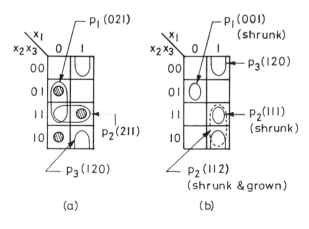

Figure 8.4.2 (a) $A(3,3,1)$ PLA P_3 on map; (b) faults $S(1,-2)$ and $S(2,1)$ occurring in combinations alter the function. Fault $G(2,3)$ masked by fault $S(2,1)$.

Design for Testability   Chap. 8

verified from Fig. 8.4.2(b). A single-fault test set, however, will not have a vector to detect this double fault. Similarly, the detectable G-fault $G(2,3)$, which is testable by minterm 2, becomes undetectable in the presence of $S(2,1)$, as may also be verified from Fig. 8.4.2(b).

8.5 THE MASKING CYCLE

To sum up we may say that the effect of undetectable faults is to reduce the multiple-fault coverage capability of an SFTS derived under the commonly employed single-fault assumption. Therefore, if all undetectable faults can be eliminated by some technique [such as the one proposed by Ramanatha and Biswas (1982, 1983)], does it mean that an SFTS for such circuits will detect 100% of all multiple faults? Unfortunately the answer is "no." This is because masking can occur even among detectable faults. Agarwal (1980) states two theorems that set forth the masking relationships among crosspoint faults in a crosspoint irredundant PLA. They are restated below with our notation. Proofs may be obtained from (Agarwal, 1980).

Theorem 8.5.1 (Agarwal, 1980). A fault from the set $G \cup A$ on a product term p_i in a PLA can be masked only by a fault from the set $S \cup D$ existing on the same product term p_i.

Theorem 8.5.2 (Agarwal, 1980). A fault from the set $S \cup D$ on a product term p_i in a PLA can be masked only by a fault from the set $G \cup A$ existing on some other product term p_j $(i \neq j)$.

From the theorems above it may be deduced that if a multiple-crosspoint fault is to go undetected, even when each of its component faults is testable by an SFTS, there must exist at least two product lines in the PLA having two faults each on them. This means that all double- and triple-crosspoint faults will be detected by a test set T for all single-crosspoint faults in a crosspoint irredundant PLA, whereas multiple faults of size 4 or more may elude detection. We illustrate this with a simple example. Consider the single-output PLA function that has been plotted on the map as in Fig. 8.5.1(a).

This PLA does not have any undetectable crosspoint fault. A test set for all single-crosspoint faults is given by $T = \{5,7,10,11,13,14\}$ and is shown by shaded circles in Fig. 8.5.1(a). Figure 8.5.1(b) shows the PLA function after the multiple-crosspoint faults $\{G(1,2), S(1,4), G(2,4), \text{and } S(2,2)\}$ have occurred. It is obvious that T fails to detect this multiple fault. This is because of the following masking cycle:

$G(1,2)$ on p_1 masked by $S(1,4)$ on p_1 with respect to T
$S(1,4)$ on p_1 masked by $G(2,4)$ on p_2 with respect to T
$G(2,4)$ on p_2 masked by $S(2,2)$ on p_2 with respect to T
$S(2,2)$ on p_2 masked by $G(1,2)$ on p_1 with respect to T

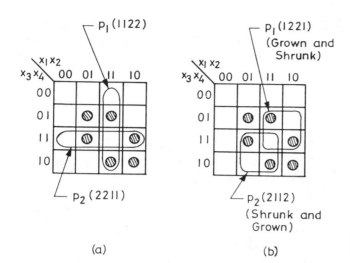

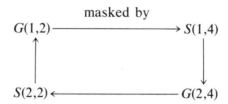

Figure 8.5.1 $A(4,2,1)$ PLA P_4 illustrating a masking cycle.

(a)

(b)

The analysis of such masking cycles, although rather complex, can be used to arrive at lower bounds on the multiple-fault coverage of SFTS. Agarwal (1980) has employed such an analysis to show that 98% or more of multiple-crosspoint faults of size 8 (eight multiple faults occurring simultaneously) or less will be detected by any test set for single-crosspoint faults in a crosspoint irredundant PLA. This result, however, is not applicable to most practical PLAs that have redundant crosspoint faults.

If we must have a very high level of confidence, in the multiple-fault coverage of SFTS, we must first ensure that the circuit does not contain any undetectable single faults. This may not be feasible in most practical situations. Even if we design irredundant circuits, we cannot still rule out the possibility of masking cycles that may corrupt the circuit function but can still elude detection. Hence the feasible alternative is to employ design for testability (DFT) techniques, which generally involve the use of additional hardware. We discuss such techniques in the next two sections, with reference to PLAs.

8.6 DESIGN FOR TESTABILITY

The major goals of testable designs are the following:

1. Tests should remain valid in the presence of undetectable faults.
2. Compact test sets should also be computationally simple to derive.

3. The design procedure to achieve testability must not add undue complexity to the logic design process.
4. The extra hardware needed to enhance testability must be low.
5. The speed of operation must not deteriorate.
6. It must be possible to apply the tests and evaluate the response using simple hardware, so as to provide built-in self-test (BIST) capability, if possible.
7. The test set derived must have very high coverage of all multiple faults.

The techniques that are evolved to meet these goals are classified as design for testability (DFT) techniques. They aim at reducing both the complexity and cost of test pattern generation and testing, ensuring at the same time very high coverage of all multiple faults of interest.

Since test generation for PLAs has been a challenging task, several DFT schemes for PLAs have been proposed in the past (Hong and Ostapko, 1980; Fujiwara and Kinoshita, 1981; Daehn and Mucha, 1981; Fujiwara, 1984; Khakbaz, 1984). A feature common to most of these approaches is the use of a shift register to facilitate the selection of individual product terms during testing. The earlier among these schemes (Hong and Ostapko, 1980; Fujiwara and Kinoshita, 1981) required expensive parity trees in addition to shift register and were not very practical. However, later DFT schemes avoided the parity trees and also improved the fault coverage. We discuss two such techniques briefly, one proposed by Fujiwara (1984) and the other an improved method proposed by Biswas and Jacob (1985). Notable among other DFT schemes without the shift register are the control input procedure of Ramanatha and Biswas (1982, 1983, 1988) and the pass transistor approach of Reddy and Ha (1987). An excellent survey of various DFT techniques appears in Somenzi and Gai (1986).

8.7 DFT SCHEMES

The augmented PLA in Fujiwara's DFT scheme for PLA P_4 of Table 8.7.1 is shown in Fig. 8.7.1. We have converted the NOR–NOR structure discussed in (Fujiwara, 1984) to the equivalent AND–OR PLA structure for simplifying the discussion. The primary advantage of this scheme is that such an augmented PLA

TABLE 8.7.1 PM OF PLA P_4

	PT				OV		
	x_1	x_2	x_3	x_4	z_1	z_2	z_3
p_1	1	0	0	2	1	0	0
p_2	0	1	1	2	0	1	1
p_3	1	0	2	1	1	0	1
p_4	2	0	0	2	0	0	1

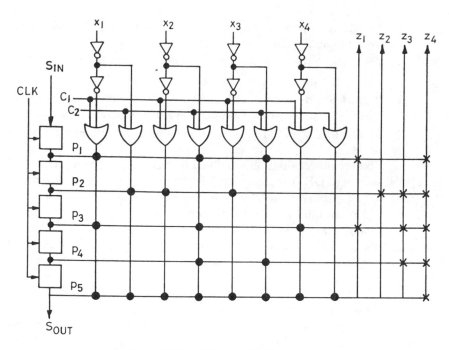

Figure 8.7.1 Fujiwara's DFT scheme.

can be tested for all multiple faults by function independent or universal test patterns, thus rendering explicit test pattern generation unnecessary.

Taking a general case, let the original PLA have n inputs x_1 to x_n, m product lines p_1 to p_m, and q output lines z_1 to z_q. Now we discuss the augmentation required to convert the original PLA to a testable PLA. An extra product line p_{m+1} is added which realizes the AND function of all input variables and their complements (i.e., $p_{m+1} = x_1 x_1' x_2 x_2' \cdots x_n x_n'$). An extra output line z_{q+1} is added, which realizes the OR of all product terms (i.e., $z_{q+1} = p_1 + p_2 + \cdots + p_m + p_{m+1}$). There are two control inputs, c_1 and c_2. c_1 is connected to all uncomplemented input lines x_j and c_2 to all complemented input lines x_j' via OR gates (In NOR–NOR scheme OR gates are not necessary; only a pull-down transistor is needed for each line x_j and x_j'). By putting a logic 1 on c_1, all bit lines representing true variables x_j's can be set to 1 independent of the logic values on input x_j (for $j = 1$ to n). Similarly, making c_2 equal to 1, all bit lines representing complementary variables x_j''s can be made 1, irrespective of their actual logic values.

The $(m + 1)$-bit serial-in serial-out shift register (SR) is used to select individual product terms during testing. The product lines p_1 to p_{m+1} are ANDed to the corresponding SR bits. During normal operation, all SR cells will have a logic 1. If we want to isolate p_j for testing, we can set $S_j = 1$ and all other SR bits to 0. This will cause all product line outputs p_1 to p_{m+1} except p_j to become logic 0. Therefore, to test the presence or absence of a device at a crosspoint (i, j), that is, on the x_j line of product term p_i, we must make the ith cell of SR 1 (the rest 0), $c_1 = 0$ and $c_2 = 1$, so that all bit lines x_j's are 1. Then we must put into the input lines $x_j = 0$ and the rest 1. Then if a device is present at (i, j), the output z_4 will be 0. Otherwise, it will be 1. So the test vector to test the crosspoint (i, j) will be as given in TV(a) and TV(b) below:

	c_1	c_2	x_1	x_2	$\cdots$	x_j	$\cdots$	x_n
TV(a)	0	1	1	1	$\cdots$	0	$\cdots$	1
TV(b)	1	0	0	0	$\cdots$	1	$\cdots$	0

It can be seen that TV(b) will test the crosspoint $(i, -j)$. Thus the test patterns are function independent. Hence the test set is called universal test set. It can be seen that we require $2n$ number of test vectors to test all the $2n$ crosspoints of a product line.

It has been proved in (Fujiwara, 1984) that this universal test set will detect any combination of multiple stuck-at, crosspoint, and bridging faults in the augmented PLA. The total number of test patterns is given by $2nm + 2n + m + 3$. All these patterns can be derived independently of the PLA function. Although the test patterns are function independent, the responses are function dependent. Fujiwara's method has a major drawback, however. The number of extra I/O pins required to implement this DFT scheme is six (two for control inputs c_1 and c_2, one each for S_{in}, S_{out}, and Clk of the SR, and one for z_{q+1}). This can be rather unacceptable in practical situations. Khakbaz (1984) has proposed an improved DFT scheme wherein the number of extra I/O pins is reduced to four. Further, the number of test patterns is also reduced to $nm + m + 2$. However, the test patterns are function dependent, although they can easily be derived from the personality matrix of the PLA.

Biswas and Jacob (1985) proposed a testable PLA design that is essentially an improvement on the designs of both Fujiwara and Khakbaz. Since independent control of product lines is the key to testable designs, the shift register (SR) has been retained in this design. All the extra lines, such as control inputs for bit lines, extra product and output lines, have been eliminated, thereby reducing the additional pin requirements to 3. Due to the limitations of packaging technology for ICs, keeping the number of pins to the minimum is a major requirement for any DFT scheme. The hardware design in this approach is similar to that of Khakbaz. However, the extra output line has been removed and instead, an observable line called a watch-line (W-line), which realizes the AND of all SR bits, is introduced. The schematic for a (4,4,3) PLA is shown in Fig. 8.7.2. The W-line adds a self-checking feature to the PLA in that it continually checks for any fault in the SR during normal operation of the PLA. Since the SR is a memory element, to save chip area the use of dynamic circuitry is proposed for its implementation. Therefore, the SR cells will be more vulnerable to faults such as transient errors than will other parts of the PLA. Since the SR outputs are ANDed to the corresponding product terms in the PLA, all SR cells must have a logical 1 during normal mode of operation of the PLA, and hence the W-line realizes a logical 1. Due to some fault, if one or more SR bits change to a 0, this will also cause the W-line to change to 0 for the duration of the fault. The W-line can be monitored continually to warn the system of the fault.

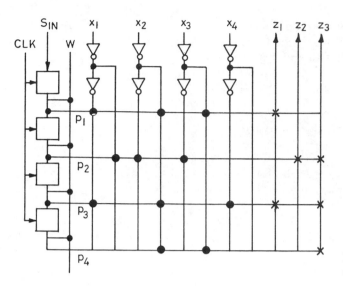

Figure 8.7.2 DFT scheme of Biswas and Jacob.

The test set can easily be derived from the PM of a PLA. The test set T_c consists of three subsets, T_1, T_2, and T_3. The application of the test is so sequenced that the response to two subsets, T_2 and T_3, is universal (hence requiring no storage of correct responses) and the response to the other subset T_1 is a mapping of the OV matrix of the PLA. The number of test patterns required is given by $k_f nm + 3m$, where k_f is a constant dependent on the density of used crosspoints in the AND array. For almost all practical PLAs, this test set requires considerably fewer vectors than that of the earlier designs. The three extra pins required are for the clock and shift-in terminals of the SR and the W-line output. The shift-out terminal of the SR need not be brought out since the SR can be checked completely through the W-line, thus reducing the pin count for the extra hardware to three, which is lower than that of both the earlier designs. Consider a (4,4,3) PLA whose PM is as given in Table 8.7.1. The schematic of this PLA with the required augmentation is shown in Fig. 8.7.2.

We shall now describe how to derive a test set for detecting all crosspoint faults in the PLA, using the SR to select or deselect appropriate product terms. During the normal operation all the shift register bits S_1 to S_m are set to logical 1. This will not affect the PLA product terms since it is equivalent to adding an extra control input to an AND gate and maintaining it at logical 1. However, during testing, each product line (AND gate) is tested independently by isolating it from all other product lines. Let $S(i)$ denote the shift register pattern that selects product line p_i while deselecting all other product lines. For example, in Fig. 8.7.2 to select p_3, we set bit S_3 of the SR to 1 and all other bits to 0. Hence $S(3)$ = 0010. This pattern will cause product terms p_1, p_2, and p_4 to realize logical 0, whereas the output of p_3 will now depend on the logical values of the inputs connected to it.

Our objective is to derive a test set that will detect all multiple-crosspoint faults in a PLA. However, we first restrict our attention to single-crosspoint faults

Design for Testability   Chap. 8

and derive a test set T_c that detects every single-crosspoint fault. Then we will show that T_c will indeed detect all multiple-crosspoint faults as well. Further, T_c can be shown to detect any combination of multiple-crosspoint, stuck, and bridging faults of interest in the PLA.

To test for any S-fault on p_i, we first isolate p_i by the SR. Then, as we have discussed earlier, we choose two opposite minterms in the cube of p_i. Call these two TVs $X(i)_0$ and $X(i)_1$. If an S-fault is present on p_i, it will cause p_i to realize the logical value 0 when either $X(i)_0$ or $X(i)_1$ is applied. This is different from the fault-free output of 1 and can be detected via any of the output lines fed by p_i. Further, any A- or D-fault on p_i will also be detected by the two tests above. Let $OV(i)$ denote the output vector corresponding to p_i in the PM of the PLA. If the observed output vector $\neq OV(i)$ for one or both of these tests, we conclude that a fault has occurred. If an S-fault is present, we obtain an all-zero output vector for at least one of these tests. If any $A(D)$-fault has occurred, then the corresponding bit in the output vector changes to 1(0) for both these tests.

$X(i)_0$ and $X(i)_1$ are obtained for each product line p_i. These patterns, together with their corresponding $S(i)$ and $OV(i)$ vectors, constitute a test set T_1 for all single-crosspoint faults of types S, A, and D in the PLA. T_1 for the PLA in Fig. 8.7.2 is shown as a subset of T_c in Table 8.7.2. To detect all G-faults on p_i, we will require as many tests as there are *used* crosspoints on p_i. Let R^i denote an index set consisting of the used variables on p_i. For example, in the PLA of Fig. 8.7.2, $R^2 = \{1,2,3\}$; $R^4 = \{2,3\}$. R^i is formed for each $i = 1 \cdots m$. Let $X(i - j)_0$ denote the input vector, which is the same as $X(i)_0$ except that the jth variable in $X(i)_0$ is complemented. $X(i - j)_0$ places a 0 on the crosspoint, corresponding to the variable X_j on p_i and a 1 on all other used decoder lines on p_i. If there is a G-fault at the crosspoint, p_i realizes a logical 1 when it is isolated using $S(i)$ and $X(i - j)_0$ is applied. This can be observed on each of the output lines fed by p_i and differs from the fault-free output of all zeros. We obtain $X(i - j)_0$ for each $j \in R^i$ with respect to each product term p_i, $i = i \cdots m$. This forms a test set T_2 for all single G-faults in the original PLA. T_2 for the example PLA appears as a subset of T_c in Table 8.7.2. Note that the total number of vectors in T_2 is 11, which is the same as the number of used crosspoints in the AND array for the PLA.

However, we have not yet considered the missing crosspoint faults that can occur in the additional hardware. These are the G-faults on the W-line and those at the junction of the SR cells and product lines. The former will be termed G_w-faults and the latter, G_{sr}-faults. To test for G_w-faults we circulate a single 0 through the SR, with all other SR bits remaining 1. If any crosspoints on the W-line is missing, it will be detected as a 0–1 change on the W-line output. Further, these tests will also detect the SA1 fault on the W-line. After the 0 is circulated out of the SR, an all-1 pattern remains in the SR, which serves as a test for an SA0 condition on the W-line. The W-line also checks for any SA1, SA0 condition in the SR cells since a SA1 or an SR cell is equivalent to a G_w-fault on the corresponding crosspoint, and an SA0 in an SR cell is equivalent to the W-line SA0. Thus the S_{out} terminal of the shift register need not be made an observable output, unlike in previous schemes. This is so as the SR can be completely

TABLE 8.7.2 TEST SET T_c FOR PLA P_4 OF FIG. 8.7.2

Selected p_i	S_1	S_2	S_3	S_4	x_1	x_2	x_3	x_4	z_1	z_2	z_3	
	S(i)				X(i)				OV(i)			
p_1	1	0	0	0	1	0	0	0	1	0	0	
	1	0	0	0	1	0	0	1	1	0	0	
p_2	0	1	0	0	0	1	1	0	0	1	1	
	0	1	0	0	0	1	1	1	0	1	1	T_1
p_3	0	0	1	0	1	0	0	1	1	0	1	
	0	0	1	0	1	0	1	1	1	0	1	
p_4	0	0	0	1	0	0	0	0	0	0	1	
	0	0	0	1	1	0	0	1	0	0	1	
p_1	1	0	0	0	0	0	0	0	0	0	0	
	1	0	0	0	1	1	0	0	0	0	0	
	1	0	0	0	1	0	1	0	0	0	0	
p_2	0	1	0	0	1	1	1	0	0	0	0	
	0	1	0	0	0	0	1	0	0	0	0	
	0	1	0	0	0	1	0	0	0	0	0	T_2
p_3	0	0	1	0	0	0	0	1	0	0	0	
	0	0	1	0	1	1	0	1	0	0	0	
	0	0	1	0	1	0	0	0	0	0	0	
p_4	0	0	0	1	0	1	0	0	0	0	0	
	0	0	0	1	0	0	1	0	0	0	0	
None	0	0	0	0	1	0	0	0	0	0	0	
	0	0	0	0	0	1	1	0	0	0	0	
	0	0	0	0	1	0	0	1	0	0	0	T_3
	0	0	0	0	0	0	0	0	0	0	0	

checked through the W-line. Now we can test G_{sr}-faults at the intersection of the SR cells and the corresponding product lines. To test for these faults, we shift in the all-zero pattern into the SR so as to deselect all product terms and apply $X(i)_0$ for $i = 1 \cdots m$. If there is no G_{sr}-fault on p_i, an all-zero output vector is obtained. On the other hand, in the presence of this fault the output vector equals OV(i). Let T_3 denote this set of tests. Then the complete test set is $T_1 \cup T_2 \cup T_3$. Table 8.7.2 gives T_c for the example PLA. We can see from Table 8.7.2 that the response to T_1 is a mapping of the OR array of the PLA, whereas the response to T_2 and T_3 is independent of the PLA function and thus universal.

We have shown how T_c detects all single-crosspoint faults in the PLA. Thus the testable PLA is shown to be *crosspoint irredundant*. It is well known that a complete single-fault test set T for an irredundant circuit can fail as a multiple-fault test set if there occurs any multiple faults such that each of its component faults is masked by another component fault of this multiple fault, with respect to test set T. This phenomenon is known as a masking cycle and was illustrated with an example in Section 8.5. Now if we can show that masking cycles among crosspoint faults cannot occur in the testable PLA with respect to T_c, then we can be sure that T_c will detect all multiple-crosspoint faults.

Agarwal (1980) has shown that in a crosspoint irredundant PLA, a test set T_c for all single-crosspoint faults, will detect all multiple-crosspoint faults of sizes 2 and 3. Hence in the scheme of Biswas and Jacob a masking cycle requires at least four faults. The masking relationships among crosspoint faults were stated earlier as Theorems 8.5.1 and 8.5.2. From these theorems it is clear that for a masking cycle to occur, there must at least be two product terms in the PLA such that there is one fault from the set $G \cup A$ and one from the set $S \cup D$ present on each of these lines. Simultaneous activation of one product line while testing for faults from the set $S \cup D$ on the other product line is also a must for a masking cycle to occur, as is clear from Theorem 8.5.2. This can happen only if there are G_{sr}-faults present on both the lines involved in the masking cycle.

Theorem 8.7.1 (Biswas and Jacob, 1985). T_c will detect all multiple-crosspoint faults in the enhanced PLA.

Proof: Let p_i and p_j be product lines with a G_{sr}-fault and one fault from the set $S \cup D$ existing on each of them, and let $OV(i) = OV(j)$, giving rise to a potential masking cycle. The G_{sr}-fault on p_i is tested by the vector $X(i)_0$ in T_3 of T_c. This fault can be masked by a fault from $S \cup D$ on p_i, provided that $X(i)_0$ causes $p_i = p_j = 0$. $X(i)_0$ along with $S(i)$ in T_1 of T_c acts as a test for the fault from $S \cup D$ on p_i. Since $X(i)_0$ causes $p_j = 0$, the fault from $S \cup D$ on p_i cannot be masked even though a G_{sr}-fault is present on p_j. Hence this multiple fault is detected by T_c and no masking cycle can occur. Therefore, T_c will detect all multiple-crosspoint faults in the enhanced PLA. Q.E.D.

The cardinality of the test set T_c is given by $|T_c| = k_f nm + 3m$. The constant k_f for a PLA is given by $k_f =$ (total number of crosspoints used in the AND array/nm) and will depend on the density of crosspoints in the AND array. The value of k_f is always less than 1, and since most practical PLAs are sparse, k_f can have values lower than 0.5, especially in the case of large PLAs. The example PLA given in Fig. 8.7.2 is not sparse and requires 23 test patterns. Assuming a PLA with 20 inputs, 200 product lines, and 20 outputs, and taking the value of k_f as 0.5, the number of test patterns required in the Biswas–Jacob scheme is 2600. This is considerably lower than the 8243 tests required in Fujiwara's scheme and the 4402 patterns required in Khakbaz's scheme.

8.8 BUILT-IN SELF-TEST

So far we have been concerned with external testing; that is, test inputs were applied and the responses evaluated by a tester external to the chip or circuit under test. Such external testers are rather expensive. Further, the costs of test pattern generation and test application are increasing rapidly as the complexity of circuits to be tested increases, even though the cost of test generation can be contained to a large extent by using DFT techniques. Apart from these factors, external testing approach has some fundamental limitations.

1. Access to internal points of a chip is limited because internal points can be controlled or observed only through the external I/O pins of the chip. As ICs become more and more dense, the device/pin ratio (which is the ratio of the number of devices inside the chip to the number of I/O pins) keeps increasing. This results in poorer ability to access the internal points, to control or observe the logic values on them. It is this factor that makes test generation more difficult and expensive.

2. The speed at which test vectors can be applied to the circuit under test is limited by the characteristics of the external tester. Often, testing at the maximum operating speed of the chip is not possible, and some timing-dependent faults may elude detection.

Built-in self-test (BIST) techniques are aimed at overcoming the problems and limitations of external testing. Here, additional circuitry is placed on the chip to facilitate testing of internal modules, and hence access to the internal points is easy. Further, testing can be done at the normal operating speed. Circuits designed for BIST will have two modes of operation, a normal mode and a test mode. When placed in the test mode, the chip executes a self-test and gives a pass/fail indication. With advances in integration, the costs of putting extra circuitry on chip is decreasing, making BIST an attractive and feasible alternative to external testing.

There are several approaches to BIST, but the feature common to most of them is that test patterns are generated and responses compressed and evaluated on chip by the use of linear feedback shift registers (LFSRs). The technique of data compression using LFSRs is popularly known as *signature analysis*. We discuss briefly how an LFSR is used for pattern generation as well as response evaluation via signature analysis. More detailed discussion may be found in McCluskey (1986).

An LFSR basically consists of an interconnection of D flip-flops, XOR gates, and constant multipliers, forming a shift register with feedback. Figure 8.8.1

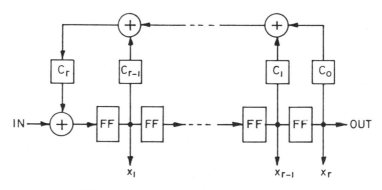

Figure 8.8.1 General structure of an LFSR.

shows an r-bit LFSR, which can do data compression for the input data stream by polynominal division. The constants $c_1, c_2, \ldots, c_r$, which are multiplier constants indicate a connection (no connection) to the XOR gates in the feedback path when $c_i = 1(0)$. The n-bit input data stream can represent a polynomial such as

$$p(x) = p_n \cdot x^n + p_{n-1} \cdot x^{n-1} + \cdots + p_1 \cdot x + p_0$$

The binary-valued coefficients of the polynomial appear on the serial input line with the higher-order coefficients appearing first. The LFSR has a characteristic polynomial defined by the constants $c_1, c_2, \ldots, c_r$ and is given by

$$c(x) = c_r \cdot x^r + c_{r-1} \cdot x^{r-1} + \cdots + c_1 \cdot x + c_0$$

The LFSR can divide any input polynomial $p(x)$ by its characteristics polynomial $c(x)$. The dividend $p(x)$ is serially shifted in and the coefficients of the quotient appear serially on the output line. After n shifts, the entire quotient has appeared on the output, and the residue is left in the SR. This residue is a function of the input data stream and is called its *signature*. Figure 8.8.2 shows a four-stage LFSR used as a signature analyzer.

Now we shall give a qualitative analysis of the effectiveness of signature analysis to detect errors in the input data stream. Let a k-bit input data sequence (coming from the output of a circuit under test) be compressed by an r-bit LFSR to yield an r-bit signature. There are 2^k possible input data sequences, out of which only one sequence (data stream) represents the correct (fault-free) response. Since 2^k possible input streams map into 2^r possible signatures, 2^{k-r} data streams map into each signature. Only one of the 2^r signatures is taken for the correct signature. However $2^{k-r} - 1$ faulty sequences also map into this correct signature. Therefore, the probability of failing to detect an error, assuming that all errors are equiprobable, is

$$\frac{\text{undetectable errors}}{\text{total errors}} = \frac{2^{k-r} - 1}{2^k - 1}$$

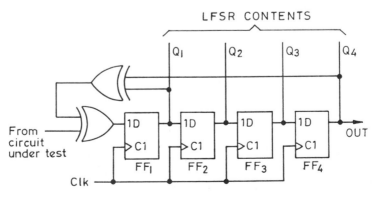

Figure 8.8.2 A four-bit LFSR as signature analyzer.

When $k \gg r$, this ratio tends to 2^{-r} and hence the fault coverage tends to $1 - 2^{-r}$. For a 16-bit LFSR, this translates to a fault coverage of 99.998%. These measures, although derived using simplistic assumptions, give us an idea of the effectiveness of signature analysis. Similar results also hold for multiple-input LFSRs, which can compress parallel input data.

It is also possible to use LFSRs as pseudorandom pattern generators. Such LFSRs do not have the serial external input line and are called autonomous LSFRs (ALFSRs). By suitably choosing the characteristic polynomials, we can cause an r-bit ALFSR, when initialized to a nonzero value to run autonomously and generate an output sequence whose period is $2^r - 1$. This means that no subsequence of r consecutive bits will repeat within an output sequence of $2^r - 1$ bits. Such an LFSR with period $2^r - 1$ for its output sequence is said to be a maximum-length LFSR. Figure 8.8.3 shows a 16-bit ALFSR that can generate $2^{16} - 1$ consecutive 16-bit vectors, which can be obtained by taking the outputs simultaneously from the 16 flip-flops.

Hassan and McCluskey (1983) have proposed a BIST scheme for PLAs that make use of LFSRs. The overall scheme is shown in Fig. 8.8.4. Maximum-length ALFSR G is used to randomly generate all the binary input combinations. Multiple-input LFSR, which is LS configured as a multiple-input signature register (MSR), compresses the output response of the PLA (for the input patterns generated by G) into a signature. Similarly, two other MSRs, L_1 and L_2, compress the outputs on the true and complemented input bit lines. L_1 and L_2 check for all faults on the input decoders. LS is used to detect faults in the AND and OR

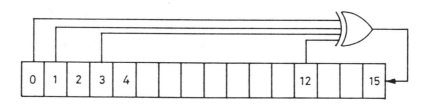

Figure 8.8.3 A sixteen-bit ALFSR of maximum length.

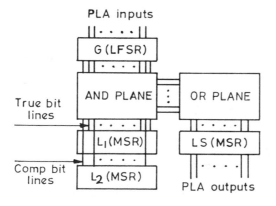

Figure 8.8.4 Hassan and McCluskey's BIST PLA.

planes of the PLA. Since exhaustive testing is done by generating all possible input combinations by the ALFSR G, all multiple faults will be detected with a very high probability. However, this scheme is suitable only for PLAs with a limited number of inputs, since the testing time is exponential in the number of inputs. A survey of other BIST schemes for PLAs may be found in McCluskey (1986).

REFERENCES

AGARWAL, V. K. Multiple fault detection in programmable logic arrays, *IEEE Trans. Comput.*, Vol. C-29, No. 6, June 1980, pp. 518–522.

AGRAWAL, V. D., AND S. C. SETH. *Test Generation for VLSI Chips*. Silver Spring, Md.: IEEE Computer Society, 1988.

BARDEL, P. H., W. H. MCANNEY, AND J. SAVIR. *Built-in Test for VLSI: Pseudorandom Techniques*. New York: John Wiley & Sons, Inc., 1987.

BISWAS, N. N., AND J. JACOB. A testable PLA design with minimal hardware and test set, *Proc. International Test Conference,* November, 1985, pp. 583–588.

BOSE, P., AND J. A. ABRAHAM. Test generation for programmable logic arrays, *Proc. 19th Design Automation Conference,* June 1982, pp. 574–580 [reproduced in Agrawal and Seth (1988), pp. 94–100].

DAEHN, W., AND J. MUCHA. A hardware approach to self testing of large programmable logic arrays, *IEEE Trans. Comput.,* Vol. C-30, No. 11, Nov. 1981, pp. 829–833.

DANDAPANI, R. On the design of logic networks with redundancy and testability considerations, *IEEE Trans. Comput.,* Vol. C-23, No. 11, November 1974, pp. 1139–1149.

FRIEDMAN, A. D. Fault detection in redundant circuits, *IEEE Trans, Electron. Comput.,* Vol. EC-16, No. 2, Feb. 1967, pp. 99–100.

FUJIWARA, H. A new PLA design for universal testability, *IEEE Trans. Comput.,* Vol. C-33, No. 8, Aug. 1984, pp. 745–750.

FUJIWARA, H., AND K. KINOSHITA. A design of programmable logic arrays with universal tests, *IEEE Trans. Comput.,* Vol. C-30, No. 11, Nov. 1981, pp. 823–828.

HASSAN, S. Z., AND E. J. MCCLUSKEY. Testing PLAs using multiple parallel signature analyzers, *Proc. 13th Fault-Tolerant Computing Symposium,* June 1983, pp. 422–425.

HONG, S. J., AND D. L. OSTAPKO. FITPLA: a programmable logic array for function independent testing, *Proc. 10th Fault-Tolerant Computing Symposium,* pp. 131–136, 1980.

KHAKBAZ, J. A testable PLA design with low overhead and high fault coverage, *IEEE Trans. Comput.,* Vol. C-33, No. 8, Aug. 1984, pp. 743–745.

MCCLUSKEY, E. J. *Logic Design Principles*. Englewood Cliffs, N.J.: Prentice Hall, 1986.

RAMANATHA, K. S., AND N. N. BISWAS. A design for complete testability of programmable logic arrays, *Proc. International Test Conference,* 1982, pp. 67–74.

RAMANATHA, K. S., AND N. N. BISWAS. A design for testability of undetectable crosspoint faults in programmable logic arrays, *IEEE Trans. Comput.,* Vol. C-32, No. 6, June 1983, pp. 555–557.

RAMANATHA, K. S., AND N. N. BISWAS. Design of crosspoint irredundant PLA's using minimal number of control inputs, *IEEE Trans. Comput.,* Vol. C-37, No. 9, September 1988, pp. 1130–1134.

REDDY, S. M., AND D. S. HA. A new approach to the design of testable PLAs, *IEEE Trans. Comput.*, Vol. C-36, No. 2, February 1987, pp. 201–211.

ROBINSON, M., AND J. RAJSKI. An algorithmic branch and bound method for PLA test pattern generation, *Proc. International Test Conference,* Washington, D.C., 1988, pp. 784–795.

SMITH, J. E. Detection of faults in programmable logic arrays, *IEEE Trans. Comput.*, Vol. C-28, No. 11, Nov. 1979, pp. 845–853.

SOMENZI, F., AND S. GAI. Fault detection in programmable logic arrays, *Proc. IEEE,* Vol. 74, No. 5, May 1986, pp. 655–668.

WEI, R. S., AND A. L. SANGIOVANNI-VINCENTELLI. PLATYPUS: a PLA test pattern generation tool, *IEEE Trans. Comput.-Aided Des.*, Vol. CAD-5, No. 4, Oct. 1986, pp. 633–644.

PROBLEMS

8.1. Plot the following PLA on the map. Identify the undetectable faults.

x_1	x_2	x_3	x_4	z_1	z_2
0	2	2	1	1	0
2	1	1	2	1	1
0	1	2	1	0	1

8.2. For the PLA of Problem 8.1, derive a minimal test set for all detectable G-, S-, A-, and D-faults. Name those faults for which there exists only one test vector capable of detecting it.

8.3. With the help of a map, determine the minimal test set for the following PLAs. Also list undetectable faults, if any.

(a)

x_1	x_2	x_3	x_4	z_1	z_2
1	2	0	1	1	0
2	0	1	1	1	0
1	1	0	2	1	1
0	1	1	0	0	1

(b)

x_1	x_2	x_3	x_4	z_1	z_2	z_3
0	0	2	1	0	1	0
2	1	0	2	1	0	1
1	1	0	0	1	1	1
1	2	2	1	0	0	1
2	0	1	1	0	1	1

8.4. With the help of a map, determine a minimal test set of the following PLA. List the undetectable faults.

x_1	x_2	x_3	x_4	z_1	z_2	z_3
1	1	0	2	0	1	0
2	1	0	2	1	0	1
1	0	2	2	0	1	1
0	0	2	1	1	1	0

8.5. Plot the given PLA on map. Product term p_2 has six shrinkage faults. Are all of them detectable? Give a minimal test set capable of detecting all S-faults on p_2.

PT	x_1	x_2	x_3	x_4	z_1	z_2
p_1	2	1	0	2	1	0
p_2	2	1	2	2	0	1
p_3	0	2	0	1	1	1
p_4	1	2	1	1	1	1
p_5	1	2	0	0	1	1
p_6	0	2	1	0	0	1

8.6. Identify all the undetectable S-faults in the PLA of Problem 8.5. Determine all the faults detected by the minterms 9 and 13.

8.7. In the PLA of Problem 8.5, $A(1,2)$ is undetectable. Does the occurrence of $A(1,2)$ lead to the generation of any second-generation redundant fault? If so, identify it.

8.8. If the product term p_1 of PLA P_1 (shown on the map of Fig. 8.2.1) is modified to 0200, the undetectable S-fault on the product line gets eliminated. This procedure is known as elimination of an undetectable fault by modification of the personality matrix of the PLA. Investigate if the elimination of the undetectable S-fault introduces any other undetectable fault in the PLA. Rewrite the PM of PLA P_1 eliminating all existing undetectable faults. Show the new PM on map, and in the map find new undetectable faults, if any. Show the faulty cubes on the map by dashed lines. Also, label all the undetectable faults.

8.9. The S-fault introduced by the ANDing of a variable x_j (either in the true or in the complemented form) in a product term p_i, and the G-fault introduced by the elimination of a variable x_j (either in the true or in the complementary form) from a product term p_i are complementary to each other. Now state if the following statement is true or false. Justify your answer. The elimination of an undetectable $S(G)$-fault by modifying the personality of a PLA is always followed by the introduction of the complementary $G(S)$-fault.

8.10. Show that in PLA P_2 of Fig. 8.4.1(a), the detectable fault $G(4,3)$ is masked by the undetectable fault $S(4,-1)$ with respect to the test vector 13.

8.11. Figure 8.5.1(a) and (b) illustrate a masking cycle. The detectable multiple fault $\{G(1,2), S(1,4), G(2,4), S(2,2)\}$ could not be detected by the single-fault test set $T = \{5,7,10,11,13,14\}$. How would you augment T so that the multiple fault is detected by the augmented test set?

8.12. Discuss the following conjecture: In a PLA having no undetectable fault, a single-fault test set (SFTS) will detect all multiple faults if each of its product term has distinct (not shared by another product term) test vectors to detect all its shrinkage and growth faults. As an example, solve and study the answer of Problem 8.11. Can you construct a counterexample?

8.13. In the testable PLA design shown in Fig. 8.7.2, identify the SR pattern and input vector that will detect the following faults: (1) $G(1,2)$; (2) $S(2,4)$; (3) $D(4,3)$; (4) line x_1—SA1; (5) AND-type bridging fault on lines x_3' and x_4.

8.14. Consider the PLA P_2 of Fig. 8.4.1(a). It can be seen that the undetectable $A(4,1)$- and $S(4,-1)$-faults on product term p_4 can be made detectable if the product terms p_1 and p_3 can be made to vanish while testing p_4. This can be done by adding an extra input line to the PLA hardware as shown in Fig. P.8.14. Note that the extra input line c_1 has been connected to the product terms p_1 and p_3. In the normal mode c_1 is held at logical 1. In test mode it is made 0 while testing the product term p_4. Hence the test vector to test the $A(1,4)$ has an additional bit to be assigned to c_1. Thus the TV to test $A(4,1)$ as a function of the input variables (now augmented by c_1) will be the minterm 7 preceded by a 0 bit for c_1. Hence for $A(4,1)$ the $TV(c_1 x_1 x_2 x_3 x_4)$ = 00111. Similarly, for the S-fault $S(4,-1)$, the TV will be the augmented minterm 15, that is, $TV(c_1 x_1 x_2 x_3 x_4)$ = 01111. For testing the product terms p_1 and p_3, c_1 must be 1, whereas for testing p_2 it may be 0 or 1. Note that here the extra input lines isolate the product term under test by removing the interfering product terms. Now apply this procedure to make all the undetectable faults of PLA P_1 of Fig. 8.2.1 detectable. Try to use the minimum number of control input lines. It should be noted here that the problem of making the entire PLA completely testable by adding the minimum number of control inputs is more complex. Various aspects of this problem have been discussed in Ramanatha and Biswas (1982, 1983, 1988).

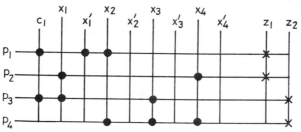

Figure P.8.14

8.15. Make the PLA P_2 of Fig. 8.4.1(a) crosspoint irredundant by the control input procedure. Do not use more than two control inputs.

8.16. With the help of a map, list all the undetectable faults of PLA P_4 of Table 8.7.1. Make all these faults detectable by using extra control input lines. Use the minimum number of control inputs.

8.17. In the control input procedure, if to isolate a product term p_i, the product terms p_j, p_k, and p_r are to be made to vanish; then the isolation requirement is written as $(i:j,k,r)$. Now a PLA has the following isolation requirements to make it completely testable by adding extra input lines.

$$(1:2,3,5) \quad (2:4,5) \quad (3:1,4,5) \quad (4:1,2) \quad (5:1,2,3)$$

Derive its minimal control input matrix.

8.18. Can you suggest an improvement over the control input procedure or an entirely new method without using a shift register such that a PLA can be made completely testable in the presence of a masking cycle?

9

Counters and Shift Registers

9.1 INTRODUCTION

In the preceding chapters we have discussed various types and aspects of combinational circuits whose outputs are determined completely by their inputs. An important property of these circuits is that there is no feedback from the output to the input. The moment we introduce this feedback, we get a new type of circuit with a new capability: the capability to store bits of information. In other words, the circuit also acquires *memory*. Depending on the contents of its memory, we say that the circuit is in a certain *state*. Therefore, a change in the contents of the memory implies a change in the state of the circuit. The output of such a circuit with memory is not always the same for the same input, as is the case with a combinational circuit but also depends on its present state. Note that we have used the word "present" in the last sentence. This means that the next state as well as the output depend not only on the present input but also the present state. Hence the element of time also comes in. Such combinational circuits with feedback, having memory or internal states, are called *sequential circuits*. A formal definition of sequential circuits or the more general term *sequential machines* is given in Chapter 10. In this chapter we discuss two special types of sequential machines: counters and shift registers. The building blocks of these sequential circuits, or for that matter, of all types of sequential circuits, are the *flip-flops*. A flip-flop is the most elementary sequential machine having only two states. These are therefore bistable circuits. Although the flip-flops may differ in their electronic compositions, they exhibit certain definite logical properties. In fact, all flip-flops, irrespective of their internal circuit implementation, can be classified into a few types according to their logical behavior. In subsequent sections we first discuss a few typical types of flip-flops and then we see how these flip-flops produce various types of counters and shift registers depending on their interconnections.

9.2 THE S–R FLIP-FLOP

Consider the circuit shown in Fig. 9.2.1. It is a combinational circuit *with feedback*. It has only two NOR gates, with the output of one gate being fed to the input of the other. Now let us study the outputs of the circuit Z_1 and Z_2 for the four different combinations 00, 01, 10, and 11 of the two input lines S and R.

When $S = 0$, Z_1 becomes 1(0) depending on if $Z_2 = 0(1)$ (since $Z_1 = S'Z_2'$), that is, $Z_1 = Z_2'$. Similarly, when $R = 0$, $Z_2 = Z_1'$ (since $Z_2 = R'Z_1'$). Thus when $SR = 00$, the values of Z_1 and Z_2 depend only on them, and it is always $Z_1 = Z_2'$. It can now be verified that with $SR = 00$, if $Z_1Z_2 = 10$ or 01, they retain these output values. In other words, the outputs remain unchanged. However, the situation changes if $S = 1$ and $R = 0$, then the 1 on the S-line will force the output Z_1 to be 0, irrespective of the value of Z_2. Therefore, Z_1 becomes 0. This forces Z_2 to become 1, as both input lines of gate G_2 become 0. Hence when $SR = 10$, the circuit has a stable state with $Z_1Z_2 = 01$. Similarly, it can be found that the circuit has another stable state with $SR = 01$ and Z_1Z_2 becoming 10. Now, let us investigate what happens if $SR = 11$. In this situation the 1 on the S-line will force Z_1 to be 0, and the 1 on the R-line will force Z_2 to be 0. So under this condition, when $SR = 11$, the output will be $Z_1Z_2 = 00$, and this will also be a stable state. Now, let S and R both become 00 simultaneously. Then both NOR gates, G_1 and G_2, will "see" 00 at their inputs simultaneously, and their outputs will tend to become 11. Now let the output Z_1 of gate G_1 change to 1 much earlier than Z_2 of gate G_2. Then the 1 at Z_1 will prevent Z_2 to become 1, and Z_2 will continue to remain 0. Now it can easily be checked that the output $Z_1Z_2 = 10$ with $SR = 00$ is also a stable state. However, when S and R become 00 simultaneously, if Z_2 would have become 1 much earlier than Z_1, the output will stabilize at the value of $Z_1Z_2 = 01$. Thus the outputs become unpredictable and depend on the operating delays of the gates G_1 and G_2. Even if these two

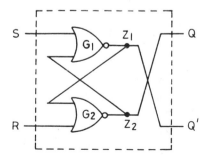

Figure 9.2.1 *S-R* flip-flop circuit from two NOR gates with feedback.

delays are identical, there is a serious problem. In that case it can be verified that the outputs will oscillate between the values 11 and 00. These are very undesirable operating conditions for the flip-flop. Thus although $SR = 11$ and $Z_1Z_2 = 00$ is a stable state, it may introduce serious anomalous situations in operation of the flip-flop. Hence to eliminate this possibility entirely, an additional restriction, that the S- and R-lines should not be made 1 simultaneously, is accepted in the definition of an S-R flip-flop.

Definition 9.2.1. An *S-R flip-flop* has two input lines, S and R. When S is 1, the flip-flop is set to state 1. When R becomes 1, the flip-flop is reset to state 0. When both S and R are 0, the flip-flop continues to be in the same state. The S- and R-lines are never made 1 simultaneously. When the flip-flop is in state 0(1), the output of the flip-flop Q is also 0(1).

This definition yields the truth table in Table 9.2.1, where q denotes the present state and Q the next state of the flip-flop. The truth table defines Q as a function of the three variables S, R, and q. As a sum of minterms it can be expressed as

$$Q(SRq) = \Sigma(1,4,5) + \phi\Sigma(6,7)$$

Minimizing Q on the map (not shown), we get

$$Q(SRq) = S + R'q$$

This function is known as the *characteristic function* of the S-R flip-flop. Note that a change of state of the flip-flop will always take some finite time, however small it may be. For this reason, q has been called the present state, and Q the next state. Thus the characteristic function of the flip-flop has an element of time inherent in it and is indicated by the two notations for the same flip-flop, namely q and Q.

TABLE 9.2.1 TRUTH
TABLE OF *S-R* FLIP-FLOP

S	R	q	Q
0	0	0	0
0	0	1	1
0	1	0	0
0	1	1	0
1	0	0	1
1	0	1	1
1	1	0	ϕ
1	1	1	ϕ

9.3 THE *J-K* FLIP-FLOP

While discussing the *S-R* flip-flop circuit (Fig. 9.2.1), we found that when both *S* and *R* become 1 simultaneously, we may not get a stable state. To overcome this difficulty, we stipulated the condition that *S* and *R* should not be made 1 simultaneously. The insurance of this condition can be built in the circuit of an *S-R* flip-flop by modifying the circuit in two different ways. These two modifications produce two new flip-flops, called the *J-K* and the *D* flip-flops. In this section we discuss the *J-K* flip-flop, and the *D* flip-flop is discussed in Section 9.4. Figure 9.3.1 shows one of the modifications made to the *S-R* flip-flop. Here the input signal does not go to the *S* input of the *S-R* flip-flop directly but is gated via an AND gate. The *J* input of the AND gate is one of the input lines of the new flip-flop. The other input of the AND gate is the *Q'* output of the flip-flop. Similarly, the *K* line is the other input of the new flip-flop. This is also fed to another AND gate, whose other input is the *Q* output of the flip-flop. The output of this AND gate is connected to the *R* input of the *S-R* flip-flop. It can now be seen that the feedback to one of the AND gates is *Q*, whereas the feedback to the other AND gate is *Q'*. Consequently, the two AND gates cannot produce the output 1 simultaneously. This ensures that the *S* and *R* lines of the *S-R* flip-flop do not become 1 simultaneously. The circuit of Fig. 9.3.1 is called a *J-K* flip-flop. When *J* and *K* are 1 simultaneously, it can be verified that the flip-flop will change state. Consequently, we may define the *J-K* flip-flop as follows.

Definition 9.3.1. A *J-K flip-flop* has two input lines, *J* and *K*. When *J* is 1 and *K* is 0, the flip-flop is set to 1, whereas when *K* is 1 and *J* is 0, the flip-flop is reset to 0. When *J* and *K* are both 1, the flip-flop changes state.

The truth table for the *J-K* flip-flop can be written in the same way as for the *S-R* flip-flop. This will give the characteristic function as $Q(JKq) = \Sigma(1,4,5,6)$. On minimization the characteristic function becomes

$$Q = Jq' + K'q$$

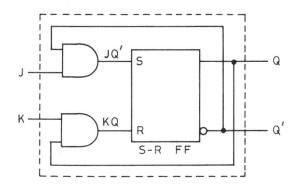

Figure 9.3.1 *J-K* flip-flop circuit obtained by modifying the *S-R* flip-flop circuit.

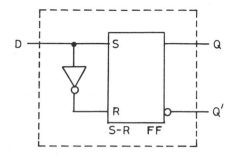

Figure 9.4.1 *D* flip-flop circuit obtained by modifying the *S-R* flip-flop circuit.

9.4 THE *D* FLIP-FLOP

Consider the circuit given in Fig. 9.4.1. This has been obtained by introducing the second modification in the circuit of an *S-R* flip-flop. This gives a new flip-flop called a *D* flip-flop. The *D* flip-flop has only one input line, called the *D*-line. This is connected directly to the *S* input of the *S-R* flip-flop. The *D*-line is also connected to the *R* input of the *S-R* flip-flop via an inverter. This ensures that the *S* and *R* inputs will always be the complement of each other, and will never become 1 simultaneously. It can be seen that whenever *D* is 0, the output of the flip-flop *Q* becomes 0; and when *D* is 1, the output *Q* becomes 1. The truth table of the *D* flip-flop can be formed easily, and its characteristic function turns out to be

$$Q = D$$

9.5 THE *T* FLIP-FLOP

As we discussed in Section 9.3, the *J-K* flip-flop has the property of changing state when both *J* and *K* inputs are 1. Hence if the *J*- and *K*-lines of the *J-K* flip-flop are short-circuited and made into a single input, we get another kind of flip-flop, as shown in Fig. 9.5.1. The single input line is called the *T*-line and a 1 on this line will make the flip-flop change the state or toggle. This flip-flop is also therefore called a toggle flip-flop. Its characteristic function turns out to be

$$Q = Tq' + T'q$$

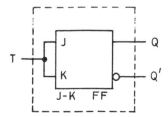

Figure 9.5.1 *T* flip-flop circuit obtained from a *J-K* flip-flop circuit.

9.6 EXCITATION TABLE

In previous sections we discussed four types of flip-flops. Each of these is an elementary sequential machine having two states and is the building block of large sequential machines having more than two states. The truth table of a flip-flop tells us the next state that the flip-flop assumes for a given input combination and its present state. For example, if a *J-K* flip-flop is in state 0 and it receives the input combination 11 on the *J*- and *K*-lines, the next state of the flip-flop becomes 1. However, for the synthesis of large sequential machines we should also know a "reverse" table called the excitation table for each of these flip-flops. While the truth table tells us the next state that the flip-flop assumes for a given input combination and the present state, the excitation table tells us what should be the input combination to drive a flip-flop from a particular present state to a particular next state. The excitation table can be derived from the information contained in the truth table of the flip-flop. For example, the truth table of the *J-K* flip-flop shows that to drive the flip-flop from present state 0 to the next state 1, the required input combination on the *J*- and *K*-lines can be either 11 or 10. Hence the required input combination is actually 1 on the *J*-line, and the *K*-line can be either 1 or 0. In other words, the entry for the *K*-line will be a don't-care term. Similarly, we may find the required input combination for the three other types of transition of the flip-flop: from 0 to 0, from 1 to 0, and from 1 to 1. The various required input combinations for the four different transitions of the *J-K* flip-flop are shown in Table 9.6.1.

In the same way the excitation tables for the three other types of flip-flops can also be found from their respective truth tables. The excitation tables for all the four flip-flops are given in Table 9.6.2.

TABLE 9.6.1 EXCITATION TABLE FOR *J-K* FLIP-FLOP

q	Q	J	K
0	0	0	ϕ
0	1	1	ϕ
1	0	ϕ	1
1	1	ϕ	0

TABLE 9.6.2 EXCITATION TABLES FOR *S-R, J-K, D,* AND *T* FLIP-FLOPS

q	Q	S	R	J	K	D	T
0	0	0	ϕ	0	ϕ	0	0
0	1	1	0	1	ϕ	1	1
1	0	0	1	ϕ	1	0	1
1	1	ϕ	0	ϕ	0	1	0

9.7 TRIGGERING OF FLIP-FLOPS

There are usually two ways by which a flip-flop can be triggered or driven from a certain present state to a certain next state. The flip-flop can respond to a level voltage on its input or it can respond to a pulse that becomes incident on its inputs. In both cases one must ensure that the triggering voltage, whether level or pulse, is present on the input for sufficient time so that the internal circuitry of the flip-flop can go through necessary changes. This time is called the *propagation time or delay* of a flip-flop. Another condition that must be kept in mind during triggering is that the flip-flop must undergo only one change for one occurrence of the pulse or a level voltage at its input. Therefore, it should also be ensured that the cause for triggering should not be large enough to produce multiple changes of state. It is obvious that a *J-K* or a *T* flip-flop that responds to a level voltage can operate reliably only if the level voltage is applied for a period greater than the propagation time but less than twice the propagation time. Thus for the *J-K* and *T* flip-flops, when the triggering voltage is in the form of a pulse, it must be broad enough to effect one change and at the same time not too broad to produce multiple changes. Quite often it is extremely difficult to have pulses of such accurate duration. Consequently, the circuit of a flip-flop is made more complex with additional gates so that it can trigger on either the rising or falling edge of the pulse. A flip-flop operating in this mode is known as *edge-triggered*. If the flip-flop changes state at the rising edge, it is called *positive* edge-triggered, and if it changes state on the falling edge, it is called *negative* edge-triggered.

So far we have not mentioned another pulse, or rather, a train of pulses that plays a vital role in the operation of a large number and types of sequential machines. These are the synchronizing or clock pulses, having a regular time period or repetition frequency. Since flip-flops are the elementary building blocks of a sequential circuit, a flip-flop, if need be, must also be capable of operating with a clock pulse. These flip-flops are known as clocked flip-flops. The clock pulse really works as an "enable" pulse of the flip-flop. A clocked flip-flop therefore responds to the input pulse only when the clock pulse is either high (active high) or low (active low) but not both. Let us assume that the flip-flop is required to change state at the rising edge of the clock pulse. To understand the timing requirements of both the input and clock pulses of a clocked flip-flop it is essential to have a close look at the rising edge of the clock pulse, as shown in Fig. 9.7.1. The time t_r is the *rise time* of the pulse. However, the input pulse must attain its stable value much earlier than the arrival of the clock pulse. Some flip-flops require this time to get ready to respond when the clock pulse arrives. This time is known as the *setup time*. Again, after the clock pulse has risen to its high value after the elapse of the rise time, the input pulse must be held at its stable value for some more time. This time is known as the *hold time* (see Fig. 9.7.1). For any flip-flop, these times are specified in the manufacturer's catalog. The sum of the three timings t_s, t_r, and t_h is the *propatation time or delay* t_p of the particular flip-flop. For some flip-flops the setup time may be zero. Again for some others, the hold time may be zero. When a flip-flop changes its state at the edge of the

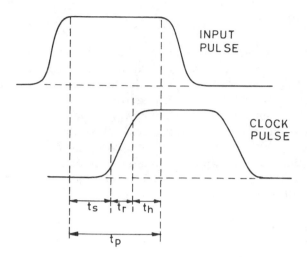

Figure 9.7.1 Setup, rise, and hold times of a flip-flop with respect to an input and a clock pulse.

clock pulse, it is called *edge-triggered* (ET). When a flip-flop is triggered by the rising (falling) edge of the clock pulse, it is called *positive* (*negative*) edge-triggered. Usually, these flip-flops have two more input lines, the set (also called preset) and the reset (also called clear) lines. A logical 0 signal on the set (reset) line overrides any other signal on the input or clock lines and sets (resets) the flip-flop to state 1(0). These signals are usually used for initializing the states of a flip-flop. In normal working mode these are held at logical 1. The circuit and the symbol of a positive edge-triggered D flip-flop with set and reset lines are shown in Fig. 9.7.2. The triangle at the C1 input of the symbol means that the flip-flop is edge-triggered, and the triggering takes place at the rising edge of the pulse. An inversion bubble in front of the triangle indicates triggering at the falling edge. No triangle before the C1 input means that the flip-flop responds to the level or amplitude of the clock pulse, and it acts when the level is high (active high). An inversion bubble indicates that the flip-flop responds when the clock pulse is low (active low). Similarly, the inversion bubbles after the S- and R-lines indicate that both the set and reset operations take place when these lines are low (active low).

Another configuration that allows reliable operation of flip-flops is the master–slave configuration. Here two flip-flops are connected in cascade. The master flip-flop is followed by the slave. The input is applied to the input line of the master, and the output is taken out from the output line of the slave. Both master and slave are triggered by the level of the input pulse. These flip-flops are therefore not edge-triggered but are level-sensitive. The same train of clock pulses is applied to the master and slave. However, the clock is fed directly to the master but via an inverter to the slave [see Fig. 9.7.3(a)]. As a result, when the input pulse is being copied by the master at the positive half of the clock pulse, the slave remains disabled or inactive. In the negative half of the clock pulse, the slave is active and copies the output of the master into it, which arrives at its output. Both the D and J-K flip-flops can be operated in this condition, and the

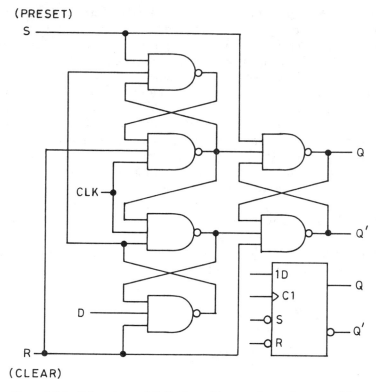

(PRESET)

(CLEAR)

Figure 9.7.2 Edge-triggered D flip-flop with set and reset inputs, and its symbol.

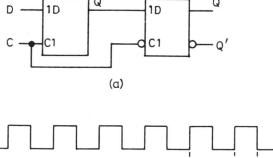

(a)

(Master - Slave D FF)

(b)

Figure 9.7.3 Master–slave D flip-flop: (a) logic diagram; (b) waveforms.

circuits are available as standard IC chips (Texas Instruments, 1987). Although both the edge-triggered and the master–slave configurations render reliable operation by ensuring only one output during the entire time period of a clock pulse, the master–slave configuration requires an additional safeguard. Here, to eliminate any uncertainty of operation, the data inputs must be held stable for the entire positive half of the clock pulse. If not, the output waveform may be unpredictable. See Fig. 9.7.3(b), which depicts such a situation.

To introduce an extra input for the clock pulse, additional AND gates are required. Such a circuit for an *S-R* flip-flop is shown in Fig. 9.7.4(a). The all NAND circuit is shown in Fig. 9.7.4(c). It should be mentioned that the clock (C1) input of a flip-flop may also be pulsed by an irregular or arbitrary pulse train, which does not have a regular time period of a clock pulse. When a flip-flop works with such a pulse train, it is called a gated rather than a clocked flip-flop. A more appropriate name for the circuit of Fig. 9.7.4 is an *S-R* latch rather than an *S-R* flip-flop. Let us explain this in the next section, where we study the difference between the working of a flip-flop and a latch. The term *bistable* will be used to mean both flip-flop and latch.

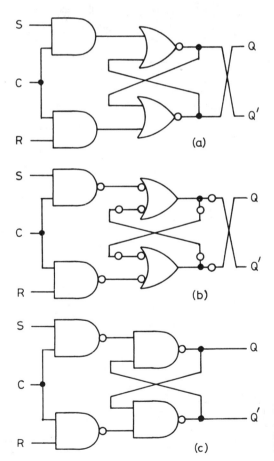

Figure 9.7.4 Gated *S-R* latch: (a) AND–NOR circuit; (b) intermediate circuit with inversion bubbles; (c) all-NAND circuit.

9.8 FLIP-FLOPS AND LATCHES

There are many applications, where a bistable may not have a gate or a clock pulse. In such a situation the bistable is said to work in an asynchronous mode. The ungated S-R and D latches work in this fashion. In such a mode of working the latch may be thought of functioning as a delay element since the output of the latch is exactly the same as the input but has been delayed by an amount of time equal to the propagation time of the bistable. However, the important difference between a delay element and the latch is that whereas in the delay element the output disappears after the input ceases to act, in the latch the last value of the input (logical 0 or 1) remains stored. In other words, the bistable remains "latched" in this condition. Hence a bistable, working in this manner, is called a latch and the term *flip-flop* is used for those bistables that are triggered. See the response of a D flip-flop and an asynchronous D latch in the waveforms of Fig. 9.8.1. Note how the asynchronous D latch faithfully copies the input pulse level, whereas the D flip-flop does not. This capability of the latch to copy faithfully the input pulse is known as *transparency property*. Many authors use the term *flip-flop* to mean both flip-flops and latches. However, it will be better to use the term *bistable* to mean both these types, and the bistable with the transparency property as a *latch,* and one without the transparency property as a *flip-flop*. This usage has become more relevant as IC chips of latches have simpler circuits than those of edge-triggered or master–slave flip-flops. Figure 9.8.1 also shows the response of a gated or clocked D latch. Here the transparency capability gets blocked during the inactive half of the gate or clock pulse C. Hence the response of the gated D latch is different from both the edge-triggered D flip-flop and the asynchronous D latch. A common property of both the asynchronous and the gated latch is that both are level sensitive, and any change

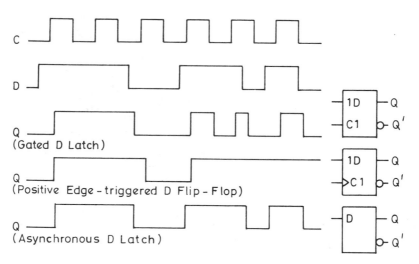

Figure 9.8.1 Waveforms of latches and flip-flops. Shows three different waveforms for three D-type bistables for the same input waveform.

in the level of the input pulse appears at the output delayed by only the propagation time, unless the change at the input gets blocked by the clock or gate pulse in the case of a gated latch.

9.9 RIPPLE COUNTERS

A binary ripple counter can be obtained by a very simple interconnection of a number of gated T flip-flops. Consider the circuit of three such flip-flops as connected in Fig. 9.9.1(a). At any instant of time these three flip-flops can store any one of the eight different combinations of the binary number. The three flip-flops are negative edge-triggered, that is, they change state at the falling edge of the gate pulse. Note that the pulse to be counted, x, triggers only the flip-flop Q_0. Q_0 triggers Q_1, and so on. Let the initial states of all the flip-flops be zeros. At the falling edge of the first pulse, the flip-flop Q_0 changes state. The pulses to be counted become incident only at the input C1 of the flip-flop Q_0, which alone changes state due to the incoming pulse. The change of state in Q_0 triggers the

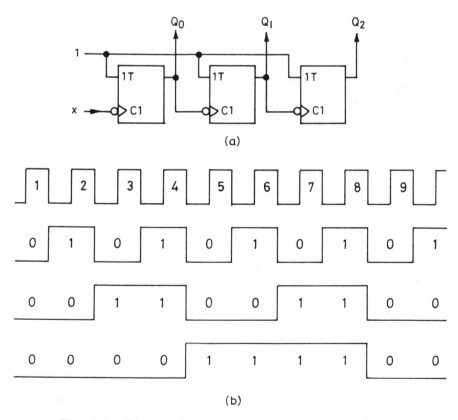

Figure 9.9.1 Binary ripple counter (up-counter): (a) logic diagram; (b) waveforms.

change in the next flip-flop Q_1, and the change of state in Q_1 triggers the next flip-flop Q_2. Consequently, we get the waveforms as shown in Fig. 9.9.1(b).

The circuit of the three-stage binary ripple counter of Fig. 9.9.1(a) counts from 0 to 7 (modulo 8) upwards. Such a counter is called an up-counter. For a counter that will count downward, that is, in the sequence 7,6,5, . . . ,0 (called a down-counter) the waveforms will be as shown in Fig. 9.9.2(a). The waveforms indicate clearly that the flip-flops must change state at the rising edge of the pulse. The flip-flops should therefore be positive edge-triggered. The circuit then becomes as shown in Fig. 9.9.2(b).

In the circuits discussed above, an m-stage ripple counter acts as a mod-2^m counter. Sometimes it may be necessary to have a counter of a modulo value less than 2^m. Suppose that we want a three-stage counter to work as a mod-5 counter. This can be achieved by connecting an AND gate that will detect the count 5. As soon as the AND-gate output is 1, it is made to clear all the flip-flops, that is, to reset them to 0-state. For this reason each flip-flop must also have an additional input line known as a reset (or clear) line which resets all the flip-flops to the 0-state whenever a 0 comes on this line. The circuit is shown in Fig. 9.9.3. It should

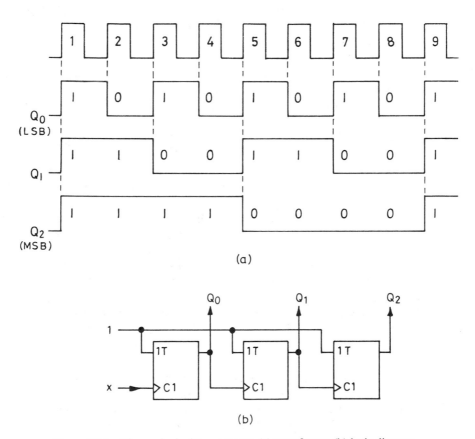

(a)

(b)

Figure 9.9.2 Binary ripple down-counter: (a) waveforms; (b) logic diagram.

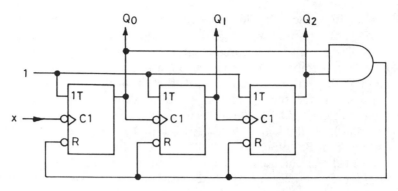

Figure 9.9.3 Modulo 5 ripple counter.

be noted that the AND gate does not have any input from the flip-flop, which is in 0-state for the number 5(101), namely, the flip-flop Q_1. This decoding AND gate will therefore also produce an output when the 0-state flip-flop Q_1 becomes 1. However, in all such cases the decoder must have at its input a number that is greater than the number at which the counter is reset to the "all-0" or the initial state. Since this number is always greater than K, this will never appear in a mod-K counter.

The waveforms of the ripple counter as shown in Figs. 9.9.1 and 9.9.2 are for ideal flip-flops that toggle instantaneously. In actual practice, the change of state of a flip-flop occurs after a finite delay called the propagation delay of the flip-flop. Taking this into consideration, the actual waveforms will be as shown in Fig. 9.9.4. It will be clear from the waveforms of this figure that before the counter assumes the stable state, there are one or more spurious states. Figure 9.9.4 shows that before the counter assumes the value of 2(010) from the previous count of 1(001), it has a short spurious state given by 0(000). The worst case is encountered when for an m-stage counter all the m-flip-flops are required to change state to assume the next count value. In case of the three-stage mod-8 counter, this happens when the count changes from 3(011) to 4(100). In this case two spurious states, 2(010) and 0(000), are produced (Fig. 9.9.4). This phenomenon of spurious states is a typical feature of all asynchronous operations, where there is no clock pulse to regulate the time period at which the output should be sampled. Consequently, in a ripple counter which is an asynchronous counter, when a decoder is used to obtain the counts, we get spurious decoding spikes in between the genuine count outputs. The decoding spikes can be avoided by providing an enable line to all the gates of the decoder unit, the timing of which is adjusted so that it keeps the AND gates of the decoder disabled during the transition period between two genuine counts. Another disadvantage of a ripple counter is that it is slow in operation since the count has to ripple through the flip-flops serially one after the other. Thus the delay becomes cumulative and quite appreciable if the number of stages of the counter is large.

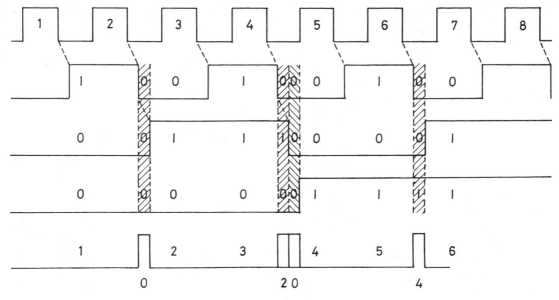

Figure 9.9.4 Spurious states in a ripple counter.

9.10 SYNCHRONOUS COUNTERS

The two drawbacks of the ripple counter, the occurrence of spurious states and long delay, are avoided in a synchronous counter, where flip-flops change their states simultaneously. The excitation function of each of the flip-flops in a synchronous counter is therefore a function of all the flip-flops as well as the external signal. Obviously, the combinational circuit that realizes these excitation functions becomes a global circuit interacting with all the flip-flops and input signals. Therefore, to achieve reliable operation that will avoid all transient states and will make the circuit immune to propagation delay, a regular train of pulses, known as clock pulses, is used to synchronize the operations of various units of the circuit.

Let us illustrate the synthesis of a synchronous counter by designing a mod-5 counter. As the counter has to store five distinct states, it will require three flip-flops (since $\lceil \log_2 5 \rceil = 3$). Let us also assume that it counts the clock pulses. Then the mod-5 counter must have a transition table as shown in Table 9.10.1, which shows the present state of the three flip-flops given by $y_2\, y_1\, y_0$ and the next state given by $Y_2 Y_1 Y_0$.

Let the states of the three flip-flops represent the count. For example, when the present states of the three flip-flops $y_2\, y_1\, y_0$ are, say, 001, it represents a count of 1. With the arrival of the next pulse, the count must be augmented by 1, and therefore the next states of the three flip-flops must be 010, that is, 2. In this way Table 9.10.1 can be constructed for the five counts (0 to 4). It can be seen that

TABLE 9.10.1 TRANSITION TABLE OF MOD-5 COUNTER

y_2	y_1	y_0	Y_2	Y_1	Y_0	T_2	T_1	T_0
0	0	0	0	0	1	(00)0	(00)0	(01)1
0	0	1	0	1	0	(00)0	(01)1	(10)1
0	1	0	0	1	1	(00)0	(11)0	(01)1
0	1	1	1	0	0	(01)1	(10)1	(10)1
1	0	0	0	0	0	(10)1	(00)0	(00)0
1	0	1	All entries are		don't cares	All entries are don't cares		
1	1	0						
1	1	1						

the flip-flops should never represent the counts 5 to 7. Hence these rows of the table are indicated by don't-care terms. Hence the corresponding next states for the present states 5 to 7 become don't-care terms. Let us now design the counter using T flip-flops. For this we must find out the values of the three excitation functions of the three flip-flops T_2, T_1, and T_0. For this, the transition of each of the flip-flops for each of the rows are to be computed. These have been shown in parentheses under the columns T_2, T_1, and T_0. Once the transitions are known, the values of Ts can be computed from the excitation table of T flip-flops, as given in Table 9.6.2. These are shown in Table 9.10.1. From this, the excitation functions for T_2, T_1, and T_0 as sums of minterms are given as follows:

$$T_2(y_2\, y_1\, y_0) = \Sigma(3,4) + \phi\Sigma(5\text{--}7)$$

$$T_1(y_2\, y_1\, y_0) = \Sigma(1,3) + \phi\Sigma(5\text{--}7)$$

$$T_0(y_2\, y_1\, y_0) = \Sigma(0\text{--}3) + \phi\Sigma(5\text{--}7)$$

It should now be noted that the combinational circuit realizing these three excitation functions is a multiple output circuit having three outputs: T_2, T_1, and T_0, and is a function of three inputs: the present states of the three flip-flops y_2, y_1, and y_0. The next step is to find the minimized form of these three functions. The most economical circuit having the least cost can be obtained, not by individually minimizing these three functions but by minimizing the three functions as that of a multiple-output circuit. As this is a small example, we carry out the multiple-output minimization with the help of the Karnaugh map (Fig. 9.10.1). It

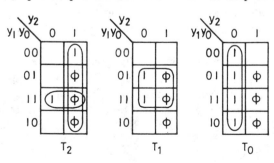

Figure 9.10.1 Multiple-output minimization of excitation functions on map.

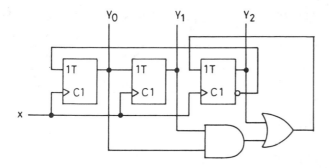

Figure 9.10.2 Implementation of a synchronous mod-5 counter with T flip-flops and AND–OR gates.

can be seen that the three excitation functions can be realized with the help of four product terms. It is interesting to note that in this case the multiple-output minimization does not produce any sharing of product terms between the functions. Thus the multiple-output minimization turns out to be the same as the single-output minimization of the three functions. However, this is a special case. Most of the time, especially for a circuit with a large number of variables, the multiple-output minimization yields the most economical circuit. The minimized excitation functions are

$$T_2 = y_2 + y_1y_0, \quad T_1 = y_0, \quad \text{and} \quad T_0 = y_2'$$

Implementing the three excitation functions by AND and OR gates, the circuit of the counter becomes as shown in Fig. 9.10.2.

9.11 RING COUNTERS

Another class of very useful counters are the ring counters. Here m stages of flip-flops are connected in the form of a ring, and at any instant of time only one of the flip-flops is in state 1, while the rest are in state 0 (one "hot"). At the incidence of a pulse on the pulsing line, the hot flip-flop of the ring becomes 0 and the next flip-flop becomes 1. Consider the design of a four-stage ring counter with edge-triggered D flip-flops. The transition table showing the present and next states of the four flip-flops y_1, y_2, y_3, and y_4 is shown in Table 9.11.1. For D flip-flops the excitation functions are the same as the next-state functions. Hence

$$D_1(y_1\,y_2\,y_3\,y_4) = Y_1 = \Sigma(1) + \phi\Sigma(0,3,5\text{–}7,9\text{–}15)$$

$$D_2(y_1\,y_2\,y_3\,y_4) = Y_2 = \Sigma(8) + \phi\Sigma(0,3,5\text{–}7,9\text{–}15)$$

$$D_3(y_1\,y_2\,y_3\,y_4) = Y_3 = \Sigma(4) + \phi\Sigma(0,3,5\text{–}7,9\text{–}15)$$

$$D_4(y_1\,y_2\,y_3\,y_4) = Y_4 = \Sigma(2) + \phi\Sigma(0,3,5\text{–}7,9\text{–}15)$$

Minimizing these functions, we get

$$D_1 = y_4, \quad D_2 = y_1, \quad D_3 = y_2, \quad \text{and} \quad D_4 = y_3$$

The implementation of the ring counter with these equations is shown in Fig. 9.11.1(a). The figure also shows an initializing circuit that is necessary for

TABLE 9.11.1 TRANSITION TABLE OF A FOUR-STAGE RING
COUNTER

m_i	Present state				Next state			
	y_1	y_2	y_3	y_4	Y_1	Y_2	Y_3	Y_4
8	1	0	0	0	0	1	0	0
4	0	1	0	0	0	0	1	0
2	0	0	1	0	0	0	0	1
1	0	0	0	1	1	0	0	0
Remaining rows or minterms (0,3,5–7,9–15)					All entries are don't cares			

proper working. In the normal working mode, the initialize input I is held at logic
1. To initialize, it is made 0. This sets the flip-flop y_1 to 1, and resets the remaining
flip-flops to 0. This state 1000 for the flip-flops $y_1 \, y_2 \, y_3 \, y_4$ is the initial state of the
ring counter (see the present state at the first row of the transition table, Table
9.11.1). After initialization, I is brought back to 1, and the counter starts
functioning normally. If due to noise, more than one flip-flop become 1 at some
time, the counter will start malfunctioning.

To remedy this situation, instead of the simple initialize input, an additional
AND-gate circuit is required to bring back the circuit to one of its valid states
from the spurious states. Here the excitation function D_1 of flip-flop y_1 is modified
to be

$$D_1 = y_1' \, y_2' \, y_3'$$

This function, known as the self-correction function, is provided by an additional
AND gate, as shown in Fig. 9.11.1(b). It can be shown that in the modified self-
correcting counter circuit, if the counter enters into a spurious state, it comes
back to a valid state after a few pulses. For example, it can be found by studying
the working of the circuit that if the counter enters into the spurious state 6,
corresponding to the minterm 6($y_1 \, y_2 \, y_3 \, y_4 = 0110$), it gets to the spurious state
3($y_1 \, y_2 \, y_3 \, y_4 = 0011$) and then to the valid state 1($y_1 \, y_2 \, y_3 \, y_4 = 0001$).

An ingenious variation of the ring counter is the *Johnson* or *Mobius counter.*
Such a counter is also called a *twisted-ring* or *switch-tail counter,* for reasons
that will be obvious when we get to its circuit. In a Johnson counter the number
of count states gets doubled; that is, an m-stage counter can act as a modulo $2m$
counter. However, a decoding circuit is required to obtain the $2m$ states, although
each individual decoder requires a simple two-input AND gate. It is also not a
"one-hot" counter. On the other hand, in the initial state all the flip-flops are in
the 0 state. Then the flip-flops become 1, one after the other until all the flip-flops
become 1. Then the flip-flops start becoming 0, one after the other until all flip-
flops return to 0 state once again. The transition table of a Johnson counter of
four stages is shown in Table 9.11.2. Following the same procedure as in the one-

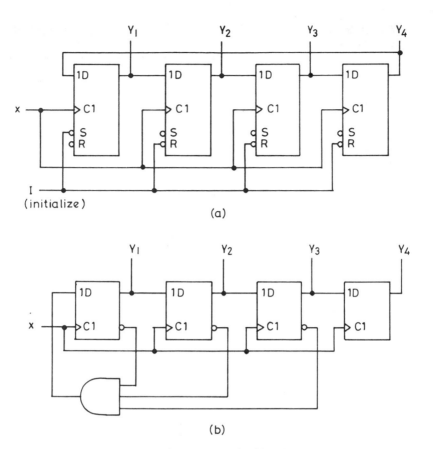

Figure 9.11.1 Four-stage ring counter: (a) with only initialization; (b) with self-correcting circuit.

hot ring counter of Table 9.11.1, the excitation functions of the four flip-flops can be found to be

$$D_1(y_1\ y_2\ y_3\ y_4) = \Sigma(0,8,12,14) + \phi\Sigma(2,4\text{--}6,9\text{--}11,13)$$

$$D_2(y_1\ y_2\ y_3\ y_4) = \Sigma(8,12,14,15) + \phi\Sigma(2,4\text{--}6,9\text{--}11,13)$$

$$D_3(y_1\ y_2\ y_3\ y_4) = \Sigma(7,12,14,15) + \phi\Sigma(2,4\text{--}6,9\text{--}11,13)$$

$$D_4(y_1\ y_2\ y_3\ y_4) = \Sigma(3,7,14,15) + \phi\Sigma(2,4\text{--}6,9\text{--}11,13)$$

After minimization

$$D_1 = y_4',\quad D_2 = y_1,\quad D_3 = y_2,\quad \text{and}\quad D_4 = y_3$$

Note that the excitation functions are similar to those of an ordinary ring counter, except that D_1 equals y_4' and not y_4. The basic circuit of the four-stage counter is shown in Fig. 9.11.2(a). The circuit clearly tells why the counter is called a twisted-ring or switch-tail counter. Figure 9.11.2(b) shows the additional circuitry required for self-correction.

TABLE 9.11.2 TRANSITION TABLE OF A FOUR-STAGE JOHNSON COUNTER

m_i	Present state				Next state				Decoder
	y_1	y_2	y_3	y_4	Y_1	Y_2	Y_3	Y_4	
0	0	0	0	0	1	0	0	0	$Y_1 Y_2'$
8	1	0	0	0	1	1	0	0	$Y_2 Y_3'$
12	1	1	0	0	1	1	1	0	$Y_3 Y_4'$
14	1	1	1	0	1	1	1	1	$Y_1 Y_4$
15	1	1	1	1	0	1	1	1	$Y_1' Y_2$
7	0	1	1	1	0	0	1	1	$Y_2' Y_3$
3	0	0	1	1	0	0	0	1	$Y_3' Y_4$
1	0	0	0	1	0	0	0	0	$Y_1' Y_4'$
	The remaining rows or minterms (2,4–6,9–11,13)				All entries are don't cares				

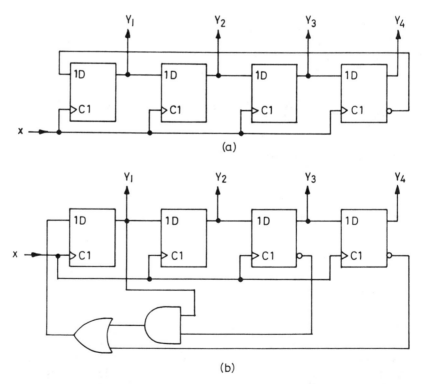

(a)

(b)

Figure 9.11.2 Four-stage Johnson counter: (a) basic circuit; (b) with self-correcting circuit.

9.12 SHIFT REGISTERS

The shift registers are very helpful and versatile modules that facilitate the design of many sequential circuits whose design may otherwise appear very complex. In its simplest form, a shift register consists of a series of flip-flops having identical interconnections between two adjacent flip-flops. Two such registers are the shift-right and the shift-left registers, shown in Fig. 9.12.1(a) and (b). In the shift-right register, the bits stored in the flip-flops shift to the right when the shift pulse is active. For example, in the three-stage shift register shown in Fig. 9.12.1(a), if the sequence of bits stored in the flip-flops Q_1, Q_2, and Q_3 at a given instant is, say, 001, and if a 1 comes to its serial data in (SDI) input at the next pulse, then this 1 gets stored in the flip-flop Q_1, the content of Q_1 shifts to the next right flip-flop, Q_2, and the content of Q_2 shifts to the next right flip-flop, Q_3. Thus the shift register will now store the bit sequence 100. If at the next pulse another 1 comes to the SDI input, it can be verified that the new bit sequence stored in the shift register will be 110. The three flip-flops of the shift-right register of Fig. 9.12.1(a) are D flip-flops and the Q output of the ith flip-flop is connected to the D input of the $(i + 1)$th flip-flop.

In the shift-left register shown in Fig. 9.12.1(b), serial data are fed to the D input of the last stage, and the Q output of the ith stage is fed to the D input of

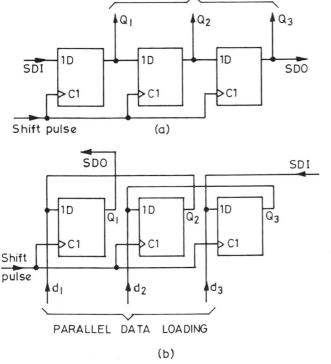

(a)

(b)

Figure 9.12.1 Three-bit shift registers: (a) right-shift register with serial data input, and serial and parallel data outputs; (b) left-shift register with serial data input and serial data output, and parallel data loading.

the $(i - 1)$th stage. The serial data output (SDO) is available from the Q output of the first stage. It can also be seen that the content of the various flip-flops can also be read in parallel by having three extra lines coming out from Q_1, Q_2, and Q_3. A shift register providing this facility is said to have parallel out capability. Many facilities can be built into a shift register in a number of different combinations by adding extra hardware. One such register is shown in Fig. 9.12.2, which acts as a shift-right register when the mode control line MC is 0, and as a left-shift register when MC is 1. The circuit has been obtained by adding a few 2-to-1 multiplexers and a 1-to-2 demultiplexer. The working of the shift register will be obvious. Shift registers having various facilities are available in the form of IC modules.

In the shift registers above, specific patterns are shifted through the register. There are applications where instead of specific patterns, random patterns are more important. Shift registers can also be built to generate such patterns, which are pseudorandom in nature. Called *linear feedback shift registers* (LFSRs), these are very useful for encoding and decoding error control codes. LFSRs used as generators of pseudorandom sequences have proved extremely useful in the area of testing of VLSI chips. In fact, we have already discussed such an application of LFSR in the built-in self-test section of Chapter 8. Figure 8.8.1 shows the general circuit of an LFSR. These are usually made of serially connected D flip-flops, like any other shift register. The important difference is that the outputs of some of the subsequent flip-flops are fed back to the D input of the first flip-flop through an XOR gate. Figure 8.8.2 shows a 4-bit LFSR, where

$$D_1 = q_1 \oplus q_4, \quad D_2 = q_1, \quad D_3 = q_2, \quad \text{and} \quad D_4 = q_3$$

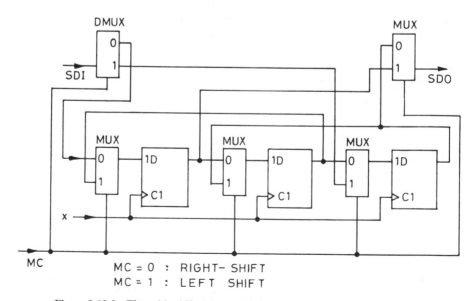

Figure 9.12.2 Three-bit shift-right and shift-left register with mode control.

Two 3-bit LFSRs with different connections are shown in Fig. 9.12.3(a) and (b). In (a), $D_1 = q_1 \oplus q_2$, whereas in (b), $D_1 = q_2 \oplus q_3$, where q_1, q_2, and q_3 are the present states and Q_1, Q_2, and Q_3 are the next states. Let us compute the sequence that will be generated in (a). Initially, introduce the combination 111 in the three flip-flops. The subsequent combinations can then be calculated by the equations

$$Q_1 = q_1 \oplus q_2, \quad Q_2 = q_1, \quad \text{and} \quad Q_3 = q_2$$

Now

Q_1	Q_2	Q_3
1	1	1
0	1	1
1	0	1
1	1	0
0	1	1

We see that the LFSR cycles through the three combinations in the following sequence:

$$011(3), \quad 101(5), \quad \text{and} \quad 110(6)$$

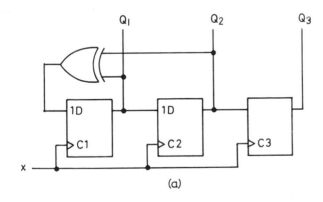

(a)

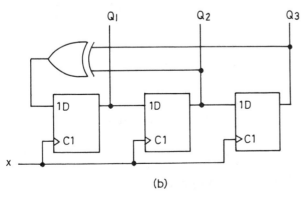

(b)

Figure 9.12.3 Three-bit linear feedback shift register: (a) limited length; (b) maximum length.

Repeating the computations for the LFSR of Fig. 9.12.3(b), it can be seen that it cycles through the following sequence of combinations: 111, 011, 001, 100, 010, 101, 110, 111, that is, in decimal, 7, 3, 1, 4, 2, 5, 6, 7. Here the LFSR cycles through all eight possible 3-bit combinations except 000. The all-0 combination is not desirable in an LFSR, since once the LFSR enters into this combination, it remains in it. This is because the XOR function of any number of zeros is always a zero. Thus the maximum number of combinations that an LFSR can generate and cycle through is $2^m - 1$ for an m-bit LFSR. Such an LFSR is called an LFSR of *maximum length*. It is significant to observe how the feedback connection makes all the difference. The LFSR of Fig. 9.12.3(a) has a length of only three. By a simple alteration of the connection, the LFSR of Fig. 9.12.3(b) becomes a maximum-length LFSR. It is known (Bardel et al., 1987) that for an m-bit LFSR there always exists a connection that will make its length maximum. Such an LFSR plays a very important role in the area of testing, especially in the built-in self-test that we discussed briefly in Chapter 8.

REFERENCES

BARDEL, P. H., W. H. MCANNEY, AND J. SAVIR. *Built-in Test for VLSI: Pseudorandom Techniques*. New York: John Wiley & Sons, Inc., 1987.

HILL, F. J., AND G. R. PETERSON. *Introduction to Switching Theory and Logical Design,* 3rd ed. New York: John Wiley & Sons, Inc., 1981.

MCCLUSKEY, E. J. *Logic Design Principles*. Englewood Cliffs, N.J.: Prentice-Hall, 1986.

MORRIS, R. L., AND J. R. MILLER (Eds.). *Designing with TTL Integrated Circuits*. New York: McGraw-Hill Book Company, 1971.

Texas Instruments. *The Bipolar Digital Integrated Circuits Data Book*. Texas Instruments, Dallas, Tex., 1987.

PROBLEMS

9.1. Treating the truth table of a *J-K* flip-flop as a transition table, it can be implemented by an *S-R* flip-flop. Find the excitation functions S and R. Show that they are given by

$$S(JKq) = \Sigma(4,6) + \phi\Sigma(1,5) = Jq'$$

$$R(JKq) = \Sigma(3,7) + \phi\Sigma(0,2) = Kq$$

9.2. Following the principle of Problem 9.1, obtain (a) a *D* flip-flop from an *S-R* flip-flop, and (b) a *T* flip-flop from a *D* flip-flop.

9.3. A flip-flop that may be called a *T-G* flip-flop has two lines, the *T*-line and the *G*-line. The flip-flop takes the value of the *T*-line as long as *G* is 1. When *G* is 0, the state of the flip-flop does not change irrespective of the values on the *T*-line. Obtain the circuit of the *T-G* flip-flop from an *S-R* flip-flop.

9.4. Explain how the circuit of Fig. 9.7.2 works as an edge-triggered *D* flip-flop.

9.5. Modify the circuit of the ripple counter of Fig. 9.9.1(a) such that all the T flip-flops are positive edge-triggered, and still the counter acts as an up-counter.

9.6. Design a three-stage mod-8 binary ripple counter with T flip-flops, such that it acts as an up-counter when a mode control signal MC is 1, and acts as a down-counter when MC is made 0.

9.7. Design a decade ripple counter. Also determine the values of the spurious decoding spikes during its count starting from 0 through 9.

9.8. Design a synchronous decade counter using J-K flip-flops and a PLA to implement the excitation functions.

9.9. Design a synchronous counter using D flip-flops and AND–OR gates that counts in the sequence (1,5,3,2,7,6,1).

9.10. Find the sequence of spurious states that the ring counter of Fig. 9.11.1(b) goes through before it comes to a valid state, when it enters into the spurious state corresponding to $y_1 \, y_2 \, y_3 \, y_4$ being **(a)** 0000, **(b)** 0101, **(c)** 0111, and **(d)** 1111.

9.11. Show that in a self-correcting ring counter circuit such as in Fig. 9.11.1(b) having m stages, the counter will return to a valid state after at most $m - 1$ pulses, when it enters into a spurious state.

9.12. Show how you can make a four-stage ring counter work as a divide-by-2 and a divide-by-4 pulse divider.

9.13. Design with minimal hardware a circuit that acts as a divide-by-2 and a divide-by-3 pulse divider.

9.14. Derive the self-correcting functions of the counters of Figs. 9.11.1(b) and 9.11.2(b).

9.15. Find the cycling sequence of combinations in 4-bit LFSRs given by the following feedback functions. Identify the maximum-length LFSR, if any.
  (a) $D_1 = q_1 \oplus q_2 \oplus q_4$ **(b)** $D_1 = q_2 \oplus q_3$
  (c) $D_1 = q_1 \oplus q_4$ **(d)** $D_1 = q_1 \oplus q_3$

9.16. Write a computer program to find the pseudorandom numbers generated by an LFSR. By this program verify that the 16-bit ALFSR of Fig. 8.8.3 is really an LFSR of maximum length.

9.17. Prove that in an LFSR of maximum length, the feedback XOR gate cannot have feedback from an odd number of flip-flops.

10

Clock-Mode Sequential Machines

10.1 INTRODUCTION

The various flip-flops, counters, and shift registers that we discussed in Chapter 9 are all examples of sequential machines. All these circuits contain memory elements. As we have mentioned before, the flip-flops are the elementary memory elements. The counters and shift registers are composed of more than one such element. All the circuits are capable of assuming more than one state. Their outputs do not depend only on the inputs but also on the state in which the circuit is at the time when the input is acting on it. If we note carefully the circuits of all these elements, they have a feedback from the output to the input. In general, a sequential machine will have the following:

1. A set S containing a finite number, say p, of internal states, so that

$$S = \{S, S_2, \ldots, S_p\}$$

2. A set X having a finite number, say n, of inputs, so that

$$X = \{X_1, X_2, \ldots, X_n\}$$

3. A set Z containing a finite number, say m, of outputs, so that

$$Z = \{Z_1, Z_2, \ldots, Z_m\}$$

4. A characterizing function f that uniquely defines the next state S^{t+1} as a function of the present state S^t and the present input X^t, so that

$$S^{t+1} = f(S^t, X^t)$$

5. A characterizing function, g, which uniquely defines the output function as a function of the input and the internal state for a Mealy machine, so that

$$Z^t = g(S^t, X^t)$$

For a Moore machine, the output is a function of the internal state only, so that

$$Z^t = g(S^t)$$

A sequential machine can therefore formally be defined as follows:

Definition 10.1.1. A *sequential machine* is a quintuple, $M = (X, Z, S, f, g)$, where X, Z, and S are the finite and nonempty sets of inputs, outputs, and states, respectively. f is the next-state function, such that

$$S^{t+1} = f(S^t, X^t)$$

and g is the output function such that

$$Z^t = g(S^t, X^t) \qquad \text{for a Mealy machine}$$

and

$$Z^t = g(S^t) \qquad \text{for a Moore machine}$$

10.2 STATE TABLES AND DIAGRAMS

To describe a sequential machine, either a state table or a state diagram is used. Table 10.2.1 is a state table describing a sequential machine M_1. It can be seen that the machine M_1 has a set of four internal states A, B, C, and D, a set of two inputs I_1 and I_2, and a set of two outputs 0 and 1.

The characterizing functions f and g are depicted in a tabular form, which is the state table. For example, for the present state B when the input is I_1, the next state is D and the output is 1. Thus the table shows the next state and the output for each combination of the present state and the input. Since the output

TABLE 10.2.1 STATE TABLE OF A MEALY MACHINE M_1

Present state	Next state, output	
	Input	
	I_1	I_2
A	$A,0$	$B,1$
B	$D,1$	$A,0$
C	$B,0$	$D,1$
D	$A,0$	$C,0$

of the machine M_1 depends on both the present state and the input, it is a *Mealy machine*.

Table 10.2.2 shows the state table of a *Moore machine*. Here the output is independent of the input and depends only on the present state of the machine. Therefore, this table has a separate column defining the outputs, and two input columns defining the next state without having any output associated with it. Another interesting property of the machines M_1 and M_2 which we have depicted in the two state tables is that for all combinations of present state and input, the next state and the output are completely specified. Such machines are therefore called *completely specified sequential machines* (CSSMs). There is another class of sequential machines, where sometimes the next state or the output or both may remain unspecified. Such machines are known as *incompletely specified sequential machines* (ISSMs).

The information contained in the state table can also be shown in a graphical manner with the help of nodes connected by directed graphs. Such diagrams are called *state diagrams*. Figures 10.2.1 and 10.2.2 show the state diagrams of machines M_1 and M_2, respectively. It should be mentioned here that the term *sequential machine* is a more general term. The circuit that implements the sequential machine is known as a *sequential circuit*. Thus there can be a number of sequential circuits implementing the same sequential machine. The reader may

TABLE 10.2.2 STATE TABLE OF A MOORE MACHINE M_2

Present state	Next state Input		Output
	I_1	I_2	
A	B	C	0
B	C	D	1
C	A	C	0
D	A	C	1

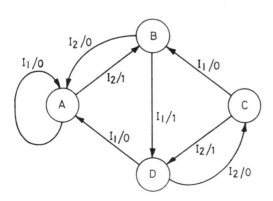

Figure 10.2.1 State diagram of Mealy machine M_1.

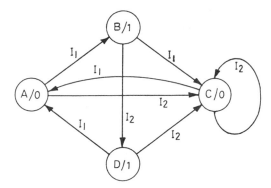

Figure 10.2.2 State diagram of Moore machine M_2.

also verify that the Mealy machine can easily be converted to a Moore machine by adding additional internal states.

10.3 INDISTINGUISHABLE STATES: EQUIVALENCE RELATION

A state table gives all informations regarding a sequential machine. The initial definition of a sequential machine is usually given in words known as the *word specification* of the machine. The next step in the synthesis of the machine is to derive a state table from the word specification. Quite often a state table so derived contains more number of states than is absolutely necessary. It is therefore essential that we have a systematic procedure to reduce a state table to one having the minimum number of states. This procedure is known as *state minimization*. However, for this purpose it is necessary to establish if and when two or more states become indistinguishable or equivalent. Every row in the state table of a completely specified sequential machine (CSSM) shows the sequence of next states and outputs, which the present state heading the row undergoes due to a sequence of input changes. Obviously, two states are indistinguishable if their next states and output sequences are identical. Take, for example, the state table of machine M_3 given in Table10.3.1. Here, if we take the states A and D, then for input I_1 both states go to state D and produce the output 0. Again for input I_2 both states go to the next state C and produce an output of 1. Clearly, these two states are indistinguishable and therefore, equivalent. To test the equivalence of two states, the first step is to check if they have identical output sequence. If the output sequences are not identical, it can immediately be concluded that the two states cannot be equivalent. If the output sequences are the same, the next-state sequences are checked for each input. Sometimes, the next states may not be identical, but they themselves may be equivalent states. In such cases also, the two states under test will be equivalent. Therefore, the equivalence relation among the various states of a sequential machine can be defined as follows.

Definition 10.3.1. Two states of a sequential machine are *equivalent* if for each input they produce the same output and their next states are either identical or equivalent.

TABLE 10.3.1 STATE TABLE
OF MACHINE M_3

Present state	Next state, output	
	Input	
	I_1	I_2
A	D,0	C,1
B	E,1	A,1
C	H,1	D,1
D	D,0	C,1
E	B,0	G,1
F	H,1	D,1
G	A,0	F,1
H	C,0	A,1
I	G,1	H,1

Applying this definition, we find states A and D of machine M_3 to be equivalent. However, if we compare states A and E of machine M_3, we find that they have the same output sequence, namely 01, for the two inputs I_1 and I_2. Hence they may be equivalent if the corresponding next states for I_1 and also for I_2 are equivalent, that is, if B and D are equivalent and C and G are equivalent. Therefore, the equivalence of A and E implies the equivalence of the two pairs BD and CG. Hence, to determine the equivalence of the various states of a given state table, it is necessary to prepare an implication matrix as suggested by Paull and Unger (1959). The *implication matrix* (IM) for machine M_3 is shown in Fig. 10.3.1. The procedure for the construction of such a matrix is as follows. First, state A is compared with state B, and in case their output sequences are not the same, a cross is put in the square of column A and row B, indicating that A and B cannot be equivalent. Then A is compared with C and again a cross is placed in the square of column A and row C since their output sequences are not the same. Comparing A and D we find that their output sequences are the same, and also the corresponding next states for both inputs are the same. Hence these two states are equivalent and a check mark ($\checkmark$) is placed in the corresponding square. Comparing A and E we find that their output sequences are the same, and the equivalence of A and E implies the equivalence of the pairs BD and CG. Therefore, both BD and CG are written in the square corresponding to the column A and row E. This procedure is continued until A has been compared with all other states. When the comparison of A with the rest of the states are complete, the same thing is repeated for state B and thereafter for state C, and so on. In this way, the initial version of the implication matrix is constructed. Thereafter, it is checked whether the implied equivalent pairs are really equivalent or not. For example, coming to the square of A and E we find from the column of B and row

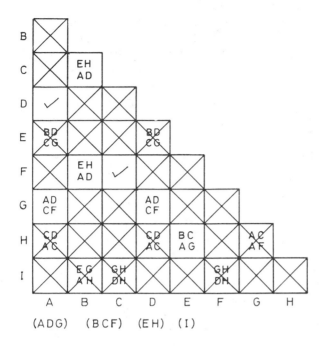

Figure 10.3.1 Implication matrix of machine M_3.

D that the pair BD is not equivalent. Hence all squares where BD appears in the implication matrix are crossed out. Again, note that after BD has been crossed out, the pair AE turns out to be a nonequivalent pair. Therefore, if AE appears in any cell of the IM, that particular cell is also crossed out. These iterations continue until no cell can be crossed out any more. Thus, in the final version of the implication matrix, some cells will be crossed out and others will remain as they are. The remaining cells that are not crossed out give the list of equivalent pairs. For example, from Fig. 10.3.1 we find that for the machine M_3 the pairs AD, AG, BC, BF, CF, DG, and EH are equivalent. It is well known that an equivalence relation must satisfy its three basic properties: that is, it must be reflexive, symmetric, and transitive. It is obvious that the equivalence relation between two states as defined in Definition 10.3.1 is both reflexive and symmetric. It must now be investigated if the relation is also transitive. For this, consider the IM of machine M_3. Here state A is equivalent to D as well as to G. Now, since D and G are both equivalent to A, their output sequences are identical, being the same as that of A. Similarly, their next states for any input are also identical or equivalent to that of A. Hence the next states of D and G for each input must also be identical or equivalent. Therefore, D and G are also equivalent. This shows that the equivalence relation indeed satisfies the transitive property.

10.4 STATE MINIMIZATION

Once the equivalent states are determined with the help of an implication matrix, the state minimization of a CSSM becomes a very simple task. Continuing our discussion of the preceding section it can easily be seen that if any column of an

IM has more than one equivalent states, they can be merged together to form a set of equivalent states. In the IM of M_3 each of the groups ADG, BCF, and EH is a set of equivalent states. Each set can therefore be merged into a single state. The state I is not equivalent to any other state, and therefore it maintains its separate identity. Hence the state table of machine M_3 can be minimized to another state table having only four states. Designating the four states to be 1, 2, 3, and 4, the reduced state table is shown in Table 10.4.1.

TABLE 10.4.1 REDUCED STATE TABLE OF MACHINE M_3

Present state	Next state, output Input I_1	I_2	Present state	Next state, output Input I_1	I_2
ADG	AD,0	CF,1	1	1,0	2,1
BCF	EH,1	AD,1	2	3,1	1,1
EH	BC,0	AG,1	3	2,0	1,1
I	G,1	H,1	4	1,1	3,1

It should be mentioned here that whereas the state minimization of a completely specified sequential machine (CSSM) is a fairly simple and straightforward procedure, that of an incompletely specified sequential machine (ISSM) is quite complex and may be quite involved, especially if the ISSM has a large number of internal states. For this reason we discuss this topic in Chapter 11.

Example 10.4.1

Find a reduced state machine that covers the machine of Table 10.4.2.

TABLE 10.4.2 STATE TABLE OF
MACHINE M_4

Present state	Next state, z $x_1 x_2$ 00	01	11	10
A	B,0	D,0	G,1	A,0
B	C,1	G,1	E,0	B,1
C	D,1	G,1	A,0	C,1
D	F,1	H,1	A,0	D,1
E	C,0	F,0	H,1	E,0
F	B,1	H,1	E,0	F,1
G	A,0	E,0	B,1	D,0
H	E,0	A,0	C,1	F,0

Clock-Mode Sequential Machines   Chap. 10

Solution Figure 10.4.1 shows the IM of machine M_4. From the IM it can be concluded that the states can be merged into three equivalent groups: AE, $BCDF$, and GH. The state table of the reduced machine covering M_4 is shown in Table 10.4.3.

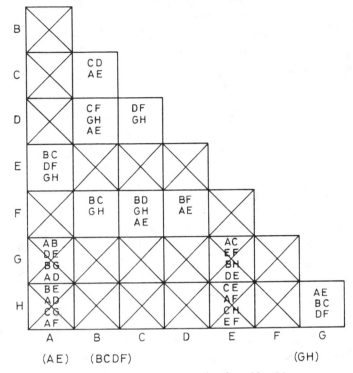

Figure 10.4.1 Implication matrix of machine M_4.

TABLE 10.4.3 REDUCED STATE TABLE COVERING M_4

Present state		Next state, z			
		$x_1 x_2$			
		00	01	11	10
AE	a	$b,0$	$b,0$	$c,1$	$a,0$
BCD	b	$b,1$	$c,1$	$a,0$	$b,1$
GH	c	$a,0$	$a,0$	$b,1$	$b,0$

10.5 FORMATION OF STATE TABLES

We have seen in previous sections that a state table or state diagram describes all the characteristics of a sequential machine. However, initially a sequential machine is described in words and it is necessary to obtain a state table from this verbal description, which is more formally known as "word specification." In this section we describe a systematic procedure by which a state table can be formed from a given word specification. Consider the synthesis of a sequence detector, which is described as follows.

A sequence detector working in the clock mode has one input line and one output line. A string of 0's and 1's are incident to its input in a serial manner. The sequence detector is required to produce a pulse output whenever the sequence 010 is detected. Assume that overlapping in the input pulse sequence is allowed.

Input: 1 0 0 1 0 0 1 0 1 0 1 1

Output: 0 0 0 0 1 0 0 1 0 1 0 0

Since the output of the machine is in the form of pulses, it will be more economical if it is designed as a Mealy machine. First, we derive from the word specification a primitive state table where the number of states may be more than the minimum number required. Once the primitive state table has been formed, the minimum state table can be obtained by applying the procedure of state minimization as we discussed in the preceding section. It is obvious that the various states of the sequential machine remember a certain amount of past history of the machine, which in these cases consist of nothing but a string of 0's and 1's that have already come to the input of the machine. The exact length of the string of bits to be remembered by a state of the machine depends on the specification of the machine. In the particular case of the sequence detector under consideration, it can easily be concluded that there must be a state that remembers a first 0 when it is received. Then there must be another state which should remember that a 1 has come immediately after this 0; that is, the sequence 01 has been received by the machine. At this time if a 0 is incident on the input line, the detector must produce an output of 1. We now proceed to form a state table having states remembering the basic requirement and introducing new states whenever required (see Table 10.5.1).

Assume that as soon as the machine is switched on, it goes to state A, which does not remember anything. Now when a 0 comes to the input line the machine goes to state B and remembers a single 0. On the other hand, if a 1 comes, the machine goes to state C and remembers a single one. In both these cases the output is 0. This is shown in the first row of the primitive state table that we are developing (Table 10.5.1). The second row describes the behavior of the machine when the present state is state B and the inputs are to 0 and 1. It can be seen that in this row when the present state is B and the input is 0, the machine need not remember the bit string 00, as it does not form a part of the sequence to be detected. So it will be adequate if the machine remembers only one 0 which has just been incident on the input line. This means that the machine need not go to any new state but can remain in the same present state B. On the other hand, when the input is 1 and the present state is B, the sequence 01 has been incident on the input line. It is obvious that this sequence should be remembered by the machine as it forms a part of the required sequence. Therefore, the machine

TABLE 10.5.1 PRIMITIVE STATE TABLE FOR THE SEQUENCE DETECTOR (OVERLAPPING ALLOWED), MACHINE M_5

Present state	Next state, z	
	x	
	0	1
$A(-)$	$B(0),0$	$C(1),0$
$B(0)$	$B(0),0$	$D(01),0$
$C(1)$	$B(0),0$	$C(1),0$
$D(01)$	$E(010),1$	$C(1),0$
$E(010)$	$B(0),0$	$D(01),0$

comes to a new state D and remembers the sequence 01. However, the output continues to be 0. This situation has been shown in the second row of the state table. The third row describes the situation when the present state is C, which has remembered a single 1 at its input. Here also when the input is another 0, the machine need not remember the sequence 10 but simply the last 0, and therefore may go to the next state, B. Next, when the input is 1, the machine need not remember the sequence 11, and remembering only the last 1 will be adequate. Therefore, it continues in state C and in both the cases the output remains 0. In the fourth row it describes the behavior of the machine when the present state is D, which remembers the sequence 01. With D as the present state when the input is another 0, the sequence 010 has been incident, and this is the sequence that should produce an output of 1, and therefore the machine goes to a new state, E, which remembers the sequence 010 and produces an output 1. On the other hand, when the input is 1 with D as the present state, the sequence received is 011, and it is clear that the machine need not remember this entire sequence but only the last 1 need be remembered. Therefore, it goes to the next state, C, which remembers a single one, and the output of the machine remains 0. The fifth row describes the behavior of the machine with E as the present state. When the input is 0, the sequence 0100 has been received and it is obvious that the machine need not remember this entire sequence. Remembering only the last 0 is adequate. Therefore, the machine goes to state B, which remembers a single 0 and the output becomes 0. When 1 is incident at the input with E as the present state, the sequence 0101 has been received. It should be noted carefully that the last two bits of the sequence, namely 01, form a part of the sequence that is desired to be detected. Since overlapping of the sequence is allowed, the 0 of the sequence 01 can be taken both as the last bit of the sequence to be detected and as the first bit of the sequence to be detected. Therefore, when the sequence 0101 has been received, the machine must remember the last two bits, namely the sequence 01, and should therefore go to state D. The output, however, will remain 0. It should be seen that in the fifth row no need has arisen to introduce any new

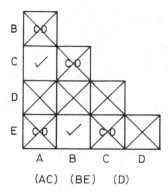

Figure 10.5.1 Implication matrix of machine M_5.

state, and also we have considered all the states that have already appeared in the state table. Hence the procedure for the formation of the primitive state table has terminated, and the primitive state table for the sequence detector has been obtained completely. The next step is to minimize this state table. To do this, it is necessary to determine the implication matrix of this machine, which has been shown in Fig. 10.5.1. From the implication matrix it can be seen that states A and C, and also states B and E, will merge. The minimized state table of machine M_5 has only three states, as shown in Table 10.5.2.

Let us now repeat the design of the sequence detector assuming that overlapping is not allowed. In other words, the bit or bits that form a part of the sequence already detected cannot be taken once again as a part of another sequence. Proceeding to form the primitive state table in the same manner as we have done for the previous case, we see that the first four rows of the primitive state table will remain the same. Coming to the fifth row, that is, when we determine the next states and outputs of the machine with E as the present state, we find that the machine should go to state B when the input is 0. However, when the input is 1, the sequence received is 0101, and since overlapping is not allowed, the machine has to remember only the last 1 and not the sequence 01, since the 0 of 01 forms the last bit of the already detected sequence 010. Therefore, the machine should go to state C, which remembers the single 1. Hence the

TABLE 10.5.2 MINIMIZED STATE TABLE FOR MACHINE M_5

Present state	Next state, z	
	x	
	0	1
$AC \rightarrow a$	$b,0$	$a,0$
$BE \rightarrow b$	$b,0$	$c,0$
$D \rightarrow c$	$b,1$	$a,0$

TABLE 10.5.3 PRIMITIVE STATE TABLE FOR SEQUENCE DETECTOR (OVERLAPPING NOT ALLOWED), MACHINE M_6

Present state	Next state, z x	
	0	1
A	$B,0$	$C,0$
B	$B,0$	$D,0$
C	$B,0$	$C,0$
D	$E,1$	$C,0$
E	$B,0$	$C,0$

primitive state table of this machine will be as shown in Table 10.5.3. After minimization this state table also becomes a three-state table, as shown in Table 10.5.4.

TABLE 10.5.4 MINIMIZED STATE TABLE FOR MACHINE M_6

Present state	Next state, z x	
	0	1
$ACE \rightarrow a$	$b,0$	$a,0$
$B \rightarrow b$	$b,0$	$c,0$
$D \rightarrow c$	$a,1$	$a,0$

It will be evident from the example of the sequence detector that from a given word specification of a sequential machine, it is possible to produce a primitive state table by introducing new states whenever it is deemed necessary. The designer need not worry about the number of states that the primitive state table may end up with. The state minimization procedure ultimately reduces the machine to one having the minimum number of states.

Example 10.5.1

Design a level-output clock-mode finite-state machine with one input and one output having the following specification. When the input bit is different from the most recent previous bit, the output becomes 1 and remains 1 until the input bit becomes the same as the last previous bit. When the latter happens, the output becomes 0 and remains 0 until the input bit once again differs from the last previous bit.

Input: 0 0 0 1 0 1 0 1 1 0 0 1 0 0

Output: 0 0 0 1 1 1 1 1 0 1 0 1 1 0

Solution It should be observed that the machine must have a level output since the outputs 1 and 0 of the machine has to remain unchanged for more than one clock period. Therefore, this machine has to be designed as a Moore machine rather than a Mealy machine, so that the output will depend only on the state and not on the input pulse. Now proceeding in the same way as we have done for machine M_6, the primitive state table for this machine M_7 can be verified to be as shown in Table 10.5.5. In the primitive state table the output is shown after a slash following a state to indicate that it is a function only of the state and does not depend on the input. The z column gives the output of each state. Note that this column is not really necessary at this stage, as this information is also contained in the present-state column.

TABLE 10.5.5 PRIMITIVE STATE TABLE FOR MACHINE M_7

Present state	Next state x 0	Next state x 1	z
$A(-)/0$	$B(0)/0$	$C(1)/0$	0
$B(0)/0$	$D(00)/0$	$E(01)/1$	0
$C(1)/0$	$F(10)/1$	$G(11)/0$	0
$D(00)/0$	$D(00)/0$	$E(01)/1$	0
$E(01)/1$	$F(10)/1$	$G(11)/0$	1
$F(10)/1$	$D(00)/0$	$E(01)/1$	1
$G(11)/0$	$F(10)/1$	$G(11)/0$	0

The reader can argue and find out how all seven states of the machine, A to G, appear in the state table. It should also be noted that since it is a Moore machine, its output appears in a separate column and is a function only of the state. Minimizing this machine the state table reduces to a five-state table, as shown in Figure 10.5.2 and Table 10.5.6.

Example 10.5.2

Repeat Problem 10.5.1 assuming that the specification now requires the output to be a pulse rather than level.

Solution Since the output is in the form of a pulse, it returns to 0 at the end of a clock pulse. Therefore, there is no need to have the second condition, which returns the output to 0 in Example 10.5.1. Consequently, the word specification of this problem has to be modified as follows: Design a clock-mode finite machine that produces a pulse output whenever the input pulse is different from the preceding pulse.

The primitive state table can be formed by arguing in the same manner as we have done before, and is shown in Table 10.5.7. Note that here the state table is

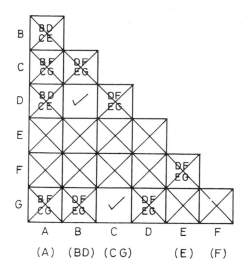

Figure 10.5.2 Implication matrix of machine M_7.

TABLE 10.5.6 MINIMIZED STATE TABLE FOR MACHINE M_7

Present state	Next state		z
	x		
	0	1	
$A \rightarrow a$	b	c	0
$BD \rightarrow b$	b	d	0
$CG \rightarrow c$	e	c	0
$E \rightarrow d$	e	c	1
$F \rightarrow e$	b	d	1

TABLE 10.5.7 PRIMITIVE STATE TABLE FOR MACHINE M_8

Present state	Next state, z	
	x	
	0	1
$A(-)$	$B(0),0$	$C(1),0$
$B(0)$	$B(0),0$	$D(01),1$
$C(1)$	$E(10),1$	$C(1),0$
$D(01)$	$E(10),1$	$C(1),0$
$E(10)$	$E(0),0$	$D(01),1$

TABLE 10.5.8 MINIMIZED
STATE TABLE FOR
MACHINE M_8

Present state	Next state, z	
	x	
	0	1
$A \rightarrow a$	$b,0$	$c,0$
$BE \rightarrow b$	$b,0$	$c,1$
$CD \rightarrow c$	$b,1$	$c,0$

that of a Mealy machine, where the output is dependent on both the present state and on the input. The primitive state table has five internal states. After minimization the state table reduces to a three-state machine as shown in Table 10.5.8.

10.6 INITIAL STATES

In Section 10.5 we have formed four state tables, two for the sequence detector and two for the finite-state machine in the clock mode with level and pulse output. In all these state tables we have one state, state A, as the starting state for the primitive state tables. While deriving the primitive state table, we have assumed that this state does not remember anything. Consider the minimized state tables for machines M_5 and M_6 shown in Tables 10.5.2 and 10.5.4. Both these tables have only three states, a, b, and c. In both these machines when power is switched on, the machine can go to any of the three internal states, a, b, and c. Now it can be seen that if the machine goes to a state other than a, the circuit may produce false output for the first two pulses. From the third pulse, however, the circuit will give proper output without making any error. Such a machine that stabilizes to a steady state, that is, does not make any error in the ouptut after a few initial pulses, is known as *fixed* or *finite memory span* circuit. If the requirement is such that a few errors at the initial stages, that is, when the circuit has been first brought into operation, can be tolerated, there is no need to start the circuit in any definite initial state. On the other hand, if the requirement is such that the circuit must not produce even a single error right from the beginning, then an initializing circuit must be provided so that the circuit always starts from a definite initial state. In the case of the sequence detector, a is the initial state. It should be mentioned here that there is many a circuit in which unless the circuit starts with a definite initial state it will not produce even a single correct output. Familiar examples of such circuits are those of counters. Unless they are started at the state representing the count 0, the circuit will continue to give wrong outputs for an indefinite time. Such circuits are called *unbounded memory span* circuits. For the two clock-mode finite machines, M_7 and M_8 (Tables 10.5.6 and 10.5.8), the output stabilizes from the second pulse. Therefore, if we can ignore the error in the first pulse, the circuit need not start at the initial state, which in our case is the state *a*. Another interesting feature that can be seen in the minimized state tables for the two machines is that the circuit starts from the state *a* but does not go back to the state at any other time. Such a state, which cannot be reached from any other state by any input sequence, is a *source state*. Similarly, a state from which the circuit can never go to any other state by any input sequence is known as a *sink state*. If in the state table of a machine each state can be reached from any other state either directly or via one or more states by an input sequence, the machine is known as a *strongly connected* machine.

It is obvious that if the error at the initial first few pulses can be ignored, a source state can be omitted from the state table. Therefore, if we accept this condition, the state *a* can be removed from both tables of machines M_7 and M_8. Machine M_7 can then be designed with only four internal states and machine M_8 with only two internal states.

Example 10.6.1

Design a clock-mode finite-state machine whose specifications are as follows. The circuit has one input line and one output line. It produces an output 1 when exactly two 1's are followed by one 0. Once the output becomes 1, it remains so until the sequence 10 is received, when the output returns to 0. Overlapping of the sequence is allowed. Is it a finite memory span machine?

Solution   Since the output remains at 1 for more than one clock pulse, the machine must have a level output. As such, the machine has to be designed as a clock-mode level-output (CM-L) Moore machine. Proceeding in the same manner as earlier, the primitive state table of the machine will be given in Table 10.6.1, and the minimized machine will be as shown in Table 10.6.2. In the primitive state table an output has been shown after a slash to indicate that it is a function only of the state and is independent of the input. A study of the minimized state table shows that the machine has a finite memory span.

TABLE 10.6.1   PRIMITIVE STATE TABLE OF M_9

Present state	Next state, z	
	x	
	0	1
$A(-)/0$	$B(0)/0$	$C(1)/0$
$B(0)/0$	$B(0)/0$	$C(1)/0$
$C(1)/0$	$B(0)/0$	$D(11)/0$
$D(11)/0$	$E(110)/1$	$F(111)/0$
$E(110)/1$	$E(110)/1$	$G(1)/1$
$F(111)/0$	$B(0)/0$	$F(111)/0$
$G(1)/1$	$H(10)/0$	$G(1)/1$
$H(10)/0$	$B(0)/0$	$C(1)/0$

TABLE 10.6.2 MINIMIZED
STATE TABLE OF M_9

Present state	Next state x 0	1	z
$ABH \rightarrow 1$	1	2	0
$C \rightarrow 2$	1	3	0
$D \rightarrow 3$	4	5	0
$E \rightarrow 4$	4	6	1
$F \rightarrow 5$	1	5	0
$G \rightarrow 6$	1	6	1

Example 10.6.2

A clock-mode finite-state machine with pulse output (CM-P) has two input lines and one output line. Strings of 0's and 1's are being incident on the two input lines. The machine produces an output 1, only when the present bit on each input line is different from the bit immediately preceding it, and also the present bits on the two input lines are different. Overlapping of sequences is allowed. Find a minimum-row state table for the machine.

$$\text{Inputs} \quad x_1: 1\ 0\ 0\ 1\ 0\ 1\ 0\ 1\ 1\ 0\ 0\ 1\ 0$$
$$x_2: 0\ 1\ 1\ 0\ 0\ 0\ 0\ 1\ 0\ 1\ 1\ 0\ 1$$
$$\text{Output} \quad z: 0\ 1\ 0\ 1\ 0\ 0\ 0\ 0\ 0\ 1\ 0\ 1\ 1$$

Solution The machine can be designed as a Mealy machine. The primitive state table of the machine will be as shown in Table 10.6.3. The minimized state table is shown in Table 10.6.4.

TABLE 10.6.3 PRIMITIVE STATE TABLE FOR MACHINE M_{10}

Present state	x_1: 0 x_2: 0	0 1	1 1	1 0
$A(-)$	$B\binom{0}{0},0$	$C\binom{0}{1},0$	$D\binom{1}{1},0$	$E\binom{1}{0},0$
$B\binom{0}{0}$	$B\binom{0}{0},0$	$C\binom{0}{1},0$	$D\binom{1}{1},0$	$E\binom{1}{0},0$
$C\binom{0}{1}$	$B\binom{0}{0},0$	$C\binom{0}{1},0$	$D\binom{1}{1},0$	$E\binom{1}{0},1$
$D\binom{1}{1}$	$B\binom{0}{0},0$	$C\binom{0}{1},0$	$D\binom{1}{1},0$	$E\binom{1}{0},0$
$E\binom{1}{0}$	$B\binom{0}{0},0$	$C\binom{0}{1},1$	$D\binom{1}{1},0$	$E\binom{1}{0},0$

TABLE 10.6.4 MINIMIZED STATE TABLE
FOR MACHINE M_{10}

Present state	Next state, z			
	$x_1 x_2$			
	00	01	11	10
$ABD \rightarrow 1$	1,0	2,0	1,0	3,0
$C \rightarrow 2$	1,0	2,0	1,0	3,1
$E \rightarrow 3$	1,0	2,1	1,0	3,0

10.7 CIRCUIT SYNTHESIS

In this section we develop the procedure that has to be followed for implementing the state table of a sequential machine. To illustrate the various steps let us implement the sequence detector whose minimized state table is shown in Table 10.5.2 (machine M_5). It can be seen that this machine has three internal states, a, b, and c. Now these internal states are realized by a combination of flip-flops. First, we must decide as to the number of flip-flops required. It is clear that m number of flip-flops can represent 2^m internal states. Each internal state will be represented by a particular combination of 0's and 1's of the flip-flops. Hence the number of flip-flops will be given by $\lceil \log_2 n \rceil$, where n is the number of states. In the present case, since the number of states is three, we require at least two flip-flops. However, two flip-flops can represent 2^2 or 4 internal states. Therefore, it must also be decided as to which combination should be assigned to each state. This problem is known as the state assignment problem. Let us assign in this case the assignment that has been shown in Table 10.7.1. Here states a, b, and c have been assigned the combination 00, 01, and 10, respectively. Note that the assignment 11 has not been used. Now the state table as shown in Table 10.5.2 has to be rewritten so that the symbols representing various states are replaced

TABLE 10.7.1 TRANSITION TABLE FOR
MACHINE M_5

Present state		Next state $(Y_1 Y_2)$					
		x					
		0			1		
y_1	y_2	Y_1	Y_2,	z	Y_1	Y_2,	z
a: 0	0	0	1,	0	0	0,	0
b: 0	1	0	1,	0	1	0,	0
c: 1	0	0	1,	1	0	0,	0
1	1			Not used			

by the state assignments on the two flip-flops that we have called y_1 and y_2 in the excitation table. The next states of the machine are now the next states of the flip-flops and are represented by Y_1 and Y_2. Such a table is known as a *transition table*.

Another decision that has to be made by the designer is to decide which type of flip-flop should be used to implement the particular transition table. We have discussed in Chapter 9 that the flip-flops commonly used are D, T, S-R, and J-K. Let us decide that we shall implement this table using J-K flip-flops. In that case it will be necessary to write the excitation tables for the two inputs J and K for each of the two flip-flops. Consequently, the excitation table for the J and K inputs of the two flip-flops, y_1 and y_2, are to be determined. For this, first rewrite the state table in the form of a truth table. (Note that the next-state functions Y_1 and Y_2 and the output function z are all functions of the input x and the present states y_1 and y_2.) Then follow the procedures of determining flip-flop input equations or excitation functions as described in Section 9.6. The truth and excitation tables of machine M_5 are given in Table 10.7.2.

It is now easy to see that the excitation and output functions of the two J-K flip-flops can be written as four equations, as given below.

$$J_1 = \Sigma(5) + \phi\Sigma(2,3,6,7)$$

$$K_1 = \Sigma(2,6) + \phi\Sigma(0,1,3,4,5,7)$$

$$J_2 = \Sigma(0,2) + \phi\Sigma(1,3,5,7)$$

$$K_2 = \Sigma(5) + \phi\Sigma(0,2,3,4,6,7)$$

$$z = \Sigma(2) + \phi\Sigma(3,7)$$

The next step is to implement these five functions, each of which is a function of the three variables x, y_1, and y_2 in a combinational circuit. At this point again the designer has to decide how to implement the combinational circuit. As we have discussed in Chapter 5, there are many ways of designing the

TABLE 10.7.2 TRUTH AND EXCITATION TABLES FOR M_5

m	\multicolumn{6}{c}{Truth table}						\multicolumn{4}{c}{Excitation table}			
	x	y_1	y_2	Y_1	Y_2	z	J_1	K_1	J_2	K_2
0	0	0	0	0	1	0	0	ϕ	1	ϕ
1	0	0	1	0	1	0	0	ϕ	ϕ	0
2	0	1	0	0	1	1	ϕ	1	1	ϕ
3	0	1	1	ϕ	ϕ	ϕ	ϕ	ϕ	ϕ	ϕ
4	1	0	0	0	0	0	0	ϕ	0	ϕ
5	1	0	1	1	0	0	1	ϕ	ϕ	1
6	1	1	0	0	0	0	ϕ	1	0	ϕ
7	1	1	1	ϕ	ϕ	ϕ	ϕ	ϕ	ϕ	ϕ

combinational circuit. Depending on the requirement, one method may be better than another. Hence it is left to the designer to decide the particular manner of implementation. Let us assume that it has been decided to implement the combinational circuit by a PLA. To ensure that the PLA has the minimum number of product lines, it is necessary to process the five functions by a multiple-output minimization or by a PLA minimizer. Since in the present case the functions are only three-variable five-output functions, we can do the minimization by the map method, as shown in Fig. 10.7.1. It shows that three product lines will be adequate to implement the five functions. Note that K_1 equals the constant 1. To minimize the area further we should now fold the PLA. However, for the sake of simplicity, we implemented the machine with an unfolded PLA. The PLA and the J-K flip-flops, together with their product lines, have been shown in Fig. 10.7.2.

It will now be apparent that the circuit of any sequential machine will always consist of (a) flip-flops as memory elements, (b) a combinational circuit feeding

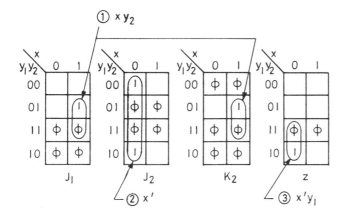

Figure 10.7.1 Multiple-output minimization of excitation and output functions.

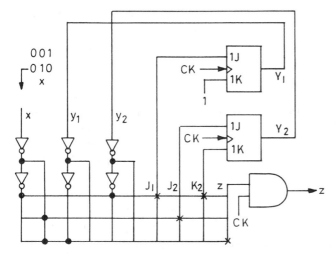

Figure 10.7.2 Implementation of machine M_5 by J-K flip-flops and a PLA.

the flip-flops and generating the outputs, and (c) feedback paths from the flip-flop outputs to the inputs of the combinational circuit (Fig. 10.7.3).

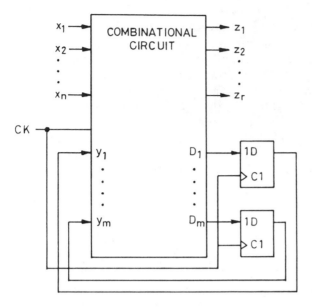

Figure 10.7.3 Generalized circuit of a sequential machine. Shows D latches as memory elements, and a combinational circuit with feedback.

We can now summarize the various steps that are to be followed in the synthesis of a clock-mode sequential machine.

1. Derive first a primitive and then a minimized state table from the word specifications.
2. Find the minimum number of flip-flops that will be required to implement the machine.
3. Decide about the type of flip-flop that should be used.
4. Decide about the state assignment that should be assigned to the various states of the flip-flops. It should be mentioned here that there are many possible assignments to implement the state table. For example, in Table 10.7.1 we have used the assignment 00, 01, and 10 for the three states a, b, and c, respectively, and the assignment 11 has not been used. Another assignment that could have been used is the combination 11 for state a, 10 for b, and 01 for c, and the combination 00 being the unused and hence the don't-care combination. Now, although it is true that one particular assignment may produce a simpler circuit compared to another, the improvement may be so marginal, especially when the circuit is implemented by ICs or embedded in a VLSI chip, that it is not worthwhile to spend valuable design time and money in finding the best or near-best assignment. Hence any arbitrary assignment is chosen to represent the states.
5. Decide what type of combinational circuits should be used to implement various functions. Most of the circuits that will be proved economical will

require multiple-output minimization of these functions. The minimized functions are then implemented by the particular device decided by the logic designer.

10.8 SHIFT REGISTER REALIZATION

So far we have designed the various sequential machines by first forming a state table and then implementing the state table with the help of flip-flops working as memory elements and the combinational circuits providing excitations to the various memory elements. For a limited class of sequential machines, they can also be designed with a different approach, the shift register realization. The sequence detectors are especially suitable for this type of approach. In this case, instead of using flip-flops and then finding their excitation functions, several flip-flops interconnected as a shift register are used as the memory elements. Let us illustrate the method by designing the sequence detector of Table 10.5.1 with the help of a shift register. In this case the sequence detector produces an output 1 when the sequence 010 is received. The shift register circuit realizing the sequence detector has been shown in Fig. 10.8.1. It can be seen that when the sequence 010 is received, the three cells of the shift register store 0, 1, and 0, respectively, and only in this case the AND gate produces an output 1. The shift register realization of the sequence detector of Example 10.6.1 is shown in Fig. 10.8.2. Here the circuit has to produce a level output. The design of the circuit is self-explanatory. However, here since an output should be produced only when exactly two 1's are followed by a 0, the shift register must receive in effect the sequence 0110, not simply 110. Hence the shift register must have not three but four cells. Again, since the output is level instead of a pulse, an S-R flip-flop is used to store the output. It gets reset when the reset sequence 10 is detected by another AND gate.

From the discussion above, the shift register realization appears to be a very attractive way of designing sequential machines. However, it is very wasteful of space if the sequence to be detected has a large number of bits. For example,

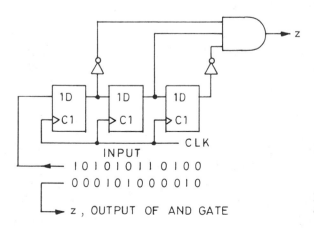

Figure 10.8.1 Shift register realization of the sequence detector, machine M_5.

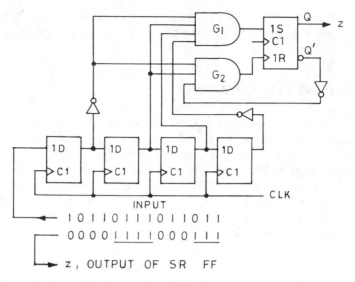

Figure 10.8.2 Shift register realization of the sequence detector, machine M_9.

it can easily be seen that the number of cells or flip-flops of a shift register must be equal to the number of bits to be detected for producing the output. On the other hand, in the state-table realization, a state table may have at best the number of states equal to the number of bits. Therefore, the number of flip-flops required will be at most $\log_2 b$, where b is the number of bits in the sequence to be detected. Therefore, the shift register realization cannot be preferred in a VLSI environment. However, it may be useful for small machines, since although the shift register realization may require more flip-flops, it will save considerable design time, which otherwise will have to be spent for going through the various steps, as we enumerated in Section 10.8.

10.9 SEQUENTIAL MACHINE TESTING

The testing of sequential circuits is a far more complex task than that of combinational circuits. In a combinational circuit the test procedure finds out if the combinational circuit satisfies the truth table that has been realized by the circuit. In a sequential circuit the test procedures must verify, by means of the implemented circuit, if a given state table functions as it should. To do this—testing sequences that have to be applied only to the input pins and responses that have to be observed only on the output pins—one has to determine the state the machine is in, and the state in which the machine goes, when a particular input is applied for a particular present state of the circuit. In a sequential circuit the states of the various flip-flops are not available to the outside world. Therefore, it is not possible to determine the state of a sequential circuit by observing the state of the flip-flops. Therefore, a particular state of a machine has to be determined by observing only the output and input sequences. Thus to identify the state uniquely it is necessary to have a sequence that will produce an output completely different from all other states for a given input sequence. Such a sequence is known as a *distinguishing sequence* of the machine. Therefore, an important condition that has to be satisfied by a machine to be tested is that it possess a distinguishing sequence. This also requires that if each state of the machine has to be determined or distinguished as a unique state, no two states in the machine should be indistinguishable or equivalent. This means that the machine to be tested must be a completely reduced machine. Again, it should be possible to check the transition of the machine from one state to another by a given input sequence. In order that all transitions of the state table can be determined, it is also necessary that there be a sequence that should enable us to take the machine from one state to another. Such a sequence is called a *transfer sequence*. It is also obvious that for a transfer sequence to exist for all pairs of states, the machine must be strongly connected. Thus the machine to be tested must satisfy two very important restrictions: namely, it must be completely reduced and should be strongly connected. However, as we shall see in Chapter 11, when a machine is not completely specified, it may be very difficult to minimize the state table so that not even a single pair of states remains indistinguishable. Thus we will have to omit from the purview of testing a large number of sequential machines: the incompletely specified machines. Unfortunately, when the number of states of the machine becomes very large, as is often the case in a VLSI situation, most finite-state machines are invariably incompletely specified, and therefore, no algorithm can guarantee that they have been completely reduced. Moreover, besides the distinguishing sequence, many other sequences, such as *homing* and *synchronizing sequences,* may have to be determined. Again, all machines, even if they are reduced and strongly connected, may not possess a distinguishing sequence. For all these and various other reasons, testing a sequential machine by verifying all the transitions and identifying all the states of the state table is a formidable task. Readers interested in the details of the various procedures of state identification and fault-detection experiments are referred to Chapter 13 of Kohavi (1978), which provides excellent coverage of various aspects of these topics.

10.10 DESIGN FOR TESTABILITY: LSSD

We have just now discussed various difficulties that are encountered in devising a method of testing the state table of a sequential machine. These difficulties are usually overcome by separating the test procedures into two different parts. In this approach the sequential machine is considered to have a combinational circuit part and a sequential circuit part consisting of bistables or flip-flops (see Fig. 10.7.3). In the normal mode, the flip-flops and combinational circuits act according to the design specifications. In the test mode, the combinational part becomes separated from the sequential part: that is, the flip-flops. Then the combinational circuits and the flip-flops are tested separately. There are many methods of testing a sequential machine in this manner. One of the popular methods is the *scan path method*. Here, in the test mode, the flip-flops are interconnected as a shift register. The required test pattern to test the combinational circuit is shifted serially into the bistables, now connected as a shift register. Then the circuit is returned to the normal mode for only one clock period when the combinational circuit, along with the input sequence, acts on the bistables or the flip-flops and stores the results in the flip-flops. Then the circuit is again placed in the test mode, and while a new test pattern is being put into the flip-flops, the previous stored data are serially scanned out. The outputs and the data stored in the flip-flops are now checked, and if they are similar to the response expected, it is concluded that the circuit is working properly. Although there are many techniques to test by the scan path method, the most popular and extensively used method is the level-sensitive scan design (LSSD) method developed by IBM (Das Gupta et al., 1978, 1981). Salient features of this method are described with the help of Fig. 10.10.1. Here, each memory element consists of two latches connected in a master–slave configuration. The master latches are the L_1 latches; whereas the slave latches are the L_2 latches. Moreover, the L_1 latches have two instead of the usual one input. There are also three clocks, which drive the circuit. Two are system clocks, CK1 and CK2, which have a phase difference of 180°; that is, when the CK1 clock is high, CK2 is low, and vice versa. The CK1 clock is connected only to L_1 latches; whereas the CK2 clock is connected only to L_2 latches. The third clock, TCK, which has the same phase as the CK1 clock, is connected to the C2 terminals of the L_1 latches. The signal on the C2 terminal of the L_1 latches acts as the control signal such that when C2 is high, the data on the 2D terminal are gated to the output of the L_1 latch, and when C2 is low, the data on the 1D terminal are gated to the output of the L_1 latch. In the normal mode (see also Fig. 10.10.2) the two system clocks, CK1 and CK2, are on, whereas the test clock, TCK, is off. In this situation, when the clock CK1 is high, the signal appears at the D outputs of the combinational logic and also at the outputs of the L_1 latches via its 1D inputs. In the second half of the clock pulse when CK1 is 0 and CK2 is 1, the output of each of the L_1 latches gets stored in its corresponding L_2 latch. During the first half of the next clock pulse, that is, when CK1 is high and CK2 is low, the input sequence $x_1, x_2, \ldots, x_n$ and also the stored values of the L_2 latches $Y_1, Y_2, \ldots, Y_m$, which are connected to the $y_1, y_2, \ldots, y_m$ terminals of the combinational logic, act only on the combinational circuits and produce the output sequence $z_1, z_2, \ldots, z_r$ and the input to the L_1 latches, namely $D_1, D_2, \ldots, D_m$. In the second half of the clock pulse, when CK2 is 1 and CK1 is 0, the values stored in the L_1 latches get transferred to the L_2 latches, become stable and ready to act upon combinational logic once again when the CK1 clock will be high. These cycles of operations go on during the normal mode. Due to the master–slave configuration of the L_1 and L_2 latches, the various data get stored and transferred when the levels of the respective clock pulses are high and are therefore independent of the delays of the individual gates and latches. For this

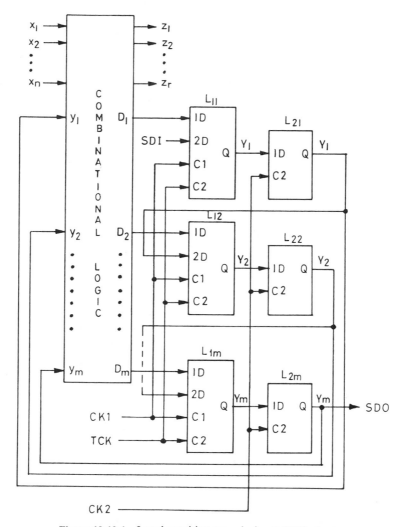

Figure 10.10.1 Level-sensitive scan design (LSSD) circuit.

reason this particular method of scan design is called *level-sensitive scan design* (LSSD).

In the test mode, the test clock TCK (which has the same phase as the system clock CK1) is turned on and the clock CK1 is turned off. The other system clock, CK2, continues to run as before. When the test clock TCK becomes 1, the outputs of the L_1 latches get connected to the 2D terminals. As can be seen from Fig. 10.10.1, the L_1 latches then get detached from the combinational circuit and assume the configuration of a shift register. Now the 2D terminal of the L_{11} latch is connected to the 1D terminal of the L_{21} latch. The output of the latch L_{21} is connected to the 2D terminal of the latch L_{12}. The output of the L_{22} latch is connected to the 2D terminal of L_{13}, and the output of L_{23} is connected to the

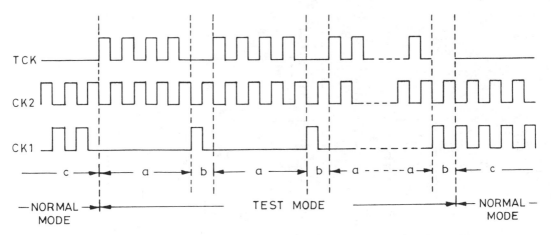

Figure 10.10.2 Timing diagram of the normal and test modes of the LSSD circuit.

input of the next pair of L_1 and L_2 latches. Now the test sequence that is desired to be stored in the flip-flops is scanned in by the serial data input (SDI) terminal of the first latch, L_{11}. While the SDI terminal scans in the required bits to be stored in the flip-flops now connected as a shift register, the serial data output (SDO) terminal scans out the data stored in the bistables.

To understand the procedure of scan in and scan out, let us study Fig. 10.10.2, which shows the operation of of an LSSD system having four internal flip-flops, that is, four pairs of L_1 and L_2 latches connected in the master–slave configuration. Assume that the machine we are testing has two inputs, x_1 and x_2, with four flip-flops (four pairs of L_1 and L_2 latches), representing its 16 internal states and having three outputs z_1, z_2, and z_3. Consider a test sequence where an input X_i takes the machine from the present state S_i to the next state, S_j, and produces an output Z_j. Let the input sequence X_i (x_1,x_2) be 01, the present state S_i (y_1, y_2, y_3, y_4) be 1011, and the next state S_i (Y_1,Y_2,Y_3,Y_4) be 0101 and output Z_j (Z_1,Z_2,Z_3) be 110. The machine is put into the test mode by turning on the test clock TCK and turning off the system clock CK1 simultaneously. When TCK becomes high, the outputs of the L_1 latches get connected to the second data line, 2D, and therefore all four pairs of latches get connected as a shift register, such that (L_{11},L_{21}) feeds (L_{12},L_{22}), which in turn feeds (L_{13},L_{23}), and so on. Since the flip-flops, y_1, y_2, y_3, and y_4, are to store 1, 0, 1, and 1, respectively, the sequence 1101 is to be put serially into the serial data input (SDI), which is connected to the 2D line of the latch L_{11}, that is, to flip-flop y_1. After four clock pulses of TCK and CK2 (which remains on), the desired sequence gets stored in four flip-flops, y_1, y_2, y_3, and y_4. At the end of the fourth pulse of the TCK, the TCK is switched off, and the system clock CK1 is switched on just for one clock pulse. Obviously, during this clock period the flip-flops lose the shift register configuration and revert to their normal-mode configuration, and hence during this clock pulse period when CK1 is 1, the input sequence x_1, x_2 and the values of y_1 to y_4 act on the combinational logic and drive the machine to the next state and produce the output Z_1. Therefore, at the end of this clock pulse the values stored in the four flip-flops will be the values of the desired next state, namely S_j; that is, the flip-flops y_1, y_2, y_3, and y_4 must store the bits 0101, respectively. Now at the end of this clock period, the clock TCK is again turned on and the clock CK1 is turned off. The situation remains like this for the next four clock pulses. During this time, the next test sequence is scanned in serially to the four flip-flops from the SDI terminal. The required values of x_1 and x_2 are also set in parallel during this period of four clock pulses. During the same period the bits stored in flip-flops Y_1, Y_2, Y_3, and Y_4 are scanned out from the SDO terminal. At the same time, the values of z_1, z_2, and z_3 are checked in parallel. If all these bits turn out to be the desired values, then it can be concluded that the combinational circuit is working all right. To ascertain that the flip-flops (the latches) are working properly, these are tested by shifting a string of 1's followed by a string of 0's through the shift register configuration. Sometimes, a more complex pattern having a mixture of 1's and 0's, such as 01100, may be shifted through the latches. Note that the LSSD method does not require the machine under test to be either strongly connected or fully reduced.

REFERENCES

DAS GUPTA, S., E. B. EICHELBERGER, AND T. W. WILLIAMS. LSI chip design for testability, *IEEE International Solid State-Circuits Conference,* San Francisco, Calif. February 15–17, 1978, pp. 216–217.

DAS GUPTA, S., R. G. WALTHER, AND T. W. WILLIAMS. An enhancement to LSSD and some applications of LSSD in reliability, availability, and serviceability, *11th Annual International Symposium on Fault-Tolerant Computing (FTCS-11),* Portland, Maine, June 24–26, 1981, pp. 32–34.

EICHELBERGER, E. B., AND T. W. WILLIAMS. A logic design structure for LSI testability, *Proc. 14th Design Automation Conference,* New Orleans, La., June 20–22, 1977, pp. 462–468.

HUFFMAN, D. A. The synthesis of sequential switching circuits, *J. Franklin Inst.,* Vol. 257, March–April, 1954, pp. 275–303.

KOHAVI, Z. *Switching and Finite Automata Theory,* 2nd ed. New York: McGraw-Hill Book Company, 1978.

MCCLUSKEY, E. J. *Logic Design Principles.* Englewood Cliffs, N.J.: Prentice Hall, 1986.

MEALY, G. H. A method for synthesizing sequential circuits, *Bell Syst. Tech. J.,* Vol. 34, September, 1955, pp. 1045–1079.

MOORE, E. F. Gedanken-experiments on sequential machines, *Automata Studies, Annals of Mathematical Studies,* No. 34. Princeton, N.J.: Princeton University Press, 1956, pp. 129–153.

PAULL, M. C., AND S. H. UNGER. Minimizing the number of states in incompletely specified sequential switching functions, *IRE Trans. Electron. Comput.,* Vol. EC-8, No. 3, Sept. 1959, pp. 356–367.

PROBLEMS

10.1. Convert the following Mealy machines into Moore machines.

<table>
<tr><td colspan="3">(a)</td></tr>
<tr><td></td><td colspan="2">Next state, z</td></tr>
<tr><td>Present
state</td><td colspan="2">x</td></tr>
<tr><td></td><td>0</td><td>1</td></tr>
<tr><td>A</td><td>B,0</td><td>C,1</td></tr>
<tr><td>B</td><td>D,1</td><td>A,1</td></tr>
<tr><td>C</td><td>A,0</td><td>D,0</td></tr>
<tr><td>D</td><td>C,1</td><td>B,1</td></tr>
</table>

<table>
<tr><td colspan="3">(b)</td></tr>
<tr><td></td><td colspan="2">Next state, z</td></tr>
<tr><td>Present
state</td><td colspan="2">x</td></tr>
<tr><td></td><td>0</td><td>1</td></tr>
<tr><td>A</td><td>A,0</td><td>B,1</td></tr>
<tr><td>B</td><td>B,1</td><td>C,0</td></tr>
<tr><td>C</td><td>C,1</td><td>D,1</td></tr>
<tr><td>D</td><td>D,0</td><td>A,0</td></tr>
</table>

(c)

Present state	Next state, z x_1x_2			
	00	01	11	10
A	A,0	B,0	C,1	B,0
B	B,0	D,1	D,1	D,0
C	C,0	A,0	A,1	D,1
D	D,0	C,1	B.1	A,1

10.2. Minimize the following state tables.

<table>
<tr><td colspan="3">(a)</td></tr>
<tr><td></td><td colspan="2">Next state, z</td></tr>
<tr><td>Present
state</td><td colspan="2">x</td></tr>
<tr><td></td><td>0</td><td>1</td></tr>
<tr><td>A</td><td>C,0</td><td>E,1</td></tr>
<tr><td>B</td><td>D,0</td><td>A,1</td></tr>
<tr><td>C</td><td>E,1</td><td>F,0</td></tr>
<tr><td>D</td><td>F,1</td><td>E,0</td></tr>
<tr><td>E</td><td>A,0</td><td>C,1</td></tr>
<tr><td>F</td><td>B,0</td><td>D,1</td></tr>
</table>

<table>
<tr><td colspan="3">(b)</td></tr>
<tr><td></td><td colspan="2">Next state, z</td></tr>
<tr><td>Present
state</td><td colspan="2">x</td></tr>
<tr><td></td><td>0</td><td>1</td></tr>
<tr><td>A</td><td>C,1</td><td>F,1</td></tr>
<tr><td>B</td><td>C,0</td><td>D,0</td></tr>
<tr><td>C</td><td>D,1</td><td>E,0</td></tr>
<tr><td>D</td><td>G,0</td><td>B,0</td></tr>
<tr><td>E</td><td>G,1</td><td>A,1</td></tr>
<tr><td>F</td><td>C,1</td><td>E,1</td></tr>
<tr><td>G</td><td>B,1</td><td>A,0</td></tr>
</table>

(c)

Present state	Next state, z			
	$x_1 x_2$			
	00	01	11	10
A	$A,0$	$F,1$	$C,0$	$B,1$
B	$B,0$	$E,1$	$C,0$	$A,1$
C	$C,0$	$B,0$	$A,0$	$C,1$
D	$D,0$	$H,0$	$G,0$	$C,1$
E	$E,0$	$G,0$	$A,0$	$C,1$
F	$F,0$	$D,1$	$H,1$	$A,0$
G	$G,0$	$D,1$	$C,0$	$G,1$
H	$H,0$	$E,1$	$C,0$	$H,1$

10.3. For each of the minimized state tables of Problem 10.2, draw the state diagram and determine if the machine is strongly connected.

10.4. Determine a minimum-row state table for a clock-mode sequence detector with one input and one output line, which produces an output 1 when one of the sequences 001, 100, and 111 is detected. Once a sequence is detected, no part of it can be taken to form part of another sequence; that is, overlapping of sequences is not allowed.

10.5. Repeat Problem 10.4 when overlapping of sequences is allowed.

10.6. A clock-mode sequential machine has two input lines, x_1 and x_2, and one output line. The machine produces an output 1 if the sequence 011 is detected on the x_1-line with x_2 remaining 1 for all 3 bits. Once the output is 1, it remains 1 until x_2 becomes 0. Construct a minimum-row state table for the machine.

10.7. In the sequence detector circuit of Fig. 10.8.2 the "enable" signal of the AND gate G_2 has been provided by inverting the Q' output of the S-R flip-flop. Will it make any difference if this signal is given directly from the Q output of the flip-flop? Discuss.

10.8. The reliable operation of the sequence detector of Fig. 10.8.2 is critically dependent on the delay introduced by one circuit element. Identify this element. Can you modify the circuit such that this operation will not be so dependent on any particular circuit element and will be absolutely reliable?

10.9. Design the sequence detector of Problem 10.4 with a shift register.

10.10. Design the sequence detector of Problem 10.5 with a shift register.

10.11. A sequence detector is to produce an output 1 only when exactly two 0's are followed by two 1's. Design the detector with a shift register.

10.12. Design the sequence detector of Problem 10.11 as a regular sequential machine. Which of the two designs has fewer flip-flops?

10.13. Implement the finite-state machines of Problems 10.4 and 10.6 with (a) a D flip-flop and (b) a J-K flip-flop. Use unfolded PLAs to implement the combinational circuit.

10.14. Analyze, that is, extract the state table of the sequential circuit of Fig. P.10.4.

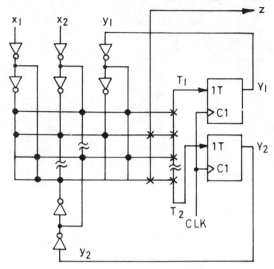

Figure P.10.14

10.15. Design a serial binary adder with pulse output with *J-K* flip-flops and AND–OR gates.

10.16. Repeat the design of the serial binary adder with level output.

10.17. Derive the state table of a sequential machine that will generate the following sequence of binary waveform:

$$1\ 0\ 1\ 1\ 1\ 0\ 1\ 1\ 1\ 0\ 1\ 1$$

10.18. Design the binary waveform generator of Problem 10.17 with a shift register.

10.19. Design the waveform generator of Problem 10.17 with ROMs and a ring counter. Which of the three designs above will be most economical, and why?

10.20. A clock-mode 5-bit odd-parity checker working in the serial mode produces an output whenever an error is detected in the 5 bits (4 data bits and 1 parity bit). Derive a minimum-row state table for the machine.

10.21. Derive a minimum-row state table for a clock-mode FSM working as an error detector in a 2-out-of-5 code data system operating in the serial mode.

11

Incompletely Specified Sequential Machines

11.1 INTRODUCTION

The sequential machines discussed in Chapter 10 had an important property. Each present state of these machines had its next state and ouptut completely specified for every input. This is a very ideal situation and may not be met in all cases. There are many machines for which either the next state or the output or both may not be completely specified. Table 11.1.1 shows the state table of such a machine, called an *incompletely specified sequential machine* (ISSM).

The state minimization of such a machine poses special problems and becomes more complicated than the straightforward way that a completely specified machine can be minimized. This is because there is a significant and fundamental difference in the relation that exists between the various states of a completely specified and an incompletely specified machine. We have seen how an equivalence relation is defined between two states of a CSSM. Suppose that we also define an equivalence relation among the states of an ISSM as follows: Two states of an ISSM are equivalent if for each input the outputs are the same when both are specified, and also the next states are equivalent when both are specified. Applying this definition to states C and F of machine M_1, these will turn out to be equivalent. Again, states D and F are also equivalent. But states C and D cannot be equivalent, as their outputs are in conflict for the input I_2.

Some materials in this chapter are reproduced by permission of the Indian Academy of Sciences, Bangalore, India, from author's paper mentioned at Reference, Biswas (1989), from their publication, *Sādhanā, Academy Proceedings in Engineering Sciences*.

TABLE 11.1.1 M_1

Present state	Next state, output			
	I_1	I_2	I_3	I_4
A	H,1	E,0	—	–,0
B	B,0	—	F,–	C,–
C	F,–	H,1	C,–	—
D	—	C,0	—	E,–
E	B,0	—	G,1	C,–
F	C,0	—	C,0	–,1
G	—	D,1	–,0	A,1
H	–,0	C,0	G,–	–,0

Therefore, the transitive property, one of the requirements for the equivalence relation, does not hold good. Hence an equivalence relation cannot be defined in case of an ISSM. Instead, a compatibility relation is defined as follows.

11.2 THE COMPATIBILITY RELATION

Definition 11.2.1. Two states of an incompletely specified sequential machine are compatible if for each input, their outputs are the same when both are specified and also their next states are compatible when both are specified.

Note that *whereas the equivalence relation is transitive, the compatibility relation is not.* Consequently, if in a CSSM, state A is equivalent to state B and B is equivalent to C, then A is also equivalent to C, and all three states, A, B, and C, can be merged into a single state. On the other hand, in an ISSM, if state A is compatible to B, and B is compatible to C, then A is not necessarily compatible to C, and the three states A, B, and C can be merged into a single state if A is also separately compatible to C. Hence a compatible class that can be merged into a single state can be defined as follows.

Definition 11.2.2. Two or more states of an incompletely specified sequential machine form a *compatible class* (CC) if they are pairwise compatible. Two states compatible to each other form a compatible class known as a *compatible pair* (CP).

Definition 11.2.3. A compatible class that cannot be included in a larger compatible class is called a *maximum compatible class* (MCC). A single state that is not compatible with any other state also forms an MCC by itself.

11.3 COMPUTATION OF MAXIMUM COMPATIBLE CLASSES

An important step in the minimization of an ISSM is the determination of all the MCCs. We now describe an algorithm for the computation of MCCs. First the compatible pairs (CPs) are found by the compatible pair implication matrix (CPIM) in the same way as the equivalent pairs are found in a CSSM. The CPIM of machine M_1 is shown in Fig. 11.3.1. From this the CPs are AD, BC, BD, BE, BF, BH, CE, CF, CG, DE, DF, DH, EH, FG, and FH. The compatibility relations given by the set of CPs are now depicted in the form of an $n \times n$ matrix, where n is the number of states of the ISSM. The rows and columns of the matrix are the states of the machine. A 1(0) is written at the intersection of a row and column when the corresponding pair of states is compatible (incompatible). Table 11.3.1 shows the compatibility matrix CM_1, showing the compatibility relations between

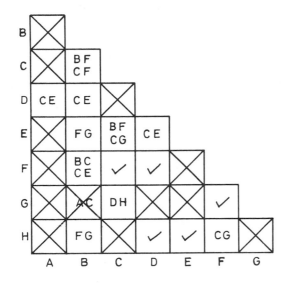

Figure 11.3.1 CPIM of machine M_1.

TABLE 11.3.1 CM_1

	A	B	C	D	E	F	G	H	α	CMCC
*A	1	0	0	1	0	0	0	0	2	AD
B	0	1	1	1	1	1	0	1	6	BCDEFH
C	0	1	1	0	1	1	1	0	5	BCEFG
D	1	1	0	1	1	1	0	1	6	ABDEFH
E	0	1	1	1	1	0	0	1	5	BCDEH
F	0	1	1	1	0	1	1	1	6	BCDFGH
G	0	0	1	0	0	1	1	0	3	CFG
H	0	1	0	1	1	1	0	1	5	BDEFH

all pairs as obtained from the implication matrix. Note that the compatibility matrix CM_1 is a symmetric matrix with an all-1 leading diagonal. This is so because each state is compatible with itself. In Table 11.3.1 two more columns are added to CM_1. One of these columns gives the number of 1's in a row, called the weight of the row.

Definition 11.3.1. The number of 1's in a row will be called its *weight*. It will be designated by α.

Again each row of the other additional column gives the collection of all states that are compatible with the state heading the row. Thus in Table 11.3.1 each of the states of *BCDEFH* is compatible with state *B*, and each of the states of *BCDEH* is compatible with the state *E*.

Definition 11.3.2. The collection of states that is compatible with a state will be called a *candidate maximum compatible class* (CMCC). The state with which each of the states of a CMCC is compatible will be called the *generating state* of the CMCC. The number of states in a CMCC will be called its *cardinality*.

Thus every state of the machine, that is, every row of the CM_1, generates a CMCC. It is also obvious that each MCC is either a CMCC itself or a subset of a CMCC. The algorithm finds all the MCCs of the ISSM from these CMCCs with the help of the following theorems and corollaries.

Theorem 11.3.1. A candidate maximum compatible class (CMCC) is a maximum compatible class (MCC) if and only if it is one of the least cardinality CMCC among all the CMCCs and all its constituent states are pairwise compatible.

Proof. IF (Sufficiency): If all the constituent states of a CMCC are pairwise compatible, the CMCC is an MCC if it is not contained in a larger MCC. Now, since the CMCC has the least cardinality, the generating state of the CMCC has all its compatible states included in the CMCC, and therefore there can be no MCC with greater cardinality that may contain the generating state within it. Therefore, the CMCC cannot be contained in another larger MCC. Hence the CMCC is an MCC.
ONLY IF (Necessity): It is obvious that the two conditions that are sufficient are also necessary to make a CMCC an MCC.   Q.E.D.

Note that all the elements of the compatibility matrix of an MCC are 1's.

Corollary 11.3.1A. A CMCC of cardinality 1 or 2 is an MCC.

The proof of this corollary is obvious.

Theorem 11.3.2. A CMCC with the least cardinality that is itself not an MCC will generate more than one MCC with the generating state as one of its members. Each MCC produces an all-1 matrix, and its columns (or rows) form a subset of the CMCC that is not contained in a larger subset.

Proof: The CMCC with the least cardinality fails to become an MCC only when one (or more) pair(s) in it is (or are) not compatible. Therefore, each of the subsets that produces an all-1 matrix has all its states pairwise compatible. Since the subset is not contained in a larger subset, it is an MCC. $\qquad$ Q.E.D.

Corollary 11.3.2A. If there are two and only two zeros in the subcompatibility matrix of a CMCC, then the CMCC produces two maximum compatible classes.

Proof: If the element a_{ij} of a subcompatibility matrix (SCM) is a 0, the element a_{ji} will also be 0, since the SCM is a symmetric matrix. Now, this pair of zeros can be eliminated from the SCM in two ways, by deleting either the row and column i or the row and column j. Hence the SCM will produce two all-1 submatrices and, therefore, two MCCs. $\qquad$ Q.E.D.

If the SCM of a CMCC has more than two zeros, then find all the MCCs by following the generalized procedure as applied to a CM.

Theorem 11.3.3. After all MCCs contained in a CMCC have been determined, the generating state of the CMCC can be deleted from the rest of the CMCCs.

Proof: A CMCC has *all* the states that are compatible with its generating state. Therefore, all MCCs having the generating state in it are determined from the CMCC, and there cannot be any other MCC that may have the generating state in it. Hence the theorem. $\qquad$ Q.E.D.

To apply Theorem 11.3.1 to CM_1 of Table 11.3.1, first the CMCC of the least cardinality is chosen. In this case it is the CMCC AD generated by state A of the ISSM and it has a cardinality of 2. By Corollary 11.3.1A, AD can be listed as an MCC without further processing. Once AD is selected as an MCC, the row and column of state A are deleted from CM_1 as a direct consequence of Theorem 11.3.3. This is how CM_2 (Table 11.3.2) is derived from CM_1.

TABLE 11.3.2 CM_2

	B	C	D	E	F	G	H	α	CMCC
B	1	1	1	1	1	0	1	6	
C	1	1	0	1	1	1	0	5	
D	1	0	1	1	1	0	1	5	
E	1	1	1	1	0	0	1	5	
F	1	1	1	0	1	1	1	6	
*G	0	1	0	0	1	1	0	3	CFG
H	1	0	1	1	1	0	1	5	

Note that while CM_1 was a matrix of order 8, CM_2 becomes a matrix of a reduced order, namely, 7. Again applying theorem 1 to CM_2, the CMCC CFG generated by the state G has the least cardinality. To check if the CMCC is an MCC, a submatrix with C, F, and G as rows and columns is derived from CM_2. This is called the *subcompatibility matrix* SCM_2 (CFG) and is shown in Table 11.3.2A. Obviously, all the states will be pairwise compatible if the submatrix is an all-1 matrix. It can be seen that the submatrix SCM_2 (CFG) is an all-1 matrix, as all the row weights are 3. Hence, by Theorem 11.3.1, CFG is an MCC. After CFG is selected as an MCC, state G is deleted from the rows and columns of CM_2, and CM_3 as shown in Table 11.3.3 is obtained.

In this table the CMCC generated by state C has the least cardinality of 4. The submatrix SCM_3 (*BCEF*) as shown in Table 11.3.3A is now derived. The row weights of the SCM are not 4 in all rows. It has two rows E and F having

TABLE 11.3.2A SCM$_2$ (*CFG*)

	B	C	G	α
C	1	1	1	3
F	1	1	1	3
G	1	1	1	3

TABLE 11.3.3 CM$_3$

	B	C	D	E	F	H	α	CMCC
B	1	1	1	1	1	1	6	
*C	1	1	0	1	1	0	4	BCEF
D	1	0	1	1	1	1	5	
E	1	1	1	1	0	1	5	
F	1	1	1	0	1	1	5	
H	1	0	1	1	1	1	5	

TABLE 11.3.3A SCM$_3$ (*BCEF*)

	B	C	E	F	α
B	1	1	1	1	4
C	1	1	1	1	4
E	1	1	1	0	3
F	1	1	0	1	3

BCE
BCF

weights 3. It can easily be seen that the submatrix of the SCM, SCM_3 (BCE), will be an all-1 matrix, as the row and column F having the 0 will be absent. Similarly, the SCM_3 (BCF) will also be an all-1 matrix, as the row and column E having the 0 will be absent. Hence, by Theorem 11.3.2, BCE and BCF are MCCs. After deleting state C from CM_3, CM_4 is derived (Table 11.3.4). Here two rows E and F have the least cardinality of 4. Hence the SCM_4 ($BDEH$) and SCM_4 ($BDFH$) shown in Tables 11.3.4A and 11.3.4B are derived. Both these turn out to be all-1 matrices and therefore produce the MCCs $BDEH$ and $BDFH$. Before deriving CM_5 from CM_4, the number of rows of CM_5 should be calculated. Here it is 3. Therefore, if CM_5 produces any MCC, its cardinality must be less than those computed from CM_4. But all such MCCs must already have been determined. Hence there is no need to derive or process CM_5. The procedure terminates here. All the MCCs of the machine are AD, CFG, BCE, BCF, $BDEH$, and $BDFH$. It should be evident now that before the algorithm derives a CM_{k+1} from CM_k, it must check if the number of remaining rows of CM_k is less than the cardinality

TABLE 11.3.4 CM_4

	B	D	E	F	H	α	CMCC
B	1	1	1	1	1	5	
D	1	1	1	1	1	5	
*E	1	1	1	0	1	4	BDEH
*F	1	1	0	1	1	4	BDFH
H	1	1	1	1	1	5	

TABLE 11.3.4A SCM_4 ($BDEH$)

	B	D	E	H	α
B	1	1	1	1	4
D	1	1	1	1	4
E	1	1	1	1	4
H	1	1	1	1	4

$BDEH$

TABLE 11.3.4B SCM_4 ($BDFH$)

	B	D	F	H	α
B	1	1	1	1	4
D	1	1	1	1	4
F	1	1	1	1	4
H	1	1	1	1	4

$BDFH$

of the MCC found in CM_k. If yes, the program produces a "stop derivation" signal that ends the procedure.

It is evident from the foregoing description of the algorithm that to determine all the MCCs, the number of compatibility matrices (CMs) that need to be derived from the previous matrices starting from CM_1 will not exceed the largest cardinality among the MCCs, and the number of all-1 submatrices to be derived and processed will not exceed the total number of MCCs. The processing of matrices also does not involve expensive matrix operations such as multiplication or inversion. For these reasons the algorithm becomes must faster than existing ones, especially for large and very large incompletely specified sequential machines.

11.4 MINIMUM CLOSED COVER

The MCCs tell us which states can be merged to produce a reduced machine to cover the original machine. The goal of state minimization is to find a reduced machine having the minimum number of states. At first sight it may appear that the minimum number of MCCs that cover all states of the machine will be the desired solution. Let us explore this possibility. For machine M_1 the MCCs are *AD, CFG, BCE, BCF, BDEH*, and *BDFH*. As there are only six MCCs, it can be found by observation that the three MCCs, *AD, CFG*, and *BDEH*, constitute the minimum number of MCCs that cover all eight states of the machine. Now it can be seen from the state table or the CPIM that if A and D are merged, states C and E must also be merged as CE is the implied compatible for AD. But in the three MCCS *AD, CFG*, and *BDEH*, there is no MCC that includes *CE*. So it will not be possible to form the reduced state table by merging *AD, CFG*, and *BDEH*. Thus *the minimum cover has to satisfy an additional property: It must also include all the implied compatibles of all the compatible classes of the solution.* This property is known as the *closure property*. The minimum cover satisfying the closure property is called a *minimum closed cover*.

It should be mentioned here that the CCs in the solution are not necessarily the MCCs. Some of them may be, and quite often are, subsets of MCCs. In fact, for machine M_1, the minimum closed cover consists of four CCs: *CFG, DH, BE*, and *A*. It is interesting to note that among the four CCs of the solution only *CFG* is an MCC. The solution also has a single state as one of the CCs. The four-state reduced machine that covers machine M_1 can be derived to be as given in Table 11.4.1.

TABLE 11.4.1 REDUCED MACHINE FOR M_1

Present state	Next state, output			
	I_1	I_2	I_3	I_4
$A \quad \rightarrow 1{:}1$	4,1	2,0	—	–,0
$BE \rightarrow 2{:}2$	2,0	—	3,1	3,–
$CFG \rightarrow 3{:}3$	3,0	4,1	3,0	1,1
$DH \rightarrow 4{:}4$	–,0	3,0	3,–	2,0

11.5 THE BREIT ALGORITHM

As a consequence of very large scale integration (VLSI), not only many hardware but also many software systems are now being designed as a collection of finite-state sequential machines. Such machines are invariably incompletely specified and have a very large number of internal states. In order that these machines can be implemented on area-efficient VLSI chips, it is imperative that these ISSMs be reduced to the maximum extent possible. Although there exist many good and efficient algorithms for the state minimization, they are suitable for small and medium-sized machines. We may tentatively define the size of a SM to be small, medium, and large if the number of its internal states is between 2 and 10, 11 and 15, and more than 15, respectively. The BREIT (*b*unch and *re*duce *i*mplication *t*rees) algorithm has proved suitable for small as well as large ISSMs. Let the algorithm be described by considering the nine-state four-input machine of Kella (1970), shown in Table 11.5.1 (machine M_2). The CPIM of the machine is shown in Fig. 11.5.1.

The computations of MCCs of this machine are shown in Tables 11.5.2 to Table 11.5.4C. The six MCCs are *ABDHI, ABCF, ABCH, BCEH, BCFG,* and *BDEH.* It was shown in the preceding section that the set of compatible classes (CCs) that form the states of the reduced machine should not only be a minimum cover, but also satisfy the closure property; that is, all the implied CCs should also be included in the set. Such a set is the end result of the minimization algorithm and is called a *minimum closed cover.* A closed cover can be represented by an *implication tree* (IT), which may be drawn as follows. Consider the MCC *ABDHI* as the root node of an implication tree. From the state table it can be seen that *ABDHI* implies the CCs *FG, BC,* and *AD* for the inputs I_1, I_2, and I_4, respectively. But *AD* is included in *ABDHI.* Hence the two CCs, *FG* and *BC,* must be in the closed cover, and therefore form two successor nodes of the node

TABLE 11.5.1 STATE TABLE OF KELLA'S MACHINE M_2

Present state	Next state, output			
	I_1	I_2	I_3	I_4
A	G,1	—	–,0	—
B	—	B,–	E,–	—
C	—	–,1	H,–	E,–
D	—	–,0	—	A,1
E	G,0	E,–	B,1	—
F	—	I,–	—	B,0
G	D,–	D,–	–,0	E,–
H	—	C,–	—	D,1
I	F,1	C,0	–,0	—

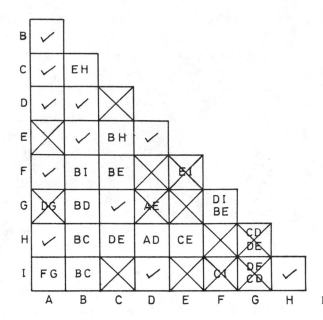

Figure 11.5.1 CPIM of machine M_2.

TABLE 11.5.2 CM₁

	A	B	C	D	E	F	G	H	I	α	CMCC
A	1	1	1	1	0	1	0	1	1	7	ABCDFHI
B	1	1	1	1	1	1	1	1	1	9	ABCDEFGHI
C	1	1	1	0	1	1	1	1	0	7	ABCEFGH
D	1	1	0	1	1	0	0	1	1	6	ABDEHI
E	0	1	1	1	1	0	0	1	0	5	BCDEH
F	1	1	1	0	0	1	1	0	0	5	ABCFG
*G	0	1	1	0	0	1	1	0	0	4	BCFG
H	1	1	1	1	1	0	0	1	1	7	ABCDEHI
I	1	1	0	1	0	0	0	1	1	5	ABDHI

TABLE 11.5.2A SCM₁ (*BCFG*)

	B	C	F	G	α
B	1	1	1	1	4
C	1	1	1	1	4
F	1	1	1	1	4
G	1	1	1	1	4
		BCFG			

TABLE 11.5.3 CM$_2$

	A	B	C	D	E	F	H	I	α	CMCC
A	1	1	1	1	0	1	1	1	7	
B	1	1	1	1	1	1	1	1	8	
C	1	1	1	0	1	1	1	0	6	
D	1	1	0	1	1	0	1	1	6	
E	0	1	1	1	1	0	1	0	5	
*F	1	1	1	0	0	1	0	0	4	ABCF
H	1	1	1	1	1	0	1	1	7	
I	1	1	0	1	0	0	1	1	5	

TABLE 11.5.3A SCM$_2$ (ABCF)

	A	B	C	F	α
A	1	1	1	1	4
B	1	1	1	1	4
C	1	1	1	1	4
F	1	1	1	1	4

ABCF

TABLE 11.5.4 CM$_3$

	A	B	C	D	E	H	I	α	CMCC
A	1	1	1	1	0	1	1	6	
B	1	1	1	1	1	1	1	7	
*C	1	1	1	0	1	1	0	5	ABCEH
D	1	1	0	1	1	1	1	6	
*E	0	1	1	1	1	1	0	5	BCDEH
H	1	1	1	1	1	1	1	7	
*I	1	1	0	1	0	1	1	5	ABDHI

ABDHI. Following the same procedure, the entire IT for the root node of *ABDHI* is constructed [Fig. 11.5.2(a)]. A node is terminated to node 0 (zero) whenever either it does not imply any CC, or the implied CC has already appeared in the IT. The IT of Fig. 11.5.2(a) has all the states of the ISSM in it. Quite often it may not be so. In such a situation the missing states are provided as single nodes in a separate branch [see Fig. 11.5.3(a)]. After an IT has been constructed, it gives a closed cover of the given ISSM. The next procedure reduces the number

TABLE 11.5.4A SCM_3 $(ABCEH)$

	A	B	C	E	H	α
A	1	1	1	0	1	4
B	1	1	1	1	1	5
C	1	1	1	1	1	5
E	0	1	1	1	1	4
H	1	1	1	1	1	5

ABCH
BCEH

TABLE 11.5.4B SCM_3 $(BDEH)$

	B	D	E	H	α
B	1	1	1	1	4
D	1	1	1	1	4
E	1	1	1	1	4
H	1	1	1	1	4

BDEH

TABLE 11.5.4C SCM_3 $(ABDHI)$

	A	B	D	H	I	α
A	1	1	1	1	1	5
B	1	1	1	1	1	5
D	1	1	1	1	1	5
H	1	1	1	1	1	5
I	1	1	1	1	1	5

ABDHI

of nodes, by bunching one or more nodes according to the following theorem, proof of which is obvious.

Theorem 11.5.1 Bunching Theorem. Two nodes N_i and N_j of an implication tree (IT) can be bunched into a single node N_s, given by $N_s = N_i \cup N_j$ and called a *compatible bunch* (CB) if the following two conditions are satisfied:
(a) $N_s \subseteq$ any MCC.
(b) Implied CCs of $N_s \subseteq$ IT.

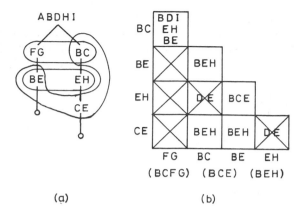

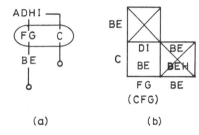

ABDHI

(a)

(b)

Figure 11.5.2 (a) Implication tree of *ABDHI*; (b) CBIM of the IT.

(a)

(b)

Figure 11.5.3 (a) Implication tree of *ADHI*; (b) CBIM of the DIT.

Definition 11.5.1. Two or more nodes of an IT form a *maximum compatible bunch* (MCB) when all nodes of the MCB are pairwise compatible and the MCB cannot be enlarged further by adding one more node to it.

To determine the MCBs a *compatible bunch implication matrix* (CBIM) similar to the *compatible pair implication matrix* (CPIM) is drawn, with each node of the IT as rows and columns. For the IT of Fig. 11.5.2(a), the relevant part of the CBIM is shown in Fig. 11.5.2(b). Each column is now compared with each row, to determine if a node N_i of row i will bunch with node N_j of row j. First compare column 1 with row 1, then row 2, and so on. *FG* and *BC* may be bunched as (*FG* $\cup$ *BC*), or *BCFG* is an MCC, provided that the implied CCs of *BCFG* are in the IT. As can be determined from the state table, the implied CCs of *BCFG* are *BDI, EH,* and *BE*. These are then written in the cell of *BC* and *FG*. The nodes *FG* and *BE* cannot be bunched as (*FG* $\cup$ *BE*), or *BEFG* is not in any MCC. Hence an $\times$ is placed in the column of *FG* and row of *BE*. In this way each cell is either crossed out or shows the implied CCs. Figure 11.5.2(b) shows the bunching requirement of the nodes of IT of Fig. 11.5.2(a). If an implied CC is already in the IT or may appear in the IT due to bunching, then the cell representing the pair of nodes can be bunched. For example, among the implied CCs of *FG* and *BC, BDI* is in *ABDHI*; *EH* and *BE* are already in the IT. Hence *FG* and *BC* can be bunched. On the other hand, the implied CC of *BC* and *EH,* namely *DE,* is neither in the IT nor will it appear. Hence this cell is crossed out.

BC and *BE* bunch into *BCE* as *BEH* may appear when *BE* and *EH* bunch. Similarly, *BE* and *EH* also bunch, due to the appearance of *BCE*. From the CBIM, MCBs are found in the same way as MCCs are found from the CPIM. The compatible bunches (CBs) of Fig. 11.5.2(b) produce the MCBs *BCFG*, *BCE*, and *BEH*. So the completely reduced tree has four nodes, as shown in Fig. 11.5.2(a). This *reduced IT* (RIT) therefore produces a four-state solution given by the closed cover *ABDHI*, *BCFG*, *BCE*, and *BEH*. However, this is not the minimum closed cover. Now, the search for an RIT giving the minimum closed cover starts with a heuristic procedure that has the following steps.

1. Take one MCC of the highest cardinality. Determine from the state table the set of implied compatibles for all the inputs. Let this be $\{C_1, C_2, \ldots, C_m\}$, and let this set be called the *implied compatible set* (ICS). An MCC with null ICS is not considered.

2. Compute the difference set DS given by

$$DS = MCC \sim \{C_1 \cup C_2 \cup \cdots \cup C_m\}$$

3. Repeat it for all the MCCs having the highest cardinality.

4. Select the DSs with the highest cardinality. Take one of these DSs. Construct the implication tree. During the construction, if at any time an implied compatible that is not disjoint with the root node is obtained, abandon this tree, go to another DS and construct the IT. Repeat this procedure until an IT with all its implied compatibles disjoint with the root node is obtained. Such a tree will be called a *distinguished implication tree* (DIT).

5. If no MCC of the highest cardinality can generate a DIT, steps 1 to 4 are repeated with MCCs of the next highest cardinality.

Definition 11.5.2. An implication tree whose all other nodes are disjoint with the root node is called a *distinguished implication tree* (DIT).

For Kella's machine, the highest cardinality MCC is *ABDHI*:

$$\text{ICS of } ABDHI = \{FG, BC\}$$

$$DS = ADHI \quad \text{and} \quad |DS| = 4$$

As *ABDHI* is the only MCC with the highest cardinality 6, *ADHI* is selected as a root node. From *ADHI*, the IT is shown in Fig. 11.5.3(a). Its two implied compatibles *FG* and *BE* are disjoint with *ADHI*. Hence it is a DIT. Its bunching is shown in the CBIM of Fig. 11.5.3(b). After the bunching is carried out, the RIT of *ADHI* generates a three state closed cover, *ADHI*, *CFG*, and *BE*. This is also the minimum closed cover. The same solution has been obtained by Kella (1970) after going through several elaborate procedures. As the procedure is heuristic, another DIT is obtained from the remaining DSs. Preference is given to a DS with the largest cardinality. In case of Kella's machine the DIT produced by the root node *CFG* (obtained from the MCC *BCFG*) produces the same three-state solution. If the second DIT produces a solution with smaller number of states, then obviously that solution will be taken. For Kella's machine the second DIT is obtained from the root node *ACF* derived from the MCC *ABCF*. This DIT yields a four-state solution with *ACF*, *BDE*, *G*, and *HI*. Hence the three-state solution obtained from the first DIT is taken as the minimal solution.

For ISSMs with a large number of states, the solution obtained by processing only two DITs may not always be absolutely minimum but will be very nearly minimum. However, such a solution may be acceptable, as processing all the DITs to obtain the absolutely minimum solution may be very expensive. For example, for a 50-state ISSM having a 20-state minimum solution, we may obtain a 21- or 22-state solution by processing only two DITs. This solution may be quite good for practical implementation purposes. For small and medium-sized ISSMs, on the other hand, it may be advisable to process all the DITs and obtain the absolutely minimum solution. For example, for a 12-state machine having a 4-state minimum solution, it is desirable to obtain this solution by processing all the DITs, whose number in such cases may not be very high.

REFERENCES

BENNETS, R. G., J. L. WASHINGTON, AND D. W. LEWIN. A computer algorithm for state table reductions, *IERE Radio and Electron. Eng.*, Vol. 42, pp. 513–520, November, 1972.

BISWAS, N. N. State minimization of incompletely specified sequential machines, *IEEE Trans. Comput.*, Vol. C-23, pp. 80–84, January, 1974.

BISWAS, N. N. Maximum compatibility classes from compatibility matrices, *Sādhanā*, Vol. 14, Pt. 3, pp. 213–218, December, 1989.

GRASSELLI, A., AND F. LUCCIO. A method for minimizing the number of internal states in incompletely specified sequential networks, *IEEE Trans. Electron. Comput.*, Vol. EC-14, pp. 350–359, June, 1965.

HOUSE, R. W., AND D. W. STEVENS. A new rule for reducing the CC tables, *IEEE Trans. Comput.*, Vol. C-19, pp. 1108–1111, November, 1970.

KELLA, J. State minimization of incompletely specified sequential machines, *IEEE Trans. Comput.*, Vol. C-19, pp. 342–348, April, 1970.

MEISEL, W. S. A note on internal state minimization in incompletely specified sequential networks, *IEEE Trans. Electron. Comput.*, Vol. EC-16, pp. 508–509, August, 1967.

PAULL, M. C., AND S. H. UNGER. Minimizing the number of states in incompletely specified sequential switching functions, *IRE Trans. Electron. Comput.*, Vol. EC-8, September, 1959, pp. 356–357.

RAO, C. V. S., AND N. N. BISWAS. Minimization of incompletely specified sequential machines, *IEEE Trans. Comput.*, Vol. C-24, pp. 1089–1100, November, 1975.

YANG, C. C. Closure partition method for minimizing incomplete sequential machines, *IEEE Trans. Comput.*, Vol. C-22, pp. 1109–1112, December, 1973.

PROBLEMS

11.1. Minimize the following state tables. Give all solutions.

<table>
<tr><td colspan="2" style="text-align:center">(a)</td><td colspan="2" style="text-align:center">(b)</td></tr>
</table>

(a)

Present state	Next state, z 0	1
A	E,1	F,–
B	D,0	—
C	A,–	E,1
D	F,1	E,0
E	C,–	A,1
F	B,0	D,–

(b)

Present state	Next state, z 0	1
A	F,0	C,0
B	A,–	D,0
C	B,0	A,–
D	F,–	—
E	–,1	D,–
F	C,–	G,0
G	B,–	–,1

11.2. Minimize the state table of the following ISSM. Bunch and reduce all the distinguished implication trees and find all the solutions if there are more than one.

Present state	Next state, z x_1x_2 00	01	11	10
A	—	C,0	B,0	D,1
B	—	F,1	A,1	E,1
C	F,0	—	E,0	F,1
D	—	—	E,1	—
E	A,0	—	—	—
F	C,0	C,1	—	—

11.3. Minimize the following state table. Is the solution unique? Give the reduced state table.

Present state	Next state, z x_1x_2 00	01	11	10
A	D,0	—	F,1	B,–
B	E,–	C,1	B,–	—
C	—	B,0	–,1	A,0
D	D,0	—	E,–	B,1
E	B,0	—	B,0	—
F	—	C,1	–,0	C,1

11.4. Justify the validity or otherwise of the following statement. If a state q_0 appears only in one MCC M_0, the MCC M_0 is an essential MCC and must be one of the

CCs of the solution. (*Hint:* Study carefully the MCCs and the solution CCs of Problems 11.2 and 11.3.)

11.5. Find a minimum closed cover of the eight-state ISSM of Meisel (1967), whose state table is given below.

Present state	\multicolumn{7}{c}{Next state, output}

Present state	1	2	3	4	5	6	7
a	a,0	—	d,0	e,1	b,0	a,-	—
b	b,0	d,1	a,-	—	a,-	a,-	—
c	b,0	d,1	a,1	—	—	—	g,0
d	—	e,-	—	b,-	b,0	—	a,-
e	b,-	e,-	a,-	—	b,-	e,-	a,1
f	b,0	c,-	-,1	h,1	f,1	g,0	—
g	—	c,1	—	e,1	—	g,0	f,0
h	a,1	e,0	d,1	b,0	b,-	e,-	a,1

11.6. Determine a minimum-state reduced machine that covers the eight-state machine of Rao and Biswas (1975) as given below.

Present state	\multicolumn{4}{c}{Next state, output}

Present state	00	01	11	10
a	—	g,0	e,1	d,-
b	a,-	d,-	—	-,0
c	c,-	-,0	—	g,1
d	e,0	—	a,-	—
e	-,1	f,-	-,1	-,1
f	-,1	e,-	a,1	-,1
g	f,-	-,1	b,-	h,-
h	c,-	—	a,0	—

The next-state/output column header for 11.6 is labeled $x_1 x_2$.

11.7. Is the following statement true? If "Yes," prove it as a theorem, else give a counterexample: For every ISSM, there always exists one minimum closed cover containing at least one MCC.

11.8. The MCCs and their implied compatible classes of a nine-state machine are given in the table below. Find a minimum closed cover of the machine. Show that you have obtained a minimum solution. Is the information contained in such a table always sufficient to yield a minimum-state solution? Justify your answer.

MCC	(3,6,7)(3,6,8)(3,5,8)(1,5,8)(6,9)(5,9)(4,5)(4,6)(2,4)(2,9)
ICS	(1,8) (4,6) (6,7) (1,5)(1,5)
	(2,9)

11.9. Justify the validity or otherwise of the following statements.
  (a) The number of MCCs is always less than the number of states.
  (b) A single state cannot be an MCC.
  (c) If the root node of an implication tree is an MCC having no implied compatible, the implication tree always produces the minimum closed cover.

11.10. Complete the state minimization of the state table of machine M_1 as given in Table 11.1.1.

11.11. The 30 MCCs of the 22-state machine of House and Stevens (1970) are as follows:

(1,2,3,4,5,7) (1,2,4,5,7,10) (1,3,5,7,21) (1,4,5,6,7,15) (1,5,6,7,9) (1,5,7,9,10)
(2,5,7,8,10,22) (3,4,12,13) (3,4,13,17) (3,11,12,13) (4,5,14,15) (4,10,12,13)
(4,10,13,17) (4,12,13,14,16) (4,13,14,15,16,17) (5,6,7,8,9) (5,6,7,8,15)
(5,7,8,9,10) (5,9,14) (5,15,18) (8,9,10,11,12,13) (8,9,11,12,13,16)
(8,10,13,17) (8,13,15,16,17) (9,12,13,14,16) (10,13,17,19) (11,12,13,16,18)
(12,13,16,20) (13,15,16,17,18) (13,16,17,19)

The machine has a nine-state solution. Construct a bunched implication tree showing one nine-state solution.

	X1	X2	X3	X4		X1	X2	X3	X4
1	1,–	2,1	–,0	8,1	12	1,1	2,0	–,–	–,–
2	–,–	3,1	5,0	9,–	13	–,–	3,0	–,–	–,–
3	–,–	4,–	6,0	10,1	14	–,–	–,–	13,1	18,1
4	–,–	–,–	–,–	11,1	15	7,0	–,–	12,–	–,–
5	1,–	–,1	–,–	–,–	16	7,–	2,0	–,1	–,–
6	1,–	3,1	12,0	–,–	17	1,0	3,0	–,–	–,–
7	–,–	4,1	–,0	–,–	18	1,–	4,–	–,1	19,–
8	–,–	2,–	–,–	14,1	19	–,0	–,0	5,–	20,1
9	7,1	–,–	–,–	15,1	20	–,1	–,0	5,–	21,1
10	7,–	–,–	6,0	16,1	21	–,1	–,1	5,–	22,1
11	1,1	4,0	5,–	17,1	22	–,0	–,1	5,–	14,1

11.12. In a six-state ($A,B,\ldots,F$) ISSM, the candidate maximum compatibles of the six states are $ABDF$, $ABCEF$, $BCDE$, $ACDE$, $BCDEF$, and $ABEF$, respectively. Find all the MCCs. Is the information supplied sufficient to compute all the MCCs?

11.13. In a 10-state ($A,B,\ldots,J$) ISSM, the compatible pairs are AJ, BH, BJ, CE, CF, CG, CJ, DE, DF, DH, DJ, EH, DJ, EH, EI, EJ, FH, FI, FJ, HI, HJ, and IJ. Find all the MCCs. Is the information supplied sufficient to compute all the MCCs?

12

Fundamental-Mode Sequential Machines

12.1 INTRODUCTION

The state table of a sequential machine tells us the next state into which a present state should change in response to a change in input. It does not, however, indicate when this change of state should take place. In the sequential machines discussed in Chapter 10, the timing of the change of state is controlled by the clock pulses. In other words, all transition of state is synchronized with the clock pulses. For this reason the clock pulses are also known as *synchronizing* pulses and the machines as *synchronous* sequential machines. In such machines all state transitions take place after a definite time interval. For many applications this feature is very desirable, and as we shall see shortly, this also makes the synthesis of a sequential circuit much easier. However, there are many applications where this timing restriction may prove detrimental and therefore undesirable. In such situations, sequential machines are not provided with clock pulses, and the various circuit elements are allowed to respond immediately to a change in the input or in the associated circuits. It can easily be seen that in such a circuit the change of input will trigger a chain of changes and may therefore have its effect on the entire circuit for quite some time. Such a circuit therefore cannot function properly until it is so arranged that an input should not change until all changes in the circuit have taken place, or in other words, until the entire circuit comes to a "stable" state. Such an operation is known as *fundamental-mode operation*.

A sequential machine operating in the fundamental mode therefore has the following characteristics.

1. No clock pulses.
2. No change in input occurs until the machine undergoes the entire chain of changes and no further change can take place.
3. In machines having more than one input, two or more inputs cannot change simultaneously. For example, for a machine with two inputs x_1 and x_2, the two inputs cannot change from 00 to 11 or from 01 to 10. The third characteristic follows from the fact that in an actual circuit, due to differential path delays, two inputs x_1 and x_2 may not be able to change from 0 to 1 in *exactly* the same time. Suppose that x_1 changes a little earlier than x_2. Then the transition from 00 to 11 of x_1x_2 will be seen by the circuit of the machine to be a transition first from 00 to 10 and then from 10 to 11 in quick succession. Obviously, the machine may not get enough time to go through the entire chain of changes warranted by the transition from 00 to 10. Therefore, the restriction imposed by the characteristic 2 implies the acceptance of restriction 3 as well.

12.2 STABLE AND UNSTABLE STATES

In a sequential circuit operating in the fundamental mode, whenever an input changes, the circuit is allowed sufficient time to undergo the entire chain of changes that would be necessitated by the present input of the machine. This condition brings about the concept of stable states in the state table of a fundamental-mode machine. Let these be discussed with reference to the state stable of machine M_1 as shown in Table 12.2.1. As we can see, if the present state of the machine is A and the input is 00, the next state is also A, and therefore the machine does not change state and remains in this state until a change in the input occurs. Therefore, state A is a stable state of the machine and has been shown by circling the state in the state table. On the other hand, if the machine were in the present state A and the input becomes 01, it goes to state E as required

TABLE 12.2.1 STATE TABLE OF MACHINE M_1

Present state	Next state, output x_1x_2			
	00	01	11	10
A	$\textcircled{A}$,0	E,0	B,0	D,1
B	E,1	$\textcircled{B}$,1	D,1	E,1
C	D,0	D,1	E,1	$\textcircled{C}$,0
D	A,0	$\textcircled{D}$,0	$\textcircled{D}$,0	E,0
E	$\textcircled{E}$,1	C,1	A,0	C,0

by the first row of the table. After a while this next state E becomes the present state and since the input is 01, the machine goes to the next state C, as is required by the last row of the state table. Then C becomes the present state and the machine goes to the next state, D. With D as the present state and 01 as input, the next state is also D and therefore the machine does not change state any further. Hence it can be seen that from the initial state A the machine transits from state A to state E, and then to C, and then to D, and these have been shown in Fig. 12.2.1 by the arrows. Such a diagram, which depicts the transition of the machine among all its states, is known as the *transition diagram* of the sequential machine. Now we can define the stable and unstable states in the following way.

Definition 12.2.1. In a fundamental-mode sequential machine, if for a particular input the machine is in such a state that it does not go to any other state but remains in that state until the input changes, then the state is known as a *stable state*. On the other hand, the state in which the machine remains for a short while before going to another state for the same input combination is an *unstable state*.

It will now be apparent that all stable states are those where the next state is equal to the present state in the state table. In Table 12.2.1 such states have been shown by circling. It can be seen that for the input combination 00, that is, in column 1 of the state table, there are two stable states, A and E. For the input combination 01, that is column 2, there are two stable states, B and D. Similarly, the input combinations 11 and 10 have one stable state each, D and C, respectively.

Let us now describe the procedure for formation of a minimum-row state table of a sequential machine operating in the fundamental mode. For this, consider a machine that has two input lines, x_1 and x_2, and one output line, z. The output z is 0 whenever x_1 is 0. While x_1 is 1, the output becomes 1 only when x_2 changes its value, and remains 1 until x_1 returns to 0.

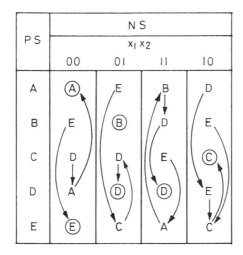

Figure 12.2.1 Transition diagram of machine M_1.

It is apparent from the word description of the machine that it has a level output. So from our experience of forming state tables of the clock-mode machines that we discussed in Chapter 10, it may appear that the machine should be designed as a Moore machine. However, we shall soon see that in the fundamental-mode operation, even a Mealy model can produce a level output. In fact, since there is no clock pulse in this mode, the concept of pulse is absent, and all the outputs and the inputs are level in nature, as they do not act for a particular period of time but may work for a prolonged period. The only restriction is that the input signal must not act for such a short time that the various elements in the circuit will not get enough time to operate and go to a stable state. So keeping the Mealy model in view, the primitive state table of machine M_2 can be derived as shown in Table 12.2.2. Here also, we observe the bits that are stored in the memory of the machine for a definite state and go on building the state table, adding a new state wherever necessary. In the state table, however, there is a significant difference from those we discussed in Chapter 10. For example, we find that in the primitive state table there are many places where both the next state and the output of the machine have remained unspecified. This is because of the restriction that in the input only one bit can change at a time. For example, take state A. It is remembering the input combination 00. Hence the machine has gone to this state when the input combination was 00. Therefore, the input combination cannot change to 11. Hence for the row having A as the present state, the next state and the output of the machine under column 11 remain

TABLE 12.2.2 PRIMITIVE STATE TABLE FOR MACHINE M_2

Present state	x_1: x_2:	Next state, z		
	x_1: 0 x_2: 0	0 1	1 1	1 0
$A\begin{pmatrix}0\\0\end{pmatrix}$	$A\begin{pmatrix}0\\0\end{pmatrix},0$	$B\begin{pmatrix}0\\1\end{pmatrix},0$	—	$C\begin{pmatrix}1\\0\end{pmatrix},0$
$B\begin{pmatrix}0\\1\end{pmatrix}$	$A\begin{pmatrix}0\\0\end{pmatrix},0$	$B\begin{pmatrix}0\\1\end{pmatrix},0$	$D\begin{pmatrix}1\\1\end{pmatrix},0$	—
$C\begin{pmatrix}1\\0\end{pmatrix}$	$A\begin{pmatrix}0\\0\end{pmatrix},0$	—	$E\begin{pmatrix}1\\1\end{pmatrix},1$	$C\begin{pmatrix}1\\0\end{pmatrix},0$
$D\begin{pmatrix}1\\1\end{pmatrix}$	—	$B\begin{pmatrix}0\\1\end{pmatrix},0$	$D\begin{pmatrix}1\\1\end{pmatrix},0$	$F\begin{pmatrix}1\\0\end{pmatrix},1$
$E\begin{pmatrix}1\\1\end{pmatrix}$	—	$B\begin{pmatrix}0\\1\end{pmatrix},0$	$E\begin{pmatrix}1\\1\end{pmatrix},1$	$F\begin{pmatrix}1\\0\end{pmatrix},1$
$F\begin{pmatrix}1\\0\end{pmatrix}$	$A\begin{pmatrix}0\\0\end{pmatrix},0$	—	$E\begin{pmatrix}1\\1\end{pmatrix},1$	$F\begin{pmatrix}1\\0\end{pmatrix},1$

unspecified. This happens for several combinations of the memory, since for every input combination there is a combination that cannot be reached by changing only one bit. In all such cases the state table has an unspecified entry. This renders the state table to be that of an incompletely specified sequential machine. The next step is minimization of the primitive state table. For this purpose we carry out two modifications. First, we circle all those next states that are the same as their present states. Obviously, these are the stable states of the machine. All other states are the unstable states. In the second modification, we make the output of all the unstable states unspecified. This is so done as the machine remains in an unstable state for a very short time, and therefore, its output is not of any real consequence for proper functioning of the machine. It is the output of the stable state that matters. Therefore, if the outputs of the unstable states, whose number is usually larger than those of the stable states, are unspecified, the possibility of getting a highly reduced machine increases. However, we shall see in the next section that the assumption that the output of an unstable state does not matter is not true unless some shortcomings on the part of the functioning of the machine can be accepted. However, it is possible to overcome these shortcomings by specifying appropriate outputs to the unstable states once again after the machine has been minimized. Hence, for the purpose of state minimization, it is desirable to make all the outputs of the unstable states unspecified. Following these modifications, the state table of Table 12.2.2 becomes as shown in Table 12.2.3. The next step is to compute the MCCs of this machine. For this, first the compatible pair implication matrix (CPIM) of the machine is determined (Fig. 12.2.2) and then the compatibility matrices. This has been done in Table 12.2.4, where two compatibility matrices reveal that there are four MCCs: AB, AC, BD, and EF. It can now be seen from the state table that none of these MCCs has implied compatibles. Therefore, the lower bound of the MCCs is the minimum closed cover, and the solution is AC, BD, and EF. Thus the state table reduces to a three-row state table as shown in Table 12.2.5. In this table, outputs of all the unstable states have been made unspecified.

TABLE 12.2.3 STATE TABLE OF
MACHINE M_2

| Present state | Next state, z | | | |
| | $x_1 x_2$ | | | |
	00	01	11	10
A	Ⓐ,0	B,–	—	C,–
B	A,–	B,0	D,–	—
C	A,–	—	E,–	Ⓒ,–
D	—	B,–	Ⓓ,0	F,–
E	—	B,–	Ⓔ,1	F,–
F	A,–	—	E,–	Ⓕ,1

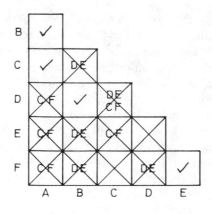

Figure 12.2.2 Compatible pair implication matrix (CPIM) of machine M_2.

TABLE 12.2.4   COMPATIBILITY MATRICES OF M_2

CM_1

	A	B	C	D	E	F	α	CMCC
A	1	1	1	0	0	0	3	ABC
B	1	1	0	1	0	0	3	ABD
$*C$	1	0	1	0	0	0	2	AC
$*D$	0	1	0	1	0	0	2	BD
$*E$	0	0	0	0	1	1	2	EF
$*F$	0	0	0	0	1	1	2	EF

AC, BD, EF

CM_2

	A	B	α	CMCC
$*A$	1	1	2	AB
$*B$	1	1	2	AB

TABLE 12.2.5   REDUCED STATE TABLE OF MACHINE M_2

Present state		Next state, z			
		$x_1 x_2$			
		00	01	11	10
AC	a	$\textcircled{a}$,0	b,–	c,–	$\textcircled{a}$,0
BD	b	a,–	$\textcircled{b}$,0	$\textcircled{b}$,0	c,–
EF	c	a,–	b,–	$\textcircled{c}$,1	$\textcircled{c}$,1

12.3 OUTPUT SPECIFICATIONS

Let us now investigate the situation when it may be necessary to specify all the outputs of the unstable states as well. Consider the unstable state b, which appears in the first row and in the input column of 01 of the reduced state table of machine M_2 (Table 12.2.5). The machine goes to this unstable state from the stable state a when the input changes from 00 to 01. Very soon the unstable state b becomes the stable state b. It should now be observed that the stable state a has an output 0, and the stable state b has an output 0. Therefore, if the output of the unstable state b remains unspecified, there remains a possibility of the output of this unstable state becoming 1 when the machine transits from the stable state a to the stable state b via the unstable state b. This output 1 will remain for a very short while and will appear as a *spike*, commonly known as a *flicker*. There may be many situations where a flicker may not be desirable. Therefore, if we want the output of the machine to be flicker-free, then the output of the unstable state b cannot remain unspecified but must be specified as 0. Now, consider the unstable c in the same row, but in the column of the input combination 11. The machine passes through the unstable state when it transits from the stable state a to the stable state c due to a change in the input from 10 to 11. It can be seen that the output of the stable state a is 0 and that of the stable state c is 1. Therefore, if the output of the unstable state c is left unspecified, it may be taken either as 0 or as 1, and there is no possibility that a spike or flicker will appear. However, if the output of the unstable state c is taken as 0, then the transition to the output of the stable state c, which is 1, is delayed for a very short while. Therefore, if this delay is not desirable, and the aim is to effect a fast change in the output, the output of the unstable state c must be specified as 1. Thus we see that if we want to make the output of the machine free of spikes or flickers, and if a change of output should be fast, then the outputs of all the unstable states should be specified. It will be apparent from this discussion that a simple way to make the output fast and flicker-free is to specify the output of each of the unstable states the same as the output of its corresponding stable state in the same input column.

12.4 CYCLES AND RACES

The state table of machine M_2 will require two flip-flops or latches for implementation. The combinations of the two flip-flops designated y_1 and y_2, representing the three states of the machine, have been shown in the transition table, Table 12.4.1. This will appear as table Y_1 and Y_2 in the transition table of machine M_2. Table 12.4.1 shows an arbitrary assignment where the combinations 00, 01, and 11 represent the states a, b, and c, respectively. The combination 10 has not been used in the state table.

In the transition tables of fundamental-mode sequential machines, new phenomena, known as races and cycles, are encountered. These can be studied in the transition table for machine M_2. Consider that the machine is in stable state

TABLE 12.4.1 TRANSITION TABLE FOR MACHINE M_2

Present state y_1y_2	Next state			
	x_1x_2			
	00	01	11	10
a:00	⓪⓪	01	11*	⓪⓪
b:01	00	⓪①	⓪①	11
c:11	00	01	①①	①①
10	Not used			

00 with the input 10. Now let the input combination change to 11. This requires that the machine go from state 00 to state 11. This means that the two latches y_1 and y_2 should change their states from 0 to 1. If these two changes of y_1 and y_2 take place at exactly the same time, the machine will transit from state 00 to state 11 and will remain in stable state 11, as can be seen from the third row of the transition table. However, it is very seldom that the operating time of the latches or the transmission time of the excitation function traveling to the input of the latches will be identical. Therefore, it will be more realistic to assume that one of the latches will operate earlier than the other. In this case, suppose that y_2 changes state from 0 to 1 earlier. Consequently, the machine goes to the state 01. State 01 now becomes the present state, and as can be seen from the second row of the transition table, state 01 is a stable state with the input 11. Hence the machine remains in this stable state and will never go to state 11. This means that the machine has gone to a wrong state and fails to reach the proper state 11. On the other hand, if latch y_1 had changed from 0 to 1 earlier, the machine would have gone to state 10 first, and since 10 is not a stable state, latch y_2 would have had enough time to change state, and the circuit would come to the desired stable state 11. Thus, whenever a transition from one stable state to another stable state involves a change in more than one secondary variable, the circuit experiences what is known as a *race* condition. If depending on the order in which the internal variables change, the circuit goes to different stable states, then a *critical race* condition is said to be present. It is obvious that it is possible to steer the circuit to the proper stable state by so designing the operating time of the latches that the appropriate latch will operate faster than the other. This will, however, mean that the various latches will have different propagation delays. But this is not a desirable situation. It will be much better if the logic designer himself or herself can overcome the critical races by incorporating some additional feature in the design of the transition table. A careful study of the critical race will reveal that a simple way to avoid a critical race is to ensure that at no time is the circuit required to go from one stable state to another stable state by incorporating more than one change in the secondary variables. This means that *any two transiting states must not differ by more than one bit in their state assignments*. This is a

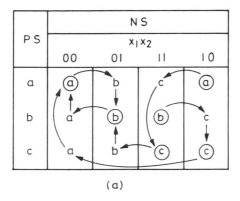

(a)

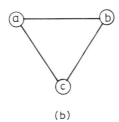

(b)

Figure 12.4.1 (a) Transition and (b) adjacency diagrams of machine M_2.

very important criterion, and if it can be achieved, no critical race will occur in the transition table. Whenever two states differ in their secondary assignments by only one bit, they are known as *adjacent states*. Therefore, we must find all pairs of states that must be made adjacent to eliminate critical races. For this, first draw the transition diagram that gives all transiting states whenever a stable state goes to another stable state. This will therefore reveal pairs of adjacent states. Now another diagram, known as an *adjacency diagram,* is drawn. Here if a state S_i is to be made adjacent, a line is drawn connecting these two states. To draw the adjacency diagram of the state table of machine M_2, we first find the transition diagram of the machine as shown in Fig. 12.4.1(a). The first row of the transition diagram shows that state *a* should be adjacent to both *b* and *c*. Similarly, the second row shows that state *b* should be adjacent to both *a* and *c*. Therefore, the adjacency diagram of the three states *a, b,* and *c* will be as shown in Fig. 12.4.1(b). How a race-free assignment is determined with the help of the adjacency diagram is discussed in the next section.

12.5 RACE-FREE ASSIGNMENTS

Definition 12.5.1.   An assignment of secondary variables that makes a state table free from critical races is known as a *race-free* or *valid assignment.*

The first step in determining the valid assignment of a state table is to determine the adjacency diagram of the state table of the machine. This diagram shows the various adjacent states of a particular stable state, as has been pointed out earlier. The next step is to find the degree of adjacency (DA) of each of the stable states.

Definition 12.5.2. The number of lines emerging from a state in the adjacency diagram is the *degree of adjacency* (DA) of the state. In other words, the DA is the number of states with which the particular state is adjacent.

We shall now describe a simple way of finding an assignment that will satisfy the adjacency requirement of all the states of a machine. It is well known that in a hypercube of dimension m, there are 2^m number of vertices, each of which is adjacent to m other vertices. Therefore, all the degrees of adjacency of an adjacency diagram of a machine can be satisfied by placing the states at appropriate vertices of a hypercube of dimension m, where m is the highest DA in the adjacency diagram. It will be very interesting to note here that to handle this problem the Karnaugh map turns out to be an extremely useful tool. As discussed in Chapter 3, the Karnaugh map excellently depicts a hypercube on a two-dimensional system. Therefore, all the adjacency requirements of a valid assignment can be satisfied by placing the various states in the appropriate cell of a Karnaugh map. It should be noted that when placed in the appropriate cell, the various states may not, and invariably cannot, satisfy all the adjacency requirements directly. This difficulty can be overcome by introducing extra unstable states that act as transiting states between two stable states of the machine. Consider three machines each having four states but exhibiting three different adjacency diagrams, as shown in Fig. 12.5.1(a), (b), and (c). In these figures (a) has the simplest and (c) the worst cases of adjacency that may occur in a four-state state table. The valid assignments for the three cases of the adjacency diagram have been shown in the Karnaugh maps of (d), (e), and (f), respectively, of Fig. 12.5.1. In case (a), each of the four states has an adjacency of two, and these can be satisfied when the four states are plotted in cells as shown in the two-variable Karnaugh map of (d). In case (b), states A and C have the maximum degree of adjacency 3, whereas B and D have DAs of 2 each. Since the maximum degree of adjacency is 3, the vertices representing the states must be placed in a 3-cube, and therefore we must plot these states in a three-variable Karnaugh map. States A, B, D, and C are so placed that A has been made adjacent to B, C, and D. This fixes the positions of all the four states of the machine. However, we now see from the map that states B and C are not adjacent, as required by the adjacency diagram. Similarly, states C and D are also not adjacent in the Karnaugh map. This problem is solved by introducing extra states. For example, when an extra state E is placed on the cell as shown in the map, state B becomes adjacent to E, which in turn becomes adjacent to C. Thus states B and C are made virtually adjacent with the help of the extra state E. In the state table, E becomes an unstable state through which states B and C transit to the respective stable states. Similarly, states C and D, which are not adjacent on the map, become virtually adjacent when the extra state F is introduced as shown in the map. In case (c), all four states have degree of adjacency 3. This is therefore the

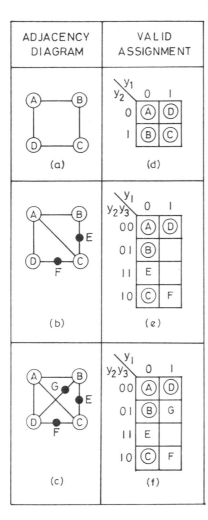

Figure 12.5.1 Adjacency diagram and valid assignment of a four-state machine.

worst case of adjacency that can be obtained in a four-state machine. After A, B, C, and D have been placed as shown in the three-variable map, the adjacency of state A only is satisfied. To satisfy the adjacency requirements of the other three states, we must introduce three extra states E, F, and G, placed as shown in the map. With these three extra states working as transiting unstable states, the adjacency requirements of all four states are satisfied either directly or virtually.

Example 12.5.1

Find a race-free assignment for the four-state machine as given in Table 12.5.1. Also, if needed, draw the augmented state table.

Solution In order to find the adjacency requirement of the machine, its transition diagram is drawn. This is shown in Fig. 12.5.2. The first row of the transition diagram shows that when the input changes from 00 to 10, the stable state A goes to the

TABLE 12.5.1 STATE TABLE OF MACHINE M_3

Present state	Next state			
	$x_1 x_2$			
	00	01	11	10
A	Ⓐ	Ⓐ	D	D
B	Ⓑ	A	Ⓑ	C
C	A	Ⓒ	D	Ⓒ
D	Ⓓ	C	Ⓓ	Ⓓ

unstable state D, then from D in the first row it goes to the stable state D in the last row. Therefore, to avoid critical race rows A and D must be adjacent. The second row tells us that states B and A, and also B and C, should be adjacent. The third row shows that state C should be adjacent to both A and D. The fourth row shows that state D should be adjacent to state C. These adjacencies are shown graphically in the adjacency diagram of Fig. 12.5.3(a). As the highest DA is 3, a three-variable Karnaugh map is needed. Figure 3.5.3(b) shows the plotting of the four states A, B, C, and D of the machine. The map also shows two extra states E and F to satisfy the adjacency requirement between states B and C and between states C and D.

The introduction of the extra states E and F is also shown in the transition diagram of Fig. 12.5.2. From this it will be apparent that state C in the second row and in the 10-input column should be made E, and C should appear in the row of the present state E and input column 10. With this modification made in the state table, when the input changes from 11 to 10 with B as the present state, the machine goes first to state E, and then from E to the stable state C. Therefore, E is an unstable state and acts only as a transiting state between the two stable states B and C, due

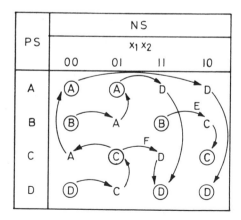

Figure 12.5.2 Transition diagram of machine M_3.

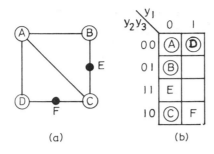

Figure 12.5.3 (a) Adjacency diagram and (b) a valid assignment for machine M_3.

(a)   (b)

TABLE 12.5.2 AUGMENTED STATE TABLE OF MACHINE M_3 WITH RACE-FREE ASSIGNMENT

Present state	Next state			
	x_1x_2			
	00	01	11	10
000:A	Ⓐ	Ⓐ	D	D
001:B	Ⓑ	A	Ⓑ	E
010:C	A	Ⓒ	F	Ⓒ
100:D	Ⓓ	C	Ⓓ	Ⓓ
011:E	—	—	—	C
110:F	—	—	D	—

to the change of input from 11 to 10. Similarly, state D in the row of the present state C and in input column 11, should be replaced by F, and D should appear in the same column but in the row of the present state F. These have been shown in the augmented state table of machine M_3 (Table 12.5.2). The valid assignment is given by the Karnaugh map of Fig. 12.5.3(b). These have also been shown in the present-state column of Table 12.5.2.

Example 12.5.2

Find a race-free assignment of machine M_2 from its adjacency diagram of Fig. 12.4.1(b). Also form the augmented state table and the transition table with the race-free assignment.

Solution From the adjacency diagram, each of the three states a, b, and c has a DA 2. Since the highest DA is 2, a two-variable valid assignment can be found from a two-variable Karnaugh map. Let state a be made adjacent to both b and c in the map, and then add a fourth state d to make b and c virtually adjacent to each other. The assignments are given by a:00, b:01, c:10, and d:11. The augmented state table and the transition table are given by Tables 12.5.3 and 12.5.4, respectively.

TABLE 12.5.3 AUGMENTED STATE TABLE OF MACHINE M_2

Present state	Next state x_1x_2			
	00	01	11	10
a	ⓐ	b	c	ⓐ
b	a	ⓑ	ⓑ	d
c	a	b	ⓒ	ⓒ
d	—	—	—	c

TABLE 12.5.4 TRANSITION TABLE OF MACHINE M_2 WITH RACE-FREE ASSIGNMENT

Present state	Next state, z x_1x_2			
	00	01	11	10
$a \rightarrow 00$	⑩,0	01,0	10,1	⑩,1
$b \rightarrow 01$	00,0	⑪,0	⑪,0	11,1
$c \rightarrow 10$	00,0	01,0	⑩,1	⑩,1
$d \rightarrow 11$	—	—	—	10,1

12.6 STATIC AND DYNAMIC HAZARDS

As we have already mentioned, in a sequential circuit operating in the fundamental mode the circuit is ever ready to respond to a change in the signal, be that in the input or in the excitation function of its memory elements. For this reason it is extremely essential to ensure that all the changes in the signal are genuine and that no spurious change appears in any part of the circuit. It is evident that if a spurious change in input or in the excitation functions occurs, it may drive the circuit to a wrong state. It is interesting to note that even a combinational circuit implementing an excitation function, which apparently appears quite harmless, may produce serious problems in the working of a fundamental mode circuit. Consider the excitation function of a D latch,

$$D = x_1 x_2' + x_2 x_3$$

shown in the Karnaugh map of Fig. 12.6.1(a), and its implementation by AND–OR gates in Fig. 12.6.1(b).

Fundamental-Mode Sequential Machines   Chap. 12

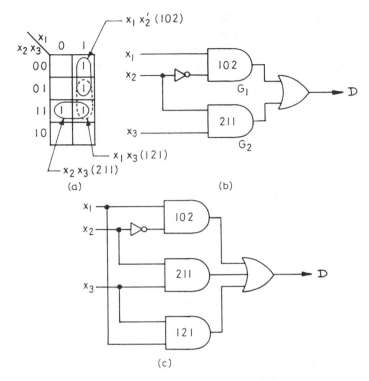

Figure 12.6.1 (a) $f = \Sigma(3,4,5,7)$ on map; (b) AND–OR implementation of f with hazard; (c) hazard-free implementation of f.

Note that when $x_1 = x_3 = 1$, the value of D remains 1 irrespective of the value of x_2. In other words, D remains 1 when $x_2 = 0$ and also when $x_2 = 1$. Therefore, a change in the value of x_2 does not alter the value 1 of D, when $x_1 = x_3 = 1$. This is, however, the condition of D at the steady state. When x_2 changes from 0 to 1, or vice versa, the value of D may momentarily be 0. Note that at the steady state, when $x_2 = 0$, the output of gate G_1 is 1 and that of gate G_2 is 0 when x_1 and x_3 are both 1. Therefore, D is 1 because of the output of gate G_1. When $x_2 = 1$, the value of D is 1 due to the output of gate G_2. Thus the steady-state value of D is being maintained at 1 by one of the gates G_1 or G_2. Now, during the transition of x_2 from 0 to 1, and vice versa, due to the different delays in the two paths, one through gate G_1 and the other through gate G_1 becomes 0 from 1 earlier than G_2 becomes 1 from 0, the value of D will be 0 for a short while during this transition period. Such a situation may drive the circuit to a wrong stable state, resulting in malfunctioning of the circuit. Therefore, this type of situation is known as a hazard. The various types of hazards that may be encountered in a combinational circuit are defined as follows:

Definition 12.6.1. A *static hazard* exists in a combinational circuit realizing a Boolean function if the function assumes momentarily a wrong value during a single change in its variables.

Sec. 12.6   Static and Dynamic Hazards

291

If the circuit produces a momentary 0 value when in fact the value should have remained constant at 1, the hazard is known as a *static 1 hazard*. On the other hand, if the circuit produces a momentary 1 value when in fact the value should have been remained constant as 0, the hazard is known as a *static 0 hazard*.

Definition 12.6.2. A *dynamic hazard* exists in a combinational circuit realizing a Boolean function, whose value must change from 0(1) to 1(0) due to a change in one of its variables, does not change in a single step.

It will be interesting to note here that once again the analysis of a static hazard on the Karnaugh map of a simple three-variable function will reveal the situations in which such a hazard exists and also how to remedy this hazard. Consider the function as shown in the map of Fig. 12.6.1(a). We see here that the two cubes that are responsible for the steady-state value 1 of the function are disjoint and adjacent to each other. It can also be seen from the map that the momentary value of 0 occurs in the function when x_2 changes from 0 to 1, because of the absence of the redundant cube $x_1 x_3$ shown dashed in the map. This cube was omitted in the minimized form of the function. Therefore, the static hazard can be eliminated if we include this redundant prime cube in the function. Hence, when implementing the function by AND–OR gates, we must provide an extra gate to realize the cube $x_1 x_3$. If this is done, then when x_1 and x_3 are both 1, the output of the OR gate will always be 1 and will remain independent of the value of x_2. From this discussion we can find the situations in which a static 1 hazard will occur and can also conclude that if we provide a redundant prime cube that acts as a bridging cube in this situation, the static 1 hazard can be eliminated from the combinational circuit. Let us state these results of the map analysis in the form of the following two general theorems.

Theorem 12.6.1. A static 1 hazard exists in the realization of a Boolean function in the form of a sum of cubes if there exist two disjoint and adjacent cubes.

Theorem 12.6.2. The static 1 hazard can be eliminated in a Boolean function expressed as a sum of cubes by providing the bridging cube for each pair of disjoint and adjacent cubes.

We have seen just now how a pair of disjoint and adjacent cubes can be found by observation on the map, and how the bridging cube can be determined from the map. When the number of variables is very large, two disjoint and adjacent cubes can be detected by bit by bit comparison of the cubes. Two cubes will be disjoint and adjacent if there is one and only one position where there is 0 in one of the cubes and 1 in the other cube. Once two cubes have been identified as disjoint and adjacent, the bridging cube can be found by observing their bit values at each position. The bits of the bridging cube will be as given in Table 12.6.1 for the three values 0, 1, and 2 of the two disjoint cubes.

TABLE 12.6.1

	0	1	2
0	0	2	0
1	2	1	1
2	0	1	2

It can easily be verified that a static 0 hazard is the dual of a static 1 hazard. Hence a static 0 hazard will exist when the Boolean function to be realized is expressed in a product-of-sum form and is realized by an OR–AND network. A static 0 hazard can also be remedied by providing the dual of the bridging cube, and a table similar to that of Table 12.6.1 can also be found for this situation.

Example 12.6.1

Implement the following Boolean function by a hazard-free OR–AND network.

$$f = \Sigma(0,2,6,7)$$

Solution To implement the function by an OR–AND network, plot the function on a Karnaugh map and minimize the 0's [Fig. 12.6.2(a)]. It can be seen from the map and from the figure that when $x_2 = 0$ and $x_3 = 1$, the function remains 0 because of gate G_1 when $x_1 = 1$, and because of gate G_2 when $x_1 = 0$. But when x_1 changes from 0 to 1, if the delay of gate G_1 is higher, G_1 becomes 0 later than G_2 becomes 1. Hence the output of the AND gate momentarily becomes 1, creating a static 0 hazard. It is now easy to see that this static 0 hazard can be eliminated by incorporating the bridging cube by a third OR gate as shown in Fig. 12.6.2(b).

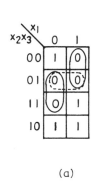

(a)

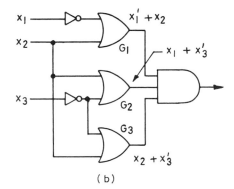

(b)

Figure 12.6.2 Hazard-free implementation of $f = \Sigma(0,2,6,7)$ by OR–AND network.

Example 12.6.2

Design a fundamental-mode mod-2 counter using D latches and AND–OR gates for its combinational circuits. The output is to be flicker-free and the combinational circuit must not contain any hazard.

Solution The primitive state table is shown in Table 12.6.2. The compatible pair implication matrix (CPIM) (not shown) will reveal that the state table cannot be reduced further. The reduced state table along with the transition arrows is shown in Fig. 12.6.3(a). Here the outputs of the unstable states have been specified to those

TABLE 12.6.2 PRIMITIVE STATE
TABLE OF Mod-2 COUNTER, M_4

	Next state, z	
Present		x
state	0	1
$A(0)$	$A(0),0$	$B(01),0$
$B(01)$	$C(010),0$	$B(01),0$
$C(010)$	$C(010),0$	$D(0101),1$
$D(0101)$	$A(0),0$	$D(0101),1$

of their corresponding stable states. This makes the output flicker-free. The transition arrows identify the pairs of adjacent states. The adjacency diagram is shown in Fig. 12.6.3(b) and the valid assignments in the map of Fig. 12.6.3(c). With these, the transition and output table is shown in Table 12.6.3.

The excitation functions D_1 and D_2 of the two latches y_1 and y_2, and the output function are now given by

$$D_1(xy_1 \, y_2) = \Sigma(1,3,6,7)$$

$$D_2(xy_1 \, y_2) = \Sigma(1,3,4,5)$$

$$z(xy_1 \, y_2) = \Sigma(6,7)$$

Carrying out multiple-output minimization on a map yields

$$D_1(xy_1 \, y_2) = 021 + 112$$

$$D_2(xy_1 \, y_2) = 021 + 102$$

$$z(xy_1 \, y_2) = 112$$

Note that the cube 021 is shared between D_1 and D_2, and the cube 112 between D_1 and z. Hence only three AND gates are required to implement the three functions.

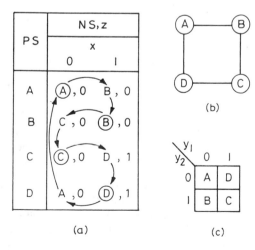

(a)

(b)

(c)

Figure 12.6.3 (a) Reduced state table along with transition arrows of machine M_4; (b) adjacency diagram; (c) a valid assignment of machine M_4.

TABLE 12.6.3 TRANSITION AND OUTPUT TABLE OF Mod-2 COUNTER, M_4

	Next state, z	
	x	
Present state	0	1
A: 00	⓪⓪,0	01,0
B: 01	11,0	⓪①,0
C: 11	①①,0	10,1
D: 10	00,0	①⓪,1

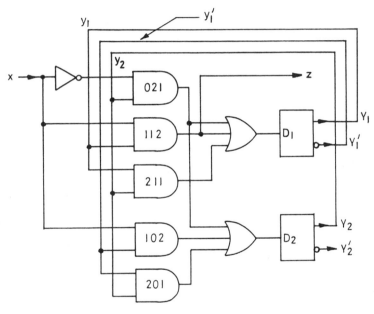

Figure 12.6.4 Mod-2 counter implemented by D latches and AND–OR gates. The combinational circuit is free of static and dynamic hazards.

However, to make the combinational circuit hazard-free, two more product terms are required. Since 021 and 112 are disjoint and adjacent, the bridging cube 211 must be added for D_1. Similarly, the bridging cube 201 must be added for D_2. The AND–OR circuit and the two D latches implementing the mod-2 counter is shown in Fig. 12.6.4.

12.7 ESSENTIAL HAZARDS

The circuit of the mod-2 counter has been so designed that it is free from any combinational circuit hazard due to any differential delay that may be introduced by any of the circuit elements. Let us now investigate this point in a little greater detail. Assume that the inverter which appears at the input of the circuit introduces considerable delay in propagating the change through it. A careful analysis will reveal that the delay of this inverter gate drives the circuit into a wrong stable state. This is a very intriguing situation that cannot be avoided by any additional circuitry that may be provided in the circuit. The only remedy is to ensure that every element of the circuit introduces an appropriate amount of delay. Such a situation is called an essential hazard, as it is inherent in the state table and not in the circuit. An essential hazard may be defined as follows.

Definition 12.7.1. An *essential hazard* exists if due to the differential delays in the transmission paths from input to different memories, a change of input drives the circuit to a wrong stable state.

It may be seen that nothing can be done in the state table to avoid an essential hazard. However, an essential hazard can be detected in the state table by the following theorem due to Unger (1959).

Theorem 12.7.1. An essential hazard exists in a fundamental-mode asynchronous sequential machine whenever the state table is such that three consecutive input changes take the circuit to different stable states than the first change alone.

An interesting consequence of Unger's theorem is that the state tables of all counters that move progressively from one stable state to another stable state will always have an essential hazard.

12.8 PULSE-MODE SEQUENTIAL CIRCUITS

In the preceding sections we have discussed the various steps and procedures that have to be followed for the successful design of a fundamental-mode sequential machine. It is evident that these are quite involved and become more complex where the number of internal states of the circuit is very high. For this reason most of the large sequential circuits, especially those encountered in VLSI systems, are designed in the clock mode. However, there are many occasions where it may not be possible to synchronize the input signals with the clock pulses. At the same time, the input signals may appear for such short times that they may be regarded as pulses. In such a restricted situation (invariably not encountered in VLSI circuits), an asynchronous circuit in pulse mode can be designed, provided that the input pulses obey the following restrictions.

1. Pulses are short enough not to trigger multiple changes in the latches or flip-flops used as memory elements. They should at the same time be broad enough to trigger at least one change in the circuit.
2. Since the clock pulse is not present to sample the input pulses, the restriction of not allowing a double change in the input as in the fundamental-mode

operation should also be imposed here, as otherwise, it will be difficult for the machine to interpret properly the change of input.

3. An additional restriction that is not present in a fundamental-mode operation is imposed on a synchronous circuit operating in the pulse mode. Here it is assumed that only one input at a time will act on the circuit. Therefore, if in such a circuit there are three inputs x_1, x_2, and x_3, input combinations that are allowed will be only 001, 010, and 100. The other combinations with two or more 1's will not appear at all. Therefore, when the primitive state table of such a circuit is constructed, only the allowable input combinations are taken into consideration. This renders the state table completely specified, and the state minimization procedure becomes fairly simple.

Thus a pulse-mode asynchronous circuit will be very easy to design if the circuit is willing to obey the restrictions mentioned above.

Example 12.8.1

An asynchronous sequential machine has two inputs. It produces an output whenever two consecutive pulses occur in one input line and no pulse is present on the other input line. Once the output becomes 1, it remains 1 until a pulse comes on the other input line. Construct a minimum-row state table for this machine.

Solution From the specifications given, it is clear that it must have a level output. Hence we must design the state table as a Moore machine. Following the same procedure as before, we first construct the primitive state table. As it is a Moore machine, outputs are shown after a slash following the memory of the state (Table 12.8.1). Figure 12.8.1 shows the implication matrix of the machine, and the minimized state table is shown in Table 12.8.2.

TABLE 12.8.1 PRIMITIVE STATE TABLE OF MACHINE M_5

Present state	Next state/output of that state x_1: 0 x_2: 1	x_1: 1 x_2: 0
$A\begin{pmatrix}0\\0\end{pmatrix}/0$	$B\begin{pmatrix}0\\1\end{pmatrix}/0$	$C\begin{pmatrix}1\\0\end{pmatrix}/0$
$B\begin{pmatrix}0\\1\end{pmatrix}/0$	$D\begin{pmatrix}00\\11\end{pmatrix}/1$	$C\begin{pmatrix}1\\0\end{pmatrix}/0$
$C\begin{pmatrix}1\\0\end{pmatrix}/0$	$B\begin{pmatrix}0\\1\end{pmatrix}/0$	$E\begin{pmatrix}11\\00\end{pmatrix}/1$
$D\begin{pmatrix}00\\11\end{pmatrix}/1$	$D\begin{pmatrix}00\\11\end{pmatrix}/1$	$C\begin{pmatrix}1\\0\end{pmatrix}/0$
$E\begin{pmatrix}11\\00\end{pmatrix}/1$	$B\begin{pmatrix}0\\1\end{pmatrix}/0$	$E\begin{pmatrix}11\\00\end{pmatrix}/1$

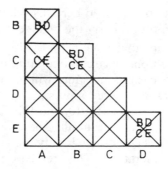

Figure 12.8.1 Implication matrix of machine M_5.

TABLE 12.8.2 STATE TABLE OF MACHINE M_5

Present state	Next state		z
	x_1x_2		
	01	10	
A	B	C	0
B	D	C	0
C	B	E	0
D	D	C	1
E	B	E	1

REFERENCES

HILL, F. J., AND G. R. PETERSON. *Introduction to Switching Theory and Logical Design,* 3rd ed., New York: John Wiley & Sons Inc., 1981.

KOHAVI, Z. *Switching and Finite Automata Theory,* 2nd ed. New York: McGraw-Hill Book Company, 1978.

MCCLUSKEY, E. J. *Logic Design Principles.* Englewood Cliffs, N.J.: Prentice-Hall, 1986.

UNGER, S. H. Hazards and delays in asynchronous sequential switching circuits, *IRE Trans. Circuit Theory,* Vol. CT-6, No. 12, March, 1959, pp. 12–25.

UNGER, S. H. *Asynchronous Sequential Machines.* New York: John Wiley & Sons Inc., 1969.

PROBLEMS

12.1. Find allowable input sequences that will take machine M_2 of Table 12.2.5 from (a) state a to state c; (b) state b to state c; and (c) state c to state a.

12.2. Determine all the races in the following state tables. Indicate which of these are critical and which are not.

	(a) Y_1Y_2			
		x_1x_2		
y_1y_2	00	01	11	10
00	01	(00)	(00)	01
01	(01)	00	11	11
10	01	(10)	01	(10)
11	(11)	01	(11)	01

	(b) Y_1Y_2			
		x_1x_2		
y_1y_2	00	01	11	10
00	11	(00)	(00)	01
01	10	10	11	(01)
10	(10)	11	11	01
11	(11)	(11)	00	(11)

12.3. Find race-free assignments for the two state tables of Problem 12.2.

12.4. A five-state $(A,B,\ldots E)$ fundamental-mode machine has an adjacency diagram where ABC is a triangle and $BCDE$ is a quadrilateral. Find race-free assignments for the machine by introducing minimum number of extra states, and using minimum number of secondary variables.

12.5. For a six-state fundamental-mode machine that has worst-case adjacency, find a valid assignment using minimum number of extra states.

12.6. Find race-free assignments of the following reduced state tables. Use a minimum number of secondary variables.

(a)

Present state	Next state			
	x_1x_2			
	00	01	11	10
a	b	(a)	c	(a)
b	(b)	c	(b)	(b)
c	(c)	(c)	(c)	a

(b)

Present state	Next state			
	x_1x_2			
	00	01	11	10
a	(a)	b	(a)	c
b	(b)	(b)	a	c
c	(c)	a	(c)	(c)
d	(d)	(d)	b	b

(c)

Present state	Next state			
	x_1x_2			
	00	01	11	10
a	c	(a)	(a)	d
b	(b)	d	e	a
c	(c)	(c)	a	(c)
d	a	(d)	(d)	b
e	(e)	b	a	(e)

12.7. Is the following statement true? Justify your answer.

Any combinational circuit implemented by an MSOP form obtained by eliminating one or more redundant prime cubes will always have static or dynamic hazard.

12.8. Discuss if the EXCLUSIVE-OR circuit made by five NAND gates and the EXCLUSIVE-OR circuit made by four NAND gates as shown in Figs. 5.3.2(a) and 5.3.6, respectively, have any static or dynamic hazards.

12.9. Prove Unger's theorem of essential hazard as has been stated in Theorem 12.7.1.

12.10. Analyze the following state table for the presence, or otherwise, of an essential hazard. Implement the circuit with D latches. What steps should be taken to eliminate the essential hazard, if any?

Present state	Next state, z x_1x_2 0	1
0	0 ,0	1,0
1	①,0	2,0
2	2 ,0	3,1
3	3 ,1	0,0

12.11. Find a minimum-row state table for each of the following fundamental-mode sequential machines, having two inputs, x_1 and x_2, and one output, z.
   (a) Output z becomes 1 only when x_1 becomes 1 first and then x_2 becomes 1. Once 1, the output remains 1 until x_1 becomes 0.
   (b) Output z becomes 1 only when x_1 becomes 1 twice with the value of x_2 remaining 1 during this period. Once 1, the output remains 1 until x_2 becomes 0.

12.12. Modify the state tables of the two machines of Problem 12.11 so that the output is fast and flicker-free. Also find race-free assignments of these two tables.

12.13. A fundamental-mode sequential machine has two inputs, x_1 and x_2, and one output, z. The output z becomes 1 only when x_1 changes from 1 to 0 while $x_2 = 1$. Once 1, the output remains 1 and returns to 0 only when x_2 changes from 1 to 0 while $x_1 = 1$.
   (a) Determine a race-free assignment for the state table.
   (b) Derive hazard-free excitation and output equations. Assume that the machine is being implemented by D latches.

12.14. A fundamental-mode sequential machine has two inputs, x_1 and x_2, and two outputs, z_1 and z_2. z_1 becomes 1 when x_1 changes its value preceded by a change in value in x_2. z_2 becomes 1 when x_2 changes its value preceded by a change in value in x_1. Once 1, both z_1 and z_2 return to 0 only when both x_1 and x_2 become 0.
   (a) Derive a minimum-row state table having fast and flicker-free output.
   (b) Determine a race-free assignment.

12.15. A sequential lock circuit has two pushbuttons, A and B, which cannot be pressed simultaneously. It has one output, z. The output becomes 1 and opens the lock only when the buttons are pressed in the sequence $ABBA$. Find a reduced state table for the lock circuit.

12.16. A sequential lock circuit has 12 pushbuttons, similar to a telephone dial. The lock opens only when the buttons are pushed in the sequence 2*508.
   (a) Derive a minimum-row state table for the lock circuit.
   (b) Determine a race-free flow table of the circuit.
   (c) Derive hazard-free excitation and output equations, assuming that the circuit is being implemented by S-R flip-flops.

12.17. A traffic light controller is to be installed at the level crossing of a single-track railway line. With no train approaching, the green light will be on. When a train approaches the level crossing and is within 2000 ft of the crossing, the light changes from green to red. The light changes from red to green when the entire train has crossed over and the rear of the train is 200 ft away from the crossing. Assume that the length of the train does not exceed 1500 ft. Design an economical circuit for the traffic controller using D latches.

12.18. Design a fundamental-mode mod-3 counter with S-R flip-flops and unfolded PLAs.

12.19. Design a pulse-mode asynchronous mod-3 counter with D latches. What is the difference in operation of this circuit from that of a similar counter operating in the clock mode?

12.20. An asynchronous sequential machine operating in the pulse mode has two inputs, x_1 and x_2, and one output, z. The output becomes 1 when two consecutive pulses occur in the x_1-line with no pulse appearing on the x_2-line. Assume that output 1 is a pulse coincident with the x_1 pulse. Derive a minimum-row state table for the machine. Implement the circuit with T flip-flops.

Index

U

Unate functions, 58
Unbounded memory span, 242
Uncommitted logic arrays, 116
Uniqueness property, 4
Universal logic module, 102
Universal test set, 191
Unstable states, 278

V

Valid assignment, 285
Valid selective prime cube, 80
VLSI, 115
VLSI processor arrays, 140
VSPC, 80

W

Weight, 64, 157
  significant, 161
Word specification, 94, 231, 236

X

XOR, 33